THE RACE SET

BEFORE US

Thomas R. Schreiner
& Ardel B. Caneday

*A Biblical Theology
of Perseverance & Assurance*

IVP Academic

An imprint of InterVarsity Press
Downers Grove, Illinois

Inter-Varsity Press
Nottingham, England

InterVarsity Press, USA
P.O. Box 1400, Downers Grove, IL 60515-1426, USA
World Wide Web: www.ivpress.com
Email: email@ivpress.com

Inter-Varsity Press, England
Norton Street, Nottingham NG7 3HR, England
Email: ivp@ivpbooks.com
Website: www.ivpbooks.com

InterVarsity Press® is the book-publishing division of InterVarsity Christian Fellowship/USA®, a movement of students and faculty active on campus at hundreds of universities, colleges and schools of nursing in the United States of America, and a member movement of the International Fellowship of Evangelical Students. For information about local and regional activities, write Public Relations Dept., InterVarsity Christian Fellowship/USA, 6400 Schroeder Rd., P.O. Box 7895, Madison, WI 53707-7895, or visit the IVCF website at < www.intervarsity.org >.

Inter-Varsity Press, England, is closely linked with the Universities and Colleges Christian Fellowship (formerly the Inter-Varsity Fellowship), a student movement linking Christian Unions in universities and colleges throughout the Great Britain, and a member movement of the International Fellowship of Evangelical Students. For information about local and national activities write to UCCF, 38 De Montfort Street, Leicester LE1 7GP, email them at email@uccf.org.uk, or visit the UCCF website at www.uccf.org.uk.

All Scripture quotations, unless otherwise indicated, are the authors' translation.

Cover photograph: iStockphoto

USA ISBN 978-0-8308-1555-5
UK ISBN 978-0-85111-551-1

Printed in the UK by 4edge Limited

Library of Congress Cataloging-in-Publication Data

Schreiner, Thomas R.
  The race set before us : a biblical theology of perseverance & assurance / Thomas R. Schreiner & Ardel B. Caneday.
    p. cm.
  Includes bibliographical references.
  ISBN 0-8308-1555-4 (pbk. : alk. paper)
    1. Perseverance (Theology)—Biblical teaching. 2. Assurance (Theology)—Biblical teaching. 3. Christian life—Biblical teaching. 4. Bible. N.T.—Criticism, interpretation, etc. I. Caneday, Ardel B. II. Title
BS2545.P58 S34 2001
234—dc21

                                                                                    00-054444

British Library Cataloguing In Publication Data

A catalogue record for this book is available from the British Library.

P	24	23	22	21	20	19	18	17	16	15	14	13	12	11	10	9	8	7
Y	25	24	23	22	21	20	19	18	17	16	15	14	13	12	11	10		

CONTENTS

Preface

We count it an unusual and remarkable gift from the Lord to offer this book to our readers. "What is so unusual about this book?" you may ask. It is not just a book; it is a book about a highly controversial theological subject. Yet even more than that, it is a *coauthored* book about a controversial topic.

As professors who devote our lives to the study of biblical theology, we know how rare and refreshing it is to find two people who agree so deeply and broadly as we do on the matter of Christian perseverance and assurance. God gave to both of us a passion for this subject, so that on a beautiful spring day a few years ago as we walked and talked on the campus of Bethel Theological Seminary in Minnesota, the idea for this book was born.

We do not claim to have written the definitive statement on perseverance and assurance, but our hope is that others will interact seriously and biblically with the perspective offered. We have written our chapters independently, but we discussed extensively the contents of the book and revised each other's work. We have attempted to write the book in such a way that the author of individual chapters cannot be discerned. (Perhaps those who are skilled in source criticism will demonstrate that we have not succeeded!)

We want to thank Dan Reid, our editor at InterVarsity Press, for his encouragement and his suggestions on how to improve the work. We are also grateful to Terry Tiessen for his careful evaluation of our manuscript. And a special thanks goes to Northwestern College student Josh Jipp, who put in many hours helping us compile the subject index.

Finally, we dedicate this book to all those along life's pathway who have admonished us to persevere in God's grace to the end. We especially dedicate this book to our wives, Diane Schreiner and Lois Caneday, who encourage us as partners and heirs together of the grace of life.

INTRODUCTION

God is not unjust; he will not forget your work
and the love you have shown him as you have helped his people
and continue to help them. We want each of you to show this same
diligence to the very end, in order to make your hope sure.
We do not want you to become lazy, but to imitate those who through faith
and patience inherit what has been promised. (Heb 6:10-12 NIV)

As a new millennium dawns, Christians continue to ponder the same questions and address the same issues that have unsettled believers since the early days of the church. Two of these issues concern perseverance in holiness and assurance of salvation. Each generation of believers must address questions that arise concerning both. Will all believers persevere in faithfulness to Christ Jesus? Is it possible for a Christian to have eternal life and subsequently perish forever? Can a believer be assured of final salvation before he or she dies? Is it not presumptuous to believe that a Christian can be assured of salvation? Is not belief in the necessity of perseverance in faithfulness to Christ simply a different form of believing in salvation by works? Do not the biblical warnings indicate that it is possible for believers to apostatize and be lost eternally? Is not the real issue at stake with all these biblical warnings simply a matter of rewards, not salvation? These and many other questions swirl about discussions concerning perseverance and assurance. Christians stand divided on how they respond to these questions. That is regrettable, but even more regrettable is the animus that attaches to this division. Listen to any discussion of Hebrews 6:4-6 on a Christian college campus or in the student lounge at a theological seminary. The conversation will likely be spirited, if not heated. We trust that our discussion of perseverance and assurance will cast more light on the subject and lower the thermostat on such discussions.

In recent years much of the discussion concerning perseverance has sounded like a battle between advocates of lordship salvation and those who claim to believe in free grace.[1] We have endeavored to compose a book that avoids the tendencies that accompany such battles. Our objective is to be irenic in spirit, careful in exegesis and interpretation, thoughtful in theological expression and pastoral by encouraging readers to continue to persevere in faithfulness to Christ Jesus and to lay claim to the bold assurance that springs from faith.

Restraints compel us to focus our discussion on the New Testament, the area in which we both primarily teach. While our discussion delves deeply into a range of selected biblical texts, all things considered, we restrict it primarily to the New Testament. Since we have adopted these limitations, some may wonder at our subtitle: *A Biblical Theology of Perseverance & Assurance.* By using the designation "biblical theology" we do not suggest that our coverage is exhaustive. We use the subtitle for two reasons: (1) to indicate an inductive method in contrast to a systematic theological approach; and (2) to note that, though our consideration of the Bible's instruction on the subject is not exhaustive, it is substantial and representative.

Therefore, we offer this biblical theology of perseverance and assurance for three principal reasons. First, we believe that any proper formulation of a Christian doctrine of perseverance and assurance must derive from the biblical text. Biblical theology is the soil from which all Christian theology must grow. Second, a dearth of exegetical books on the subject beckons us to offer a fresh word on the subject. The last exegetical work on the subject was by Judith Gundry Volf: *Paul and Perseverance: Staying In and Falling Away.*[2] However, her

---

[1]The battle's primary "generals" have been Zane Hodges on the free grace side and John MacArthur on the lordship side. See, e.g., Zane Hodges, *The Gospel Under Siege: A Study on Faith and Works,* 2nd ed. (Dallas: Rendención Viva, 1991); *Absolutely Free! A Biblical Reply to Lordship Salvation* (Grand Rapids, Mich.: Zondervan, 1989); John F. MacArthur Jr., *The Gospel According to Jesus* (Grand Rapids, Mich.: Zondervan, 1988); *Faith Works: The Gospel According to the Apostles* (Dallas: Word, 1993). Two British advocates of Hodges's view are R. T. Kendall (*Once Saved, Always Saved* [Chicago: Moody Press, 1983]) and Michael Eaton (*No Condemnation: A New Theology of Assurance* [Downers Grove, Ill.: InterVarsity Press, 1995]).

[2]Judith M. Gundry Volf, *Paul and Perseverance: Staying In and Falling Away* (Louisville, Ky.: Westminster John Knox, 1990). For an excellent history of interpretation on the matter of perseverance and apostasy see B. J. Oropeza, *Paul and Apostasy: Eschatology, Perseverance, and Falling Away in the Corinthian Congregation,* Wissenschaftliche Untersuchungen zum Neuen Testament 2:115 (Tübingen: J. C. B. Mohr, 2000), pp. 1-

book, showing a Calvinistic orientation, was aimed at a scholarly audience and thus never achieved the popularity that British Wesleyan scholar I. Howard Marshall's book *Kept by the Power of God* achieved twenty-five years ago.[3] From the Reformed and Calvinist side, the last book on perseverance that had measurable popular influence was *Faith and Perseverance* by Dutch theologian G. C. Berkouwer.[4] The third reason we wrote this book is that we recognize a need for believers to hear an urgent pastoral appeal to persevere in faithfulness to Jesus Christ. We pray that, to the degree that we have been faithful to the Word and the gospel, this book will be useful to spur readers on "to love and good deeds" (Heb 10:24), that they may be "imitators of those who through faith and patience inherit the promises" (Heb 6:12 NRSV).

Our discussion throughout this book endeavors to assist readers to recognize the full range of biblical evidence one must include in any theological formulation concerning perseverance and assurance. Our objective is to lay out the biblical evidence and offer an interpretation consistent with that evidence that will help readers integrate it into a coherent and consistent whole. We will explore eight types of passages that must be considered in a biblical theology concerning perseverance and assurance.

First, certain passages reflect the gospel's announcement of conditional promises as it calls for us to receive salvation in Christ. God promises to give salvation to everyone who believes the gospel by following Jesus Christ. That is, the gospel calls for initial belief ("Believe in the Lord Jesus, and you will be saved—you and your household," Acts 16:31), but it also summons all who believe to persevere in belief. Here we offer three conditional promises from the letters to the seven churches in Revelation: "To him who overcomes, I will give the right to eat from the tree of life, which is in the paradise of God"

---

34. Oropeza investigates 1 Corinthians 10:1-13 and argues for an Arminian position. Unfortunately Oropeza's work appeared after this work was completed, so we are unable to interact with it in more detail.

[3] I. Howard Marshall, *Kept by the Power of God: A Study of Perseverance and Falling Away* (1969; reprint, Minneapolis: Bethany Fellowship, 1974). Another book of some import from the Arminian tradition is Robert Shank, *Life in the Son: A Study of the Doctrine of Perseverance,* 2nd ed. (Springfield, Mo.: Westcott, 1976).

[4] G. C. Berkouwer, *Faith and Perseverance,* trans. Robert D. Knudsen (Grand Rapids, Mich.: Eerdmans, 1958).

(Rev 2:7); "He who has an ear, let him hear what the Spirit says to the churches. He who overcomes will not be hurt at all by the second death" (Rev 2:11); and "He who overcomes will, like them, be dressed in white. I will never blot out his name from the book of life, but will acknowledge his name before my Father and his angels" (Rev 3:5).[5]

A second type of passage contains God's promise to preserve his people unto final salvation. No more assuring promise could be spoken than the one Jesus gave beside the tomb of Lazarus: "I am the resurrection and the life. He who believes in me will live, even though he dies; and whoever lives and believes in me will never die. Do you believe this?" (Jn 11:25-26).

The gospel often beckons its hearers with a third type of passage: conditional warnings and admonitions that require believers to persevere in faithfulness to Christ to be saved. Though the New Testament is filled with warnings and admonitions of this kind, we select one from the closing chapter of the Bible: "I warn everyone who hears the words of the prophecy of this book: If anyone adds anything to them, God will add to him the plagues described in this book. And if anyone takes words away from this book of prophecy, God will take away from him his share in the tree of life and in the holy city, which are described in this book" (Rev 22:18-19).

In a fourth type of passage the gospel announces that everyone who believes in Christ Jesus needs to persevere in faithfulness to him because they will face opposition and hatred from the world.

> We also rejoice in our sufferings, because we know that suffering produces perseverance; perseverance, character; and character, hope. And hope does not disappoint us, because God has poured out his love into our hearts by the Holy Spirit, whom he has given us. (Rom 5:3-5)

> Everyone who wants to live a godly life in Christ Jesus will be persecuted. (2 Tim 3:12)

A fifth type of passage summons us to examine whether our behavior matches what the gospel requires of all who believe. For example, the apostle John tells us, "We know that we have come to know him if

---

[5]Throughout this list of eight kinds of passages every biblical citation derives from the NIV. Throughout the remainder of the book, unless we note otherwise, biblical quotations reflect our own translations.

we obey his commands. The man who says, 'I know him,' but does not do what he commands is a liar, and the truth is not in him. But if anyone obeys his word, God's love is truly made complete in him. This is how we know we are in him: Whoever claims to live in him must walk as Jesus did" (1 Jn 2:3-6).

The Bible explains in a sixth type of passage that people who fail to remain loyal to Christ never were genuine believers. Once again the apostle John explains: "Dear children, this is the last hour; and as you have heard that the antichrist is coming, even now many antichrists have come. This is how we know it is the last hour. They went out from us, but they did not really belong to us. For if they had belonged to us, they would have remained with us; but their going showed that none of them belonged to us" (1 Jn 2:18-19).

In a seventh type of passage the New Testament explains that all who persevere in loyalty to Jesus Christ do so because God is at work in them by his grace, causing them to desire and to do what pleases him. Two passages stand out in this category: "This is the verdict: Light has come into the world, but men loved darkness instead of light because their deeds were evil. Everyone who does evil hates the light, and will not come into the light for fear that his deeds will be exposed. But whoever lives by the truth comes into the light, so that it may be seen plainly that what he has done has been done through God" (Jn 3:19-21); "Therefore, my dear friends, as you have always obeyed—not only in my presence, but now much more in my absence—continue to work out your salvation with fear and trembling, for it is God who works in you to will and to act according to his good purpose" (Phil 2:12-13).

Finally, the writers of the New Testament teach us that everyone who believes in Christ Jesus and perseveres in faithfulness to him does so because of God's grace alone: "For it is by grace you have been saved, through faith—and this not from yourselves, it is the gift of God—not by works, so that no one can boast. For we are God's workmanship, created in Christ Jesus to do good works, which God prepared in advance for us to do (Eph 2:8-10). Salvation, from election to glorification, is all grounded in and secured by God's grace.

We integrate these eight kinds of passages into our eight chapters. Some chapters focus primarily on one type of text, while others span two or three. Because the athletic metaphor appears frequently in the

New Testament and suitably portrays the Christian's faith and quest of the prize of salvation, we adopted it as the motif for our title and chapters. We do not slavishly develop this motif, nor do we seek to elevate it above other biblical imagery for salvation. Rather, our chapter titles, derived from aspects of the imagery of the runner, should prompt our readers' imaginations to recognize how the familiar New Testament metaphor aptly portrays the Christian's persevering pursuit of eternal life. Chapter subtitles link the athletic metaphor to their corresponding aspects of biblical theology. To make these connections clear, we have included a suitable biblical passage at the head of each chapter, as appears under the title of this introduction.

Chapter one—"The Race Set Before Us: What Is There to Win or Lose?"—lays out the principal points of disagreement among Christians concerning perseverance and assurance, points of disagreement that prompted us to write this book. Disagreement concerning perseverance and assurance primarily focuses on biblical warnings and admonitions. One's understanding of them regulates (1) whether or not one believes in the necessity of perseverance, (2) one's belief concerning how Christians persevere and (3) one's perspective on whether or not Christians can have assurance that they will persevere to the end and be saved. In this chapter we present four popular approaches to warnings and admonitions. We endeavor to describe each approach as accurately and fairly as possible in order to show its beliefs and legitimate concerns. We seek to bring into sharp focus the different ways Christians read biblical passages such as "The one who perseveres to the end will be saved" (Mt 10:22). How one understands this passage is a gauge concerning one's view of perseverance and assurance. Though there are elements of these four popular explanations of warnings and admonitions with which we agree, we explain why we find each to be deficient.

Having surveyed four popular approaches to this issue, we propose in summary form a fifth view that has been expressed clearly in prior generations but not recently. Each of the subsequent chapters, moreover, unpacks the biblical evidence that led us to adopt this fifth view. We have arranged these chapters to engage readers in what we believe is a reasonable and orderly development of biblical ideas. Since we build our argument in a systematic and orderly way, readers who skip chapters one through three to read chapter four will likely have an impaired understanding of our approach, for we have intentionally placed our extensive exposition of biblical warnings and admonitions after two crucial chapters that provide necessary biblical perspectives showing the multifaceted nature of both salvation and faith.

Chapter two—"The Prize to Be Won: Our Present and Future Salvation"—is foundational to all that we do in the next six chapters. We believe that a right understanding and use of biblical warnings and admonitions is bound up with acquiring a biblical orientation on salvation that is multidimensional: salvation is a gift and possession from God that we already have but do not yet have in its fullness. So in this chapter we make the case that Christians have tended to think of salvation in abstracted categories of systematic theology: justification, sanctification and glorification. We seek to correct these overly simplified categories by showing that a biblical concept of salvation is multifaceted, adequately portrayed only through a number of metaphors. We discuss six categories of biblical imagery, each with a variety of metaphors that portray the splendor and glory of God's salvation. Our goal in chapter two is also to correct a somewhat static and retrospective view of salvation by showing how the biblical concept of salvation entails both already and not-yet aspects. For example, the Bible portrays salvation as a gift we already possess (Eph 2:8-9) but also as a prize for which we hope (Rom 8:24-25; 13:11). Without an understanding of this already-but-not-yet perspective on salvation, one's grasp of perseverance and assurance will be truncated.

Chapter three—"The Race to Be Run: The Necessity of Obedient Faith"—begins to address the first two categories of passages identified earlier. Here we sketch a biblical portrayal of faith to show that the biblical concept of faith is like a multifaceted gem that can be described only with a number of metaphors. To establish the connection between faith and reward, we begin our discussion of faith from Hebrews 11:6: "Without faith it is impossible to please God, for whoever would approach him must believe that he exists and that he rewards those who seek him." Following brief discussions on the relationship between faith and faithfulness and between faith and understanding, we focus attention on the multifaceted biblical metaphors for faith, with athletic imagery leading the way.

Chapter four—"Running to Win the Prize: Heeding God's Admonitions and Warnings"—is the largest of our chapters because it addresses the central concern that prompted this book. This chapter focuses attention on the first and third kinds of biblical passages noted above. These admonitions and warnings are the theological watershed in the biblical teaching concerning perseverance. We make our case that they function as a necessary means for believers to persevere unto final salvation. We show how they underscore the dynamic and prospective nature of our salvation. They draw our focus to the not-yet aspect of salvation without doing damage to the fact that believers already have salvation. Biblical admonitions and warnings link the already and the not yet. We propose a view that takes them seriously while at the same time retaining present and full assurance of receiving salvation in the day of Christ Jesus. We show how God uses warnings and admonitions to secure the salvation of his children.

Chapter five—"Reflecting on Fallen Runners: Who Are Those Who Have Fallen Out of the Race?"—addresses a number of biblical examples of individuals who fell away from the gospel of Christ. In particular, this chapter addresses passages that fit categories four and six above. We address two instructive passages on falling away—John's perspective on those who have left the church (1 Jn 2:18-19) and Jesus' parable of the soils (Lk 8:1-15)—then round out the chapter with a consideration of certain "fallen" ones: Alexander, Hymenaeus, Philetus, Demas, Judas and Peter. We address each relevant passage and weigh carefully the biblical evidence. We end the chapter by emphasizing the biblical distinction between the complete and final apostasy of Judas and the temporary lapse in faithfulness by Peter. We purposely conclude this chapter with a discussion of Peter's triple denial and restoration by Christ, for it is Jesus Christ's intercession that is our only hope to persevere in faithfulness to him.

Chapter six—"Drawing on God's Grace: Going the Distance by God's Power"—comments on passages that fit category seven above. We examine what four New Testament writers—Peter, John, Jude and Paul—say about how and why believers do persevere in loyalty to Jesus Christ. Tying this chapter with the previous one, we begin with Peter. We show how Peter and each of the others make the case that, if anyone does persevere in God's grace and love, it is because God is the one who enables those who persevere. Hence, the view that we espouse in this book cannot be labeled works-righteousness, for we are simply reminding readers of what Augustine said long ago: God gives what he demands.[6]

Chapter seven—"Running with Confidence: Being Assured That We Shall Win the Prize"—discusses select passages that fit categories five and seven above. We closely examine these passages and make the case that assurance is integral to Christian faith. We endeavor to show that Christian assurance can be thought of as having three legs— God's promises, the fruit of the Spirit and the witness of the Holy Spirit. Every leg is important for Christian assurance, but the promises of God are the most important of all, for God's promises are the foundation of all Christian assurance.

Chapter eight—"Running by Divine Appointment: Who Are Those Who Run to the End and Win?"—expounds the eighth kind of biblical passage. This chapter reminds us that we run the race to the end only because of God's election. Those who run in the arena of faith and finish the race will not boast about their fortitude but will praise God that he has given them his grace.

As we integrate the eight kinds of biblical passages throughout this book, our paramount concern is faithfulness to Scripture. With pastoral concern we appeal to our readers to submit to the coherent biblical message, which simultaneously assures us (that God secures all who are in Jesus Christ) and admonishes us (that we must persevere in loyalty to Jesus Christ or else enter into eternal death). We hope to demonstrate, through careful attention to the biblical text, that assurance and admonition function in harmony, for God's promise grounds God's warning. This is a crucial and ever timely message for believer and unbeliever alike, for the matters we address are of the essence of the gospel's call for faith in Jesus Christ.

---

[6]This is a paraphrase of Augustine *Confessions* 10.39. See Augustine, *Confessions,* trans. William Watts, Loeb Classical Library 27 (Cambridge, Mass.: Harvard University Press, 1997), pp. 148-49.

1

THE RACE SET BEFORE US

What Is There to Win or Lose?

Therefore, since we are surrounded by so great a cloud of witnesses,
let us also lay aside every weight and the sin that clings so closely,
and let us run with perseverance the race that is set before us,
looking to Jesus the pioneer and perfecter of our faith. (Heb 12:1-2 NRSV)

The New Testament frequently uses the imagery of the footrace to portray the Christian life. This imagery aptly represents various aspects of our salvation. God calls us to this race (Phil 3:14). We train for this race (1 Tim 4:7-8). Our training entails strict self-control (1 Cor 9:25). Anyone who runs this race must compete according to the rules (2 Tim 2:5). There is a prize to be won (1 Cor 9:24), and anyone who seeks to win the prize must run with singular devotion, with one's eyes set on the prize who is Jesus Christ (Heb 12:1-2).[1]

Throughout this book we will discuss these and many other analogies between the athlete and the Christian. Presently, however, our concern is to consider the nature of the race set before us. One question comes to the foreground as we begin to ponder the Christian race, namely, the urgency of the race. What is there to win or lose? Not all Christians agree on the answer, though all appeal to Scripture.

It may seem quite simple to answer this question from Scripture. However, we all come to the Bible with biases. All of us read the Bible

---

[1]For a development of the athletic imagery in the Bible, see Erich Sauer, *In the Arena of Faith: A Call to the Consecrated Life* (Grand Rapids, Mich.: Eerdmans, 1955).

with a point of view already in place, a point of view that needs to adjust to Scripture. Therefore, we tend to read biblical passages through our point of view so that, without intending to do so, we adjust words and phrases and clauses to fit our perceptions and biases. None of us ever completely escapes this. Nevertheless, every time we come to Scripture, we must strive to rid ourselves of prejudices that impede our reading of the biblical text and to read it for what it actually says. This is what we seek to do for our readers, just as we seek this for ourselves.

Therefore, we begin this book by focusing on a variety of interpretations of biblical passages that portray the Christian life as a footrace in pursuit of a prize. What is the prize to be won or lost? Christians offer varied responses. These varied responses principally derive from how they view biblical warnings and admonitions that urge us to persevere to the end in order that we may lay hold of the prize. For example, consider the exhortation that appears below the title to this chapter: "Therefore, since we are surrounded by so great a cloud of witnesses, let us also lay aside every weight and the sin that clings so closely, and let us run with perseverance the race that is set before us, looking to Jesus the pioneer and perfecter of our faith" (Heb 12:1-2 NRSV).

One will find varied explanations of this admonition in the commentaries. Some, believing that the goal of the race set before us is salvation itself, are convinced that it is necessary to persevere to the end in order to be saved. Others contend that perseverance is the evidence that one is already saved. Still others argue that the outcome of this race cannot be salvation, for, they believe, the salvation issue has been settled already. Therefore, they argue that perseverance has nothing to do with salvation but only with rewards that even real Christians may lose without losing their salvation. Yet others believe that admonitions such as Hebrews 12:1-2 indicate that it is possible for authentic Christians to fall away and perish forever. Some contend that admonitions indicate that all who are saved will persevere to the end and not fall away and that warnings address those who have fallen away, proving that they never truly did believe. Finally, some believe that admonitions say nothing concerning our salvation. These and many other differences exist among well-meaning believers who read the Bible to find encouragement and hope in living the Christian life.

While our book offers an exposition of Scripture's teaching regarding Christian perseverance and assurance, our central concern is to show how the Bible places side by side both God's promises of complete and final salvation for all his people and God's admonitions or warnings that call on his people to persevere to the end in order to be saved. Long before we began to think about the biblical teaching on perseverance and assurance, many Christians had already wrestled to explain the biblical relationship between warnings and promises. The juxtaposition of promise and warning continues to be the source of the disputes we sketched above and has given birth to at least four different popular views. Therefore, it is only right that we consider briefly how others have tried to explain the relationship of promise and warning before we offer our proposed explanation.

Our objective for this chapter is twofold. First, we will explain four major interpretations of the relationship between God's promises and his admonitions or warnings and how both relate to assurance. We will do so excluding our own view. Our objective is not to offer a critique of these four popular views but to explain them accurately and fairly.[2] We do this because we believe each of these views has legitimate concerns that Christians need to hear as we strive to settle on a biblically conceived understanding of the tension. To clarify distinctions among the various views, we include pictorial representations of each view. Second, we will offer a succinct introduction to our own explanation of the relationship between biblical promises and admonitions or warnings. The remainder of the book lays out the biblical evidence that grounds our understanding of how Scripture integrates God's promises and warnings without contradiction. Each subsequent chapter examines vital biblical evidence that must be factored into a cohesive and comprehensive biblical theology concerning perseverance and assurance.

Four Popular Views on Warnings and Assurance

Loss-of-salvation view. Though many Christians believe that the Bible addresses warnings and admonitions to believers, some insist that these warnings and admonitions indicate that believers can and

---

[2]See also a summary of views by Thomas R. Schreiner, "Perseverance and Assurance: A Survey and a Proposal," *Southern Baptist Journal of Theology* 2 (1998): 32-62.

sometimes do abandon their faith and consequently lose their salvation. According to the loss-of-salvation view, the Bible's warnings and
admonitions make it clear that heirs of God's promise can, by forsaking Christ, fail to persevere in faithfulness and longsuffering, and thus
lose the inheritance of salvation. I. Howard Marshall engages a careful study of the New Testament in his attempt to resolve this question, "whether it is possible for a man who has truly become a
Christian and an heir of the life of heaven to fall away from his faith
and be finally lost."[3] He concludes that though the possibility of losing
one's salvation is "slight on the whole, nevertheless it is a real possibility."[4] Marshall attempts to position his view between the Arminian
and Calvinist views by adopting what he calls a Wesleyan view.[5]

John Wesley, with whom Marshall identifies, held that biblical
warnings are the starting point for explaining biblical words of promise and hope. Wesley insisted that every biblical promise of God's
preservation of his chosen ones needs to be qualified with warnings.
For example, Wesley argued that we properly understand Romans
8:28-39 only by recognizing that the certainty of God's preservation of
his chosen people is contingent on their perseverance. Thus he contended that the warning of Romans 11:22 must be imported into a
reading of Romans 8:28-39. He claimed this because he believed that
Paul's unbroken chain—election, predestination, calling, justification
and glorification—must be understood conditionally. Wesley com-
mented, "And whom he justified—provided they 'continue in his
goodness,' Romans 11:22, he in the end glorified—St. Paul does not
affirm, either here or in any other part of his writings, that precisely
the same number of men are called, justified and glorified."[6] So both
Wesley and Marshall conclude that Paul "does not deny that a believer
may fall away and be cut off between his special calling and his glorification."[7] Thus, even though Marshall wants to distance himself from

---

[3] I. Howard Marshall, *Kept by the Power of God: A Study of Perseverance and Falling Away*
(1969; reprint, Minneapolis: Bethany Fellowship, 1974), p. 24.
[4] Ibid., p. 75.
[5] Ibid., p. 208.
[6] John Wesley, *Explanatory Notes upon the New Testament* (London: Epworth, 1952), p. 551.
G. C. Berkouwer wisely observes, "The opponents of the doctrine of perseverance knew
these passages, of course; but they always stress that the 'if,' the conditional, must always
be understood in the text, even though it is not found there in so many words" (*Faith and
Perseverance,* trans. Robert D. Knudsen [Grand Rapids, Mich.: Eerdmans, 1958], p. 90).
[7] Wesley, quoted by Marshall, *Kept by the Power of God,* p. 103.

Arminianism, he and Wesley are both Arminians, for they affirm that believers may fall away from Christ and perish.[8]

Recently other scholars have argued the case for the loss-of-salvation view to explain the function of the biblical warnings (see figure 1.1).[9] Of these the best argument is that made by Scot McKnight, who focuses on the epistle to the Hebrews.[10] McKnight carefully examines

The race track represents salvation. Christians may abandon the race and lose salvation.

Figure 1.1. Loss-of-salvation view of warnings and admonitions

all five warning passages (Heb 2:1-4; 3:7—4:13; 5:11—6:12; 10:19-39; 12:1-29) together as he makes a strong case that all the warnings do at least three things: (1) they interpret one another, (2) they address believers, and (3) they warn believers that they will perish if they for-

---

[8]This has become a cardinal teaching of Arminianism. However, the original followers of Arminius, the Remonstrants, did not at first fully affirm that true believers can apostatize and lose salvation.

[9]See, e.g., Grant R. Osborne, "Soteriology in the Epistle to the Hebrews," in *Grace Unlimited* (Minneapolis: Bethany House, 1975), pp. 144-66; Robert Shank, *Life in the Son: A Study of the Doctrine of Perseverance,* 2nd ed. (Springfield, Mo.: Westcott, 1976); Dale Moody, *The Word of Truth: A Summary of Christian Doctrine Based on Biblical Revelation* (Grand Rapids, Mich.: Eerdmans, 1981), esp. pp. 337-65; and Dale Moody's polemical work *Apostasy: A Study in the Epistle to the Hebrews and in Baptist History* (Greenville, S.C.: Smyth & Helwys, 1991).

[10]Scot McKnight, "The Warning Passages of Hebrews: A Formal Analysis and Theological Conclusions," *Trinity Journal* n.s. 13 (1992): 21-59.

sake the salvation announced by the Lord in these last days. Mc-Knight also contends that apostasy in Hebrews is deliberate and willful. Two features of McKnight's case deserve emphasis. He argues that the author of Hebrews threatens authentic believers with eschatological judgment if they apostatize from Jesus Christ. He also maintains that the author of Hebrews principally conceives of salvation in future terms. Therefore, believers who now partake of the present aspects of salvation, which is already inaugurated, may wander from the pathway and perish before they experience the eschatological salvation.

Do the warnings indicate that it is possible for authentic believers to perish in the end? One of the questions we intend to address is whether or not the biblical evidence, including Hebrews, warrants the conclusion that true believers can apostatize and thus perish eternally. However, we will demonstrate that there is a primary question that we need to answer first. It concerns the function of warning passages.

Loss-of-rewards view. Christians who embrace the loss-of-rewards view as the explanation of biblical warnings hold two beliefs in common with the loss-of-salvation view. Both agree that biblical warnings address true believers. Both also believe that one of the functions of biblical warnings is to indicate a possible loss for true believers. The two views radically disagree, however, concerning what the believer who fails to persevere will lose.

The designation loss of rewards accurately describes this view and distinguishes it from the previous interpretation because its advocates contend that the biblical admonitions and warnings threaten believers with a possible loss. However, the loss that a Christian may encounter concerns "rewards" only, not salvation or eternal life, which comes to us only by faith in Jesus Christ.[11] The strongest advocates of this view have made this their theological mission. Indeed, in 1986 Robert Wilkin established the Grace Evangelical Society, which now has its own journal and website.[12] According to the society's mission statement, "The goal of Grace Evangelical Society is to focus worldwide attention on the distinction between the freeness of eter-

---

[11]This may be confusing in light of the paragraph above. We will clarify this double use of terms such as *salvation* and *eternal life* by advocates of this view.

[12]*Journal of the Grace Evangelical Society.* See < www.faithalone.org >.

nal life and the costliness of eternal rewards." Their view concerning biblical warnings maintains popular support among American evangelicals. The popularity of this interpretation is partly owing to the earlier influence of the notes in *The New Scofield Reference Bible*, particularly the note concerning 1 Corinthians 3:14:

> God in the N.T. Scriptures offers to the lost, salvation; and for the faithful service of the saved, He offers rewards. The passages are easily distinguished by remembering that salvation is invariably spoken of as a free gift (e.g., Jn. 4:10; Rom. 6:23; Eph. 2:8-9), whereas rewards are earned by works (Mt. 10:42; Lk. 19:17; 1 Cor. 9:24-25; 2 Tim. 4:7-8; Rev. 2:10; 22:12). A further distinction is that salvation is a present possession (Lk. 7:50; Jn. 3:36; 5:24; 6:47), whereas rewards are a future attainment, to be given at the rapture (2 Tim. 4:8; Rev. 22:12).[13]

Two important concerns motivate advocates to adopt this explanation of biblical passages that warn believers against eternal loss. First, advocates of the loss-of-rewards view endorse a radical version of "eternal security." Like many, they appeal to texts such as John 6:37-44, 10:28-30 and Romans 8:28-39 to affirm that no one who believes in Jesus Christ will fail to have eternal life and that no one who has eternal life will ever perish. However, they radicalize eternal security by insisting that security in Jesus Christ guarantees that even those who fail to persevere in faithfulness to Christ and his gospel will never perish but are saved and will remain saved forever. The second motivation that prompts people to adopt the loss-of-rewards view is a defense of the gospel against any intrusion of works-righteousness. Advocates of this view see themselves as guardians of the gospel, the only consistent preachers of the free grace of the gospel of Jesus Christ and the champions against others who introduce the idea of meriting or earning salvation.[14] Their concern is to keep the biblical warnings separate from salvation, for otherwise salvation and eternal life would be earned

---

[13]*The New Scofield Reference Bible* (New York: Oxford University Press, 1967), p. 1235. Charles C. Ryrie similarly states, "Salvation is a free gift, but rewards, for those who are saved, are earned" (*The Ryrie Study Bible*, NASB [Chicago: Moody Press, 1978], p. 1730). It is curious that commentators, theologians and preachers who adopt this view argue vigorously against a doctrine of human merit with regard to salvation yet speak of meriting rewards from God.

[14]Both expressions, "consistent" and "free grace," are their own. For this, see various publications of the Grace Evangelical Society, including comments made at <www.faithalone.org>.

by works.[15] They insist that anyone teaching that believers must persevere in doing good works in order to be saved is proclaiming a different gospel that falls under Paul's anathema in Galatians 1:8-9.[16] They take such a strong stand because they say that the gospel requires only faith for salvation; there is no role at all for obedience or good works in salvation. If obedience or good works are necessary in any sense, then the gospel's offer of eternal life is no longer free and salvation is no longer a free gift. Furthermore, no one could have assurance of salvation, because a Christian's assurance would be conditioned on works. Christians would always be in a state of uncertainty.

Loss-of-rewards advocates agree that biblical warnings address true Christians, but because believers cannot lose their salvation, the threat of loss concerns rewards that would otherwise be received in the age to come. For example, R. T. Kendall contends that anyone who believes the gospel *"will go to heaven when he dies no matter what work (or lack of work) may accompany such faith."*[17] Kendall asks, " 'What if a person who is saved falls into sin, stays in sin, and is found in that very condition when he dies? Will he still go to heaven?' The answer is yes."[18] He then concludes, "I therefore state categorically that the person who is saved—who confesses that Jesus is Lord and believes in his heart that God raised Him from the dead—will go to heaven when he dies no matter what work (or lack of work) may accompany such faith."[19] Likewise, Charles Stanley affirms, "The Bible clearly teaches that God's love for His people is

---

[15]Recent works that argue for the loss-of-rewards view include Zane Hodges, *The Gospel Under Siege: A Study on Faith and Works,* 2nd ed. (Dallas: Rendención Viva, 1991); *Grace in Eclipse: A Study on Eternal Rewards* (Dallas: Rendención Viva, 1985); *Absolutely Free! A Biblical Reply to Lordship Salvation* (Grand Rapids, Mich.: Zondervan, 1989); Robert Wilkin, *Confident in Christ: Living by Faith Really Works* (Irving, Tex.: Grace Evangelical Society, 1999); Charles Stanley, *Eternal Security: Can You Be Sure?* (Nashville: Thomas Nelson, 1990); and Erwin W. Lutzer, *Your Eternal Reward: Triumph and Tears at the Judgment Seat of Christ* (Chicago: Moody Press, 1998). Two British authors defending this perspective include R. T. Kendall (*Once Saved, Always Saved* [Chicago: Moody Press, 1983]) and Michael Eaton (*No Condemnation: A New Theology of Assurance* [Downers Grove, Ill.: InterVarsity Press, 1995]).

[16]Robert Wilkin, "What Is the Anathema of Galatians 1:8-9: Are All Who Preach a False Gospel Eternally Condemned?" *Grace in Focus,* March-April 1994. Wilkin argues that Paul's anathema does not entail eternal punishment.

[17]Kendall, *Once Saved, Always Saved,* p. 49, emphasis in the original.

[18]Ibid., pp. 50-51.

[19]Ibid., pp. 52-53.

of such magnitude that even those who walk away from the faith have not the slightest chance of slipping from His hand."[20] He explains further, "Even if a believer for all practical purposes becomes an unbeliever, his salvation is not in jeopardy."[21] There is no danger of eternal condemnation because "believers who lose or abandon their faith will retain their salvation, for God remains faithful."[22]

Consider how this view interprets one biblical warning. Paul sharply warns the Corinthians, "Do you not know that wrongdoers will not inherit the kingdom of God? Do not be deceived! Fornicators, idolaters, adulterers, male prostitutes, sodomites, thieves, the greedy, drunkards, revilers, robbers—none of these will inherit the kingdom of God" (1 Cor 6:9-10 NRSV). Zane Hodges explains this warning as follows:

> In speaking of heirship in 1 Corinthians 6:9, 10, the Apostle did not threaten his readers with the loss of eternal salvation. He did not even raise a question about their salvation. But he warned them plainly that, if they did not correct their unrighteous behavior, they confronted a serious consequence. They would not inherit the Kingdom of God.[23]

This may sound like double talk. However, Hodges and fellow advocates of this view distinguish between inheriting the kingdom of God and entering the kingdom of God. Hodges explains: "Many have assumed, without much thought, that to 'inherit' the Kingdom must be the same as entering it."[24] But for Hodges there is a great difference. He contends that entrance into the kingdom is of grace, and therefore free, because it is based on Christ's work for us. However, inheritance of the kingdom is based on the merits of our deeds for Christ and thus is costly.[25]

Advocates of the loss-of-rewards view have a doctrine of perseverance, but for them perseverance has nothing to do with salvation in the sense of deliverance from eternal punishment. If it did, salvation

---

[20]Stanley, *Eternal Security,* p. 74.

[21]Ibid., p. 93.

[22]Ibid., p. 94.

[23]Hodges, *Gospel Under Siege,* p. 134.

[24]Ibid. See also Hodges, *Grace in Eclipse,* pp. 67-81. He devotes the entire chapter to drawing his distinction between "inheriting" and "entering." Compare Eaton, *No Condemnation,* pp. 214-17.

[25]See Hodges, *Grace in Eclipse,* pp. 66-81, esp. pp. 72-75.

would be earned by works. Furthermore, they contend, if perseverance were necessary for salvation, then the loss-of-salvation view
would be correct, since, they insist, many believers do not persist in
faithfulness. So they agree with the loss-of-salvation view that biblical warnings indicate that a real loss for the believer is possible. The
point at which the two views disagree, however, is with regard to
what is lost. Advocates of the loss-of-salvation view take phrases
such as "eternal life," "salvation" and "inherit the kingdom" at face
value. Advocates of the loss-of-rewards view, on the other hand,
adopt a novel reading of the text. They reject the Arminian and Wesleyan understanding of biblical warnings because they are convinced that the Bible warrants belief in eternal security. However,
because they find no biblical support for the assurance that believers will persevere in faithfulness to Jesus Christ, they reject the
classical Calvinist or Reformed view of biblical warnings (yet to be
discussed).[26]

Robert Wilkin, for example, argues that biblical warnings and
commands "to persevere would be pointless if all believers persevere."[27] Rather, advocates of this view insist, the Bible makes it clear
that many believers will not persevere in loyalty to Christ. Some
will become apostates yet continue to be Christians.[28] For advocates
of the loss-of-rewards view, perseverance is the attainment and
earning of the right to inherit the kingdom and to rule with Christ
Jesus.[29] Perseverance has nothing to do with salvation for two reasons: (1) salvation would be based on works, and (2) God does not
assure believers that we will persevere. Wilkin notes, "The Scriptures repeatedly command perseverance, but they never promise
it."[30] Even the apostle Paul was uncertain if he would persevere in
faithfulness to the gospel (1 Cor 9:26-27). That is, "Paul knew he was
eternally secure" (2 Tim 1:12), but he did not know if "he would
reign with Christ" (2 Tim 2:12).[31]

---

[26]Eaton identifies his loss-of-rewards view as Calvinist, but he draws a clear distinction
between his version of Calvinism and what he calls "developed Calvinism" (*No Condemnation*, pp. 15-25).

[27]Wilkin, *Confident in Christ*, p. 175.

[28]Hodges, *Gospel Under Siege*, p. 78.

[29]Wilkin, *Confident in Christ*, pp. 133-34.

[30]Ibid., p. 133.

[31]Ibid., p. 134.

The race track represents salvation. Christians may abandon the race and lose rewards.

Figure 1.2. Loss-of-rewards view of warnings and admonitions

For Hodges and his fellow advocates of the loss-of-rewards view, "perseverance in holiness is an indispensable condition" for attaining one's reward, but it has no function whatsoever concerning salvation and eternal life (see figure 1.2).[32] According to this view, texts to which Christians often appeal for confidence and assurance that God will preserve them in faithfulness to him unto the end turn out to have nothing to do with salvation.[33] Because of this, adherents of this view carefully separate salvation from perseverance in holiness.

Tests-of-genuineness view. One of the most common views in evangelicalism today may be called the tests-of-genuineness view. Those who hold this view contend that the Bible poses many warnings and admonitions because of hypocrisy. People may profess faith in Christ but have nothing more than a false salvation.[34] Michael Eaton refers to this view as "developed Calvinism,"[35] while Zane Hodges and other

---

[32]Ibid., p. 116.

[33]See, e.g., John F. Hart, "Does Philippians 1:6 Guarantee Progressive Sanctification?" *Journal of the Grace Evangelical Society* 9, no. 16 (1996): 37-58.

[34]Eaton calls this "unreal salvation" (*No Condemnation,* p. 21).

[35]Ibid., pp. 15-25. Though we do not agree fully with Eaton's assessment of "developed Calvinism" (popular Calvinism, our term), we concur that its general treatment of biblical warnings and admonitions tends to evoke introspection. We believe Eaton's criticism of Puritanism's introspective bent is correct, though he seems to have overreacted against English Puritanism.

American evangelicals who adopt the loss-of-rewards view use the designation "lordship salvation." We will call this perspective the tests-of-genuineness view.[36]

How does this view differ from the two we have already considered? We have shown that Christians who adopt either the loss-of-rewards or the loss-of-salvation view to explain biblical warnings agree that the warnings address true believers and that one of the functions of biblical warnings is to indicate a possible loss for true believers, though they disagree over what the believer might lose. By way of contrast, those who advocate the tests-of-genuineness view believe that the biblical warnings are addressed to people who profess faith in Jesus Christ but who prove to be false or disingenuous in their confession. Second, this view does not regard the threatened loss to be a possible loss of something already possessed. Rather, the warnings function as tests to prove that the "disingenuous believer" never possessed true salvation. Thus, biblical admonitions and warnings distinguish pseudobelievers from true believers.

Here it is important to recognize points of agreement between this view and the first two we described. In terms of defining *salvation,* advocates of the tests-of-genuineness view concur with those who hold to the loss-of-rewards view. Both fundamentally conceive of salvation as already possessed and as something that, once possessed, cannot be lost. However, when the two views apply this conviction to biblical warnings, they come to radically different conclusions. On the other hand, adherents to the tests-of-genuineness view agree with proponents of the loss-of-salvation view that good works are necessary for salvation. However, in the context of warnings and admonitions, their agreement diverges because those who view biblical warnings as tests of faith regard good works retrospectively only as evidence that one is saved. Advocates of this view carefully explain that though perseverance is

---

[36]Note the subtitle of Hodges's book *Absolutely Free! A Biblical Reply to Lordship Salvation.* Review the theological firestorm swirling about John MacArthur and Zane Hodges. See particularly John F. MacArthur Jr., *The Gospel According to Jesus* (Grand Rapids, Mich.: Zondervan, 1988), juxtaposed with Zane Hodges, *Absolutely Free! A Biblical Reply to Lordship Salvation.* For a Reformed critique of this conflict, see Michael Horton, ed., *Christ the Lord: The Reformation and Lordship Salvation* (Grand Rapids, Mich.: Baker, 1992).

necessary as evidence of authentic faith, perseverance has no role in the means of salvation, for then salvation would be of works and not of grace.[37]

It is characteristic of those who hold the tests-of-genuineness view to insist that authentic faith in Christ inevitably perseveres as it produces good works (Eph 2:10). Yet, while good works are both the inevitable fruit and necessary evidence of faith, advocates of this view vigorously oppose any notion of works-righteousness. They do not separate good works from faith as if one were justified by faith and good works. Instead, faith is the root that yields its fruit of good works.[38] Those defending this view of biblical warnings argue that perseverance in loyalty to Christ and in holiness is essential for salvation, because perseverance is the necessary evidence that belief is genuine. Therefore, preachers who hold this view of biblical admonitions and warnings are understandably concerned to call on their congregations: "Test yourselves, whether you are in the faith. Examine yourselves!" (2 Cor 13:5). They use biblical admonitions and warnings as tests of genuine faith, citing 1 John 2:19 to support their case. There the apostle John says, "They went out from us, but they did not belong to us; for if they had belonged to us, they would have remained with us. But by going out they made it plain that none of them belongs to us" (NRSV). Because there are many who make a false profession of faith in Christ, a significant aspect of faithful preaching, for advocates of this view, is to call on people to test the genuineness of their faith, for saving faith produces the fruit of the Spirit (Gal 5:22-23).

For the time being we offer two examples to show how the tests-of-genuineness view handles biblical admonitions and warnings. We will interact with other examples during our interpretive work in the biblical text. John MacArthur writes:

---

[37]This is the viewpoint expressed by John F. MacArthur Jr. in various books, including *Gospel According to Jesus; Faith Works: The Gospel According to the Apostles* (Dallas: Word, 1993); *Saved Without a Doubt* (Wheaton, Ill.: Victor, 1992).

[38]See Kim Riddlebarger, "What Is Faith?" in *Christ the Lord: The Reformation and Lordship Salvation,* ed. Michael Horton (Grand Rapids, Mich.: Baker, 1992), pp. 81-105, for a discussion of how both Zane Hodges and John MacArthur articulate the relationship between faith and good works.

Certainly Scripture seems to be filled with warnings to people in the church lest they should fall away (cf. Heb. 6:4-8; 1 Tim. 1:18-19; 2 Tim. 2:16-19). . . . But God does not contradict Himself. The warning passages do not negate the many promises that believers will persevere. . . . And, it might be added, the warning passages like Jude 21 reveal that the writers of Scripture were very keen to alert those whose hope of salvation might be grounded in a spurious faith. Obviously the apostolic authors were not laboring under the illusion that every person in the churches they were writing to was genuinely converted.[39]

It seems evident that MacArthur believes that biblical admonitions and warnings address the "mixed church" as a way of sifting the "tares" from the "wheat" (cf. Mt 13:24-30).[40]

S. Lewis Johnson Jr. agrees with this approach to biblical admonitions and warnings. Consider his explanation of Colossians 1:21-23, which indicates that Christ Jesus will present us holy and blameless before God in the day of judgment, "if [we] remain in the faith."

But what about the "if"? we hear someone say. Is not the whole program in jeopardy? Does it not all depend upon us ultimately? Suppose our faith fails? Now, we must not dodge the "ifs" of the Word. They are tests for professors. If faith fails, that is the evidence that the faith was not valid saving faith (cf. 1 Jn. 2:19). On the other hand, the genuine believer will persevere in faith, not by human strength, but by divine strengthening. . . . The *ei* (AV, "if"), it may be noted, introduces a first-class condition, determined as fulfilled. The apostle assumes the Colossians will abide in their faith.[41]

Unlike adherents to either the loss-of-salvation or the loss-of-rewards views, Johnson regards the admonitions and warnings to be retrospective tests of faith. They prompt believers to review their progress in faith to assess whether or not there is evidence that faith is genuine. Johnson does not explain Colossians 1:21-23 as having a

---

[39]MacArthur, *Faith Works*, pp. 179-80.

[40]In chapter four we will return to evaluate MacArthur's appeal to the idea of the "mixed church" to explain biblical warnings and admonitions. Here it is sufficient to note I. Howard Marshall's objection that this idea that the church "contains men whose belief is superficial and unreal" is not "adequate to explain the whole of the evidence" (*Kept by the Power of God*, pp. 200, 201).

[41]S. Lewis Johnson Jr., "Studies in the Epistle to the Colossians: IV. From Enmity to Amity," *Bibliotheca Sacra* 119 (1962): 147. See also Willard M. Aldrich, "Perseverance," *Bibliotheca Sacra* 115 (1958): 16.

prospective orientation, as the other two views do.[42] By *prospective* we mean forward-looking, particularly to the consummation of salvation. This view of admonitions and warnings turns us both retrospectively and introspectively to assess the beginning and continuation of our faith, whether or not growth, good works and fruit have been and continue to be present. Others support Johnson's explanation of these verses in Colossians. F. F. Bruce comments, "If the Bible teaches the final perseverance of the saints, it also teaches that the saints are those who finally persevere—in Christ. Continuance is the test of reality."[43]

Earlier we took note of how John Wesley introduces the language of a biblical warning ("if") from Romans 11:22 into Romans 8:29-30 to explain the language of promise.[44] Those who hold the tests-of-genuineness view do the same thing, only in an inverted way. Whether overtly or implicitly in their explanations of the text, they import language of promise to explain biblical warnings and admonitions.

When advocates of the tests-of-genuineness read biblical warnings and admonitions, they reject the idea that the loss to be avoided is merely loss of a reward. Though they believe that the warnings are concerned with eternal loss, they disagree with the loss-of-salvation view by arguing that the warnings in a text like Hebrews 6 are addressed to those people who have externally joined themselves to the church and have experienced many blessings attached to the gospel but who are not actually Christians. The warnings address people "who experienced many blessings and then fell away," and by their falling away prove that they "had never truly been saved in the first place."[45]

---

[42]Contrast, for example, Robert Shank's concern: "Let us, then, heed the many warnings against the peril of turning aside from Him who is our hope, our peace, and our life. We dare not ignore the fateful contingency with which Paul confronts us: God, who has reconciled us to Himself through the death of His Son, will ultimately present us . . . 'Holy and unblameable and unreproveable before him' in His own holy presence—if we continue in the faith, grounded and settled, and be not moved away from the hope of the Gospel which we have heard" (*Life in the Son*, p. 71). Also see Hodges's explanation of the text as a prospective warning against loss of rewards (*Gospel Under Siege*, pp. 89-90).

[43]F. F. Bruce, *The Epistles to the Colossians, to Philemon, and to the Ephesians*, New International Commentary on the New Testament (Grand Rapids, Mich.: Eerdmans, 1984), p. 79. Compare the approval of this view by Judith M. Gundry Volf, *Paul and Perseverance: Staying In and Falling Away* (Louisville, Ky.: Westminster John Knox, 1990), p. 197 n. 231.

[44]See note 6 above and the corresponding discussion it supports.

[45]Wayne Grudem, "Perseverance of the Saints: A Case Study of Hebrews 6:4-6 and the Other Warning Passages in Hebrews," in *Still Sovereign: Contemporary Perspectives on Election, Foreknowledge, and Grace*, ed. Thomas R. Schreiner and Bruce A. Ware (Grand Rapids, Mich.: Baker, 2000), p. 173.

The race track represents salvation. To abandon the race proves one was never saved. Christians run with their back toward the goal to assess their progress on the track.

Figure 1.3. Tests-of-genuineness view of warnings and admonitions

It is apparent that those who hold the tests-of-genuineness approach to biblical warnings adopt this view as a way to preserve the promise of security in Jesus Christ for everyone who truly embraces him for salvation. Advocates of this view want to take the warnings seriously because they administer caution against the sin of apostasy. However, this viewpoint often interprets the biblical warnings from the retrospective vantage point of apostasy completed rather than from the prospective threat lest someone fall away. In other words, this view often interprets biblical warnings as though the loss warned against is already a reality for the persons being warned (see figure 1.3). If professing Christians forsake Christ and the gospel, such apostasy proves that they were never truly part of Christ's household. The warnings against apostasy in Hebrews 6 do not address authentic believers, for that would entail their loss of salvation. Clearly for this view the warnings do not have that function, because there is no possible loss of salvation for anyone who is truly a believer.

If the Bible warns spurious believers against apostasy, do these warnings have any function for true believers? Wayne Grudem, who adopts this view, claims at the close of his essay on the warnings in

Hebrews that "these warnings will often be the very means God uses
to keep his own from turning away."[46] However, it is at least curious
that Grudem makes this statement, because he consistently argues
that Hebrews addresses the warnings to people who have already
fallen or who are about to fall, and in every case those people prove
not to be Christians. Evidently Grudem means that one's response to
the warnings is the test of faith. Just as failure to persevere is evidence that one does not belong to God's people, so all who respond to
the warnings by persevering in loyalty to Christ prove that they are
genuine believers and members of Christ's household.

Hypothetical-loss-of-salvation view. It is not necessary to devote much
space to the hypothetical view because this interpretive viewpoint
emerges principally in discussions of warnings in Hebrews. Some who
comment especially on the threats in Hebrews adopt this fourth viewpoint as they attempt to avoid problems they see in each of the other
three views. For advocates of this fourth interpretive viewpoint, the
problem with the loss-of-salvation view is that it contradicts biblical
promises of security in Jesus Christ for everyone who believes. The
problem with the loss-of-rewards view is that it minimizes the awful-
ness of apostasy, for, they insist against Hodges, an apostate is not a
Christian. This fourth view also seeks to avoid two problems with the
tests-of-genuineness view: its insistence that the warnings do not
address authentic Christians and its retrospective reading of the warning passages in Hebrews. Contrary to Grudem's claims, the sin of apostasy that the author of Hebrews warns against has not yet happened; it
is a projected supposition. Otherwise, why administer the warning?[47]

The fourth view contends that the warnings, particularly in
Hebrews, focus on correcting "wrong ideas" by making it clear that if
a Christian could apostatize, it would be impossible for that person to
become a Christian again. The warnings address genuine believers to
correct the wrong idea that apostasy is not serious, as though one
could continue to oscillate between Christianity and Judaism without

---

[46]Ibid., p. 182. Grudem adds, "This does not imply that a true believer could lose salvation, but it does imply that the impossibility of losing salvation does not rest ultimately in any inherent ability in the believer himself or herself, but in the power of
God at work, usually in many different internal and external ways, in the believer's
life."

[47]See Homer A. Kent Jr., *The Epistle to the Hebrews: A Commentary* (Grand Rapids,
Mich.: Baker, 1972), pp. 111-13.

eternal loss.[48] The warnings threaten Christians with eternal and irremediable loss lest they flirt with such apostasy from Christ. Succinctly expressed, this interpretive viewpoint claims that any believer who fails to persevere in faithfulness to the gospel (and this is impossible) will not be saved (see figure 1.4).

Various scholars who adopt the hypothetical-loss view express it

The race track represents salvation. One who is already saved cannot abandon the race.

Figure 1.4. Hypothetical loss-of-salvation view of warnings and admonitions

differently. However, all point to B. F. Westcott as the modern source of the view.[49] Commenting on Hebrews 6:4-6, Westcott says, "The case is hypothetical. There is nothing to show that the conditions of fatal apostasy had been fulfilled, still less that they had been fulfilled in the case of any of those addressed. Indeed the contrary is assumed."[50] However, careful attention to Westcott's phrasing indicates that he does not hold the view that Thomas Hewitt ascribes to him concerning Hebrews 6:4-6.[51] Hewitt explains the warning as follows: "If such a

---

[48]Ibid., p. 113.

[49]See Kent, *Epistle to the Hebrews*, p. 114. Also see Thomas Hewitt, *The Epistle to the Hebrews: An Introduction and Commentary*, Tyndale New Testament Commentaries (Grand Rapids, Mich.: Eerdmans, 1960), p. 111.

[50]B. F. Westcott, *The Epistle to the Hebrews* (Grand Rapids, Mich.: Eerdmans, 1974), p. 165.

[51]Marshall correctly demonstrates that Hewitt wrongly uses Westcott to support his own view (*Kept by the Power of God*, p. 146).

falling away could happen, he is saying, it would be impossible to renew them again unto repentance unless Christ died a second time, which is unthinkable."[52] While Westcott says that "the case is hypothetical" ("if one apostatizes . . ."), Hewitt goes beyond the simple conditional by using a different type of hypothetical construction, namely, a contrary-to-fact supposition, for he says, "if such a falling away could happen." Notice the difference. Westcott is saying, "Suppose someone falls away." Hewitt is saying, "Suppose someone could fall away." Hewitt, and those who follow his lead, fail to realize that Westcott's commentary does not support their view.[53]

The concern that motivates the hypothetical view is the desire to avoid the apparent contradiction between biblical warnings and God's promises to secure his own people. Kent's comments on the warning of Hebrews 10 make this clear.

> Are true Christians ever guilty of complete apostasy? The Arminian says yes, and interprets this passage as denoting true believers who lose their salvation. Calvinists, however, recognize that salvation is eternally secure for true believers, and interpret this passage in other ways. Some regard the apostates as mere professors who finally depart. It might be tempting to weaken the punishment so as to make it less than loss of salvation, but this expedient has not satisfied many in the light of the nature of the offense. A more reasonable explanation would seem to be that the passage warns true believers what the outcome would be if apostasy would occur.[54]

We have surveyed four major interpretive approaches concerning the relationship between biblical warnings and promises. We have offered little critique of these viewpoints as we have attempted to represent each one fairly and accurately. We do not intend to suggest that these are rigid categories so that someone who advocates one view never crosses over to another view when interpreting another biblical warning. Rather, we have identified categories by prominent

---

[52]Hewitt, *Epistle to the Hebrews*, p. 111.

[53]For example, Homer Kent does not properly distinguish between Hewitt's and Westcott's views (*Epistle to the Hebrews*, p. 114). His misfortune is that he confuses his own view by appealing both to Hewitt and to W. H. Griffith-Thomas. He quotes Griffith-Thomas: "The passage is apparently a supposed case to correct their wrong ideas, and the argument seems to be that if it were possible for those who have had the experiences of verses 4-6 to fall away, it would be impossible to renew them unless Christ died a second time" (p. 114).

[54]Kent, *Epistle to the Hebrews*, pp. 206-7.

interpretive tendencies that will help our readers understand the issues at stake with regard to how the biblical text holds warnings and promises together. Of course, there is a fifth view that we have not yet discussed: our own. We will briefly introduce it in the following section, then use the remainder of the book to develop it and demonstrate its biblical basis.[55]

Promises and Warnings: God's Means of Saving His People

In our earlier days of Christian understanding, we both sat under preaching and teaching that led us to certain conclusions about the relationship between biblical promise and warning. We first believed that those who hold the loss-of-reward view explained the relationship best, but later we came to agree with those who teach that warnings are tests of the genuineness of one's faith. In truth, our spiritual pilgrimages took us through various understandings until the Scriptures convinced both of us that we were continually asking the wrong question concerning the biblical warnings. Thus, we now believe that biblical warnings are a crucial means God uses to protect his people for "the salvation that is ready to be revealed in the last time" (1 Pet 1:5 NIV).

What is the function of biblical admonitions and warnings? Advocates of all four popular views surveyed above are consumed with addressing one principal question, which they believe the biblical warnings and admonitions raise in view of God's promises: Is it possible for authentic believers to apostatize and perish forever? Advocates of each view offer contrary answers, depending on other theological commitments. Many Christians believe that the admonitions and warnings are proof that Christians are free to forsake Jesus Christ and perish eternally, and that some do. Therefore, they hold the loss-of-salvation view. Yet other Christians believe that, if God's promises are true, no genuine believer can fall away and perish forever. It is not surprising, then, that their explanations of biblical warnings sound very different. However, the explanations of this second group are quite diverse, as our overview above shows, which leads to three

---

[55]We should mention another interpretive view. Gerald L. Borchert believes that we must maintain a certain tension between passages that offer assurance to the believer and warning passages. He believes the proper approach is to let both kinds of texts stand as they do by preaching both but not making an effort to explain how they fit together (*Assurance and Warning* [Nashville: Broadman, 1987]). For interaction with this view see Schreiner, "Perseverance and Assurance," pp. 40, 51-52.

divergent interpretations within this one group.

None of the advocates of the four popular views arrive at their interpretations of biblical warnings on the basis of the warning passages themselves. Rather, they read the warning passages in view of their prior assumptions concerning the possibility of falling away and perishing under God's wrath. Because they all seek to protect their prior conclusions concerning falling away, whether consciously or not, all four views fail to ask the right question concerning biblical warnings. We believe the right question concerns the function of biblical warnings in relation to biblical promises. This question does not seem to occur to those who adopt one of the four popular interpretations of biblical warnings.

Advocates of both the loss-of-salvation view and the loss-of-rewards view appeal to admonitions and warnings to prove that believers have the freedom to forsake Christ Jesus. The basic function of warnings seems to be to indicate that it is possible to fall away and suffer loss. While it is true that the apostasy and consequential loss differ substantially between these two views, they hold in common the notion that admonitions and warnings, framed as suppositions, necessarily imply a doubtful outcome.

Those who endorse either the tests-of-genuineness view or the hypothetical-loss-of-salvation view seem concerned to avoid the implications the other two views find in suppositional warnings and admonitions. They also seem to assume that suppositional warnings imply some kind of uncertainty. Convinced, however, that all who are in Christ Jesus are secure forever, these Bible interpreters unwittingly modify the suppositional warnings to avoid conflict with God's sure promises. Earlier we showed how S. Lewis Johnson's interpretation of Colossians 1:21-23 turns the prospective admonition into a retrospective test of faith's sincerity. Consequently, the function of admonitions and warnings is to call on believers to assess whether or not their belief is authentic. Similarly, Thomas Hewitt recasts suppositional warnings to mean that if a believer could fall away, then it would result in eternal perishing. Thus, the function of admonitions and warnings is to correct incorrect reasoning that apostasy is not serious. However, the call for perseverance is only indirect.

What distinguishes our proposal from the other four views? While the other four interpretations of biblical warnings do not allow the suppositional language of biblical warnings its ordinary function, we seek to do just that. Whereas the other four explanations of biblical admonitions and warnings smuggle theological conclusions into their explanations of the warning passages, unwitting though it may be, we believe we avoid both implicitly and explicitly imposing a theological grid on the warnings. Instead, we concentrate our interpretive efforts on the grammar and context of biblical texts that admonish and warn, and we do the same for biblical promises of God's assuring grace to preserve his own. We refuse to impose suppositional warnings on God's promises, as advocates of the loss-of-salvation view do. We equally resist superimposing God's promises on admonitions and warnings, as those who endorse the other three views do. We believe that God's promises have their own function, namely, to establish belief in the God who keeps his promises and to assure us that he is faithful to his people. We also believe that God's warnings and admonitions have their distinctive function. They serve to elicit belief that perseveres in faithfulness to God's heavenly call on us. Thus, God's promises and God's warnings do not conflict. Rather, the warnings serve the promises, for the warnings urge belief and confidence in God's promises. Biblical warnings and admonitions are the means God uses to save and preserve his people to the end (see figure 1.5).

The race track represents salvation. If one abandons the race one will not receive the prize.

Figure 1.5. God's means-of-salvation view of warnings and admonitions

Conditional promises and conditional warnings. What do biblical warnings look like? Most biblical warnings use suppositional or conditional language to express a threat or a promise. It may be helpful to identify what conditional language entails. A condition expresses a contingent relationship. Ordinarily we express this contingency with a conditional sentence that consists of two clauses: (1) a dependent clause ("if"), also called the protasis, and (2) an independent clause ("then"), also called the apodosis. Another word to describe a condition is *supposition*. English readers usually think of the word *if* as the indicator of a condition. Though perhaps most conditional expressions in English do use the word *if,* there are other ways to express a conditional idea. We often use the imperative, a command, to express a contingency, such as, "Swallow arsenic, and you will die." Sometimes we simply express a condition by saying, "Suppose you swallow arsenic—you will die." But we also use other grammatical structures to express a contingency. For example, we regularly use a relative clause for this purpose: "Whoever swallows this bottle of arsenic will die." We also use a gerund: "Swallowing arsenic will kill you." Or we may rephrase it, "The one who swallows arsenic will die." What is true in English is also true in the biblical languages, Hebrew and Greek.[56]

As we read the New Testament, we find many warnings and admonitions that seem to have immediate and direct application to Christians. We will look briefly at two main kinds of New Testament passages in this segment. We will call these two categories of passages (1) conditional promises and (2) conditional warnings and admonitions. At this point we will simply introduce the kind of biblical language that will become the primary focus of chapter four. Here we will illustrate what we mean by conditional promises and conditional warnings. We have carefully selected two passages with the hope that readers will agree that these fit our two categories. In addition, we expect that all will agree that the alternative the text presents in both passages is eternal life or eternal perishing. We are also reasonably confident that not all will fully agree with our discussion of these texts.

The following passage represents a conditional promise: "To the one who is thirsty, I will give freely from the spring of the water of

---

[56]For a helpful discussion of conditional sentences in the Greek New Testament, see Daniel B. Wallace, *Greek Grammar Beyond the Basics* (Grand Rapids, Mich.: Zondervan, 1996), pp. 679-712.

life. The one who overcomes will inherit these things, and I will be
God to that one and that one will be a son to me" (Rev 21:6-7). The
passage expresses the promise conditionally, for receiving the thirst-
quenching drink of eternal life is conditioned on thirsting, and inheriting all that God has promised is contingent on overcoming. This
promise seems to be nothing more nor less than an elaboration of the
gospel's initial conditional call to believe the good news of Jesus
Christ. Who could doubt that this passage announces the gospel's
command to both believer and unbeliever? It is clear that the two
metaphors—thirsting and inheriting—depict our profound need and
God's abundant provision. Furthermore, the passage uses the common biblical imagery of water to depict eternal life (cf. Jn 4:7-15; Rev
7:17; 22:1, 17). But how does this conditional promise elaborate the
call of the gospel? It does so by inviting believer and unbeliever alike
to consider the outcome of extended belief, here designated by two
Greek participles: "the one who is thirsty" and "the one who overcomes." Thus, eternal life, according to this conditional promise,
belongs to anyone who exercises belief that endures against trials,
belief that is characterized as thirst that is determined to be
quenched.[57]

An example of a passage that administers a conditional warning is
Revelation 22:18-19:

> I warn everyone who hears the words of the prophecy of this book: if
> anyone adds to them, God will add to that person the plagues described
> in this book; if anyone takes away from the words of the book of this
> prophecy, God will take away that person's share in the tree of life and
> in the holy city, which are described in this book. (NRSV)

As before, this passage uses conditional language, but here it
expresses the warning. If one adds to the book of Revelation, God will
add to that person the horrible plagues described in this book. If one
subtracts from the book, God will snatch away from that person his or
her share "in the tree of life and in the holy city." As with the promise, the warning uses metaphors for eternal punishment ("plagues")
and for eternal life ("share in the tree of life and in the holy city"). To

---

[57]Though we nuance our discussion of gospel conditions and of the relationship
between faith and obedience, we essentially concur with John Piper's discussion of
"conditional promises." For his discussion see *The Purifying Power of Living by Faith in
Future Grace* (Sisters, Ore.: Multnomah, 1995), pp. 231-59.

"add to" or to "take away from" the book is imagery that depicts the consequences of unbelief or unfaithfulness. It should be apparent, now, that the two passages are similar, for both promise and warning employ conditional language.

However, there is an important difference between the two classes of passages. The first passage assures a promise of eternal life with a condition attached. The second trumpets a warning lest anyone who has a share in eternal life forfeit it. Though there is a distinction between the two passages, it is important to study both classes of passages together because the warning is a corollary of the promise. By corollary, we mean that the warning accompanies the promise by complementing it. One may readily see this complementary relationship by reading Revelation 22:17, the verse that immediately precedes the warning we have cited: "The Spirit and the bride say, 'Come.' And let everyone who hears say, 'Come.' And let everyone who is thirsty come. Let anyone who wishes take the water of life as a gift" (NRSV). Clearly, this verse reiterates the conditional promise of Revelation 21:6-7. Thus it confirms our earlier observation that the conditional promise of those verses is the gospel's sustained call for protracted belief, belief that endures. It also confirms our observation that the warning of verses 18-19 complements the conditional promise by reinforcing the fact that the promise is conditioned on persistent belief. The conditional promise (Rev 21:6-7; 22:17) sustains and elaborates the gospel's initial command to believe by reiterating the call for belief that persists to the end. The conditional warning (Rev 22:18-19), as a corollary to the promise, also elaborates or sustains the call of the gospel for faithfulness and loyalty to Christ that endures to the end.

Biblical warnings and admonitions point us toward the last day. Another significant difference between our proposal and the general orientation of the other four interpretations of warnings is what we call an eschatological orientation. A passage such as 1 Peter 1:5—"who are being protected by the power of God through faith for a salvation ready to be revealed in the last time" (NRSV)—makes the point, if we will hear it, that salvation has an eschatological or last-day orientation. *Salvation,* in other words, is not only a term to describe what God has already done by justifying and converting us but also a word that portrays what God has not yet done when he will bring us to "the goal of our faith, the salvation of our souls" (1 Pet 1:9).

Much of the theological wrangling that has taken place between Calvinists and Arminians, between defenders of so-called lordship salvation and the self-designated advocates of free grace, has been due to a failure to take seriously and consistently the biblical evidence for the already-but-not-yet elements that fill the pages of the New Testament.[58] Each of the four theological groups we have identified earlier in this chapter talks past the others because each has ignored one strand of evidence or another while also exaggerating out of biblical proportion one or another strand. The way forward and through the impasse of this theological dispute is to acknowledge that the biblical lines of evidence indicate that our salvation in Christ Jesus is properly portrayed with evenhanded accent on both the already and the not-yet aspects.

In the next chapter we will demonstrate that the Bible portrays salvation with many and varied metaphors, as a reality that is already ours by rights as heirs but that we have not yet inherited. This is so because the heavenly Son of God offered himself as a sacrifice once to do away with sin, but he has not yet returned to bring salvation to us who are waiting for him (Heb 9:26-28). We recognize how tempting it is to draw simplistic conclusions concerning this tension between the already and the not yet. Some evangelicals tend to exaggerate the not-yet-attained consummation of salvation as they insist that the biblical warnings and admonitions prove that Christians can lose their salvation. Many other evangelicals exaggerate what we already possess in Christ Jesus so that they collapse the not-yet-attained aspects into the already-received aspects. The result is that either the warnings have nothing to do with salvation (as per the loss-of-rewards view) or the warnings lose their prospective orientation and take on a retrospective function as tests to uncover hypocrites and spurious believers in the church.

We believe that holding a proper tension between the already and not-yet aspects of God's gracious gift of salvation leads us to recognize that biblical warnings are prospective, designed to elicit faith that perseveres to the end in order to lay hold of the eternal prize of life. We

---

[58]See the critique of the so-called lordship salvation debate between Hodges and MacArthur, in *Christ the Lord,* ed. Michael Horton (Grand Rapids, Mich.: Baker, 1992).

believe that not only must we accept the intended functions of both promise (assurance) and warning (admonition), but we must also accurately represent their functions in our writing, our teaching and our preaching if we want to do justice to the biblical evidence. This is especially true because how we explain the relationship of promise and warning has profound implications for us personally, interrelationally in the home and in the church, and pastorally.

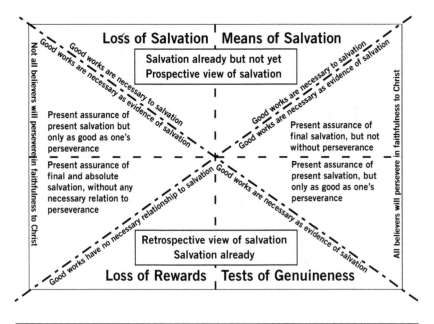

Figure 1.6. Comparative chart of four views of perseverance and assurance, with a focus on warnings and admonitions (excluding the hypothetical-loss-of-salvation view)

2

THE PRIZE
TO BE WON

Our Present & Future Salvation

Not that I have already arrived or have already been perfected,

but I pursue it, if I also may lay hold of that for which I

was laid hold of by Christ Jesus. Brothers and sisters, I do not yet regard

myself as having laid hold of it. But one thing I do:

forgetting what lies behind and straining forward to what lies ahead,

I pursue the goal to attain the prize of the upward call

of God in Christ Jesus. (Phil 3:12-14)

The Christian life is like a race, and we run to win a prize. Winning this race is the most important matter in our lives. If we lose this race, everything else we achieve in life is meaningless. Paul exhorts us in 1 Corinthians 9:24 to "run in such a way as to get the prize." The prize is described in verse 25 as "a crown that will last forever." To win the prize, believers must go into "strict training" (v. 25) and run diligently (v. 26). We must exercise discipline and perseverance so that we "will not be disqualified for the prize" (v. 27). Paul also uses racecourse imagery in Philippians 3:12-14. During this life we have not yet obtained the prize or reached the goal. So we "press on" (vv. 12, 14) and "strain" (v. 13) toward the goal. We run hard and long to receive the prize at the conclusion of the race.

Believers must train diligently to receive the prize at the end of the race, and we can also be confident while running the race that we will win the prize. When Paul approached the end of his life, he reflected on his effort in the arena of life. He was confident that "the crown of righteousness" awaited him (2 Tim 4:8). The reason for his assurance is explained in the famous words "I have fought the good fight, I have finished the race, I have kept the faith" (2 Tim 4:7). The crown of righteousness is not reserved for Paul alone; it belongs "to all who have longed for his [Christ's] appearing" (v. 8). Two truths stand out in Paul's assessment of his life. First, he was confident that he had lived in a way that pleased God. Paul knew that the crown of righteousness awaited him. Second, the reason for Paul's assurance was his perseverance in running the race. He had not quit halfway into the race; he had not abandoned the faith.

The previous paragraph raises a question. What is the prize that believers are running to win? Some Christians are convinced that it cannot be eternal life. They understand the prize to be rewards, which are an additional gift beyond eternal life. They insist that believers already have eternal life, so there is no need to win eternal life as a prize on the last day. They also fear that any talk of winning the prize smacks of salvation by works.

In this chapter we shall attempt to show that our salvation is both present and future. This is important because almost every view we criticize fails to understand correctly the already-but-not-yet character of salvation. We will discover that this is particularly true of the view of the Grace Evangelical Society, which we described in chapter one, but even the tests-of-genuineness view tends to fix our attention onto the past instead of the future.

Both the present and future dimensions of salvation should be viewed as two aspects of an indivisible whole.[1] Almost inevitably the impression that separable parts are intended will tend to creep into readers' minds, but we must fix in our minds from the beginning that wholes instead of parts are in view. The present possession of all the gifts we will describe is ours because the eschaton (the end time) has invaded history. The blessings we enjoy today, therefore, are anchored in the cross and resurrection of Jesus Christ, which constitutes the invasion of God's end-time work into this present age.

Salvation is not merely a past reality; it is also our future destiny. Actually, the word *salvation* is simply one metaphor used in the Scrip-

---

[1]For this insight, see Mark A. Seifrid, *Christ, Our Righteousness: Paul's Theology of Justification* (Downers Grove, Ill.: InterVarsity Press, 2001).

tures to describe God's action in Christ on our behalf. No single metaphor can encompass God's saving work, for our salvation exceeds the capacity of any image or metaphor. We have chosen to classify God's work on our behalf into five different types of metaphors: (1) deliverance, (2) renewal, (3) family, (4) cultic and (5) legal.

Deliverance Metaphors

When biblical writers think of our new life in Christ, they often describe it in terms of deliverance. Three major metaphors or pictures are used to portray deliverance: salvation, the kingdom of God and redemption. *Salvation* means that we have been rescued from sin and death as well as from God's wrath. Believers are delivered from the realm of Satan and transferred to the *kingdom of God's Son* (Acts 26:18; Col 1:12-13). The word *redemption* signifies that believers are liberated from the power of sin and Satan. All three terms describe the deliverance that God has accomplished for his people. We will consider each of these three terms in more detail.

Salvation. Almost all Christians think of salvation exclusively in terms of the past. Believers often say, "I have been saved," or ask someone else, "Have you been saved?" We will argue that most evangelical Christians do not use the word *salvation* as it is usually used in the Bible, where the term denotes our future salvation. Hence, the emphasis of the biblical text often gets lost when we speak about salvation.

The word *salvation* denotes rescue from some danger or plight. Luke relays the meaning of the word in the story of the storm that buffeted Paul's ship. The storm was so fierce that those on the ship "gave up all hope of being saved" (Acts 27:20). The word *saved* indicates that they gave up all hope of being rescued from the storm; they were certain that death awaited them. The Scriptures use the noun *salvation* and the verb *save* to denote our rescue from sin and God's wrath. Once again the term finds its antecedents in the Old Testament. Salvation, like redemption, occurred when God saved his people out of Egypt (Ex 14:13; 15:2; Ps 106:8, 10). The term is often used to denote God's intervention to deliver his people in other situations, such as during the period of the judges (Judg 2:16; 3:9, 31; 6:14) and in answer to the prayers of the psalmist (e.g., Ps 6:4; 7:1). God also promises to save his people in the future and to bring in his kingdom (Is 35:4; 45:17; 46:13; 49:6, 25; 52:10; Jer 31:7-9; Ezek 36:29). We must understand again that the term *salva-*

tion flows out of the Old Testament and that the salvation portrayed in the New Testament fulfills what the Old Testament promised.

When we examine the New Testament, some texts indicate that our salvation has already been accomplished and is our present possession. For instance, Ephesians 2:5 and 8 clearly speak of salvation as an accomplished reality. God "made us alive with Christ even when we were dead in transgressions—it is by grace you have been saved. . . . For it is by grace you have been saved, through faith—and this not from yourselves, it is the gift of God" (NIV). The words "have been saved" demonstrate that salvation now belongs to believers. Three other texts in Paul also attest that salvation is the present possession of believers: "He saved us, not because of righteous things we had done, but because of his mercy. He saved us through the washing of rebirth and renewal by the Holy Spirit" (Tit 3:5 NIV); God "has saved us and called us to a holy life—not because of anything we have done but because of his own purpose and grace. This grace was given us in Christ Jesus before the beginning of time" (2 Tim 1:9 NIV); "For in this hope we were saved. But hope that is seen is no hope at all. Who hopes for what he already has?" (Rom 8:24 NIV). In all three verses past tenses are used to denote our salvation. We conclude from this construction that believers are already saved.

When we study the New Testament writers, however, we discover something quite surprising. Though they occasionally describe salvation as the present possession of believers, they usually envision salvation as something that will occur in the future. For example, Jesus says, "All men will hate you because of me, but he who stands firm to the end will be saved" (Mt 10:22 NIV; cf. also Mt 24:13). Matthew does not say that the one who endures to the end has been saved or that this person shows evidence that he or she was saved. Matthew says that the one who stands fast and perseveres will be saved, that is, will be saved on the future day of the Lord.

Paul usually conceives of salvation in future terms as well: "Since we have now been justified by his blood, how much more shall we be saved from God's wrath through him! For if, when we were God's enemies, we were reconciled to him through the death of his Son, how much more, having been reconciled, shall we be saved through his life!" (Rom 5:9-10 NIV). Notice the logic in both verses: since we are now justified and reconciled, we can be sure that we shall be saved.

Paul does not say that we can be sure that we are saved but that we *will* be saved. He thinks of salvation as a future blessing that we shall receive. Paul conceives of salvation in a similar way in 1 Thessalonians 5:8-9: "But since we belong to the day, let us be self-controlled, putting on faith and love as a breastplate, and the hope of salvation as a helmet. For God did not appoint us to suffer wrath but to receive salvation through our Lord Jesus Christ" (NIV). Salvation must be a future gift, since Paul speaks of the hope of salvation. Of course, Paul says elsewhere that believers are saved, so apparently salvation must be conceived of as both a present possession and a future reality, and 1 Thessalonians 5:9 confirms the future dimension of our salvation. God's wrath refers to his wrath that he will inflict on the wicked on the day of judgment (cf. Rom 5:9). Believers are not appointed to receive wrath on the day of judgment; instead, we shall obtain the gift of salvation promised to us.

In Romans 13:11-14 Paul exhorts the church to godly living. He begins his exhortation as follows, "And do this, understanding the present time. The hour has come for you to wake up from your slumber, because our salvation is nearer now than when we first believed" (Rom 13:11). We should live a godly life because "our salvation is nearer now." Paul does not say here that we should strive for godliness because we are saved or have been saved. We are summoned to live godly lives because salvation lies before us.

Paul does not promise salvation to all.[2] For example, Paul exhorts the church to excommunicate the man committing incest by handing him over to Satan "for the destruction of the flesh, so that his spirit may be saved in the day of the Lord" (1 Cor 5:5 NRSV). The verse does not promise salvation for the man, nor does it proclaim his certain judgment. Paul simply informs the Corinthians that the purpose of handing him over to Satan is so that he will experience salvation. The hoped-for salvation is obviously future, since it will occur "in the day of the Lord." Likewise, Paul summons Timothy to godliness and sound teaching in 1 Timothy 4:11-16, then sums up his exhortation by saying, "Watch your life and doctrine closely. Persevere in them, because if you do, you will save both yourself and your hearers" (1

---

[2]We already saw this in Mt 10:22. For a further explanation of these texts, see chapter three.

Tim 4:16 NIV). The salvation contemplated here is clearly future. Persevering in godly behavior and sound teaching are necessary to obtain salvation, both for Timothy and those to whom he ministers. A similar statement is found in 1 Timothy 2:15: "But women will be saved through childbearing—if they continue in faith, love and holiness with propriety" (NIV). This verse is quite controversial, but there are good reasons to believe that the word *salvation* retains its usual sense here.[3] In any case, our interest is not in explaining the entire verse but in noting that salvation is a future reality, as in 1 Timothy 4:16, and women must practice godly behavior to receive it.

A stimulating text is 1 Corinthians 3:15, where Paul speaks of the inadequate work of some of God's ministers: "If it [the minister's work] is burned up, he will suffer loss; he himself will be saved, but only as one escaping through the flames" (NIV). This verse raises a number of questions, for we are told that some will be saved who have done shoddy work. At this juncture, we observe that the salvation is future, since the fire that consumes the work will occur on the day of the Lord (1 Cor 3:13). Even at the close of his life Paul considers his own salvation to be future: "The Lord will rescue me from every evil attack and save me for his heavenly kingdom. To him be the glory forever and ever. Amen" (2 Tim 4:18 NRSV). The verb *sōsei* is rightly translated by the NRSV as "save," and it is a future tense verb. That the salvation is on the last day is clear since it will involve induction into the Lord's heavenly kingdom.

Other New Testament writers also emphasize that salvation is future. Hebrews 1:14 says angels "are sent to those who will inherit salvation." Salvation is depicted as a future inheritance, not a present possession. Similarly, Hebrews 9:28 says that "Christ was sacrificed once to take away the sins of many people; and he will appear a second time, not to bear sin, but to bring salvation to those who are waiting for him." Doubtless the salvation is future here, since it will be given at Christ's second coming. Peter also describes salvation as a future reality. The salvation of believers is a future inheritance (1 Pet 1:4), and it is impending: "the salvation that is ready to be revealed in

---

[3]For a fuller defense of the interpretation of this verse, see Thomas R. Schreiner, "An Interpretation of 1 Timothy 2:9-15: A Dialogue with Scholarship," in *Women in the Church: A Fresh Analysis of 1 Timothy 2:9-15*, ed. Andreas J. Köstenberger, Thomas R. Schreiner and H. Scott Baldwin (Grand Rapids, Mich.: Baker, 1995), pp. 146-53.

the last time" (1 Pet 1:5 NIV). Similarly, 1 Peter 1:9 implies that salvation is eschatological, since "the goal of your faith is the salvation of your souls." Salvation, according to this verse, is not the present possession of believers; it is the *telos,* that is, the "goal" or "outcome" of our faith. James also conceives of salvation as future. He exhorts his readers to "humbly accept the word planted in you, which can save you" (Jas 1:21 NIV). The idea is not that they are saved but that the Word is able to save them. Apparently, the work of salvation is not completed, since the Word planted in them must be given free rein so that they will ultimately experience salvation.

We conclude that it is wrong to conceive of salvation exclusively in terms of the past. Believers have been saved, yet the New Testament emphasizes even more that we shall be saved on the last day. We are already saved, yet our salvation has not yet been completed or consummated. We must uphold the tension in the New Testament between the already and not yet when we think of salvation in the New Testament. Believers today are prone to oversimplify the biblical teaching and to think of salvation only in terms of the present. When this happens, a crucial element of biblical teaching is surrendered, and we shall see that abandoning part of the biblical teaching has practical consequences that are of great importance.

The kingdom of God. The New Testament often uses the term "kingdom of God," especially in the Synoptic Gospels. Matthew prefers the term "kingdom of heaven," but it is almost universally agreed that "kingdom of God" and "kingdom of heaven" are synonyms. The Jews were hesitant to use the name of God, so the term *heaven* was substituted for the word *God.* Because Matthew writes to Jewish believers, he normally follows this convention in referring to the kingdom. We shall assume throughout our discussion, therefore, that "kingdom of God" and "kingdom of heaven" are synonymous.

A full understanding of the kingdom of God would warrant an entire book.[4] We want to focus here on the future and present dimensions of the kingdom, but we begin by saying a word about the mean-

---

[4]See especially George E. Ladd, *The Presence of the Future: The Eschatology of Biblical Realism* (Grand Rapids, Mich.: Eerdmans, 1974); G. R. Beasley-Murray, *Jesus and the Kingdom of God* (Grand Rapids, Mich.: Eerdmans, 1986); Herman Ridderbos, *The Coming of the Kingdom,* ed. Raymond O. Zorn, trans. H. de Jongste (Philadelphia: Presbyterian & Reformed, 1962).

ing of the term "kingdom of God." Most scholars agree that "kingdom of God" refers to God's ruling power.[5] God's kingdom exists where he exerts his saving power over human beings. Thus, the emphasis is not on the place or realm where God reigns but on his actual rule over human beings. At the beginning of Jesus' ministry he announces that God's kingdom is near (Mt 4:17; Mk 1:15). This should not be interpreted to mean that God did not rule in the Old Testament. For example, Psalm 103:19 says, "The LORD has established his throne in heaven, and his kingdom rules over all" (NIV). God has always been the sovereign of the universe (cf. *1 Enoch* 84:2-3). In fact, when Jesus announced the good news of the kingdom, he was referring to God's saving promises in the Old Testament Scriptures.

The Old Testament does not typically use the term "kingdom of God," but many texts in the Old Testament promise that God will bring in a new era in which Israel will be saved from her enemies and enjoy the fullness of the covenantal blessings promised to Abraham and David (e.g., Gen 12:1-3; 2 Sam 7:11-16; Ps 22:22-31; Is 11:1-9; 35:1-10; Zech 14:1-21). We also know that Jews during New Testament times longed for the fulfillment of these promises (e.g., *Pss. Sol.* 17:1—18:12). The people who gave us the Dead Sea Scrolls, for example, left Judean society and established an outpost in the wilderness to prepare for the kingdom of God. Likewise, the hope for the coming kingdom is expressed in the Testament of Moses: "Then his kingdom will appear throughout his whole creation. Then the devil will have an end" (*T. Mos.* 10:1).[6] Thus, the impending kingdom of God proclaimed by Jesus did not merely guarantee that God would begin to reign over the world. He had always exercised his sovereignty over all things, even though his rule was inscrutable at times (Ps 103:19). The Jews of Jesus' day would have understood his promise of the kingdom of God to refer to God's promises to enter history and save his people. Zechariah (the father of John the Baptist) nicely captures what Jews were expecting when he says that the Messiah will bring "salvation from our enemies and from the hand of all who hate us" (Lk 1:71 NIV), that the covenant with Abraham will be fulfilled (Lk 1:72), so that we will

---

[5]See E. P. Sanders, *Jesus and Judaism* (Philadelphia: Fortress, 1985), p. 127.

[6]The citation is from J. Priest's translation in *Apocalyptic Literature and Testaments*, vol. 1 of *The Old Testament Pseudepigrapha*, ed. J. H. Charlesworth (Garden City, N.Y.: Doubleday, 1983), p. 931.

"serve him without fear in holiness and righteousness before him all our days" (Lk 1:74-75 NIV). Jesus proclaims that God's age-old promise to save Israel is about to be fulfilled. God will destroy Israel's enemies and inaugurate the age when they rule over the world as God's people.[7]

The centrality of the kingdom of God in Jesus' teaching is evident from the number of times he uses the term. Jesus uses the phrase "kingdom of heaven" over thirty times in Matthew's Gospel, while in Mark and Luke the term "kingdom of God" is uttered by Jesus fourteen and over thirty times respectively. The importance of the kingdom is also signaled by Jesus' proclamation of the kingdom at the inception of his ministry in Matthew and Mark (Mt 4:17; Mk 1:15). Moreover, when Matthew and Luke summarize Jesus' ministry, they describe it in terms of his proclamation of the kingdom (Mt 4:23; 9:35; Lk 8:1; 9:11; Acts 1:3). However, the preaching of the kingdom cannot be confined to the ministry of Jesus. Jesus commissioned the twelve and seventy-two to preach the kingdom of God (Mt 10:7; Lk 10:9). Luke sums up the preaching of both Philip (Acts 8:12) and Paul (Acts 19:8; 28:23) by saying that they proclaimed the kingdom of God. We conclude that the pervasiveness of the term "kingdom of God" in Jesus' and his followers' teaching confirms its importance.

Has the kingdom of God already come, or do we still await its arrival? The biblical text does not yield an either-or answer. The kingdom of God has come, yet we still await the coming of the kingdom. The kingdom is already inaugurated, but it is not yet consummated. The future dimension of the kingdom is evident from a number of texts. For example, Jesus teaches the church to pray, "your kingdom come" (Mt 6:10; Lk 11:2). Such a prayer would be superfluous if the kingdom were already here in all its fullness! Jesus promises that those who belong to him will have table fellowship in the coming kingdom (Mt 8:11; Lk 22:30), and he anticipates drinking from the fruit of the vine in the coming kingdom (Mt 26:29; Mk 14:25; Lk 22:16, 18). Sitting at Jesus' right hand in the kingdom is reserved for those whom the Father has appointed (Mt 20:21-23). Jesus instructs his disciples that the consummation of the kingdom will not occur

---

[7]Of course, the way the kingdom of God was fulfilled through Jesus was a surprise to many in Israel, but it is not our task to explain that feature of the kingdom here.

immediately (Lk 19:11) and that they will know it is near when certain signs occur (Lk 21:31).

Furthermore, believers do not yet possess the full blessing of the kingdom, for they have not yet inherited what is promised. When the Son of Man returns (Mt 25:31), then the righteous will inherit "the kingdom prepared for you since the creation of the world" (Mt 25:34 NIV). Before entering the kingdom we are buffeted by many pressures. Paul and Barnabas say to their new converts on the first missionary journey, "We must go through many hardships to enter the kingdom of God" (Acts 14:22 NIV). Indeed, the sufferings of believers are necessary for us to "be counted worthy of the kingdom of God" (2 Thess 1:5 NIV). Jesus warns that merely calling him Lord does not guarantee entrance into the kingdom; the kingdom is reserved for those who do his will, not for evildoers (Mt 7:21-23). Paul threatens the Corinthians with the words that "the wicked will not inherit the kingdom of God" (1 Cor 6:9 NIV; cf. v. 10). Obviously, a future judgment is intended. Similarly, in Galatians he asserts that those who practice the works of the flesh "will not inherit the kingdom of God" (Gal 5:21 NIV). That the kingdom of God is still future is confirmed in 1 Corinthians 15. Believers still await the resurrection of the body, and "flesh and blood cannot inherit the kingdom of God" (1 Cor 15:50 NIV). Paul does not mean to say that physical bodies cannot enter the kingdom. His point is that our corruptible bodies cannot enter the kingdom. Our bodies must be transformed and changed to enter the kingdom.

We have ample evidence, therefore, that the kingdom of God is a future reality that we await. The New Testament also teaches, however, that the kingdom of God has now arrived and is a present reality. For instance, after expelling a demon from a man who was blind and mute, Jesus says, "But if I drive out demons by the Spirit of God, then the kingdom of God has come upon you" (Mt 12:28 NIV; cf. Lk 11:20). Jesus does not say that his expulsion of demons is a sign that the kingdom will come; he asserts that the kingdom has come. The kingdom is inaugurated in the ministry of Jesus. The present reality of the kingdom is also communicated when the Pharisees ask Jesus when the kingdom will come (Lk 17:20). He replies that the kingdom "is among you" (Lk 17:21 NRSV). The NIV translates the Greek phrase *entos hymōn* as "within you." It is doubtful, though, that this is the fitting translation. Nowhere else does Jesus speak of the kingdom as an internal reality. People enter the kingdom, but the idea of the kingdom being inside people is not a biblical expression. It is also unlikely that Jesus would say to the Pharisees that the kingdom resides within them. We would expect him to say this to his disciples rather than to the Pharisees. When Jesus says the kingdom is "among you," he confronts the Pharisees with himself; the kingdom has arrived in his person and his ministry.[8] Their speculation on the future kingdom is futile, since they fail to see that the kingdom is manifest in Jesus himself. Jesus also communicates the presence of the kingdom to John the Baptist (Mt 11:2-15). The exact meaning of Matthew 11:12 continues to bedevil interpreters, but we need not linger to explain this difficult text. The context of the passage testifies to the inauguration of the kingdom in Jesus' ministry. Jesus assures John that he is indeed the coming one by pointing to his ministry of healing and preaching (Mt 11:2-5). His works fulfill what is prophesied in Isaiah 35, and that passage in turn reflects a fulfillment of the promises made to Abraham. In other words, even though the word *kingdom* is not used in Isaiah 35, its content is such that it is equivalent to kingdom promises, and Jesus assures John that this kingdom power is present in his miraculous signs and preaching.

The parables of Jesus also teach the presence of the kingdom. For reasons of space we will confine ourselves to the parables of the mustard seed and leaven (Mt 13:31-33). Both parables indicate that the kingdom begins as something small and grows until it becomes absolutely dominant. The absolute dominance of the kingdom will occur when the kingdom is consummated, when our prayer "your kingdom come" is answered. What is crucial for our purposes is to see that the kingdom begins as something small. It does not crush all its adversaries when it first arrives. This conception of the kingdom astonished the Jews. They expected the kingdom to overwhelm the whole world immediately and to involve a decisive vanquishing of

---

[8]For interpretations that are compatible with that adopted here, see I. Howard Marshall, *The Gospel of Luke: A Commentary on the Greek Text*, New International Greek Testament Commentary (Grand Rapids, Mich.: Eerdmans, 1978), pp. 655-56; Joseph A. Fitzmyer, *The Gospel According to Luke X-XXIV: Introduction, Translation, and Notes*, Anchor Bible (Garden City, N.Y.: Doubleday, 1985), pp. 159, 1161-62; and especially Darrell L. Bock, *Luke 9:51-24:53*, Baker Exegetical Commentary on the New Testament (Grand Rapids: Mich.: Baker, 1996), pp. 1415-19.

their enemies. Instead, Jesus teaches that the kingdom arrives almost invisibly, like a mustard seed or yeast in dough. We could examine many other issues in these parables. We have clearly seen, however, that the kingdom is already present in Jesus' ministry, even if it is as small as a mustard seed. Jesus maintains (cf. Mt 13:16-17) that the disciples are blessed because they see the inauguration of the kingdom, even if its beginning is surprisingly small. These parables are of crucial importance in formulating our understanding of the kingdom. We cannot restrict the kingdom to its future manifestation when God's rule over all people is absolute and complete. The kingdom has arrived—like the planting of a mustard seed or the insertion of leaven in dough—but it has not yet been consummated.

Believers also enjoy the present blessings of the kingdom: "Blessed are the poor in spirit, for theirs is the kingdom of heaven" (Mt 5:3 NIV; cf. Lk 6:20). Similarly, Jesus says to those who are persecuted that "theirs is the kingdom of heaven" (Mt 5:10 NIV). Jesus does not say that "theirs will be the kingdom of heaven," but "theirs is the kingdom of heaven." This is not to deny a future dimension to the kingdom, but the text plainly teaches that believers enjoy the blessings of the kingdom now.

In summary, the kingdom is inaugurated but not yet consummated. It has begun but is not completed. We must not assign the kingdom exclusively to the future or to the present. The New Testament teaching is complex, and we must retain this complexity when we think of the prize that is to be won in the Christian life. We must not collapse New Testament teaching so that one dimension of the kingdom disappears, with the result that we fix only on the presence of the kingdom or the future of the kingdom. We are tempted to seize on one pole of the truth and to neglect the other. To be faithful to the Scriptures, we must retain the biblical tension that the kingdom is both present and future.

Redemption. Another metaphor that connotes deliverance is redemption. Redemption signifies our liberation from that which binds us. In the Old Testament, redemption often refers to the liberation of Israel from Egypt (Ex 6:6; 15:13; Deut 7:8; 13:5; 24:18; 2 Sam 7:23; Neh 1:10; Ps 74:2; 77:15; 106:10; 111:9). The liberation from Egypt functions as a type and anticipates the redemption that is ours in Jesus Christ. Even after being redeemed from Egypt, Israel continued to long for redemption. The psalmist prays, after Israel has entered the land of promise, "Redeem Israel, O God, from all their troubles" (Ps 25:22 NIV), and when enemies afflict Israel the psalmist prays, "Rise up and help us; redeem us because of your unfailing love" (Ps 44:26 NIV). The psalmist also confidently proclaims that God "himself will redeem Israel from all their sins" (Ps 130:8 NIV). Isaiah conceives of Israel's future glory in terms of redemption (Is 35:9). Israel's release from Babylon functions as a second exodus (Is 44:22-23; 51:11; 52:1-6). New Testament writers were convinced that these Old Testament promises of future redemption were fulfilled in Jesus Christ.

What we want to investigate is whether redemption is exclusively past or future. In popular circles redemption is almost always related to a past reality. Believers confess and sing that they "have been redeemed." There is no doubt that this captures a dimension of the New Testament message. The promise made to Israel regarding redemption has now been fulfilled in Christ. Paul asserts in Ephesians 1:7 that in Christ "we have redemption through his blood, the forgiveness of sins" (NIV; cf. Col 1:14). Redemption is the present possession of believers. Likewise, 1 Peter 1:18-19 teaches that redemption is now ours: "You were redeemed from the empty way of life handed down to you from your forefathers . . . with the precious blood of Christ" (NIV; cf. also Tit 2:14). Romans 3:24 also refers to an accomplished redemption. Believers "are justified freely by his grace through the redemption that came by Christ Jesus" (NIV). This text teaches that believers are now justified through redemption. Since the justification spoken of is a present gift, we can safely conclude that the justification becomes ours through the redemption that Christ has already accomplished for us. We have "obtained eternal redemption" through the blood of Christ (Heb 9:12). It is imperative to see in all four texts that redemption in the New Testament is from the bondage of sin. The New Testament does not teach that our fundamental problem is that others have mistreated us. We are not fundamentally victims of the sins of others. God has redeemed us from our guilt (Eph 1:14; Heb 9:12) so that we are now righteous before God (Rom 3:24) and freed from our futile way of living (1 Pet 1:18-19). In 1 Corinthians 1:30 Paul likewise teaches that our redemption has been accomplished: "It is because of him that you are in Christ Jesus, who has become for us wisdom from God—that is, our righteousness, holiness and redemption" (NIV). Christ is already the wisdom of God for believers, and this wisdom of God is further explained by the terms *righteousness, holiness* and *redemption.*[9]

We could conclude from the above that redemption is exclusively a present reality for believers. Someone could say, "Either you are redeemed or you are not redeemed." The actual teaching of the New Testament, however, is more complex than this. Believers have been redeemed, yet they still await their redemption. We must beware of polarizing the issue, for then we would concentrate on only one dimension of the biblical witness. Several texts clarify that redemption is also a future reality. Luke describes the terrors that will precede the coming of the Son of Man (Lk 21:25-27), then remarks, "When these things begin to take place, stand up and lift up your heads, because your redemption is drawing near" (Lk 21:28 NIV). In other words, your redemption is not yet accomplished, but it will become a reality when the Son of Man returns. Paul also locates redemption in the future: "Not only so, but we ourselves, who have the firstfruits of the Spirit, groan inwardly as we wait eagerly for our adoption as sons, the redemption of our bodies" (Rom 8:23 NIV). Believers have the firstfruits of the Spirit now, but they long for something more, namely, their future adoption, which is described as "the redemption of our bodies." Our redemption will not be complete until we receive our resurrected bodies on the last day. The same idea is found in Ephesians 1:13-14: "You also were included in Christ when you heard the word of truth, the gospel of your salvation. Having believed, you were marked in him with a seal, the promised Holy Spirit, who is a deposit guaranteeing our inheritance until the redemption of those who are God's possession—to the praise of his glory" (NIV). Those who believe in Christ are sealed with the Holy Spirit, and this Spirit guarantees our inheritance, which consists of our redemption. The connection between inheritance and redemption demonstrates that redemption in this text is future. Thus, the redemption of "God's possession" refers to the resurrection of our bodies, which will complete the work God has already begun in us.

Is redemption past or future? Yes! It is both. We have been redeemed by the blood of Christ, freed from the power of sin and our guilt. Yet redemption still awaits us. We have not received our resur-

---

[9]For this interpretation, see Gordon D. Fee, *The First Epistle to the Corinthians*, New International Commentary on the New Testament (Grand Rapids, Mich.: Eerdmans, 1987), pp. 185-87.

rection bodies, and complete freedom from sin is not yet ours. Redemption, like the kingdom of God, is already ours, yet the fullness of redemption still lies in the future.

Renewal Metaphors

The Scriptures utilize metaphors of deliverance to denote God's work on behalf of his people. We are transferred into God's kingdom, yet we await the fullness of his kingdom. God has redeemed us, yet we have not yet obtained the redemption of our bodies. God has saved us, yet salvation is still before us and will be obtained on the last day. New Testament writers also depict our salvation in terms of our renewal and transformation. Our salvation should not be understood only in terms of deliverance; we have also been renewed and transformed by God's work. Some of the terms that describe our renewal are *regeneration, new creation, resurrection, conversion* and *eternal life.* We shall examine them one by one.

Regeneration. The term *regeneration* conveys the transformation we have experienced. Believers are not the same persons they were upon physical birth. They have "been born again" (Jn 3:3). The Scriptures typically use this metaphor to denote what is true now, so that regeneration is an accomplished reality for believers. Of course, Jesus says that Nicodemus must be "born again" or, perhaps better, "born from above" (Jn 3:3 NRSV). But Jesus admonishes Nicodemus precisely because he was not yet truly part of the people of God. When speaking of believers, New Testament writers conceive of regeneration as a past reality. John says that those who have received Jesus have been born of God (Jn 1:12-13). John in his first letter always uses the perfect tense to designate those who have been born again. Those who do what is righteous, love one another, believe that Jesus is the Messiah and overcome the world have been born of God (1 Jn 2:29; 3:9; 4:7; 5:1, 4, 18). God's regenerating work precedes faith, love and a righteous life. Believers have been born again through the resurrection of Jesus Christ (1 Pet 1:3) and through the Word of God (1 Pet 1:23). Paul also locates our rebirth *(palingenesia)* in the past: God "saved us through the washing of rebirth and renewal by the Holy Spirit" (Tit 3:5 NIV). We see that salvation is conceived of here as a past reality, and our rebirth is concomitant with that salvation. This rebirth is also described here in terms of renewal *(anakainōsis).* Both

regeneration and renewal suggest that believers have been transformed and changed. One could infer from the deliverance metaphors alone (although we think this would be mistaken) that believers
are rescued from evil and sin but not changed from within. Regeneration, however, indicates that believers have been transformed.

New creation. The renovation that God has accomplished in believers
is also conveyed by the teaching that believers are a new creation.
Under this category we will include the term "new creation" *(kainē ktisis)*
and the terms relating to renewal and newness. Paul uses the language
of new creation on two occasions. In both instances, he speaks of an
already accomplished reality. He says in 2 Corinthians 5:17, "If anyone
is in Christ, he is a new creation; the old has gone, the new has come!"
(NIV). In Galatians 6:15 Paul implies that believers are already a new
creation: "Neither circumcision nor uncircumcision means anything;
what counts is a new creation" (NIV). God required circumcision for
induction into Israel under the old covenant, but now that the new era
has dawned, what matters is whether one is a new creation. Galatians
6:14 suggests that believers are already a new creation, for Paul says he
has been crucified to the world. In other words, he has left the old
world behind and has now become a new creation.

The verb *create (ktizō)* is also used in two instances to denote the
renewal of believers. Interestingly, in Ephesians 4:24 it is linked with
"new person" *(kainos anthrōpos)*. The new person ("a new self" in the
NIV) has been "created like God" (Eph 4:24). In other words, the decisive work of creation has already been accomplished; believers are
new persons in Christ. Similarly, Ephesians 2:10 implies that we have
already been created in Christ Jesus as "God's workmanship" (cf. Eph
2:15). "New creation" and "create" are not used of the future destiny of
believers. Believers have been ushered into a new world and a new
existence at conversion.

We have already seen that the term *renewal,* like the term *regeneration,*
denotes the dramatic change that has occurred in believers (Tit 3:5). We
have also seen that believers have been created as new persons (Eph
4:24). The old person is who we were in Adam, but that old person has
been crucified with Christ (Rom 6:6).[10] There is an already-but-not-yet

---

[10]The new self or new person is probably Christ himself in Paul's thinking, for he is the
new Adam (Rom 5:12-19) who succeeded where Adam failed. For the idea that Christ
is the new self, see also Eph 2:15 and Col 3:10-11.

dimension, however, to the language of newness in the New Testament. The old person has died with Christ, and believers have put on the new self (Col 3:10) and have "taken off your old self with its practices" (Col 3:9 NIV). Nonetheless, believers must also "put off your old self" to "put on the new self" (Eph 4:22, 24 NIV).[11] There is an ongoing work of transformation in the lives of believers. Thus, in Colossians 3:10 Paul says that the new self "is being renewed" and in 2 Corinthians 4:16 that "inwardly we are being renewed day by day" (NIV). Believers are a new creation in Christ, yet there is still a process of renewal that will not be complete until the final day of redemption. Paul tells us to "be transformed by the renewing of your mind" (Rom 12:2 NIV), to "be made new in the attitude of your minds" (Eph 4:23 NIV). Believers must make a conscious effort to "walk in newness of life" (Rom 6:4 NRSV) and in the "newness of the Spirit" instead of the "oldness of the letter" (Rom 7:6 NASB).

We are new persons in Christ who have been decisively changed, yet our renewal is not yet complete. We are not yet all that we will be. We await the day when "we shall be like him, for we shall see him as he is" (1 Jn 3:2 NIV). We are new persons, yet we are also in the process of renewal. To deny either truth would be disastrous. If believers repudiate that they are a new creation, they call into question their conversion. But if they deny the need for renewal in this life, a godless life could easily be defended on the basis that we are already renewed and can do no wrong. To deny the twin features of the biblical theme invites either works-righteousness or antinomianism: works-righteousness in the sense that we might try to earn or merit salvation, antinomianism in the sense that we might conclude that we can do whatever we wish apart from any concern for God's standards.

Resurrection. The language of resurrection is almost exclusively confined to the future, for it typically denotes the resurrection from the dead that will occur on the last day. Thus, even John, who emphasizes the present possession of eternal life (see below) locates the resurrection of the body to the last day (Jn 5:28-29; 6:39-40, 44, 54;

---

[11]Some scholars doubt that the infinitives here are imperatives. For a defense of the interpretation adopted here, see F. F. Bruce, *The Epistles to the Colossians, to Philemon, and to the Ephesians*, New International Commentary on the New Testament (Grand Rapids, Mich.: Eerdmans, 1984), pp. 358-59; and Douglas Moo, *Romans 1—8*, Wycliffe Exegetical Commentary (Chicago: Moody Press, 1991), pp. 391-92.

11:24). Paul dismisses as heretical those teachers who claim that the resurrection has already occurred (2 Tim 2:18), insisting that the resurrection of the body will only occur in the future (cf. 1 Thess 4:13-18). Paul probably counters similar false teaching in 1 Corinthians. Some Corinthians had probably succumbed to an overrealized eschatology, concluding that there was no future resurrection (1 Cor 15:1-58; cf. 1 Cor 4:8-13).[12] Paul insists emphatically that the resurrection of believers is future (1 Cor 15:20-57). Even though God has already raised Christ from the dead, Christ is raised as the firstfruits, and believers will not be raised until Christ returns. Paul anticipates the day when he will "attain to the resurrection from the dead" (Phil 3:11 NIV). We will share the resurrection of Christ on the final day (Rom 6:5).[13] Even though we have the Holy Spirit, our bodies are still "dead because of sin" (Rom 8:10). We anticipate the day when our mortal bodies will receive life (Rom 8:11). Presently we groan as we await "the redemption of our bodies" (Rom 8:23; cf. 2 Cor 5:1-5).

When New Testament writers refer to the resurrection, they emphasize the not yet. We could cite many other texts that locate the resurrection of believers in the future. However, we should also see that the resurrection of the dead, which is an end-time phenomenon (Dan 12:1-3), has invaded the present evil age, for Jesus Christ has been raised from the dead (Mt 28; Mk 16; Lk 24; Jn 20—21; Rom 1:4; 1 Cor 15 and so on). Jesus' resurrection from the dead signals that the age to come has penetrated the present evil age. His resurrection is the firstfruits that guarantees the resurrection of believers at the end of history (1 Cor 15:50-58). Since the resurrection has infiltrated history through the resurrection of Jesus, believers have resurrection power now to live new lives (Rom 6:4). Because of Christ's resurrection, believers are "alive to God" (Rom 6:11). We know "the power of his resurrection" (Phil 3:10), even though the resurrection of our bodies is future (Phil 3:11). We "have been born anew to a living hope through the resurrection of Jesus Christ from the dead" (1 Pet 1:3 RSV). Since Jesus is "the resurrection and the life," the one who believes in

---

[12]Supporting the thesis that overrealized eschatology was the problem in 1 Corinthians is Anthony C. Thiselton, "Realized Eschatology at Corinth," *New Testament Studies* 24 (1978): 510-26.

[13]Some interpreters understand the resurrection here to be present. In defense of the interpretation proposed here, see Thomas R. Schreiner, *Romans*, Baker Exegetical Commentary on the New Testament (Grand Rapids, Mich.: Baker, 1998), pp. 312-13.

Jesus "will live, even though he dies" (Jn 11:25 NIV). That is, on the basis of Jesus' resurrection life, believers have eternal life now. By virtue of Christ's resurrection we are already raised up together with Christ (Eph 2:6; Col 2:12; 3:1).

Resurrection, then, mainly denotes the future destiny of believers, the assurance that we will be raised from the dead. Nonetheless, a few texts teach that resurrection has invaded the present age through the resurrection of Christ. Thus, believers are born again, have newness of life and are raised with him in the heavenly places because of Christ's resurrection. We can conclude, then, that the already-but-not-yet dynamic of New Testament teaching is even to be found in the New Testament teaching on the resurrection. Of course, the emphasis is on the not yet. Our bodies are dying and groaning, awaiting their full liberation. We are warned against an overrealized eschatology relative to the resurrection. Overrealized eschatology promises heaven on earth, as though we have already received all of God's promises in the present world. Those who dismiss the future resurrection of the body have allowed the already to swallow up and destroy the not yet. But to deny our being raised with Christ now severs the cord between our present new life and our future resurrection. We who have been raised with Christ are confident that we will receive the future resurrection. The already in every instance guarantees the not yet.

Conversion. Conversion also designates the renewal that God has accomplished in believers. The Greek word translated "conversion" simply means "turn." The verb is used of Jesus turning and looking at his disciples (Mk 8:33), but the term *conversion* is also used to refer to turning to God in response to the proclamation of the gospel. A representative example is found in 1 Thessalonians 1:9, where Paul says that the Thessalonians "turned to God from idols to serve the living and true God" (NIV). Conversion is closely associated with repentance, since the former denotes turning to God and the latter turning away from sin. Thus, Peter says in Acts 3:19, "Repent, then, and turn to God, so that your sins may be wiped out, that times of refreshing may come from the Lord" (NIV). In examining the book of Acts it is clear that conversion, repentance, faith and baptism are alternate and overlapping ways of describing coming to Christ for salvation (e.g., Acts 2:38, 41; 3:19, 26; 4:4; 5:14, 31; 8:12-13, 36-38; 9:18, 42; 10:43; 11:17-18, 21; 13:12, 39, 48; 14:1, 9, 15, 27; 15:7, 9, 11, 19; 16:31-34; 17:30, 34; 18:8,

27; 20:21; 24:24; 26:18, 20; 28:27).[14] We do not need to detain ourselves long with these terms but will make a brief comment on conversion and repentance. Both of these words denote something humans do in response to hearing the gospel, namely, turn from sin and turn towards God. Both repentance and conversion depict the revolutionary alteration that has transpired in Christians.

Eternal life. Eternal life by definition is life of the age to come. Jews typically believed during the Second Temple period that there were two ages: this age and the age to come. The New Testament also teaches the division between the two ages. Jesus says that blasphemy against the Spirit "will not be forgiven, either in this age or in the age to come" (Mt 12:32 NIV). Paul tells us that Jesus will rule "not only in the present age but also in the one to come" (Eph 1:21 NIV). A number of texts in Matthew refer to the end of the age (Mt 13:39-40, 49; 24:3; 28:20), and anxiety and worry are intrinsic to this age (Mt 13:22; Mk 4:19). Paul refers to "the rulers of this age, who are passing away" (1 Cor 2:6 NASB). The wisdom of this age is characterized as foolish (1 Cor 3:19), the present age is designated as evil (Gal 1:4) and unbelievers are under the dominion of the "god of this age" (2 Cor 4:4). Thus, believers are exhorted not to be conformed "to this age" (Rom 12:2, *tō aiōni toutō*).[15] Marriage is characteristic of this age, but those who are worthy of the age to come will experience the resurrection (Lk 20:34-35). Paul also argues that the age to come has penetrated the present age: "These things happened to them as examples and were written down as warnings for us, on whom the fulfillment of the ages has come" (1 Cor 10:11 NIV). Although the age to come has invaded the present evil age, the present evil age has not yet ended; both the age to come and the present evil age coexist until the cessation of this present evil age.

Jesus forges a link between the age to come and eternal life in Mark 10:29-30, where he says, "no one who has left home or brothers or sisters or mother or father or children or fields for me and the gospel will fail to receive a hundred times as much in this present age (homes, brothers, sisters, mothers, children and fields—and with

---

[14]For more extended support of this thesis, see Robert H. Stein, *Difficult Passages in the Epistles* (Grand Rapids, Mich.: Baker, 1988), pp. 116-26.

[15]This is our translation since the NIV, NRSV, NASB and RSV all translate the word *aiōn* as "world."

them, persecutions) and in the age to come, eternal life" (NIV). Those who leave all for Jesus will receive eternal life in the age to come, and thus we can conclude that eternal life is a gift of the coming age (cf. Lk 18:30). A number of other texts agree that eternal life is a future gift. The rich young man asks Jesus, "What must I do to inherit eternal life?" (Mk 10:17 NIV; cf. Mt 19:16; Lk 18:18). The collocation of the words *inherit* and *eternal life* demonstrate that the life longed for is eschatological. At the conclusion of the parable of the sheep and goats, the Son of Man concludes with the statement that the wicked "will go away to eternal punishment, but the righteous to eternal life" (Matt 25:46 NIV). Obviously, both the punishment and life are obtained on the day of the Lord, since they are given at the coming of the Son of Man.

Likewise, Paul typically locates eternal life in the future. Those who do good works will receive eternal life (Rom 2:6-7). Death is the wages of sin, but eternal life is God's gift (Rom 6:23). Those who sow to the flesh "will reap destruction," but those who sow to the Spirit "will reap eternal life" (Gal 6:8). Life is a treasure that is acquired on the last day (1 Tim 6:19). Paul refers to the "hope of eternal life" (Tit 1:2; 3:7), indicating that it is something believers do not yet possess. James assures his readers that a "crown of life" is promised to those who endure testings (Jas 1:12), and John assures those who are faithful until death that they will receive a "crown of life" (Rev 2:10).

The preceding texts demonstrate that eternal life is a gift of the coming age. But John regularly maintains that eternal life is something that believers possess now. He says that "whoever believes in the Son has eternal life" (Jn 3:36). John does not say that believers will have eternal life but that they have eternal life. In fact, John emphasizes often that eternal life is a present gift, as the following texts demonstrate:

> I tell you the truth, whoever hears my word and believes him who sent me has eternal life and will not be condemned; he has crossed over from death to life. (Jn 5:24 NIV)

> I tell you the truth, he who believes has everlasting life. (Jn 6:47 NIV)

> Whoever eats my flesh and drinks my blood has eternal life, and I will raise him up at the last day. (Jn 6:54 NIV)

> And this is the testimony: God has given us eternal life, and this life is in his Son. He who has the Son has life; he who does not have the Son of God does not have life. I write these things to you who believe in the

name of the Son of God so that you may know that you have eternal
life. (1 Jn 5:11-13 NIV)

If we wish to represent the New Testament correctly, we cannot
say that eternal life is exclusively a present or a future gift. It is both
present and future. We already possess eternal life by believing in
Jesus as the Christ, yet we will not inherit eternal life nor acquire the
inheritance of eternal life until the last day. The term "eternal life"
also emphasizes the renewal and renovation that have gripped us. We
were formerly in the throes of death, but now we have the life of the
age to come and anticipate enjoying it in its fullness in the future. We
must also see that the present possession of eternal life guarantees
that we will receive eternal life in the age to come. Still, we must not
use this promise to explain away the New Testament admonitions, for
good works and following Jesus (Rom 2:6-7; Mk 10:29-30) are also necessary to obtain eternal life on the last day. As interpreters of Scripture, we must maintain the balance and tension of the New
Testament instead of choosing which of the two themes we prefer.

Family Metaphors

As we have already seen, the Scriptures portray God's work on behalf
of believers in terms of deliverance and renewal. God rescues us from
that which would destroy us and transforms us by his grace. No metaphor, however, embraces all that God has done for us. God's deep love
and delight for us is also conveyed by family metaphors. As believers
we are adopted, reconciled, made children of God and granted the status of heirs. We are not only delivered and changed by God; we are
also made friends of God.

Adoption. The New Testament does not often speak of believers
being adopted (Rom 8:15, 23; Gal 4:5; Eph 1:5). Even though the term
adoption is not used in the Old Testament, the conception of adoption
probably hails from the Old Testament portrayal of God's relationship
to Israel (Rom 9:4).[16] As believers, we already enjoy the status of adoption. When Paul reflects on the conversion of his readers, he deems it
the occasion of their adoption: "For you did not receive a spirit of sla-

---

[16]James M. Scott makes a good argument for the view that the adoption metaphor in
the New Testament derives from the Old Testament Scriptures (*Adoption as Sons of
God: An Investigation into the Background of "Huiothesia" in the Pauline Corpus,* Wissenschaftliche Untersuchungen zum Neuen Testament 2, no. 48 [Tübingen: Mohr, 1992]).

very to fall back into fear, but you have received a spirit of adoption"
(Rom 8:15 NRSV). This is confirmed by Galatians 4:5, where God's purpose in redeeming people through Christ is "so that we might receive
adoption as children" (NRSV). Most likely Ephesians 1:5 also refers to
adoption as the current status of believers, since adoption is said to be
the result of God's predestining work. We might conclude from this
that we could simply say to a person, "Either your adoption as God's
child is already complete, or you don't belong to him." Paul, however,
also locates our adoption in the future. He says that we "who have the
first fruits of the Spirit, groan inwardly while we wait for adoption,
the redemption of our bodies" (Rom 8:23 NRSV). Here adoption is said
to become ours when our bodies are redeemed, that is, on the last
day. We conclude, then, that there is an already-but-not-yet dimension to adoption as well. As Christians we are adopted into God's family, yet we will not experience the consummation of our adoption
until the day of the resurrection. The danger of making simplistic
either-or statements about adoption is apparent.

   Children of God. To say that believers are adopted is probably just
another way of saying that they are children of God. In both Romans
8:14-17 and Galatians 4:4-7 Paul oscillates between believers being children of God and being adopted, which suggests that they are different
ways of enunciating the same reality. It is probably also the case that we
should not sharply distinguish the terms "children of God" *(tekna theou)*
and "sons of God" *(huioi theou).* Most scholars agree that the terms are
synonymous. Paul seems to confirm this in Romans 8:14-17, gliding from
"sons of God" to "children of God" without any discernible difference in
meaning. Thus, in the following discussion we will assume that the
terms "children of God" and "sons of God" are synonyms.

   In the Old Testament, Israel was identified as God's son (Ex 4:22;
Deut 14:1; 32:5-6; Hos 1:10), and in the intertestamental period Israel
as God's son was destined to inherit his saving promises (*1 Enoch*
62:11; *Jub.* 1:24-25; 2:20; *Pss. Sol.* 17:30; 4 Ezra 6:58; *2 Apoc. Bar.* 13:9).
When New Testament writers, therefore, identify the church as God's
children and sons, the implication is that the promises made to Israel
are now being fulfilled.[17] The church is the new eschatological people

---

[17]One should not conclude from this, however, that there is no future salvation for ethnic Israel (see Rom 11:25-32).

of God. This is confirmed by Galatians 3:7, where Christian believers are identified as Abraham's sons (cf. Rom 9:7-8), and by Galatians 4:28, where believers, like Isaac, are said to be the true children of promise. Indeed, Paul's burden in Galatians is to establish that believers need not receive circumcision to become the children or seed of Abraham. They belong to the seed of Abraham by virtue of belonging to Christ (Gal 3:16). They are sons of God now in Christ Jesus (Gal 3:26), and, since they have been incorporated into Christ, they are the true seed of Abraham (Gal 3:29; cf. Gal 6:16). Now that the age of fulfillment has arrived and God has sent his Spirit, believers are God's sons (Gal 4:6-7; cf. Heb 2:10; 12:5-11).

Paul also argues elsewhere that believers are now the children of God. Believers are "dearly loved children" (Eph 5:1), "children of light" (Eph 5:8) and "sons of the light" (1 Thess 5:8). They have the internal witness of the Spirit that they are God's children (Rom 8:16), and their leading by the Spirit attests that they truly belong to God's family (Rom 8:14). John also emphasizes that believers currently enjoy the status of being God's children. To those who receive and believe in Jesus, "he gave the right to become children of God" (Jn 1:12 NIV). Indeed, John emphasizes particularly that believers are presently the children of God (1 Jn 3:1-3) by saying, "now we are children of God" (1 Jn 3:2 NIV), removing any doubt that this is only confined to the future. Why do the New Testament writers stress our current status as God's children? Probably because they want to confirm that God's promises to Abraham are now being fulfilled. The new community of God's people exists in the world now, and it is made up of people from every ethnic group.

We are not denying the future dimension of being the children of God. Matthew locates being called a son of God to the future: "Blessed are the peacemakers, for they will be called sons of God" (Mt 5:9). Paul, in the same context in which he stresses that believers are God's children (Rom 8:14-17), also implies that the fullness of our family relationship will not be manifested until creation is renewed: "The creation waits in eager expectation for the sons of God to be revealed" (Rom 8:19 NIV). Philippians 2:15 should probably be interpreted eschatologically, since believers become "blameless," "pure" and "children of God without fault" on the last day. Thus, the theme that believers are children of God contains the same tension between the present and the future that we have seen elsewhere, though the present realization of the promise to be God's children receives the emphasis.

Heirs. In the Old Testament Yahweh promises Israel an inheritance: the land of promise. A careful reading of the promise to Abraham (Gen 12:1-3), however, also implies that ultimately Israel will be heir of the whole world. God will reclaim the world that is opposed to him and bring it back under his rule. Paul certainly understands the promise to Abraham this way. Abraham is to "be heir of the world" (Rom 4:13). The author of Hebrews sees this inheritance fulfilled in the heavenly city and country (Heb 11:10, 13-16). If believers have through Christ become what Israel was—children of God—it is not surprising that they are also heirs to what was promised to Israel. Paul argues for this indissoluble connection between sonship and heirship in both Galatians 3:26-29; 4:4-7 and Romans 8:14-17. Certainly we would expect that those who are children would also become heirs.

The language of inheritance and heirship is such that it is naturally used to convey the future blessing that will be given to believers. Believers will inherit eternal life (Mt 19:29; Mk 10:17; Lk 10:25; 18:18; Tit 3:7), the kingdom (Mt 25:34; 1 Cor 6:9-10; 15:50; Gal 5:21; Eph 5:5; Jas 2:5), the earth (Mt 5:5), the promises (Heb 6:12) and a blessing (1 Pet 3:9). Only those who overcome will inherit the promises (Rev 21:7), and believers have a sure "inheritance that can never perish, spoil or fade—kept in heaven for you" (1 Pet 1:4 NIV). The language of inheritance, then, casts its eyes toward the future, to the promises that await believers. We are heirs now (Rom 8:17; Gal 3:29; 4:7; Tit 3:7), but we have not yet obtained the inheritance laid up for us. Inheritance focuses on the not-yet dimension of salvation, on what still awaits us. We are the children of God now, but we have not yet obtained the inheritance promised to us.

Reconciliation. God as our Father has adopted us, made us his children and promised us an inheritance. The tenderness of his love is also expressed by the term *reconciliation.* We are now friends of God through the work of his Son, Jesus Christ. Paul uses the term *reconciliation* to depict what is already accomplished in the lives of believers. For instance, in Romans 5:10-11 he says, "For if, when we were God's enemies, we were reconciled to him through the death of his Son, how much more, having been reconciled, shall we be saved through his life! Not only is this so, but we also rejoice in God through our Lord Jesus Christ, through whom we have now received reconciliation" (NIV). Reconciliation is a past act based on the death of God's Son. Colossians 1:22 confirms this (cf. also 2 Cor 5:18): "now he has reconciled you by Christ's physical body through death" (NIV). Both Jews and Gentiles are reconciled through the work of Christ on the cross (Eph 2:16).[18]

If heirship focuses on the not yet, reconciliation brings the already to the forefront. The Scriptures do not say that we will be reconciled at the last day. They emphasize that we are reconciled now, that our friendship with God has been accomplished, that we are in a new relationship with him. It would be a mistake to conclude from this that there is no future dimension to our salvation, but reconciliation itself should not be interpreted in future terms.[19]

Cultic Metaphors

In the Old Testament Israel is God's holy people, set apart specially for him (Ex 19:6). The New Testament appropriates the cultic language (language that relates to the temple and holiness) from the Old Testament and applies it to the church so that now believers are a "holy nation" (1 Pet 2:9). Believers are saints, sanctified and called to perfection. Cultic metaphors are used to describe God's work on our behalf, because we are not only delivered from sin and friends of God but are also made holy and sanctified by him. Those whom God has rescued and befriended he has also changed and transformed. The cultic metaphors, like the renewal metaphors, emphasize the moral transformation that has occurred in the people of God.

When we examine the words relevant to this metaphor (*hagiazō*, to sanctify; *hagiasmos*, sanctification; *hagioi*, holy ones/saints; *hagiōsynē*, holiness), it is apparent that we are holy and sanctified now but that

---

[18]Colossians 1:20 indicates that all things have been reconciled through Christ. It seems that the reconciliation here is still in the past. What is controversial is the extent of the reconciliation, namely, "all things." For the purposes of this book, we cannot take the time to examine or solve the latter issue.

[19]Someone could object that the exhortation "be reconciled to God" (2 Cor 5:20) demonstrates that reconciliation is eschatological. We would argue, however, that Paul is calling on people to be reconciled to God now; he is not thinking of the day of judgment as the day of reconciliation here.

holiness and sanctification will not be ours until the day of redemption.[20] The present holiness of believers is apparent from Paul's custom of calling them "saints" (Rom 1:7; 1 Cor 1:2; 2 Cor 1:1; Eph 1:1; Phil 1:1; Col 1:2). All believers from the time of their conversion are designated as saints or holy ones; the term is not reserved for the specially righteous. Paul says that the church in Corinth is "sanctified in Christ Jesus" (1 Cor 1:2), emphasizing that holiness is their present possession. Similarly, in 1 Corinthians 1:30 "righteousness, holiness and redemption" now belong to those who are in Christ Jesus. The holiness spoken of in this verse was probably theirs at conversion, since the righteousness and redemption spoken of here are gifts since the inception of a believer's life.

Paul, in 1 Corinthians 6:11, almost certainly locates sanctification at conversion: "You were washed, you were sanctified, you were justified in the name of the Lord Jesus Christ and by the Spirit of our God" (NIV). Sanctification in this text should not be understood as a process subsequent to conversion. The danger of imposing our categories from systematic theology on biblical texts arises here. Sanctification does not invariably refer to a process of Christian growth after conversion. If Paul were thinking in terms of systematic theology, he would not have put sanctification before justification! The order of the text is (1) washing, (2) sanctification and (3) justification. All three terms here refer to conversion. Believers were cleansed and washed in baptism, made holy at conversion and declared righteous. When biblical writers speak of holiness or sanctification as something that is true of believers from conversion, we could capture what the text says by speaking of definitive or positional sanctification.[21] Such definitive sanctification is already ours because the age to come has penetrated this present age. Believers are already holy and sanctified, that is, they are now clean in God's sight because of the death and resurrection of Christ. Believers are also really changed by the work of God in Christ. But they have not yet attained the fullness of holiness that will be theirs on the last day.

---

[20]The Greek words for perfection *(teleios, teleiōs* is and *teleioō)* yield similar results, and we will indicate some of the relevant verses in the discussion.

[21]For an especially insightful and helpful treatment of sanctification, see David Peterson, *Possessed by God: A New Testament Theology of Sanctification and Holiness* (Grand Rapids, Mich.: Eerdmans, 1997).

The author of Hebrews conceives of holiness similarly. The sacrifice of Jesus Christ has made us holy: "We have been made holy through the sacrifice of the body of Jesus Christ once for all. . . . By one sacrifice he has made perfect forever those who are being made holy" (Heb 10:10, 14 NIV). The definitive work for our holiness has been accomplished on the cross, and it has effected a real and permanent change in us. We are "perfect forever" through Christ's sacrifice, yet we are in the process of "being made holy." Nonetheless, Christ's atonement guarantees our future holiness.

We know that believers must grow in holiness, for we are summoned to be holy on a number of occasions in the New Testament (e.g., Rom 6:19-22; 2 Cor 7:1; Col 1:22; 1 Thess 4:3-8; 1 Tim 2:15; 1 Pet 1:15-16; cf. Mt 5:48; 1 Jn 3:3). Exhortations to holiness would be superfluous if believers were already perfectly holy. Presumably we will not need to be encouraged to pursue holy living in heaven. Thus, the exhortations demonstrate that even though believers are now holy, there is a not yet in our experience of holiness. One cannot say that these directives are given only to churches that were doing poorly, such as the Corinthians. One of Paul's most sustained calls to holy living is in 1 Thessalonians 4:3-8, and Paul says on a number of occasions that the Thessalonian church is doing quite well (1 Thess 1:2-10; 2:13; 3:6-9; 4:1, 9-10). It is fair to conclude, therefore, that all Christians need exhortations to holiness, that all believers without exception have further to go. Paul makes it patently clear in Philippians 3:12-16 that he has not obtained perfection and that such perfection will not be ours until the day of resurrection (cf. Phil 3:11). Nor is growing in holiness optional. The author of Hebrews says, "Make every effort to live in peace with all men and to be holy; without holiness no one will see the Lord" (Heb 12:14 NIV). Holiness is necessary to see God, that is, to experience eternal life.

A number of texts also seem to indicate that we will be made holy on the last day, the day of our final redemption. For instance, Paul prays in 1 Thessalonians 5:23, "May God himself, the God of peace, sanctify you through and through. May your whole spirit, soul and body be kept blameless at the coming of our Lord Jesus Christ" (NIV). The words "at the coming of our Lord Jesus Christ" suggest that this prayer will be fulfilled at the coming of our Lord, though we should not erect an absolute barrier between present growth in holiness and future vindication because of holiness. The future tense of 1 Thessalonians 5:24 seems to point in this direction as well: "The one who calls you is faithful and he will do it" (NIV). That is, even though the church is holy now, God will sanctify the church fully in the future so that on the day of the Lord she will be holy and blameless. The consummation of holiness also seems to be located at the coming of our Lord in 1 Thessalonians 3:13: "May he strengthen your hearts so that you will be blameless and holy in the presence of our God and Father when our Lord Jesus comes with all his holy ones" (NIV). Again, present growth in holiness is surely implied, but there is also the suggestion that the completion and perfection in holiness will be ours at the coming of the Lord.

Similarly, Paul informs us in Ephesians that God's design in Christ's work on the cross was "to make her [the church] holy, cleansing her by the washing with water through the word, and to present her to himself as a radiant church, without stain or wrinkle or any other blemish, but holy and blameless" (Eph 5:26-27 NIV; cf. 4:13). The verb *present* suggests that an eschatological presentation before God is in view. Christ's work on the cross has secured our future sanctification on the day of the Lord. Colossians 1:22 is similar to the Ephesian text: "Now he has reconciled you by Christ's physical body through death to present you holy in his sight, without blemish and free from accusation" (NIV). Again, an eschatological presentation is probably in view, though we shall see later that a condition must be met for this presentation to occur (Col 1:23). Finally, God chose us to be his people before the world began "to be holy and blameless in his sight" (Eph 1:4). This text emphasizes that God's goal in choosing us was our holiness, and it is likely that Paul thinks of our perfection in holiness on the day of our redemption.

It is crucial to preserve the tension between the future and the present in constructing our theology of holiness. Those who espouse some form of entire sanctification or perfectionism nullify the not yet that permeates Paul's theology of holiness, while those who limit holiness now to "positional sanctification" are in danger of squelching the real transformation that Paul understood to be part and parcel of the Christian life. We see again that understanding the already-but-not-yet dimensions of New Testament theology is immensely practical. It spares us from utopian visions in the present and rationalistic excuses for ungodly living. Understanding the already and the not yet is not merely abstract theology. Those who fail to grasp it may fall prey either to perfectionism or give way to a libertine view of the Christian life.

Legal Metaphors

We have just seen that God's work on our behalf is portrayed in cultic terms: we are holy and sanctified ones. Images from the legal or penal realm are also utilized to describe our salvation. We will investigate two of those images here: our sins have been forgiven, and God has declared us righteous. Forgiveness of sins is our greatest need before God and the basis on which all other blessings become ours. In that sense, forgiveness and justification are fundamental to God's saving work.

Forgiveness of sins. The picture here is of God as the divine judge and of us as guilty before him. We are guilty because we have sinned and therefore deserve judgment and God's eschatological wrath (Rom 1:18—3:20; Eph 2:1-3). The Scriptures declare, however, that those who put their faith in Jesus and confess him as Lord (cf. Rom 10:9) are forgiven of their sins (Acts 2:38; 10:43; 13:38; 26:18) by the divine judge. They are not guilty before his tribunal. When the Scriptures speak of forgiveness, they almost invariably emphasize that we are forgiven of our sins now: "In him we have redemption through his blood, the forgiveness of sins" (Eph 1:7 NIV; cf. Col 1:14). Forgiveness of sins is not a future gift; we enjoy it as a present possession.

Similarly, the author of Hebrews eloquently contends for the superiority of the new covenant and Christ's sacrifice over the old covenant and animal sacrifices (Heb 9:1—10:18). The sacrifice of Christ is definitive and final precisely because it is effective. Animal sacrifices never really brought forgiveness of sins or the cleansing of the conscience (Heb 10:2). They only foreshadowed the sacrifice that could secure forgiveness. The sacrifice of Christ, however, has ushered us into the very presence of God. The forgiveness of sins through Christ, therefore, fulfills the new covenant promise of Jeremiah 31:31-34. The sacrifices under the old covenant pointed to and anticipated the forgiveness of sins available through believing in Christ. The author remarks that, if "sins and lawless acts" are forgotten, then these miscues "have been forgiven" and no further sacrifice for sin is needed

(Heb 10:17-18). Since Christ's sacrifice is effective and final, forgiveness belongs to us now. We can "draw near to God with a sincere heart in full assurance of faith, having our hearts sprinkled to cleanse us from a guilty conscience and having our bodies washed with pure water" (Heb 10:22 NIV). Cleansing and washing illustrate our once-for-all forgiveness of sins.

Actually, the language of cleansing and washing hearkens back to the cultic sphere that we examined above. It is not surprising that some of these metaphors overlap. Forgiveness relates to both the legal and the cultic spheres. We are not guilty before our judge, and we are cleansed from our defilement. Forgiveness is portrayed, therefore, in John 13:10 as a bath in which we are cleansed from that which stains us. Such cleansing is closely associated with baptism, for in baptism our sins are washed away. The forgiveness of sins in baptism is probably described in Ephesians 5:26, where Paul says that the church was cleansed "by the washing with water through the word." Similarly, Titus 3:5 describes the new birth of Christians in terms of "the washing of rebirth," indicating that we should not divide baptism from regeneration.[22] Forgiveness, then, is always a present gift. New Testament writers want us to have confidence that God accepts us and loves us so that we have boldness to enter his presence. What do we say, however, about 1 John 1:9, which says, "If we confess our sins, he is faithful and just and will forgive us our sins and purify us from all unrighteousness" (NIV)? If our sins are already forgiven, do we need to continue to confess our sins to be forgiven by God?

Some maintain that John could not possibly intend such a thought, since we are already forgiven by our divine judge. They think, therefore, that John merely means that we must confess our sins to maintain fellowship with God. In their view, fellowship is not the same thing as salvation, for fellowship means that one has a richer and more satisfying Christian life. This interpretation is mistaken, for fellowship in these verses cannot be separated from salvation. In this context John counters the teaching of secessionists who had left the church. These secessionists claimed to be without sin (1 Jn 1:8) and asserted that they had not sinned since their conversion (1 Jn 1:10), yet John says they "walk in darkness" (1 Jn 1:6). John argues that if

---

[22]We believe this is an argument that points to believer's baptism.

we make such claims then we are not Christians. This is what he means when he says that "his word has no place in our lives" (1 Jn 1:10) and that "the truth is not in us" (1 Jn 1:8). Those who have fellowship with John and Jesus Christ and the Father (1 Jn 1:3) belong to the redeemed people of God. Thus, John really means that we must confess our sins in an ongoing way to be forgiven by God.

Of course, this does not mean that believers must frantically try to recall every transgression ever committed to be "clean" before God. It means that we must ask God to forgive the sins we remember. The stubborn refusal to admit such sins is lethal. What are we to make of the objection that our sins are already forgiven? The already-but-not-yet dynamic of New Testament thinking helps us here. Yes, we are already forgiven. But we have not yet arrived in the heavenly city. We cannot use the promise of present forgiveness as a wedge to deny the need to confess sins as we commit them. We are already forgiven, yet we must continue to confess sins in order to be forgiven. The Scriptures teach both truths, and we ignore either of them to our peril. Jesus himself makes it quite clear that we must forgive the sins of others to be forgiven by God (Mt 6:14-15). How tempting it is to explain these verses away! But Jesus is dead serious, and people who ignore these verses and do not forgive others will find themselves in hell. Of course, there is the danger of perfectionism and demanding a "perfect" forgiveness of others to be saved, so that we fall into a works-righteousness and legalism. But there is also the danger of ignoring verses such as 1 John 1:9 and Matthew 6:14-15. We must integrate these two themes wisely, and in this book we shall try to help the reader do so.

Righteousness. One of the most famous metaphors for our salvation is righteousness, what is commonly called justification. Justification hails from the forensic sphere and denotes the right standing of believers before God. Paul especially emphasizes that God's righteousness has now been manifested and revealed in Christ (e.g., Rom 1:17; 3:21-26), particularly in his cross and resurrection (Rom 4:25). It is crucial to understand that the conception of God's righteousness stems from the Old Testament, and in the Old Testament God's righteousness often denotes his promise to save his people in accord with the promises made to the patriarchs. Thus, in a number of Old Testament texts God's righteousness is parallel to salvation, truth, steadfast love and faithfulness. For example, Psalm 36:5-6 states, "Your stead-fast love, O LORD, extends to the heavens, your faithfulness to the clouds. Your righteousness is like the mighty mountains, your judg-ments are like the great deep; you save humans and animals alike, O LORD" (NRSV). God's righteousness here is his saving righteousness based on his steadfast love. Psalm 40:10 confesses, "I do not hide your righteousness in my heart; I speak of your faithfulness and sal-vation. I do not conceal your love and your truth from the great assembly" (NIV). Note again the parallels between righteousness, faithfulness, salvation, love and truth. The Old Testament linkage between righteousness, salvation and God's faithfulness is clearly a part of the warp and woof of the Old Testament (cf. Ps 51:5-8; 71:2, 15; 98:2-3).

These texts indicate that the saving righteousness of God spoken of in the New Testament fulfills Old Testament promises. It is a mistake to abstract Paul from the Old Testament context when he refers to God's righteousness.

When the New Testament speaks of the righteousness of God, is the text speaking of a divine activity or a gift given to human beings? We do not need to resolve that debate here, though we do wish to say that righteousness is fundamentally forensic.[23] Paul emphasizes that righteousness is a gift that human beings now receive by faith (Rom 1:17; 3:21-22; Phil 3:9). Similarly, the tax collector was justified before God when he acknowledged his sinfulness and pled for mercy (Lk 18:14). "Everyone who believes is justified" (Acts 13:39), showing that righteousness becomes theirs when they believe. Righteousness is given to all now when they believe through God's grace (Rom 1:17; 3:21-22, 24, 28, 30; 4:3, 5-6, 9, 11, 13, 22; 5:1; 8:30, 33; 9:30; Gal 3:6; Phil 3:9; Tit 3:7). Paul specifically says, "We have been justified now by his blood" (Rom 5:9 NIV; cf. 5:1). The word *now* indicates with certainty that righteousness is a present gift. In the vast majority of instances, righteousness is said to belong to believers now. As with forgiveness, New Testament writers wanted to emphasize that believers are right with God in this life.

This does not mean, however, that righteousness is not an end-

---

[23]This is a matter of prolonged and intense debate. See the discussion under Rom 1:17 in Schreiner, *Romans,* pp. 63-71, for a summary of the debate.

time gift and verdict. The Old Testament language of righteousness shows that it is part of God's promises to Israel, that Israel would receive the gift of righteousness when salvation became theirs. Paul maintains that the eschatological gift of righteousness has penetrated history now and has been given to the church. Thus, righteousness is part of the pattern that we have found in the rest of the metaphors for salvation in the New Testament. Some texts indicate that righteousness is a future gift believers do not yet have: "For through the Spirit, by faith, we eagerly wait for the hope of righteousness" (Gal 5:5 NRSV). Righteousness here is almost certainly future, since "we eagerly await" it and it is the content of our "hope."[24] Paul is confident of receiving the gift of righteousness, yet he locates it in the final day. Romans 2:13 and 3:20 also reveal that righteousness will be declared on the final day, for the future tense "will be declared righteous" most probably refers to a declaration on the day of judgment. There are indications, therefore, that righteousness should be included in the already-but-not-yet tension that informs New Testament soteriology. Believers are righteous now, yet they still await the gift of righteousness that will be theirs on the day of redemption. We should not use the texts that speak of righteousness being ours now to nullify those that refer to righteousness as a future reality.

The Prize: An Athletic Metaphor

Another conclusion can be drawn from the material presented in this chapter. Various metaphors are used to designate the same prize that we are striving to win. Our future prize may be described as the kingdom, salvation, redemption, eternal life, resurrection, sonship, an adoption, an inheritance, sanctification, perfection and righteousness. Yet in every case the prize is the same: the possession of the eternal inheritance in the kingdom of God. We do not claim that we have presented every metaphor used in the Scriptures. Biblical writers, for instance, also use the language of glorification or glory (Rom 5:2; 8:17-18, 21, 30; 1 Pet 5:4). Our point is that there is a diversity of metaphors that convey the idea that our salvation has been inaugurated but is not yet consummated. Sometimes writers speak of inher-

---

[24]For the eschatological understanding presented here, see John Reumann, "Righteousness" in the New Testament: "Justification" in the United States Lutheran–Roman Catholic Dialogue (Philadelphia: Fortress, 1982), pp. 58-59.

iting the kingdom (Mt 25:34; 1 Cor 6:9; 15:50; Gal 5:21; Eph 5:5; Jas 2:5) and on other occasions of inheriting eternal life (Mt 19:29; Mk 10:17; Lk 10:25; 18:18). It would be a serious error to conclude that inheriting the kingdom is distinct from inheriting eternal life.

Michael Eaton attempts to forge a distinction between the justification that is present and by faith alone and the inheritance that is future and by works.[25] But Eaton does not think inheritance always relates to the future. Thus, "inheriting the promises" in Hebrews 6:12 is said to "clearly" refer "to what is achieved in this life."[26] Against Eaton, it is much more probable that the promises relate to the future eschaton, and nowhere is it clear that inheritance relates to present enjoyment of promises. The more fundamental problem with Eaton is his sharp distinction between inheritance and justification. He fails to explain adequately that justification also has a future dimension. Even more damaging to his thesis is the biblical claim that one must have works to be justified on the last day (Rom 2:6-13; Jas 2:14-26). This suggests that Eaton's confinement of the eschatological inheritance to a reward that is distinct from eternal life is questionable.

Rather, the metaphors of kingdom and eternal life are two different ways of presenting the same reality. Similarly, inheriting the earth (Mt 5:5), the promise (Heb 6:12) and a blessing (1 Pet 3:9) all refer to our eternal inheritance, to what Christians have typically called heaven. Likewise, our future reward can be designated as adoption or as the redemption of the body. Of course, these two terms do not have the same meaning. But the consummation of our adoption and the redemption of the body will both occur at the same time, when we receive our eternal inheritance. Another way of portraying what will happen to us on that future day is resurrection. "Redemption of the body" and "resurrection" do not have the same meaning, but both promise freedom from our corruptible sinful body at the coming of our Lord Jesus Christ. The Scriptures can also speak of our future inheritance in terms of our sanctification, holiness and perfection. When Jesus returns we shall be perfected and sanctified; we shall be transformed into his likeness. We have also seen that the Scriptures often speak of this future blessing as salvation. We shall be saved on

---

[25]Michael A. Eaton, *No Condemnation: A New Theology of Assurance* (Downers Grove, Ill.: InterVarsity Press, 1995), pp. 175-85.
[26]Ibid., p. 178.

the day of the Lord from God's wrath by virtue of Christ's work on the cross.

Writers, therefore, who attempt to distinguish the kingdom of God from eternal life, so that the former refers only to blessings in the present life, are seriously mistaken. The same criticism applies to those who try to keep salvation distinct from the kingdom of God or our inheritance. They define these latter two terms so that they relate to rewards above and beyond eternal life or to fruitfulness in our lives now. We are not arguing that all three terms mean the same thing. We are saying that they often all refer to our heavenly inheritance.

Probably the most effective way to demonstrate this point is to conduct a study of a particular text where many of these terms are used. Matthew 19:16-30 (see the parallels in Mk 10:17-31; Lk 18:18-30) is of remarkable help in this regard. The rich man approaches Jesus and inquires, "What good thing must I do to get eternal life?" (Mt 19:16 NIV). Note that eternal life is his desire, and Jesus responds that, if he wants "to enter life"—another way of describing eternal life—he must "obey the commandments" (Mt 19:17). The man replies that he has kept the commandments that Jesus specifies (Mt 19:18-20), but Jesus summons him to sell all he owns and to follow him (Mt 19:21). Jesus says that he must do this in order to be "perfect" and to "have treasure in heaven" (Mt 19:21). The perfection demanded here is not a call to extraordinary commitment and sacrifice that only some Christians attain, as it has often been interpreted in the Roman Catholic tradition. Remember that the man's question was how he could obtain "eternal life," and Jesus says he must give up everything! Thus, "perfect" and "treasure in heaven" here are simply alternate expressions for eternal life. We have noted above that *perfect* may be used to designate the future inheritance of believers, and that is the point here. It is telling that Zane Hodges does not direct readers to the fact that kingdom of God, eternal life and saved are used as alternate expressions of the same reality. Instead, he introduces the idea of belief from John's Gospel to silence what this text says.[27]

---

[27]Zane Hodges, *Absolutely Free! A Biblical Reply to Lordship Salvation* (Grand Rapids, Mich.: Zondervan, 1989), pp. 183-89. We should also note, though we do not have space to explore it here, that one of Hodges's major errors is his definition of faith. He fails to see that faith involves by definition a delight in and satisfaction with God. For a brilliant and practical exposition of this theme, see John Piper, *The Purifying Power of Living by Faith in Future Grace* (Sisters, Ore.: Multnomah, 1995).

The young man was unwilling to part with his riches and departed downcast and dejected. Jesus remarks that "it is hard for a rich man to enter the kingdom of heaven," so hard that "it is easier for a camel to go through the eye of a needle than for a rich man to enter the kingdom of God" (Mt 19:23-24 NIV). The disciples do not reply by saying, "Well, it sure is hard to get rewards," or "Not many Christians live fruitful lives of discipleship," or "At least the rich man is saved, even though he is not willing to part with all his wealth." No! When the disciples exclaim, "Who then can be saved?" (Mt 19:25) Jesus replies, "With men this is impossible" (v. 26). Clearly they understand Jesus' statement about entering the kingdom of heaven as relating to salvation! "If the rich cannot enter the kingdom, then who can enter the kingdom and be saved?" ask the disciples. We have good exegetical warrant for concluding that "eternal life," "the kingdom of heaven," "salvation," "perfect" and "treasure in heaven" are alternate ways of referring to the same reality. Interpreting these terms to refer to different realities confounds the story incredibly. A final piece of evidence conspires to validate our interpretation. After the disciples exclaim, "Who then can be saved?" Jesus does not say, "I am not talking about salvation. Of course, he is saved. I am talking about entering the kingdom." Jesus assumes that salvation and entering the kingdom of heaven are the same reality, so he declares, "With man this is impossible, but with God all things are possible" (Mt 19:26 NIV). In other words, no one can be saved apart from the miraculous intervention of God to transform that person.

Charles Ryrie says that the young man should have lingered to hear that he did not have to sell his riches to enter the kingdom, for Jesus goes on to explain that salvation is impossible for human beings so no one can do what is necessary to enter the kingdom.[28] This interpretation is implausible. It virtually teaches that Jesus evangelized in an inferior way, for he never got around to telling the young man what was needed for eternal life and he let the man get away before telling him! Indeed, Jesus could have pursued him and told him the truth but instead allowed the young man (according to Ryrie's view) to walk away without correcting his misperception. Contrary to

---

[28]Charles C. Ryrie, *So Great Salvation: What It Means to Believe in Jesus Christ* (Wheaton, Ill.: Victor, 1989), p. 86.

Ryrie's view, Jesus' saying should be understood to teach that the saving power of the kingdom is so great that the young man's desires would be transformed so that he would be willing to sell all for the kingdom. Only God can accomplish such a heart transformation in a person's life. Ryrie regularly asks "how much" a person must be willing to sacrifice to be a believer and worries that no one perfectly gives his or her life to the Lord. Ryrie is correct in warning us about the dangers of perfectionism, but we must also be on our guard lest we evacuate the calls to discipleship of their significance and fail to follow the Lord.

When the Scriptures speak of winning the prize, occasionally the image of a crown is utilized. For example, believers will obtain a crown of life (Jas 1:12; Rev 2:10), a crown of righteousness (2 Tim 4:8) and a crown of glory (1 Pet 5:4). Some interpreters understand these terms to refer to a reward that is above and beyond eternal life, reserved only for "faithful Christians." On the contrary, we maintain that each of these crowns is a metaphor for obtaining the heavenly inheritance. That is, apart from receiving these crowns, no one will be saved on the final day, for to be saved is nothing short of being crowned with life, righteousness and glory. We have already seen that the terms *life, righteousness* and *glory* are used elsewhere to denote our eternal inheritance. The metaphor of crown is added to them to emphasize that eternal life, salvation, glory and righteousness are prizes worth striving for and winning.

What evidence is there for the interpretation proposed here? Each of the seven letters in Revelation concludes with an exhortation to overcome. Those who overcome will receive a reward. But what is the reward for overcomers? We would argue that it is eternal life itself. Two texts show this plainly. Revelation 2:11 says, "He who overcomes will not be hurt at all by the second death" (NIV). The implication is that those who do not overcome will be hurt by the second death, which is clearly identified in Revelation 20:14 as the lake of fire. Thus, the second death is hell itself, and in order to escape the second death one must overcome, according to Revelation 2:11. What does overcoming involve for the church of Smyrna? It means that one must "suffer persecution" and be cast into prison. However, if these church members are "faithful, even to the point of death," then "I will give you the crown of life" (Rev 2:11). In other words, they must not deny Jesus even if it costs them their lives. Those who deny Jesus will not be saved; they will not receive the crown of eternal life. Paul himself said, "If we deny him, he will also deny us" (2 Tim 2:12 NRSV), and this Pauline teaching hearkens back to Jesus' own words: "Everyone therefore who acknowledges me before others, I also will acknowledge before my Father in heaven; but whoever denies me before others, I also will deny before my Father in heaven" (Mt 10:32-33 NRSV). Those who are not faithful to death, those who deny knowing Jesus, will not obtain the crown of life. In other words, they will experience the second death, the lake of fire.

This interpretation is confirmed by another "overcomer" text in Revelation 2—3. At the conclusion of the letter to Sardis, Jesus says, "He who overcomes will, like them, be dressed in white. I will never blot out his name from the book of life, but will acknowledge his name before my Father and his angels" (Rev 3:5 NIV). Those who acknowledge Jesus will be acknowledged before the Father, according to Revelation 3:5. Matthew 10:32-33 makes the same statement and adds that those who deny Jesus will be denied by Jesus before the Father. We conclude, then, that to be acknowledged by Jesus is to enter the new heavens and new earth (Rev 21:1—22:5). By implication those who refuse to acknowledge Jesus and fail to overcome will be judged in the lake of fire. From these two overcomer texts it seems fair to conclude that the reward in view in every overcomer text is eternal life itself. Thus, the crown of life in Revelation 2:10 is not a reward above and beyond eternal life; it is eternal life itself.

We suggest the same interpretation for the crown-of-life metaphor in James: "Blessed is the man who perseveres under trial, because when he has stood the test, he will receive the crown of life that God has promised to those who love him" (Jas 1:12 NIV). One could understand this to refer to a reward that is given in addition to eternal life. But a canonical reading of James suggests that eternal life itself is the reward. James contends in his most famous passage that faith without works is dead and that "faith" that lacks works cannot save (Jas 2:14-26). This fits with the idea that the test of genuine faith is persevering under trial. Those who do so will receive the reward of eternal life. Those who wilt under trials have a faith without works. Similarly, James says that those who hear the word without keeping it "deceive" themselves (Jas 1:22). That is, they claim to be believers but deny it by the way they live. Similarly, those who endure trials

will receive the crown of life and an eternal inheritance. Those who
crack under trials so that they abandon their faith forever will not
receive the crown of life, for they have deceived themselves by
thinking they were believers. In other words, enduring under trials is
not optional for believers, nor is there a special unique reward for
believers who persist when tested. All believers must stand fast
when buffeted in order to obtain the crown of eternal life. We are not
suggesting, of course, that believers do not fail or sin when experiencing trials, for James himself says we all stumble in many ways
(Jas 3:2). Persevering under trials does not suggest some kind of perfectionism; it means that we do not forsake Jesus Christ when tested.

The crown of righteousness in 2 Timothy 4:8 denotes the righteousness necessary to enter the heavenly kingdom (cf. 2 Tim 4:18).
Paul says, "Now there is in store for me the crown of righteousness,
which the Lord, the righteous Judge, will award to me on that day—
and not only to me, but also to all who have longed for his appearing"
(2 Tim 4:8 NIV). The crown of righteousness is not only for Paul but
for all believers who long for Jesus' appearing. Nor is it likely that the
desire for the Lord's appearing is confined to some Christians only,
while other Christians do not yearn for his coming. Longing for the
Lord's coming is characteristic of all believers. Paul will receive the
crown of righteousness because he "fought the good fight," "finished
the race" and "kept the faith" (2 Tim 4:7). Notice that one must keep
the faith to obtain the crown of righteousness. This strongly suggests
that the crown of righteousness refers to entrance into the heavenly
kingdom, for those who do not keep the faith will not enter heaven.
Keeping the faith, fighting the good fight and finishing the race are
not optional for believers; they are essential for obtaining the eternal
reward, the crown of righteousness by which we stand in the right
before God.

Peter says that elders who serve well "will receive the crown of
glory that will never fade away" (1 Pet 5:4 NIV). Some interpret this to
be a special and unique reward for those who have served in ministry. It is more probable, though, that the crown of glory is the glorification believers will receive when they enter upon their eternal
inheritance. Shepherds who persist in the ministry because of con-
straint, to satisfy their greed or to dominate those under their charge
(1 Pet 5:2-3) will not receive the crown of glory. That is, they will not

be glorified at all. They will experience the deprivation of being separated from God. Again, this is not to say that pastors never fall prey to coercion, greed or tyranny. If these sins characterize a pastor's life, however, we have an indication that such a person does not truly belong to God.

We conclude by saying that the prize to be won is nothing other than eternal life itself, entrance into the heavenly kingdom and final redemption. Nothing less than our eternal inheritance is at stake, and thus the issue of perseverance is weighty indeed. Many worry that such teaching undermines assurance, teaches that we must merit salvation by good works and fosters an unhealthy perfectionism. We urge readers to investigate all that we say in this book before jumping to conclusions on these issues, for we categorically deny that salvation can be earned by works, we believe that our teaching promotes assurance instead of destroying it, and we are not commending any form of perfectionism or second-blessing theology. We are simply saying this: the prize to be won is eternal life, and as Paul said, we must strive to win that prize.

3

THE RACE
TO BE RUN

The Necessity of Obedient Faith

Compete in the good competition of faith; lay hold of eternal life,
to which you were called and for which you made the good confession
before many witnesses. (1 Tim 6:12)

In chapter one, where we surveyed the four popular views of
how biblical warnings and admonitions relate to our Christian
lives and then offered a summary of our own explanation, it
became apparent that the various views understand faith differently.
Some believe that faith can completely fail, yet those who believe this
do not agree on the consequences. For some faith's failure brings loss
of salvation, but for others it simply results in loss of rewards. Some
believe that there are different kinds of faith. Faith that gives out or
fails is spurious, but faith that perseveres is genuine. Against this, others find no biblical evidence to warrant such distinctions. Those who
believe that faith can fail generally conclude, for example, that three
of the soils in Jesus' parable of the soils represent genuine believers,
though two fall away and perish. Again, some believe the two lose
eternal life, while others think they lose only rewards. Generally,
those who believe that Scripture describes a variety of responses to
the gospel as faith also believe that faith is a gift God grants to us who
"were dead in our sins," just as God breathed life into the lifeless body of
Adam. Others object that faith cannot be God's gift, because we are the
ones who believe and we are the ones who can cease believing. These
disagreements signify substantial differences concerning how various

Christians understand the gospel's call for faith.

Few disagreements, however, are as divisive and generate as much heat as the conflict that concerns the nature of faith's relationship to obedience and good works. The familiar motto *sola fide* ("by faith alone") was central to the Protestant Reformation of the church. This was the source of the famous disputation between the reformer Martin Luther and Desiderius Erasmus, the Roman Catholic.[1] Since the Reformation, Protestants have continued to debate the meaning of "by faith alone." Each generation debates this Protestant motto, usually with some acrimony, because few issues concerning the gospel of Jesus Christ are as crucial as the question concerning the relationship of faith and obedience. Some sever obedience from faith and insist that one can be a Christian and yet have no deeds that accompany one's faith. In fact, they say, a Christian can abandon faith itself and never return but still be saved. This, of course, alarms many who contend that the gospel binds faith and obedience together. Yet it is no small task to explain how the gospel binds them together.

We concluded chapter two by saying that the prize to be won is eternal life, and we noted that Paul the apostle said we must strive to win that prize. The "race set before us" is an uncommon footrace, for the victor's wreath of life that we pursue is the life that already courses through our mortal bodies by God's Spirit (Rom 8:11). This is not the rhetoric of a sports commentator reporting on the marathon at the Olympics: "The runners are already empowered by the gold." It is much more than desire for the gold that invigorates runners in this uncommon race. For we have affirmed that although eternal life is God's prize of salvation that we pursue with eager hope, eternal life is also the gift of grace that already invigorates us with resurrection life so that we run the race with perseverance. Eternal life is the reward that we trust God will give to us who faithfully endure to the end of the race. Yet eternal life is also the very breath of heaven that already fills our hearts by God's Spirit and enlivens our "feeble arms and weak knees" (Heb 12:12) to "run the race set before us" (Heb 12:1).

As we have pondered the eternal value of the prize to be won at the end of the race, now we focus on how the prize is attained. One

---

[1]Martin Luther, *The Bondage of the Will*, trans. J. I. Packer and O. R. Johnston (Old Tappan, N.J.: Fleming H. Revell, 1957).

gains the prize of eternal life only by running the race. Faith that perseveres not only receives God's approval now but also God's final commendation in the day of judgment. Yet this obedient faith contributes nothing to God's gracious salvation accomplished in the redeeming work of Jesus Christ. So before we proceed, we need to clarify what we mean by the phrase "how the prize is attained."

The *how* of which we speak in this chapter is not the sacrificial death and resurrection of Jesus Christ, who is the pioneer and perfecter of faith (Heb 12:2). Christ's redemptive act is the objective basis of salvation. Rather, the how that is our concern is the subjective means of salvation. We must exercise faith in Jesus Christ in order to receive the prize of eternal life. Biblical writers are fond of portraying belief, the subjective means of salvation, as running a footrace. We must "run with perseverance the race that is set before us" (Heb 12:1 NRSV). We make this crucial distinction between the objective basis and the subjective means of salvation to make it clear from the outset that what believers do in order to attain the prize of eternal life does not add to or nullify God's grace in the saving work of Jesus Christ. The reward we receive by faith in Christ is based on grace alone; it is not grounded on our achievement. Only those who exercise faith in the one true God will receive this reward, for Scripture says, "Without faith it is impossible to please God, for whoever would approach him must believe that he exists and that he rewards those who seek him" (Heb 11:6 NRSV).

Faith and Reward

Hebrews 11:6 is a good place to begin to offer a biblical portrayal of faith. We highlight two elements in the verse. First, the author speaks of being justified before God through the language of pleasing God and of God's rewarding those who seek him. The whole of Hebrews 11 provides a glimpse, ahead of time, to the future day of judgment. God's righteous commendation in that day is already ours by faith. This glimpse indicates that God only commends people whose behavior is governed by faith in him; he passes over their sins without mentioning them. For example, Noah's drunkenness is not mentioned, nor does the author of Hebrews bring up Abraham's lying. God commends people who believe in him. "God's commendation" is this author's expression for saying what Paul means when he talks of "justification before God." Both *commendation* and *justification* concern approval under the scrutiny of God's discriminating judgment (cf. Heb 4:12). Hebrews 11, therefore, is about salvation and our inheritance of righteousness (cf. Heb 11:7).

The second component in Hebrews 11:6 worth highlighting is the author's description of the kind of faith that receives commendation or justification from God. People who are pleasing to God believe two essential truths about him: that God exists and that God rewards those who seek him. This verse indicates that God commends all who penetrate beyond the veil of things seen to understand that they are made from things that are not seen (Heb 11:3) and that the things that are seen testify that God exists. Hebrews 11:6 also makes it clear that all who approach God must believe not only that he exists but also that he rewards those who seek him. The last phrase of Hebrews 11:6 is significant for our discussion because it affirms two important truths. First, the metaphorical use of the active verb *seek* or *search* replaces the word *believe*. This substitution makes it clear that faith is not only a passive repose on God but an active quest for him. Second, God rewards people who seek him. We must be careful lest we misunderstand what Hebrews means by *reward*. Therefore, we pause to reflect on the text of Hebrews 11:6, in order to avoid two common errors concerning the words "he rewards those who seek him" and to clarify the nature of the reward.

God's reward for us is not earned wages. First, though it is true that the word used in this verse literally means "one who pays wages" *(misthapodotēs),* the author of Hebrews does not mean that we achieve the reward by meriting it. According to Hebrews 11:6 and the context, the reward God gives to those who seek him is his commendation, the verdict of righteousness (cf. Heb 11:7). Verse 2 functions as a prelude to the litany of ancestors who all received God's approval by faith. Then begins the lengthy recitation of individuals, each one introduced with the words "by faith," but the author mentions only two—Abel and Enoch—and then momentarily interrupts the recital with verse 6. Why does the author interrupt? It is likely that the author recognizes that the texts of Genesis 4:4 (concerning Abel) and of Genesis 5:21-24 (referring to Enoch) do not mention faith, which verse 2 identifies as the principle to be illustrated. Therefore, the author inserts verse 6 to explain why these two ancient men are included in the litany illustrating that we receive God's approval by faith. The author finds that the biblical text implicitly mentions faith in both stories, because both men pleased God and without faith no one can please God.[2] The author of Hebrews, who knows from Genesis 15:1-6 that faith is essential for pleasing God, reasons that because Abel found favor with the Lord and because Enoch walked with God, who took him without having him pass through death, both men gained God's approval by faith, for "without faith it is impossible to please God."

But what is the relationship between faith in God and his approval of the believer? Does faith secure God's approval by earning his pleasure? Does the one who believes in God work for wages, and does God really pay out wages to those who believe in him, as though faith earns wages? Remember, the word that Hebrews 11:6 uses concerning reward literally means "one who pays wages." We will have more to say concerning the use of figurative language later, but for now it is readily apparent that the author of Hebrews is using his word figuratively, not literally. This means that there is some analogy between God who rewards those who believe in him and the employer who pays wages to those who work for him. However, since figurative language expresses analogy, we must be careful lest we literalize the figurative use of *rewards*. The relationship between the believer and God is not identical to the employee and employer relationship, but only analogical or metaphorical. While the employer pays wages out of indebtedness to the employee, God gives a reward to the believer purely out of his grace, and the author of Hebrews certainly believes this (see, e.g., Heb 4:16; 12:15). Hence, we can say from the outset that faith alone secures God's approval and our final vindication, but faith is not a meritorious act that adds something to Christ's redeeming work.

God's reward for us is not in addition to salvation. Now let us consider the second error that we need to avoid concerning Hebrews 11:6. If we do not carefully read the verse in context, we might misunder-

---

[2]Genesis 4:4-5 expressly states, "The LORD looked with favor on Abel and his offering, but on Cain and his offering he did not look with favor" (NIV). However, the Hebrew text of Gen 5:21-24 does not explicitly say what Heb 11:5 attributes to it. The words "he was commended as one who pleased God" (NIV) derive from the Greek translation of the Old Testament (LXX), which the author of Hebrews was apparently using.

stand the nature of God's reward. Some Christians read the verse as though it makes a distinction between rewards and eternal life or salvation.[3] They wrongly deduce that wherever the Bible mentions reward, it must carry the idea of merit.[4] They reason that eternal life or salvation cannot be simultaneously a prize and a gift; a prize is earned, a gift is received. However, the author of Hebrews has in mind neither a concept of merit nor a distinction between reward and salvation. Rather, the author of Hebrews uses *reward* to describe God's salvation that is of inestimable worth, which he awards to all who believe that he exists and who seek him. There are at least three reasons in the text to support this.

First, it is likely that Genesis 15:1 informs the principle that Hebrews 11:6 expresses, because in Hebrews 11:8 the author presents Abraham as a model of faith. In Genesis 15:1, the Lord announced to Abraham, "I am your shield, your very great reward" (NIV). The Lord and all that he has to give, including justification, is Abraham's great reward (cf. Gen 15:6). God rewarded Abraham's faith with justification, which is another way of saying that God commended his faith. Likewise, God commended Abel as a righteous man who by faith offered a better sacrifice than his brother Cain. So also by faith Noah condemned the world by his preaching and became an heir of righteousness. So according to the text, the reward God gives to the believer is his salvation.

Second, the context surrounding Hebrews 11:6 clarifies that the word *reward* does not refer to something that is in addition to eternal life.[5] One should not fail to recognize that Hebrews 10:35-39 already defines the reward mentioned in Hebrews 11:6.

> So do not throw away your confidence; it will be richly rewarded. You
> need to persevere so that when you have done the will of God, you will

---

[3]See, for example, Zane Hodges, *Grace in Eclipse: A Study on Eternal Rewards*, 2nd ed. (Dallas: Rendención Viva, 1987). See also Robert N. Wilkin, "The Biblical Distinction Between Eternal Salvation and Eternal Rewards: A Key to Proper Exegesis," *Journal of the Grace Evangelical Society* 9 (1996): 15-24. See our discussion in chapter one.

[4]On Hebrews 11:6, the influential *New Scofield Reference Bible* (New York: Oxford University Press, 1967), p. 1322, points readers to a note on 1 Cor 3:14: "God in the N.T. Scriptures offers to the lost, salvation; and for the faithful service of the saved, He offers rewards" (p. 1235).

[5]To our knowledge, the best discussion concerning the idea of reward in Scripture is by G. C. Berkouwer, *Faith and Justification*, trans. Lewis B. Smedes (Grand Rapids, Mich.: Eerdmans, 1954), pp. 112-29.

receive what he has promised. For in just a very little while, "He who is coming will come and will not delay. But my righteous one will live by faith. And if he shrinks back, I will not be pleased with him." But we are not of those who shrink back and are destroyed, but of those who believe and are saved. (NIV)

These verses clarify that the reward is salvation. *Confidence*, which is another word for faith in Hebrews, holds great reward, and this great reward is the promise from God that will be received after we have persevered in doing God's will. The author makes it clear that *reward* and *promise* are metaphors for salvation, for the words in verse 39 contrast shrinking back unto destruction and faith unto preservation of the soul.

Finally, the reward that the author speaks of in Hebrews 11:6 is the promised inheritance mentioned earlier in the sermon. Early in the book the author uses familiar imagery to portray salvation as a future inheritance (Heb 1:14), then sustains this imagery throughout Hebrews. In chapter 11, the reward is righteousness, which Noah was to inherit (Heb 11:7). The reward is the promise that Abraham and all his descendants of faith are to inherit, the heavenly Jerusalem (cf. Heb 11:10, 14-16, 39-40; 12:22-24; 13:14). This is why the author of Hebrews urges us to imitate Abraham by saying, "We want each of you to show this same diligence to the very end, in order to make your hope sure. We do not want you to become lazy, but to imitate those who through faith and patience inherit what has been promised" (Heb 6:11-12 NIV). Like Abraham, who waited patiently for God's firm promise, so we who are heirs of what was promised must have faith in God, who confirmed his promise with an oath, showing that it is a sure hope (Heb 6:13-20). To all who seek him, God rewards them with "the promised eternal inheritance," which is salvation (Heb 9:15).

God's reward for us is Jesus Christ, the object of our faith. It may seem that the subtitle above contradicts our burden in chapter two, where we show that eternal life is the prize or reward. There is no contradiction, however, for Paul properly summarizes our concern when he says, "that I may gain Christ" (Phil 3:8). To gain Christ is to receive all that is in him: righteousness, salvation, eternal life, redemption, sanctification, adoption, the fullness of God's good things for us. Therefore, when God revealed himself to Abraham he said, "I am your shield, your very great reward" (Gen 15:6 NIV). "In these last days," however, God has revealed himself to us more fully by his Son, for "the Son is the radiance of God's glory and the exact representation of his being" (Heb 1:2, 3 NIV). The Father directs our worship, obedience and submission to the Son (Heb 1:5-13). The Father has set forth the Son as the king before whom we must bow and the apostle and high priest whom we confess (Heb 1:3, 8-9; 3:1). Therefore we believe and obey Christ Jesus, who has announced to us God's salvation (Heb 2:1-4; 3:7-14; 12:23-25). We lay hold of Christ, who is the merciful and faithful high priest whom we confess (Heb 4:14-16). Our worship is acceptable to God only through Jesus Christ (Heb 13:15, 20-21). Finally, Jesus Christ is both the one who blazed the pathway of faith and the one on whom we set our eyes of faith as we run the race to lay hold of the prize (Heb 12:1-2). Jesus Christ is the prize that fills our vision as we press on toward the goal. So just as the Lord assured Abraham, "I am . . . your very great reward," so now that God has disclosed his fullness in Jesus Christ he assures us, who are Abraham's descendants (Heb 2:16), that his Son who has accomplished salvation for us is our great reward.

When we speak about biblical faith, such faith is not an abstract faith in God. As believers we place our faith in Jesus Christ, the crucified and risen Lord (cf. Rom 3:21-26; 9:30—10:17; Gal 2:15—3:5; Eph 3:12; Phil 3:7-11; Col 2:5). We trust in the God who has raised Jesus from the dead (Rom 4:23-25), believing that he will also grant life to our dead bodies as well (Rom 8:10-13). Biblical faith, then, should not be collapsed into a mere human disposition, so that belief receives the emphasis. The object of faith is central. We put our trust in the risen Lord who was crucified for us on Calvary so that we might have life. Nor should biblical faith be limited to belief in God, as if such faith is disconnected from the work of Jesus Christ in his cross and resurrection. Genuine biblical faith is always in the Son of God who loved me and gave himself for me (Gal 2:20). Saving faith constantly looks to Jesus Christ and his atoning sacrifice as the way of life, recognizing our inability and weakness to do anything to please God (Rom 8:5-8). We say this at the outset so that no one will misunderstand us and say that faith in God suffices apart from faith in Christ. We underscore this so that readers will fix firmly in their minds that saving faith is directed to the crucified and risen Lord, our only hope for commendation by God and before him.

Faith and Faithfulness

Throughout Hebrews 11 the author's use of the word translated "faith" actually includes two concepts: faith and faithfulness. This is because faith, by its very God-created design, springs into obedient behavior. First, as we noted earlier, Hebrews 11:6 replaces the word *believe* with the metaphorical use of the active verb *seek* or *search* when it explains why "without faith it is impossible to please God." The text reads, "for whoever would approach him must believe that he exists and that he rewards those who seek him." Carefully observe the argument in Hebrews 11. It was by faith that Abel offered to God a better sacrifice. It was by faith that Noah built an ark in order to save his family. It was by faith that Abraham obeyed and went where God led, though he did not know where he was going. It was by faith that Rahab welcomed the spies. In every case, faith sprang into faithful action. God commends each one, not merely for possessing faith, but for faith that obeys.

The inseparable link between faith and faithfulness should be evident from the argument sustained throughout Hebrews. If we conceive of Christian faith as only a passive resting on God, we have an inadequate concept. While we are correct to portray faith as reposing safely in God's arms (cf. Is 40:11), we need to hold this image alongside a variety of other pictures of faith. The author of Hebrews sketches a mental image of faith as finding rest (Heb 3:7—4:11) by stating, " Now we who have believed enter that rest" (Heb 4:3 NIV). But the author also shows no hesitation to mix images of faith, using rest and labor alongside each other: "Let us, therefore, make every effort to enter that rest, lest anyone fall in this same pattern of disobedience" (Heb 4:11).

Faith that perseveres receives God's commendation. For the author of Hebrews, faith in God—the kind that receives God's commendation—expresses itself as a diligent pursuit after the God who exists (Heb 11:6). God is pleased with faith that perseveres; God does not commend a person for a singular act of faith that fails to endure. God does not reward faith that does not go the distance. This is made clear with the admonition, "Therefore do not throw away your confidence, which holds great reward. For you have a need for perseverance in order that, after you have done God's will, you will receive the promise" (Heb 10:35-36). The faith God commends and the faithfulness he will reward with his promised salvation are indistinguishable. God's promised city of salvation, which we have not yet received but for which we continue to look (Heb 11:14-16; 13:14), will be given only to those who in this present world already have faith in God who exists and rewards all who seek him. By faith we run the distance that lies between the now and the not yet. By faith we now lay hold of God's word of promise, namely, the gospel, and reach beyond what can now be seen, in order that after we have done all that delights God, we will receive what his gospel promises us. This is what is meant when the author of Hebrews says, "These were all commended through their faith; they did not receive the promise, for God had planned something better for us in order that they would not, apart from us, be made perfect" (Heb 11:39-40).

Faithfulness is the proof of faith. Our pattern of behavior and the words we speak uncover what we truly believe. What we say, what we desire, what we do—all reveal what is in our hearts. God formed us so that there is an unbreakable and tight connection between faith and action, between creed and word, between belief and desire. Paul underscores this link: "Those who have doubts are condemned if they eat, because they do not act from faith; for whatever does not proceed from faith is sin" (Rom 14:23 NRSV). Because we act out our beliefs, we disclose to those around us what our hearts secretly believe and cherish. Regrettably, it is true that we find ourselves too easily speaking or acting contrary to a belief we profess, confirming the fact that God's gift of faith is not yet perfected in us. God's grace gives birth to our faith, and this faith governs the pattern of our behavior, so that by faith God purifies our hearts unto holiness (Acts 15:9; 26:18). Therefore, when Hebrews 11 recites the registry of those whom God commends, what the author mentions in every case is the behavior and conduct for which God commends them. God commends them for their faith, which shows itself in their faithful words and conduct (cf. Heb 11:39). All behavior is conceived in the womb of our beliefs. Therefore, all our desires, all our words and all our deeds make known what we truly believe and what we really value in our hearts.

Jesus makes the same point in Matthew 6:19-21 (NIV), when he says:

> Do not store up for yourselves treasures on earth, where moth and rust destroy, and where thieves break in and steal. But store up for yourselves treasures in heaven, where moth and rust do not destroy, and where thieves do not break in and steal. For where your treasure is, there your heart will be also.

Notice that Jesus does not explain his exhortation of verses 19-20 as some invert his saying, "For where your heart is, there will your treasure be also." Jesus expresses it as he does because he means that what we treasure discloses what truly holds the affections of our hearts. Our treasure lays bare our hearts. How we behave toward seen and unseen things uncovers what our hearts secretly value. Abel's "better sacrifice" pulled back the veil of his heart to disclose that he treasured God. Noah's faithful preaching and steadfast building of the ark proved that he valued God's commendation. Abraham's obedience, when called, unveiled his assurance concerning unseen things that God had promised to him.

When Scripture warns us of divine judgment, it tells us that God will judge the secrets of our hearts "according to our deeds" (Ps 62:12; Mt 16:27; Rom 2:6). This is the principle of God's judgment. God has formed us so that all our deeds originate from our beliefs, whether God-focused or not, whether in seen or unseen things. Therefore, because our deeds show what we truly believe, when God judges us he will assess our behavior and, in keeping with that behavior, will either reward us with eternal life or pour out his wrath on us. Though someone may play the hypocrite, one cannot mask one's true character of unbelief from God. When God judges us, he will commend us or condemn us in keeping with our deeds.

We have set our eyes on things yet unseen and have become heirs of the righteousness that comes by faith (cf. Heb 11:7). All who have not done this already dwell under God's wrath (Jn 3:18, 36; Rom 1:18). Likewise, Paul affirms with Jesus that our deeds matter when we stand before God in judgment, for he says that God "will give back to each person in keeping with his deeds. To those who by persevering in a good work seek glory and honor and incorruptibility, he will give eternal life" (Rom 2:6-7). Eternal life is the prize we shall receive from God in the day of judgment if we pursue God's reward—glory, honor and incorruptibility—by persevering in what is good. Such perseverance is not works-righteousness but the "obedience of faith" (Rom 1:5; 6:12; 15:18; 16:26).

Paul and Jesus agree. Our own words and deeds will either indict or vindicate us in the day that God judges us. Why? It is because the deeds and words that emerge from our hearts uncover what we secretly and truly trust, and God's judgment will bring to light the secrets of our hearts (Rom 2:16). Likewise, Jesus and Paul agree with the author of Hebrews: God will award the verdict of righteousness to those whose conduct in the present world is governed by faith that fixes its vision on the unseen things of the age to come. God rewards faithfulness. So faithfulness is simultaneously the obedience that derives from faith and the proof that faith is genuine.

Faith and Understanding

Our discussion of the contributions of Hebrews 11 for a proper understanding of Christian faith would be incomplete without reflecting on the relationship between faith and understanding. The author says in Hebrews 11:3, "By faith we understand that the worlds were created by the word of God, so that what is seen came into existence from what is not visible." What Hebrews affirms, not only here but throughout the whole of the book, is that God has established a relationship between invisible and visible things. We grasp this relationship only by faith, just as Hebrews 11:3 says, "Now faith is the assurance of things hoped for, the evidence of what is not seen." God indelibly imprinted his character on all that he created so that visible things reflect the splendor of invisible things, and this is because he made visible things to be earthly analogies of heavenly realities. As a result, Paul affirms that God has given universal witness to his eternal power and divine nature: "Ever since the creation of the world his eternal power and divine nature, invisible though they are, have been understood and seen through the things he has made" (Rom 1:20 NRSV).

Visible things bear analogical likeness to invisible things. The relationship is analogical and not identical. That is, visible things are earthly and shadowy copies of heavenly originals. So, for example, the sanctuary of the tabernacle constructed in the wilderness was a "copy and shadow of the heavenly one," which explains why the Lord warned Moses, "See that you make everything according to the pattern that was shown you on the mountain" (Heb 8:5 NRSV). Precisely because of this analogical relationship, we must not be dismissive toward creation, for what we see instructs us concerning the Creator whom we do not see (Ps 19:1; Rom 1:20; Heb 11:1-3). The present form of creation, which is passing away, points us toward God's enduring order, which is biblically expressed as a tangible "new creation" that we shall inhabit in our resurrection bodies.

Yet on the other hand, because the relationship between visible and invisible things is analogical, we must watch out lest we substitute visible things, which are images and shadows, for true and spiritual reality. Such an error, of course, is the essence of three great sins: unbelief, idolatry and worldliness. It is the sin of unbelief because sight of the visible replaces the eye of faith. Paul instructs us to "fix our eyes not on what is seen, but on what is unseen. For what is seen is temporary, but what is unseen is eternal," and all who please God "live by faith, not by sight" (2 Cor 4:18; 5:7 NIV). Likewise, to exchange the invisible splendor of God for the splendor of creation is the sin of idolatry. Because created things reflect God's glory and power, sinful humans are prone to turn the created thing into the thing to be worshiped. To do so is to exchange "the glory of the immortal God for images made to look like mortal man and birds and animals and reptiles" (Rom 1:23 NIV). Furthermore, substituting earthly shadow for heavenly reality is worldliness, for Christian faith acknowledges that spiritual reality is not the world that we see with our physical eyes but the world that is not seen. The world that will endure for eternity is the one that we do not see yet, except by faith. For the things that we presently see are mere shadows of the original, and these shadows are already in the process of fading away (2 Cor 4:17-18; 5:17; 1 Pet 1:8; 1 Jn 2:15-17).

Here is the principal point that Hebrews 11 makes: by faith we understand that the things we see are temporary images of the things that are unseen and permanent. The created things we see will be shaken in the day of judgment, and only those things that cannot be shaken will endure (Heb 12:25-29). It is by faith that we taste "the powers of the age to come" while we yet dwell in the present age (Heb 6:5). Therefore, by faith we understand that the visible tokens that God gives us have the same function for us that the Promised Land had for our father Abraham. This is so because visible things are signs that point away from themselves in two directions, both upward to the heavenly reality of invisible things and forward to the coming age when all that we do not yet see will be ours. By faith we understand this relationship, and we set our hope on unseen things. Therefore, we entrust ourselves to him who is invisible yet more real and enduring than all that we see with our eyes. For concerning people who do this, "God is not ashamed to be called their God, for he has prepared a city for them" (Heb 11:16 NIV).

Informed by Hebrews 11:1-6 concerning the relationship of faith to reward, faithfulness and understanding, we now need to consider the range of metaphors and images that the Bible uses to portray Christian faith.

Faith and Its Biblical Images

Christian faith is like a finely cut gemstone; it is multifaceted. Because faith is a multifaceted jewel, no single biblical metaphor is adequate to describe either the nature or function of faith. In our earlier discussion of faith in Hebrews as both resting and seeking, we hinted at the variety of images for faith. Now, as we focus on biblical images that portray faith, we draw special attention to the athletic imagery we repeatedly encountered throughout our discussion in chapter two. When we closely examined the footrace metaphor and the prize of salvation to be won, we came upon several words and phrases that describe how we must run the race in order to win. Paul says that we must "run in such a way as to get the prize," that is, we must go into "strict training" and "not run aimlessly" but with purpose (1 Cor 9:24-26). Elsewhere, using the footrace metaphor, Paul says "I press on" and "strain" toward the goal (Phil 3:12-14).[6] Paul exhorts us, "Compete in the good competition of faith; lay hold of eternal life, to which you were called and for which you made the good confession before many witnesses" (1 Tim 6:12).[7] Paul's exhortation is unambiguous, though it is often misunderstood. He clearly states that eternal life is the prize to be won by running after it with athletic vigor and

---

[6]We highly recommend John Bunyan's short treatise "The Heavenly Footman," in *The Whole Works of John Bunyan* (1875; reprint, Grand Rapids, Mich.: Baker, 1977), pp. 381-94.

[7]This is our translation. It is difficult to translate Paul's exhortation in 1 Tim 6:12 (also 2 Tim 4:7) and retain the play on words *(agōnizou ton kalon agōna tēs pisteōs)*. One's translation should reflect the fact that Paul's metaphor in these passages is the athletic arena, whereas in 1 Tim 1:18 he draws upon a military metaphor *(strateuē tēn kalēn strateian,* "Fight the good fight").

resolve. Because of the frequency and importance of these athletic metaphors in the New Testament, they will hold prominence in our discussion. However, first it will be helpful to review how metaphors function.

When we were children, our first exposure to figurative language came by distinguishing between simile and metaphor. While both make comparisons, we discovered that similes use *like* or *as* and metaphors use the verb *to be*.[8] Helpful as that distinction may be, it is less than adequate, for metaphors frequently do not use this verb. A better way to distinguish the two is to understand that similes express an explicit comparison and metaphors state an implicit comparison. Note the difference between the two. Think about Paul's exhortation: "Compete in the good competition of faith; lay hold of eternal life, to which you were called and for which you made the good confession before many witnesses" (1 Tim 6:12). Paul's implicit comparison sets our minds in motion to sketch a mental image of an arena, a footrace, a prize for the winner, an athlete and spectators, and then to draw proper correlations between the earthly analogy and the heavenly reality. What if Paul had used a simile? Would his exhortation require the same colorful imaginary work of our minds? Metaphors require more of our imaginations than similes do. They require us to engage the mental imagery more vigorously because they do not explicitly state the comparison, as similes do, but expect us to develop the analogy. Therefore, as we read biblical metaphors we must tease out the implications. This is what we will do with each group of faith's metaphors. As we do this, it will be necessary to keep in mind our earlier discussion concerning faith as the link that spans the chasm between things seen and unseen.

It is easy to forget that a metaphor sketches a mental image of an abstract idea in terms of a familiar concrete illustration. As with any symbol, a metaphor points away from the concrete comparison to the intangible thing being pictured or symbolized. Scripture teaches that God makes himself known to us analogically. This is apparent from the design of God's creation. His creation reflects his glory, for he has stamped his own invisible attributes, his eternal power and divine

---

[8]Psalm 58:8 provides a good example of a simile: "Like a slug melting away as it moves along, like a stillborn child, may they not see the sun" (NIV). A metaphor occurs in Psalm 23:1: "The LORD is my shepherd."

nature, upon creation (Rom 1:19-20). God has invested his creative work with the capacity to reflect its Creator. When God breathed life into Adam, he became a unique and living metaphor, for he is the image and likeness of God, his Creator.

Because God conveys heavenly realities by means of earthly analogies, it is only by faith that we can understand biblical metaphors of faith. For example, remember the time you first discovered a live image of yourself projected on a television screen from one of the many video cameras displayed in the electronics store. Initial curiosity probably yielded to embarrassment when you realized that the live image displayed your physical characteristics just as they are. You quickly moved, hoping to escape the snooping camera's view. Similarly, when Jesus preached and taught, his message unveiled the true characteristics of his hearers. He skillfully used word images to portray the kind of faith his gospel requires. When he sketched images of faith, his metaphorical pictures of faith required faith in order to understand them (Mk 4:1-20). Failure to understand biblical metaphors for faith uncovers a lack of faith. This may be painful and unsettling, just as it was for those who heard Jesus teach (Jn 6:60-71). Let us consider two biblical examples to illustrate how unbelief fails to grasp metaphorical language that depicts faith, while belief grasps it.

First, consider Jesus' words: "Very truly, I tell you, no one can see the kingdom of God without being born from above" (Jn 3:3 NRSV). Nicodemus, a man of the night to whom Jesus spoke, replies with mocking incredulity, "How can anyone be born after having grown old? Can one enter a second time into the mother's womb and be born?" (Jn 3:4 NRSV).[9] Jesus responds in part by saying, "Are you a teacher of Israel, and yet you do not understand these things? Very truly, I tell you, we speak of what we know and testify to what we have seen; yet you do not receive our testimony. If I have told you about earthly things and you do not believe, how can you believe if I tell you about heavenly things?" (Jn 3:10-12 NRSV). One who is born of the flesh cannot comprehend heavenly things; only as one is born of the Spirit can one understand heavenly realities conveyed through

---

[9]On the symbolic significance of "night" in Jn 3:2, see Craig R. Koester, *Symbolism in the Fourth Gospel* (Minneapolis: Fortress, 1995), p. 9; and D. A. Carson, *The Gospel According to John* (Grand Rapids, Mich.: Eerdmans, 1991), p. 186.

earthly language. Today, despite widespread talk about being born again, many fail to understand Jesus' symbolic language and actions any better than Nicodemus did. We will return to John 3 later to unpack its contributions concerning John's definition of belief.

The failure of Jesus' twelve disciples to understand the metaphors of his parabolic teaching provides a second example of those who are fascinated with signs but fail to believe in the reality to which they point. After feeding the four thousand, as Jesus got into the boat, he warned the Twelve, "Watch out—beware of the yeast of the Pharisees and the yeast of Herod" (Mk 8:15 NRSV). They failed to understand both that Jesus spoke metaphorically and that the metaphor referred to a disposition that fastens on the sign rather than the reality signified. As a result, the twelve disciples reasoned together that Jesus' mention of the "yeast of the Pharisees and of Herod" must be an indirect reproach for failing to bring enough bread for their day's excursion. While Jesus spoke concerning "things of God," the Twelve remained captivated by "human things" (cf. Mk 8:33). Jesus rebukes them: "Why are you talking about having no bread? Do you still not perceive or understand? Are your hearts hardened? Do you have eyes, and fail to see? Do you have ears, and fail to hear?" (Mk 8:17-18 NRSV). Though the Twelve do not appear to be represented by the pathway in the parable of the soils, like the Pharisees and Herod (cf. Mk 4:4, 15), they were yet unbelieving, for they failed to understand that Jesus invested earthly symbols with heavenly significance. They were still blind to heavenly things and needed a healing touch from Jesus to see and to understand. Jesus makes the point visually for the Twelve by healing the blind man of Bethsaida (Mk 8:22-26). They were like the blind man. They had been following Jesus for some time, yet they still only saw his true identity dimly. Spiritual sight, by which we understand heavenly language cast in earthly symbols, comes only by the touch of Jesus. Only then can we "see everything clearly" (Mk 8:25).

We easily misinterpret metaphorical language, as with all biblical symbolism of spiritual things. The temptation is to reify or literalize metaphor. What this means is that we are tempted to treat a metaphor as the true or authentic thing, but a metaphor is only a representation of the true thing. Thus, for example, the manna that came down from heaven in the wilderness to feed the Israelites was a representation of the authentic bread that truly comes from heaven, namely, Jesus Christ (Jn 6:32). Both the Israelites in the wilderness generation and those who heard Jesus' discourse on the bread of life regarded manna as an end in itself. They failed to recognize that God's giving of manna was a dramatized metaphor concerning God's giving the authentic bread from heaven by which he gives eternal life to the world (Jn 6:33-42). Set against the backdrop of the wilderness feeding with manna, Jesus presents himself as the "true bread out of heaven" (Jn 6:32), also calling himself "the bread of life" (Jn 6:35). Those who heard him, even many among his own disciples, grumbled against him (Jn 6:41-42, 60). Their grumbling betrays their unbelief, for they are imitating the generation in the wilderness who grumbled both before and after God rained bread from heaven (Ex 16:2, 8-9; Num 11:4-6). More than that, their grumbling led them to reenact their forefathers' unbelief in the wilderness (Jn 6:64-66). They grumbled against Jesus for his evident claim of deity. Yet ironically it was they who blasphemed God by exalting manna above Jesus, the Son of God.

Without imagery or word pictures such as metaphors, language would be dull, colorless and impoverished. We scarcely speak of anything without using figurative language, though we may not always be aware of it. Figurative speech, used in place of abstract concepts and ideas, provides definition for the words they replace. We have seen that the multitude of metaphors for salvation deeply enrich apprehension of that heavenly reality. The same is true concerning faith. As we seek to offer a biblical definition of the faith the gospel requires of us, we will take a look at the word pictures that the biblical writers sketch for us. The Bible uses many metaphors to portray belief or faith. We will discuss several metaphors arranged into helpful categories. Biblical writers use at least seven types of metaphors to portray Christian faith: (1) athletic, (2) military, (3) rational, (4) sensory, (5) bodily action, (6) discipleship and (7) endowment.

Athletic imagery. As we reflect on the athletic imagery of the biblical writers, we encourage our readers to be careful to read all the related passages. We are convinced that a believing and consistent posture distinguishes between the symbolic picture and the spiritual reality. Therefore, Christian faith does not endorse the following logic: Because eternal life is portrayed with the earthly image of a prize to be won by an athlete who runs swiftly, eternal life is an achievement to be gained by earning it from God. Once it is earned, the winner may legitimately boast of his or her accomplishment. Christian faith does not lead to this misunderstanding, for such a view superimposes the earthly symbol on the spiritual reality and thereby blurs the clarity of the biblical truth. To state it another way, such a view forces the heavenly original to be identical to the earthly copy. Christian belief does not deduce from the athletic metaphor that the use of verbs such as *run, strive, press on, compete* or *lay hold of* denotes actions called "works" that stand over against "faith." Rather, we will show that all these verbs in the athletic metaphor are symbolic representations of Christian faith. The following discussion seeks to make clear what each aspect of the metaphor of the athletic arena contributes to our understanding of faith. We have arranged our discussion in terms of the following elements: the arena of faith, the training of faith, the contest of faith, and the victor's wreath for faithfulness.

The Greek athletic arena provides the background for the several metaphors that come from various sporting events, including the footrace and boxing. The implicit comparison of the Christian life with the events of the arena recurs especially in Paul's letters. In ancient Greece there were four major athletic arenas: Olympia, Pythia, Isthmia and Nemea. Though each one hosted a festival dedicated to the worship of local deities, the New Testament writers use these pagan athletic festivals to provide a fitting picture of the Christian life. Thus, biblical writers use several words and phrases descriptive of preparation for and competition in the arena.

The ancient Greeks referred to the athletic arena as the *agōn*.[10] Originally the word referred to the place where people assembled. Then the Greeks used it to refer to the place where contests took place; thus it became synonymous with stadium. Naturally, the word *agōn* came to refer to the contest itself, and finally it referred to any kind of conflict, not just in the arena. Consequently, when the New Testament writers used the word *agōn*, of its six uses, three are meta-

---

[10]For detailed consideration of the arena metaphor in the New Testament, we suggest two books: Erich Sauer, *In the Arena of Faith: A Call to the Consecrated Life* (Grand Rapids, Mich.: Eerdmans, 1955); and Victor C. Pfitzner, *Paul and the Agon Motif: Traditional Athletic Imagery in the Pauline Literature*, Novum Testamentum Supplements 16 (Leiden: Brill, 1967).

phorical comparisons of the Christian life to an athletic contest (1 Tim 6:12; 2 Tim 4:7; Heb 12:1), and three simply use the word to refer to conflicts engaged because of the gospel (Phil 1:30; Col 2:1; 1 Thess 2:2). Though the New Testament never uses the word to refer to the arena itself, the recurring athletic metaphor certainly draws the implication that this present age is the arena of faith, the place of faith's great contest and struggle against antagonists who seek to defeat the believer. However, the New Testament uses the athletic metaphor to focus on the contest rather than the place.

In addition to referring to the arena of faith, the New Testament also addresses the training of faith. Preparation for athletic competition in the ancient arena entailed strict training of both mind and body in the gymnasium. New Testament writers take advantage of athletic training as an apt metaphor for strengthening Christian faith. We derive our word *gymnasium* from the Greek gymnasia, so named because the athletes who trained in the gymnasium exercised naked *(gymnos)*.[11] Paul is the only New Testament writer who uses the noun *gymnasia,* and he does so only once, in combination with the verb *gymnazō,* meaning "to train." He admonishes Timothy, "Train yourself for godliness, because though bodily training is beneficial for a short time, godliness is beneficial for all time, because it holds a promise of life both for the present and for the coming time" (1 Tim 4:7-8).

Paul uses both "train yourself" *(gymnaze)* and the noun "training" to form his exhortation by drawing a metaphorical connection between the spiritual and physical realms. The linkage is organic. It is not merely a convenient illustration that Paul grabs with a hope to aid understanding. Correlation between earthly and heavenly things is organic or internal, for it is built in by God, who designed and created all things.[12] The heavenly or spiritual are original; the earthly and

---

[11]One must be careful not to fall into the fallacy of reasoning that word meaning derives from word formation or etymology It would be erroneous to think that either the Greek word *gymnasia* or the English *gymnasium* refer to nakedness simply because the root *gymnos* means naked. The Greek *gymnasia* refers either to the place where athletic training took place or to the athletic training itself; similarly the English word. In Europe the word has taken on a very different meaning. Concerning word study and common fallacies see Darrell L. Bock, "New Testament Word Analysis," in *Introducing New Testament Interpretation,* ed. Scot McKnight (Grand Rapids, Mich.: Baker, 1989), pp. 97-113.

[12]See the provocative discussion by Moisés Silva, *God, Language and Scripture,* Foundations of Contemporary Interpretation 4 (Grand Rapids, Mich.: Zondervan, 1990), pp. 20-26, esp. pp. 22-23.

physical are copies (Heb 11:3). A copy bears resemblance to the original and therefore testifies to its supremacy. Glorious as the replica may be, its beauty is drab compared to the splendor of the original. Because the physical creation bears this significant relationship to unseen things that endure, Paul does not resort to monastic asceticism and dismiss the value of bodily training in his admonition. Rather, he regards it for what it is; physical training has value only for the present age. Its greater value is in its metaphorical association. Bodily training is a vivid image with spiritual significance. The analogical correspondence is not arbitrary but fashioned by God, so that while we condition the body, we ought to recognize its symbolic function as it points away from itself to spiritual conditioning of Christian faith for godly character. But the symbol does not terminate upon training for godliness as an end in itself. No, Paul contrasts bodily and spiritual exercise precisely in terms of what they yield. Bodily discipline benefits for a while, but spiritual training for godliness bears within itself the promise of life that endures, not only now but forever.

Before we unpack the athletic metaphor as it corresponds to Christian faith, it may be helpful to ponder how useful figurative language is. Paul's admonition, "train yourself for godliness," framed metaphorically, enables him to say what would be difficult to express apart from the analogical relationship between spiritual and earthly things that God embedded into creation. Paul calls for Timothy and for us to do what we can do by faith alone, namely, become godly. Yet he substitutes a word picture—"train yourself for godliness"—for an exhortation that otherwise would have been a protracted and theologically encumbered admonition. Pause for a moment and try to frame Paul's admonition without using metaphorical language. It is difficult, isn't it? Because Paul exploits an analogical image to formulate his encouragement to Timothy, one's imagination more rapidly grasps the image than one's mouth can explain it. Certainly, what he means is not inexplicable. Rather, it takes many more words to explain his meaning than it does to convey it by his chosen metaphor. If a picture is worth a thousand words, how many words does a well-chosen metaphor displace? This may be illustrated by the paragraphs that follow, which endeavor to explain Paul's metaphorical admonition.

So how do the figurative words "train yourself for godliness" move us to act in faith? Paul's words appeal to our imagination. They compel us to relate spiritual exercise to body training. Ponder the implicit comparison. The admonition calls for athletic vigor that pushes the believer to the point of pain in order to attain strength, stamina and endurance for victorious competition. From Paul's analogy, then, it is evident that there are three aspects of comparison. First, the exertion he calls for is the kind of intensity a focused athlete expends in the gymnasium. While an athlete concentrates energy to work out in a compressed span of time, the Christian must be ever vigilant to sustain the exercise without ever slackening. Paul's call to spiritual exercise is a figurative replacement for putting faith into action. This is apparent from his references to faith that punctuate the immediate context. The apostle affirms that by Timothy's faithful instruction of the church, he will be a "good servant of Christ Jesus, being reared in the words of faith" (1 Tim 4:6). Paul also calls on Timothy to be an example for "the believers" in faith and other virtues (1 Tim 4:12). Furthermore, Paul's admonition "exercise yourself for godliness" is the endeavor of believers (1 Tim 4:10).

The second aspect of comparison is the penultimate objective for this intense and rigorous spiritual exertion; it is for the purpose of godliness. Only those who have faith in God become godly; it is by faith that we become devout in character. As athletic strength comes only to one who exercises the body, so strength of character—godliness—comes only to the one who flexes spiritual muscles by the exertion of faith. Without such faith one cannot be godly, because godliness is the imitation of God. Later in the same letter, Paul uses the athletic metaphor again to urge Timothy, as a "man of God," to "pursue righteousness, godliness, faith, love, endurance, gentleness" (1 Tim 6:11). "Godliness is a means of great gain" (1 Tim 6:6), though not a gain of worldly wealth but a gain of eternal life. Therefore, one must pursue godliness, which is penultimate, in order to lay hold of eternal life, which is ultimate (1 Tim 6:12). Without discipline one cannot be godly, and without godliness one cannot gain the eternal life of the age to come.

The third feature of Paul's implicit comparison is the ultimate aim for this devout and holy workout: God's promised eternal life. Paul's exhortation does not terminate upon godliness any more than bodily exercise terminates upon athletic physique, for the ultimate goal in one's spiritual workout is not simply to acquire strong Godlike character. Godliness bears within itself the promise of life for the present. Much more than that, however, it holds the promise of life to come. Paul clarifies what he means when he says, "But exercise yourself for godly character, for though bodily exercise is profitable for a little while, godly character is profitable for all time, because it holds a promise of life now and for the coming time" (1 Tim 4:7-8). Paul accents the significance of verse 8 when he says, "Reliable is the saying and worthy of full acceptance" (1 Tim 4:9).[13] Likewise, verse 10 amplifies the motivation for exercising to strengthen godliness. Paul explains, "For unto this we labor and strive." To what do the words "unto this" refer? They have in view "godliness," which holds the promise for "life to come." Verse 10 resumes the athletic metaphor of verses 7 and 8 with the words "we labor and strive." Paul's exhortation and inducements to follow through have come full circle. First he admonishes Timothy, "Exercise yourself for godliness" (v. 7); then he offers a motivation: "godliness is profitable for all time, because it holds the promise of life" (v. 8). Paul then affirms that this is both Timothy's and his own present pursuit, a pursuit that is characteristic of all Christians. Finally, Paul explains why we "labor and strive" for godliness, which holds the promise of life. It is "because we have set our hope upon the living God who is the savior of all humanity, especially of believers" (v. 10).

Therefore, Paul's command "Exercise yourself for godliness" is a metaphorically framed admonition aimed at inciting faith to act. Paul urges Timothy and us to do what he himself does. Elsewhere he employs the athletic training motif when he elaborates on his own exercise of faith. "Everyone who competes in the games goes into strict training" (1 Cor 9:25 NIV). Likewise, we must exercise the muscles of faith to strengthen godly character with the ultimate objective to win the prize of eternal life. We train for godliness to gain victory in the contest for eternal life.

The New Testament writers also use athletic metaphors to describe, not only the arena and the training of faith, but also the contest of faith. Earlier we noted that the New Testament uses *agōn* meta-

---

[13]There is, of course, considerable dispute as to the identity of "the faithful saying." For discussion of the interpretive choices, see George W. Knight III, *The Faithful Sayings in the Pastoral Epistles,* Baker Biblical Monograph (Grand Rapids, Mich.: Baker, 1979).

phorically to refer to the contest of faith rather than the arena where the contest takes place. When the New Testament writers use *agōn* figuratively for Christian faith, they exploit the metaphor in combination with other terms from the athletic arena. Hebrews 12:1, for example, uses *agōn* with two other terms from the arena: "Let us also lay aside every encumbrance and the sin that so easily entangles us, and let us run with endurance the race that is set before us." It should be readily apparent that this urgent appeal for us to "run with endurance" is a metaphorical substitution for a call to persevere in faith. Faith is portrayed here both as casting aside all hindrances and as running with perseverance. As the athlete prepares to run a footrace by shedding all clothing, so we are to throw aside both weights and sins that would entangle and weigh us down.[14] Then the writer exhorts us to run with endurance the race that lies stretched out before us, but we must do so with our gaze fastened on the goal, just as a runner does (Heb 12:2). In this case, Jesus is the goal on which we fix our eyes, just as Moses focused on the reward (Heb 11:26). But Jesus is more than the goal and prize; he is also the champion or exemplar of faith who has finished the race with victory. The cross did not deter Jesus from running his course to gain victory, because he set his eye on the joy that could only be attained by enduring the shameful cross. Likewise, if we are to attain victory, we must fix our eyes on Jesus as the inestimable prize. Joy of winning this prize surely will sustain us through the most difficult stretches of our racecourse, so that we may be made perfect with those who have gone before us (Heb 11:39-40).

A familiar image for the Christian life that Paul develops more than any other New Testament writer is that of a runner who strives to win a wreath. When Paul warns the Philippians about the Judaizers—"Beware of the dogs, beware of the evil workers, beware of those who mutilate the flesh!" (Phil 3:2 NRSV)—he portrays his own perseverance in faith and his determination not to put confidence in the flesh. If anyone could boast in fleshly achievement, Paul could (Phil 3:3-6). The passage is significant because it is about the object of our

---

[14]One should not miss the fact that there is a distinction between *weights* and *sins*. The former are not sinful in themselves. They may be legitimate concerns of this earthly life—time, money, relationships—that become weights that impede one's stride in the race of faith.

confidence and faith. On the one hand, Paul insists that his accomplishments according to the law have no profit, so he puts no confidence in the flesh. On the other hand, he engages an arduous and olympian pursuit of Christ. As he contrasts the pursuit of "righteousness that is in the law" (vv. 6, 9) and "righteousness that is from God" (v. 9), he does not minimize endeavor and exalt reposing. Rather, as a devoted runner in the arena, Paul's faith focuses on the prize and abandons all confidence in past achievements (v. 7). By faith he concentrates every nerve, every muscle, every desire on the singular goal that lies before him: to win Christ (v. 9). For to win Christ is the only hope of being declared righteous before God in the day of judgment.

It may seem that Paul mixes metaphors—the athletic and the courtroom—for he introduces the imagery of judgment. However, because judges enforced the rules of the games in the athletic arena (cf. 2 Tim 2:5), Paul's imagery is consistent with the arena metaphor. Paul is determined to run his race with complete devotion in order that he might win Christ, which is the same as "knowing Christ" (Phil 3:8) and being "found in him" (v. 9).[15] The expression "that I may be found in him" does not deny that the Christian is already "in Christ." It is a phrase that derives from the courtroom, where the defendant is found either guilty or not guilty. Without denying his present state of righteousness in Christ, Paul makes it clear that he determines that God's righteous verdict shall be his in the day of judgment. Therefore, he portrays his own Christian faith as a race in pursuit of Christ and the wreath of righteousness that will be awarded to all who persevere in faith to the end (cf. 2 Tim 4:7-8).

Paul elaborates on the intensity of his athletic pursuit of being found in Christ when God judges. The pathway of this pursuit brings acquired knowledge of both Christ and the power resident in his resurrection, and it brings about a real participation with Christ in his sufferings as one who, like him, dies to sin. Only if we run this pathway that brings us through death to sin is there any hope that we will attain the resurrection of eternal life (Phil 3:10-11).[16] One cannot win Christ at the end without faithfully running this course now. Faith endeavors to over-

---

[15] See the comments by Peter O'Brien, *Commentary on Philippians*, New International Greek Testament Commentary (Grand Rapids, Mich.: Eerdmans, 1991), pp. 391-92.

[16] For an exposition of this passage see our discussion in chapter four.

come every obstacle of the racecourse now in order that it may victoriously clutch Christ as the prize when it attains the end.

Paul extends his use of the athletic imagery in Philippians 3:12-15, lest anyone presume to have won Christ already without the need for steadfast faith to the very end.

> Not that I have already arrived or have already been perfected, but I pursue it, if I also may lay hold of that for which I was laid hold of by Christ Jesus. Brothers and sisters, I do not yet regard myself as having laid hold of it. I do but one thing: forgetting what lies behind and straining forward to what lies ahead, I pursue the goal to attain the prize of the upward call of God in Christ Jesus. As many as are perfect, let us think like this. And if someone thinks differently, God will reveal this understanding to you also. Only let us live up to what we have already attained. (Phil 3:12-15)

Like a marathon runner, Paul disavows satisfaction with past accomplishments and sets his eye on the goal. He recognizes that because he has not yet arrived at the goal line, there are obstacles to overcome that lie between his present attainment and the goal. Continuity between the starting block and finish line of this racecourse is attained only by faith in the God who exists and who rewards all who pursue him.

Time and again Paul resorts to the arena motif. He urges Timothy to "flee from" the love of money that motivates teachers of heterodoxy. Paul carries the athletic imagery forward to frame his positive exhortation also: "Pursue righteousness, godliness, faithfulness, love, perseverance, gentleness. Compete in the good competition of faith; lay hold of eternal life, to which you were called and for which you made the good confession before many witnesses" (1 Tim 6:11-12). Earlier we noted that this admonition is unambiguous in what it says. It affirms that eternal life is the reward to be attained by those who run after it with athletic intensity and perseverance. Paul metaphorically frames his exhortations for Timothy to "pursue righteousness" and to "lay hold of eternal life" to remain steadfast in his faith, for righteousness and eternal life come only by faith. When Paul admonishes Timothy to "compete in the good competition," he only reiterates what Jesus exhorts: "Strive to enter through the narrow door; for many, I tell you, will try to enter and will not be able" (Lk 13:24

NRSV).[17] In order to "compete in the good competition of faith," we must continually train ourselves to be resolute and determined in order to "lay hold of eternal life."

As one who knows the agony and pain of striving against antagonists and obstacles that impede the course leading to eternal life, Paul admonishes us to rigorous training of faith and to indefatigable striving to attain the prize. As a missionary of the gospel, Paul indicates that he freely relinquishes use of Christian freedoms in order that he, with those who receive his gospel, will receive the eternal life his gospel promises.

> I do all this on account of the gospel, in order that I may become a beneficiary of it with my hearers. Don't you know that in a race all the runners run, but one alone receives the prize? Run in such a manner that you might win. And everyone who competes exercises strict training in every regard. They do it to receive a perishable wreath, but we do it for an imperishable one. In keeping with this manner, I run, not with uncertainty; I do not box as one who beats the air, but I strike blows to my body and master it, lest after I have preached to others, I myself become a disqualified competitor. (1 Cor 9:23-27)

In the next chapter we will consider this passage more fully. All that is necessary now is to show that Paul's athletic imagery in 1 Corinthians 9:23-27 is concerned with faith that perseveres in order to receive eternal life.

Most Bible translations place a paragraph division between verses 23 and 24. However, the athletic imagery of verses 24-27 explains why Paul is willing to forgo his own rights to accommodate the convictions of those whom he seeks to save (v. 22). Paul explains in verse 23 that his own salvation is bound up with how he ministers the gospel to others: "I do all this on account of the gospel, in order that I may become a fellow beneficiary of it." His passion to save others calls for tending carefully to himself. All that he does to win others is guided by his objective to be sure that he also receives the blessing of eternal life promised in the gospel. Paul's own race that leads to eternal life runs directly through the faithful execution of his apostolic mission: to proclaim the gospel of Jesus Christ (cf. 1 Tim 4:16). Therefore, Paul's use of the athletic motif—whether the runner or the boxer—

---

[17]Both texts use the same word, *agōnizomai*, though translated differently: "compete" (1 Tim 6:12) and "strive" (Lk 13:24).

illustrates the kind of faith that he must exercise in order to receive the salvation his own gospel promises. Verse 27 restates what Paul says in verse 23, except now he expresses it as part of the athletic metaphor: "lest after I have preached to others, I myself become a dis- qualified competitor" *(adokimos)*. The word Paul uses could also be translated "reprobate." The prize or wreath is resurrection to eternal life; the running and boxing is obedient faith (cf. Acts 20:24; 2 Tim 4:7-8).[18]

The final athletic metaphor is the victor's wreath for faithfulness. Because we have already shown in chapter two that the New Testa- ment portrays salvation and eternal life by using the metaphor of the athlete's wreath or crown, our discussion will be abbreviated here. Our only objective is to show that if the athletic wreath is indeed eter- nal life, then to "run" or to "compete," portrayed in the metaphor, must be a picture of faith. Whether the wreath is "righteousness" (2 Tim 4:8), "life" (Jas 1:12; Rev 2:10), "glory" (1 Pet 5:4) or "honor" (1 Thess 2:19; Phil 4:1), it is "imperishable" (1 Cor 9:25) and can only be attained by faith. As we have already noted in our discussion of Hebrews 11:6, God's reward is granted to us by faith and by faith alone. But, of course, the kind of faith that God rewards is one that seeks after him.

Wherever Paul uses athletic imagery to portray faith's conflict, the struggle is essentially internal. There are obstacles, hindrances and temptations that lie along the marathon course. However, in our endurance contest, our struggle is principally against sin and the desire to yield to sin's power to distract us from our holy pursuit. By faith we set our gaze on Christ in order to win him. By faith we watch the path for proper footing. By faith we strengthen our flagging arms and energize our exhausted legs (Heb 12:12-13). By faith we run with perseverance the race that is laid out before us. By faith we breathe in eternal life—the breath of God. By faith we shall endure to the end and lay hold of eternal life. But faith's struggle is not only against sin, the internal enemy; it is also against external enemies. Paul's admoni- tions, therefore, also draw on the military metaphor.

---

[18]Cf. Craig Blomberg, "Degrees of Reward in the Kingdom of Heaven," *Journal of the Evangelical Theological Society* 35 (1992): 163. See also Roman Garrison, "Paul's Use of the Athlete Metaphor in 1 Corinthians 9," *Studies in Religion* 22 (1993): 209-17. He argues that the "imperishable wreath" is an apt metaphor for the resurrection body.

Military imagery. In his letters Paul uses the athletic metaphor to emphasize (1) the goal toward which one strives and (2) the hindrances that lie between the athlete and the goal, obstructions that must be overcome in order to win. These obstacles are both within the Christian and along the racecourse. When they are external to the athlete, they are generally impersonal impediments. However, when Paul employs the military motif, his focus is on the enemy—the devil—and one's need to stand steadfastly against his hostile assaults. The enemy is personal, and in the military motif the accent is on defense rather than attack.[19] The military motif occurs in several texts. We will study two of them, one dealing with fighting the good fight, the other concerning our battle against invisible forces.

Paul employs a military motif to represent Christian belief. Earlier we distinguished Paul's admonition to "fight the good fight" (1 Tim 1:18) from his appeal to "compete in the good competition" (1 Tim 6:12; cf. 2 Tim 4:7). The latter references use the athletic motif, though translations rarely reflect it, while the former text draws on military imagery. Paul exhorts Timothy:

> I entrust this charge to you, Timothy my son, in keeping with the prophecies previously announced to you, that by them you might fight the good fight, by holding to faith and to a good conscience, which some, upon repudiating, have made shipwreck concerning faith, among whom are Hymenaeus and Alexander, whom I have handed over to Satan in order that they may be taught not to blaspheme. (1 Tim 1:18-20).

Here it is readily apparent that Paul uses warfare imagery to draw an implicit comparison between Christian faith and engaging an enemy in battle. Paul's imagery serves his admonition well, for the Christian ceaselessly clashes with enemies that are hostile to faith. The apostle explains that we must engage this warfare "by holding to faith and to a good conscience." He further clarifies that he is admonishing Timothy to steadfast faith when he points out that some have "made shipwreck concerning faith." Paul switches metaphors, but his concern is the same: perseverance in faith.

Paul's military metaphor in Ephesians 6:10-17 is probably more familiar. Here Paul admonishes Christians to be fully prepared to

---

[19]Cf. Pfitzner, *Paul and the Agon Motif,* p. 158.

fight against the assaults of the devil, because "our fight is not with flesh and blood but against the rulers, against the authorities, against the cosmic forces of this present darkness, against the spiritual forces of wickedness in heavenly realms" (Eph 6:12).

A significant contrast between the athletic and military metaphors is that the athlete strips off every excess weight and clothing so as not to be entangled or to catch the wind, and this imagery suits its spiritual counterpart. The soldier, on the other hand, puts on the full armor necessary to defend against the enemy. Paul uses the command "put on" as he does with his change-of-clothing imagery in which he exhorts Christians "to put off the deeds of darkness" and "to put on the Lord Jesus Christ" (Rom 13:12-14; cf. Eph 4:20-24; Col 3:8-10). To put on pieces of spiritual armor is an extended portrayal of Christian faith defending itself against external enemies, drawn substantially from Isaiah's imagery (cf. Is 11:5; 52:7; 59:17). Each of the words—"put on" (Eph 6:11, 14, 15), "stand against" (v. 11), "our struggle" (v. 12), "take up" (vv. 13, 16), "stand and fasten" (v. 14), "receive" (v. 17)—metaphorically signals faith in action. But Paul also identifies a piece of the armor with faith: the shield of faith to protect against the enemy's flaming arrows (v. 16). Paul's word choice sketches a mental image of a large body shield, which protects the Christian from the enemy's projectiles of temptation and allurement to yield to sin and to defect.

Paul's military metaphor portrays faith as engaging spiritual enemies from outside. To believe is to "fight the good fight" to the very end, for there is no conquest and there is no righteous pronouncement at the end apart from persevering to the end. Faith prepares itself to engage the invisible but real enemy; to dress for battle is faith in action. God fully equips the believer with the necessary armor, yet that armor is insufficient apart from continual prayer and watchfulness, prayer for oneself but also for all the saints (Eph 6:18).

Rational imagery. This and the next two groups of figures for belief derive principally from John's Gospel. Though each of the four Gospels beckons us to believe in Jesus as the Christ, the Son of God, John's purpose is most overtly expressed (Jn 20:30-31). His purpose statement has prompted much discussion among scholars, a discussion we will not enter, except to note that it is important to understand that John wrote to answer one primary question: Who is the

Messiah?[20] He answers the question when he states his purpose, which is best translated "But these things have been written in order that you might believe that the Messiah, the Son of God, is Jesus, and that by believing you might have life in his name."

For John it is axiomatic that evidence grounds belief. To believe that the Christ, God's Son, is Jesus is reasonable and grounded in evidence. It also explains why John uses the rational metaphor "know" to explain "believe." Occasionally John uses *know* or *understand* in tandem with *believe*, as in Peter's confession: "We believe and know that you are the Holy One of God" (Jn 6:69). Elsewhere John uses the rational metaphor as a substitute for "believe" or negates it for "disbelieve." In his prologue he says, "He was in the world, and the world came into existence through him, and the world did not know him. He came to his own, and his own people did not receive him. But as many as received him, to them he gave authority to become children of God, to those who believe in his name" (Jn 1:10-12). From these three verses it is evident that three expressions are interchangeable for John: know, receive, believe. To believe that the Christ is Jesus is to know him, to recognize him or to acknowledge him. Likewise, to believe in him is to receive him, which we will call the endowment or gift metaphor, to which we will return later.

Jesus says, "When you have lifted up the Son of Man, then you will recognize that I am he" (Jn 8:28). Certainly, John does not mean that all of Jesus' antagonists will believe in him when they crucify him, for they do not. Rather, if they do come to acknowledge him as the Christ, they will do so principally because of the cross.[21] The context further develops the interplay between believing and knowing. John writes, "Therefore Jesus said to the Jews who had believed in him, 'If you continue in my word, then truly you are my disciples. You will know the truth, and the truth will liberate you' " (Jn 8:31-33). This defines the kind of belief Jesus requires to lay hold of eternal life. It perseveres in Jesus' teaching and brings knowledge that liberates from bondage to sin. Belief in Jesus Christ that is void of endurance and understanding of the truth that deliv-

---

[20]For a thorough discussion of John's purpose in writing the Fourth Gospel see D. A. Carson, "The Purpose of the Fourth Gospel: John 20:30-31 Reconsidered," *Journal of Biblical Literature* 108 (1987): 639-51.

[21]Carson, *Gospel According to John*, p. 345.

ers one from sin's mastery does not lay hold of eternal life.

John 8:31-59 begs further consideration, because our explanation of the text, namely, that it describes different levels of belief, draws no mild response from some. A few insist that, as John unfolds his story, every time he uses the verb *believe,* he means "saving faith."[22] Their dispute focuses on two passages: John 2:23-24 and 8:30-31.[23] In these two passages John indicates that as the Jews heard Jesus teach, "many believed in his name" (Jn 2:23) and "many believed in him" (Jn 8:30). Because in the subsequent dialogue (Jn 8:33-59) Jesus unmistakably and repeatedly tells his listeners that they do not believe (Jn 8:42-47), some are insistent that Jesus must be speaking to another group of Jews, not to the ones who believed (Jn 8:30-32).[24] But such a reading is both remarkable and unnecessary.

To read John's words as though the Jews' belief was "saving faith" reflects a naive reading of the text at three levels. First, it unveils a simplistic understanding of word usage. This is what linguists call the prescriptive fallacy, namely, the notion that a word bears only one meaning and has the same meaning wherever it is used.[25] A second mistake, linked with the first, is the assumption that John's phrase "believe in" (Greek, *pisteuō eis*) is a "technical term" for "saving faith."[26] John's expression is not a technical term because its meaning in any context depends on its use. It is usage that determines meaning, and usage is concerned with the function of words within a context. A third indicator of a credulous reading, which follows from the first two mistakes, is an oversimplified understanding of how narratives function. Such a reading is simplistic because it requires the

---

[22]For example, see Charles C. Bing, "The Condition for Salvation in John's Gospel," *Journal of the Grace Evangelical Society* 9 (1996): 25-36. See also Zane Hodges, "Untrustworthy Believers—John 2:23-25," *Bibliotheca Sacra* 135 (1978): 139-52.

[23]For specific arguments used to support their case, see Bing, "Condition for Salvation," pp. 35-36.

[24]For consideration of the various attempts to settle the apparent problem, see Carson, *Gospel According to John,* pp. 346-48. For a popular attempt to prove that there are two distinct groups of Jews whom Jesus addresses in Jn 8:30-32 and 8:33-59, see Robert N. Wilkin, "A Faith in Christ Alone Which Won't Save? John 8:30-31," *Grace in Focus,* June–July 1988.

[25]See Bock, "New Testament Word Analysis," p. 111.

[26]Charles Bing mistakenly argues, "It is commonly agreed that the construction *pisteuō eis* is John's premier technical term for saving faith" ("Condition for Salvation," p. 35). For examples of this error see also D. A. Carson, *Exegetical Fallacies,* 2nd ed. (Grand Rapids, Mich.: Baker, 1996), pp. 45-47.

author to express an "explicit denial" if, in fact, his statements that "many believed in Jesus" were not intended to be taken at face value to describe "true faith."[27] But this is not what we should expect from the apostolic narrator. The authenticity of people's faith is not determined from the apostle's choice of expressions, but he does indicate what distinguishes spurious from authentic belief. Jesus says, "If you continue in my word, then truly you are my disciples." As John seamlessly continues to unfold the drama, the very Jews who "believed in him" (Jn 8:30-32) are the ones who joined in the retort, "We are Abraham's descendants and have never been enslaved to anyone. How can you say that we shall be liberated?" (Jn 8:33). They protest too much, for their protestation uncovers the kind of faith they exercised. The tone of their protest demonstrates that they remain enslaved to and blinded by their sinfulness. Their belief is defective. They do not hold to Jesus' words. They fail to acknowledge the truth. They remain slaves to sin.

What should we expect from John, who is both a skilled evangelist and writer, if we should not look for overt sidebar commentaries on his narrative? As he seeks to engender belief in Jesus Christ, he includes a range of illustrative responses to Jesus within his unfolding narrative. Consider the connections between John 2:23-25 and 3:1.

> Now while he was in Jerusalem at the Passover Feast, many people saw the miraculous signs he was doing and believed in his name. But Jesus would not entrust himself to them, for he knew all men. He did not need man's testimony about man, for he knew what was in a man. (Jn 2:23-25 NIV)

What follows this episode? John presents Nicodemus as an example of a man who, though exalted as "Israel's teacher" (Jn 3:10), has no sacred imagination or sense to see the invisible reality to which Jesus' signs and metaphors point. Nicodemus is a vivid representative of one who exercises a sign-focused faith, for he said, "Rabbi, we know that you are a teacher who has come from God; for no one can do these signs that you do apart from the presence of God" (Jn 3:2 NRSV). Jesus rebukes Nicodemus's failure to grasp his earthly

---

[27]Charles Bing says, "We first observe that there is no explicit denial of the reality of true faith in this passage" ("Condition for Salvation," p. 35, referring to Jn 2:23).

imagery of spiritual reality:

> You are Israel's teacher, . . . and do you not understand these things? I
> tell you the truth, we speak of what we know, and we testify to what we
> have seen, but still you people do not accept our testimony. I have spo-
> ken to you of earthly things and you do not believe; how then will you
> believe if I speak of heavenly things? (Jn 3:10-12 NIV)

John sketches another response to Jesus when he recounts the episode concerning the castaway Samaritan woman at the well. During
her dialogue with Jesus, she moved from unbelief toward belief. At
first she failed to drink the heavenly water of which Jesus was speaking with his earthly water symbol. Her words, like Nicodemus's, disclose an unbelieving heart (Jn 4:11, 15). However, before she returned to the well from the village, she came to believe.

Thus, John includes a range of responses that are illustrative of
belief and unbelief. He tells of the resolute unbelief on the part of the
Jews and religious leaders (Jn 6:36; 10:25-26), of unbelief even among
Jesus' own brothers (Jn 7:5), of fickle faith among his disciples (6:61-
64) and of belief among Samaritans (Jn 4:40-42). John also tells of a
belief among Jesus' disciples that the promised Messiah was Jesus,
though this faith would grow to flourish only after the resurrection
(Jn 2:11, 23; 20:8-9), and mentions that members of the Jewish Coun-
cil kept their belief secret for fear of the Jews, until Christ's death (Jn
12:42-43; 19:38-40).[28]

No competent storyteller insults an audience by giving an explanation of everything in the story. The story would collapse with heavi-
ness, and the storyteller would drive readers away with boredom,
exasperation or patronization. John does not unfold such a story, for
it has been said that the Fourth Gospel is like a stream in which children can wade while elephants, at the same time, can swim.[29] He
requires attentive interpretive skills from his readers to believe and
understand his symbols and metaphors, for his narration places on
them the responsibility to grasp their significance. This is the very

---

[28]It should be readily apparent that one cannot properly reason that those to whom
Jesus said, "But among you there are some who do not believe" (Jn 6:64), were all true
believers simply because John uses "disciples" (Jn 6:60). The word *disciple* is no more
a technical term than *believe,* for the band of disciples includes even Judas.

[29]This has been credited to Chrysostom. Cf. also Graham N. Stanton, *The Gospels and
Jesus,* Oxford Bible Series (Oxford: Oxford University Press, 1989), p. 102.

reason he selected the particular signs he includes, for Jesus' signs require belief to understand their significance. Because John's whole objective is to draw his readers to believe "that the Messiah, the Son of God, is Jesus," he includes within his narrative patterns of belief and unbelief, of understanding and misunderstanding. Each one has its proper function to direct us to believe and understand properly.[30] Therefore, as John unfolds his Gospel story he does not separate understanding from believing; he does not cheapen the beauty of his signs, symbols and metaphors by explaining each one for his readers. The signs John records bear God-invested significance to provide evidence for faith, but it is by believing that we understand them.

Sensory imagery. We will restrict our discussion to two sensory metaphors: seeing and hearing. Our modern use of *see* and *hear* is so colloquial that we easily pass over these two metaphors for believing without pondering their significance. As with other words, they have multiple layers of sense and meaning. We may ask a blind person, "Do you see what I mean?" and do it without insult. Parents frequently ask their children, "Did you hear me?" They do not ask whether the auditory nerve has converted sound waves to intelligible speech patterns. The question semantically means much more than it says grammatically. It actually asks, "Why are you not obeying me?" Hence, we commonly exchange *hear* for *obey,* as we substitute *see* for *understand.* The New Testament writers do the same, and John does so frequently.

The Fourth Gospel is rich with symbolism throughout.[31] It employs more metaphors for faith, perhaps, than any other portion of the New Testament. Throughout this chapter we have sustained a consistent theme regarding God's stamp of significance on his creation. It explains why we frequently find Jesus enlightening the blind and unplugging the ears of the deaf. Without minimizing Jesus' compassion, he opened eyes and ears first of all as signs with spiritual significance calling for belief.[32] Thus, we will demonstrate in this section that eyes are for seeing through the veil seen with the

[30]Cf. D. A. Carson, "Understanding Misunderstandings in the Fourth Gospel," *Tyndale Bulletin* 33 (1982): 59-89. See also R. Alan Culpepper, *Anatomy of the Fourth Gospel: A Study in Literary Design* (Philadelphia: Fortress, 1983), pp. 152-65.

[31]For a careful study of John's symbolism, see Koester, *Symbolism in the Fourth Gospel.*

[32]Cf. the words by Michael Card, "Recapture Me," Birdwing Music and BMG Songs, 1992.

eye and that ears are for hearing the Word of God.

As the Fourth Gospel forges a theology of belief, it often draws on the analogical correspondence between seeing and believing. One prominent motif that John weaves throughout the fabric of his Gospel is the theme of light versus darkness (Jn 1:4-9; 3:19-21; 8:12; 9:5; 12:35-36, 46).[33] Two motifs that support this core symbol are contrasts between day and night (Jn 3:2; 9:3-5; 11:9) and references to seeing and looking (Jn 3:3, 14; 4:48; 12:44-50), including the blindness of the sighted and sight for the blind (Jn 9:35-41). These themes are crucial for John's development of his contrasts between believing and not believing and between understanding and misunderstanding (see Jn 1:5). Though these themes are much too extensive to trace out here, we must reflect on them to some extent. As John weaves these themes into his Gospel, he argues that eyes are for seeing the true identity of Jesus through the veil of flesh by way of the signs he works.

Twice earlier we mentioned the dialogue between Jesus and Nicodemus. Because we will have occasion to return to it once more in this chapter, we will mention it only briefly here. Nicodemus, curious about Jesus' signs yet cloaking his approach with the darkness of night, accurately identifies the source of Jesus' power but greatly understates his identity with his conversation starter (Jn 3:1-2). Because Nicodemus approaches him in darkness when it is difficult to see, Jesus wisely tailors his response for the occasion, "I tell you the truth, no one can see the kingdom of God unless he is born again" (Jn 3:3 NIV). Nicodemus misses the spiritual significance of Jesus' carefully chosen metaphor of sight as he directs the conversation to explore the born again metaphor. It is important to recognize what Jesus means by the clause "see the kingdom of God." In response to Nicodemus's question about new birth, Jesus explains, "I tell you the truth, no one can enter the kingdom of God unless he is born of water and the Spirit. Flesh gives birth to flesh, but the Spirit gives birth to spirit" (Jn 3:5-6 NIV). To "see the kingdom of God" is to "enter the kingdom of God"; they are metaphors for belief, as the subsequent discourse clarifies both explicitly (Jn 3:11-12) and implicitly. An implicit

---

[33]Literary scholars identify John's light-darkness theme as a "core symbol." See Culpepper, *Anatomy of the Fourth Gospel*, pp. 180-98. See also Koester, *Symbolism in the Fourth Gospel*, pp. 5-7.

but decisive indicator occurs when Jesus says, "Just as Moses lifted up the snake in the desert, so the Son of Man must be lifted up, that everyone who believes in him may have eternal life" (Jn 3:14-15 NIV).[34] One who knows the Old Testament allusion might have expected Jesus to say, "that everyone who looks to him may have eternal life" (cf. Num 21:9). By substituting "believes in him" for "looks to him," Jesus brings closure to the metaphor with which he first responded to Nicodemus. To see means to believe; to believe in the Son of God is to look to him for life.

John sustains this metaphorical interplay between seeing or looking with believing throughout his Gospel. The words our ears expected to hear in John 3:15 are spoken in John 6:40 when allusion to the bronze serpent recurs: "For my Father's will is that everyone who looks to the Son and believes in him shall have eternal life, and I will raise him up at the last day" (NIV). Of course, we must be careful not to impose the limitations of the Old Testament type or image on the fulfillment and reality of which Jesus speaks. The dying Israelite's solitary look to the bronze serpent does not mean, as one concludes, "Could anything be more profoundly simple than that! Eternal life for one look of faith!"[35] John's text does not say that a singular act of faith receives eternal life; rather, it is "the one who believes," which means one who is characterized by believing. One look to the bronze serpent, which was only a symbol, brought relief to the anguished Israelite. It was a singular look, lest the Israelites turn the symbolic bronze serpent into an idol, as they did until Hezekiah destroyed it (2 Kings 18:4). But Jesus Christ is no mere symbol; he is the true deliverer to whom the serpent pointed. He is the one who gives life forever to those who fasten their gaze on him, which is to say, to those who believe in him and continue to believe. The point we are making is not to deny that one look of faith saves.

---

[34]It is possible to read Jn 3:15 as follows: "that everyone who believes may have eternal life in him." On John's grammatical construction, see the discussion in Carson, *Gospel According to John*, p. 202. However, against Carson's commentary, it may be that John's grammatical construction here *(pisteuōn en autō)* is intended to correspond to and complement the clear allusion to Num 21:9: "when he looked to the bronze serpent, he lived." So also, "everyone who believes in him may have eternal life."

[35]Zane Hodges, *The Gospel Under Siege: A Study on Faith and Works*, 2nd ed. (Dallas: Rendención Viva, 1991), p. 18. By way of contrast to Hodges, see Piper, *Purifying Power of Living*, pp. 231-59.

Rather, looking that does not persist does not save.

At the same time Jesus admonishes us to look to him for life, he rebukes those who look for signs: "Unless you see signs and wonders you will not believe" (Jn 4:48 NRSV). After the people had seen Jesus perform the sign of the miraculous feeding from five barley loaves, they reasoned, "This is indeed the prophet who is to come into the world" (Jn 6:14 NRSV). But Jesus knew their intentions to draft him to be their king, so he fled. When he encounters the same people later, he reproves them, "Very truly, I tell you, you are looking for me, not because you saw signs, but because you ate your fill of the loaves. Do not work for the food that perishes, but for the food that endures for eternal life, which the Son of Man will give you" (Jn 6:26-27 NRSV). Though it is incredulous, the very Jews who had already witnessed the miraculous feeding ask Jesus, "Therefore, what sign are you about to perform in order that we might see and believe? What are you about to do? Our fathers ate manna in the wilderness, just as it is written, 'He gave them bread from heaven to eat' " (Jn 6:30-31).

Along similar lines, in Jerusalem Jesus found a man born blind and healed him for a sign. There is considerable irony in this episode, for the Pharisees who had eyes to see stumbled over the sign because Jesus gave sight to a man on the sabbath. But the man who could not see Jesus before Jesus healed him nevertheless came to believe in the Son of Man, testifying before the religious leaders, "One thing I do know. I was blind but now I see!" (Jn 9:25 NIV). Later Jesus encounters him again and announces, "You have seen the Son of Man," words that conveyed spiritual sight to the man. He immediately confessed, "Lord, I believe!" (Jn 9:38).[36] Jesus punctuates the completion of his healing sign with a riddle: "For judgment I came into this world, in order that those who do not see might see and those who see might become blind" (Jn 9:39). Jesus, the light of the world, gives sight to the blind (those who are in spiritual darkness and acknowledge it) and blinds the sighted (those who think they see but live in spiritual night).[37]

This theme of judgment for having sight that does not see comes to

---

[36]Note the significance of Jesus' words in Jn 9:37, when he encounters the man born blind after he returns from the Pool of Siloam, where he washed his eyes: "You have now seen him; in fact, he is the one speaking with you" (NIV).

[37]For further discussion of this text, see Carson, *Gospel According to John*, pp. 377-78.

a climax in John 12:37-50. Why was there such extensive unbelief among Jesus' own people, the Jews (Jn 1:11)? John explains that even after they saw all the signs Jesus had done "they did not believe in him" because God intended that they should persist in unbelief, just as Isaiah prophesied:

> He has blinded their eyes
> and hardened their hearts,
> in order that they might not see with their eyes
> and understand with their hearts and turn,
> and I heal them. (Jn 12:40)[38]

For the moment, without broaching the controversy these words raise, we should recognize the prominence that John gives to the metaphor of eyes and sight. This segment (Jn 12:37-50) closes the first half of John's Gospel, which is properly designated "The Book of Signs."[39] John sums up: "Although he had performed so many signs in their presence, they did not believe in him" (Jn 12:37 NRSV). Though they looked for signs and saw them, they did not see the Son of Man because they did not look to him. Jesus explains:

> The one who believes in me does not believe in me but in the one who sent me, and the one who looks at me sees the one who sent me. I have come as light into the world in order that everyone who believes in me should not remain in the darkness. And if anyone hears my words and does not keep them, I do not condemn him, for I did not come in order to condemn the world, but to save the world. The one who rejects me and does not receive my words has one who judges him—the word which I have spoken, this will condemn him in the last day. For I have not spoken on my own, but the Father who sent me, he gave me a commandment concerning what I should speak. (Jn 12:44-49)

How great is the condemnation for those whose eyes have seen but fail to see what is before their eyes! Yet how blessed are those whose eyes see far more than what is before their eyes!

A wistful notion entrances some to suppose that, had they seen Jesus as he traversed the landscape of Palestine, their faith would have been deeper and stronger. Such is not the case at all. John's Gospel ought to destroy that myth. Consider his account of "Peter and the

---

[38]We will return to this passage later for a brief discussion of the meaning of these words for the origin of belief.

[39]Gary M. Burge, *Interpreting the Gospel of John* (Grand Rapids, Mich.: Baker, 1992), p. 76.

other disciple" who, having just received word that the Lord's body had been removed from the tomb, ran to see for themselves. Of "the other disciple," John says, "He saw and believed" (Jn 20:8). His believing was born from seeing the intact grave clothes in the empty tomb. Then he adds parenthetically, "For not yet did they understand the Scripture, that he must rise from the dead" (Jn 20:9). Likewise, with all his privileges of seeing Jesus' signs and conversing with him as they walked the countryside, even after his fellows testified that they had seen the resurrected Jesus, Thomas announced, "If I do not see in his hands the imprint of the nails and put my finger into his side, I will not believe" (Jn 20:25). Jesus obliged Thomas who, upon seeing Jesus, said, "My Lord and my God!" Then Jesus drew a connection between Thomas, as representative of his eyewitnesses, and future believers: "You have believed because you have seen me. Blessed are those who believe though they have not seen" (Jn 20:29). The faith of Jesus' own disciples, who were his eyewitnesses, did not gain depth or resilience until after his resurrection, but their eyewitness faith is crucial to all who follow them, for we believe in him "through their word" (Jn 17:20), for example, the word John wrote (Jn 20:30-31).

Our belief in Jesus Christ is not diminished because it is not aided by sight, for we joyfully receive Jesus' benediction. Though we do not look on Jesus with eyes that see his frame in a compassionate deed, hanging on the cross or risen from the tomb, we see him clearly with faith's eye, for we look to the Son of Man that we might have eternal life. We see him more clearly than most who looked on him in the flesh.[40]

Eyes are for seeing and perceiving that the one who enlightens blind eyes does so to show that he alone enlightens our hearts to trust him for salvation. Better to be as the blind man, who did not see the one who gave him sight but gladly received sight, than to have looked on him with both eyes wide open and fail to look to him for eternal life. "Though you have not seen him, you love him; and even though you do not see him now, you believe in him and are filled with an inexpressible and glorious joy, for you are receiving the goal of your faith, the salvation of your souls" (1 Pet 1:8-9 NIV).

If faith is to see through the eye what spiritually corresponds to

---

[40]Cf. Michael Card, "Through the Eye," Birdwing Music and BMG Songs, 1992.

what we see with the eye, then faith is to hear through the ear the voice of God in the Word, who is Jesus Christ. The most basic of all John's themes, though not overtly so, is that of heavenly speech, for he begins his Gospel by saying, "In the beginning was the Word, and the Word was with God, and the Word was God" (Jn 1:1). The Word underscores Jesus' identity. He is God. He is Creator. He is life. He is light. He is God's Word.[41]

To hear Jesus speak is to hear the voice of God (Jn 5:24-30, 37-40; 6:45-47; 7:16-19; 8:28-29, 46-47; 10:34-38; 12:44-50). Jesus announces, "For I did not speak of my own accord, but the Father who sent me commanded me what to say and how to say it. I know that his command leads to eternal life. So whatever I say is just what the Father has told me to say" (Jn 12:49-50 NIV). The voice of Jesus is indistinguishable from God's voice, for he is the Word: "Whoever does not love me does not keep my words; and the word that you hear is not mine, but is from the Father who sent me" (Jn 14:24 NRSV). This is why Jesus says, "Whoever believes in me believes not in me but in him who sent me. And whoever sees me sees him who sent me" (Jn 12:44-45 NRSV).

Though John does not include within his selected signs an account of Jesus opening deaf ears, as the Synoptic Gospels do (e.g., Mk 7:31-37; 9:25), the imagery of hearing punctuates his Gospel. Hearing the word, or gospel, preached is essential to believing, but hearing at that level is not in itself believing (Jn 8:43; cf. Rom 10:14). Though one cannot believe in Jesus without hearing, one can hear without believing in him (Jn 12:47). For many, even among his own disciples, heard Jesus bear witness concerning himself, yet they did not believe in him (e.g., Jn 6:60). To believe in Jesus Christ is to hear him; to hear his voice is to entrust oneself to him. Three crucial passages affirm this.

Usually, when John's Gospel contrasts belief and unbelief using the auditory metaphor, the contrast assumes hearing over against deafness. For one who gave sight to eyes that had never seen before, it would be a small thing for Jesus to claim that he could restore hearing to deaf ears. However, Jesus lays claim to much more than that. He claims authority for himself that belongs to God alone; he

---

[41]Cf. Michael Card, "The Final Word," Birdwing Music/Mole End Music, 1986.

announces that he has the power to make the dead hear.

> I tell you the truth, whoever hears my word and believes him who sent
> me has eternal life and will not be condemned; he has crossed over
> from death to life. I tell you the truth, a time is coming and has now
> come when the dead will hear the voice of the Son of God and those
> who hear will live. For as the Father has life in himself, so he has
> granted the Son to have life in himself. And he has given him authority
> to judge because he is the Son of Man. (Jn 5:24-27 NIV)

Under the imagery of hearing, Jesus affirms that he calls the dead,
who are insensible, to come out of their tombs. He has in view a dual
reference: the time that "is coming" and the time that "has now
come." Though Jesus will tell of his power to speak and cause the
dead to hear and rise from their tombs in the last day to be judged (Jn
5:28-30), he mentions his last-day authority as a reference point to
explain his present work. Resurrection in the last day is the work of
God alone, yet Jesus is already calling the dead to hear and live. This
unmistakable claim to deity draws an inseparable link between the
not yet and the already. To hear his voice now is akin to hearing him
in the final day. His voice creates hearing in the ones he calls. The
voice of Jesus is as effective as God's creative word in the beginning
(cf. Gen 1:1; Jn 1:1). Later in John's Gospel, to testify to the truth of
his claim, Jesus performs a sign at a tomb when he speaks the creative word, "Lazarus, come out!" (Jn 11:43). Already his voice effectively causes the dead to hear. Already the spiritually dead, those who
have no senses for God, hear when the Son of God calls them. To hear
his voice is to believe in him. Faith is to hear through the ear the
voice of God in the Word, who is Jesus Christ.

John 8:42-47 is the second passage that makes it clear that to hear
the voice of Jesus is to believe in him. Earlier, when we considered
the "rational metaphor," we looked at John 8:30-33. Jesus' words in
John 8:42-47 continue his dialogue with "the Jews who had believed
in him" (Jn 8:31). They persistently protest Jesus' call for them to be
truly his disciples. Though they could rightly claim physical descent
from Abraham, Jesus challenges their spiritual parentage (Jn 8:37-
47). Neither Abraham nor God is their father, for their speech and
actions are traits inherited from "your father, the devil" (Jn 8:44). The
devil's children do not have ears for heavenly language. Jesus says to
them, "Why do you not understand my form of speaking? It is

because you cannot hear my word" (Jn 8:43). Spiritually, they need Jesus' creative word to form ears for them to cause them to hear, for they are as insensible to Jesus' words from above as Lazarus was to the voices of his mourners. Jesus raises the question and answers it: "If I am speaking the truth, why do you not believe in me? Whoever is from God hears God's words. For this reason you do not hear, because you are not from God" (Jn 8:46-47).

It is mentally tempting to invert the last sentence to read, "For this reason you are not from God, because you do not hear," as if hearing God's word causes us to be born of God. Failure to hear the voice of God in Jesus' words is not the reason why people do not belong to God; rather, the reason people do not hear God's word is that they do not belong to God. This is so because hearing is a sensory gift formed in us by God's creative word just as much as our auditory sense is an endowment from the Creator. To hear through the ear the inaudible voice of God in the word Jesus speaks is to believe. But to hear is also to obey, for Jesus is indicting the Jews "who had believed in him" (Jn 8:31) for failing to "do the things Abraham did" (Jn 8:39) and for doing "what you have heard from your father" (Jn 8:38). He excoriates them, saying, "You belong to your father, the devil, and you want to carry out your father's desire" (Jn 8:44 NIV). Jesus' discourse inextricably entangles believing in him, hearing what he says, remaining in his word and doing what Abraham did. The dominant theme that Jesus presses upon us throughout John 8:31-47 is that belief in him that does not persevere in the gospel and fails to hear God's voice with obedience is not true belief and exposes one's illegitimacy; such a person is not born from God.

The good shepherd passage (Jn 10:1-30) is the third in John's Gospel to make it clear that the hearing metaphor defines belief in Jesus Christ as an act of obedience. It is neither necessary nor wise to comment on the whole passage in order to unpack the significance of the auditory metaphor, for to explain a metaphor, particularly extended metaphors and parables, is somewhat like explaining a joke: its point tends to become blunted.[42] Jesus' signs, symbols and metaphors are a kind of

---

[42] John calls his figure of speech *paroimia*, a word he uses again in Jn 16:25, 29, but the Synoptic Gospels never use this word The favored word in the Synoptics is *parabolē*. Both words translate and render the Hebrew *māšāl*, and all three words are broad enough to include proverbs, parables, maxims, similes, allegories, fables, riddles, narratives embodying certain truths, taunts and more. The feature that is common among all these is that there is something enigmatic or cryptic.

silent speech that shuts mouths and captures one's holy imagination.

Jesus introduces the shepherd motif to indict the Pharisees and religious leaders as false shepherds and to announce that he is the true and good shepherd who fulfills Old Testament prophecies. Besides Psalm 23, echoes from Ezekiel 34 are prominent. The prophet condemned "the shepherds of Israel," that is the religious leaders of Ezekiel's time, for ruling the people harshly and brutally (Ezek 34:2-4). The Lord promises to rescue his people from false shepherds, for he says, "I will set up over them one shepherd, my servant David, and he shall feed them: he shall feed them and be their shepherd" (Ezek 34:23 NRSV).

Though they knew Ezekiel's prophecy, the Pharisees failed to grasp Jesus' figure of speech, so he explained it:

> I am the gate for the sheep. . . . I am the good shepherd. The good shepherd lays down his life for the sheep. . . . I know my sheep and my sheep know me. . . . I have other sheep that are not of this sheep pen. I must bring them also. They too will listen to my voice, and there shall be one flock and one shepherd. (Jn 10:7, 11, 14, 16 NIV)

Later Jesus repeats a significant element of his extended metaphor when he says, "The works that I do in my Father's name testify to me; but you do not believe, because you do not belong to my sheep. My sheep hear my voice. I know them, and they follow me. I give them eternal life, and they will never perish. No one will snatch them out of my hand" (Jn 10:26-28 NRSV; cf. Jn 10:3, 8, 16). These verses raise a number of points for discussion, but we resist the temptation to probe the text more deeply than necessary here; we will return to this text briefly before the end of this chapter. Our concern for now is to recognize that Jesus clarifies, by his auditory metaphor within the extended figure of speech, that to hear his voice is to believe unto obedience, for he inseparably links *hear* and *follow* as metaphorical explanations of what it means to believe in him.

Jesus uses these metaphors to define and explain what he means by believing. As much as we need to avoid reifying or literalizing biblical metaphors, that is, failing to recognize that they point away from themselves to spiritual realities that they represent, we also must guard against flattening biblical metaphors by suppressing or nullifying their role to define the things they represent. Some attempt to force Jesus' use of *hear* and *follow* to fit their preconceived notions of what *believe* means. Because Jesus is not speaking "about literal sheep which physically follow a literal shepherd,"[43] they reason that "following" Jesus as sheep follow a shepherd does not define faith as obedience to Jesus' commands. They conclude that *hear* and *follow* are merely figurative substitutes for "belief in Jesus Christ," but they do not convey actual significance to the word they replace. But one is mistaken to impose one's preferred definition of *believe* on the sheep imagery. Jesus uses the metaphor of sheep, who hear and follow the shepherd, precisely because he is defining and shaping what he means by *believe*. Believing is explained as hearing and following; metaphors function to define words and concepts they replace. To reverse the analogical direction, that is, to explain *hear* and *follow* by *believe*, is to nullify or at least to suppress the metaphor. We use metaphors to define and clarify. This is why it is so crucial to select metaphors suitable to the task for which we choose them.

So while it is correct that Jesus is not truly speaking about sheep, he is speaking about "true sheep," for true sheep are people who hear and follow the good shepherd. His metaphor makes it clear that belief in Jesus Christ bears within itself obedience, which agrees with what John says early in his Gospel: "Whoever believes in the Son has eternal life; whoever disobeys the Son will not see life, but must endure God's wrath" (Jn 3:36 NRSV). To believe in Jesus Christ is to obey him. One who does not obey him also does not believe in him.

Though all creation now resides under God's curse, it is nonetheless inherently good (Gen 1:31). The created order continues to reveal the nature of its Creator: "Everything in the world is capable of 'representing' the realm and reality of its creator."[44] Therefore, Jesus fully exploits the created order to disclose himself as the Son of God. To believe in him and to understand is what eyes and ears are for.[45] To see, to look to him, to understand, to hear God's voice in the Word, to follow him implicitly as sheep follow a shepherd is to believe.[46]

Bodily action imagery. This is the third collection of images for faith in John's Gospel. We have already encountered some of these as John

---

[43]Robert N. Wilkin, "Is Following Christ a Condition of Eternal Life?" *Grace in Focus*, April 1990. See also Hodges, *Gospel Under Siege*, pp. 48-49.

[44]Culpepper, *Anatomy of the Fourth Gospel*, p. 201.

[45]Cf. Michael Card, "Recapture Me," Birdwing Music and BMG Songs, 1992.

[46]Cf. Michael Card, "Will You Not Listen?" Birdwing Music and BMG, 1992.

embeds them with both the rational and sensory metaphors. For example, John links *hear* and *follow* together in the shepherd motif (Jn 10:27). Bound together, they signal trusting obedience. Likewise, those who believe in Jesus "will not follow" a stranger's voice but will run away from him and not acknowledge him (Jn 10:5). Within contexts of passages already considered, we have come upon the bodily action imagery of entering. Jesus says, "No one can enter the kingdom of God without being born of water and the Spirit" (Jn 3:5), and later he says, "I am the gate. Whoever enters by me will be saved, and will come in and go out and find pasture" (Jn 10:9 NRSV). Jesus portrays believing as an act of entering, an intentional act of seeking safety from hostilities and enemies outside.

Coming to Jesus is a natural metaphor for believing, particularly as it is linked with two other bodily actions, namely, eating and drinking. In chapters 6 and 7 John makes this association. Jesus says, "I am the bread of life. Whoever comes to me will never be hungry, and whoever believes in me will never be thirsty. But I said to you that you have seen me and yet do not believe. Everything that the Father gives me will come to me, and anyone who comes to me I will never drive away" (Jn 6:35-37 NRSV). These words prepare ears of faith to understand his hard saying that prompted some of his disciples to abandon him, for they persisted in unbelief (Jn 6:60-66). Jesus piles up metaphors for believing: to believe is to see, to hear, to come to him, to eat true bread that is his flesh, to drink his blood that is true drink (Jn 6:44-58). All who eat his flesh and drink his blood already have eternal life and will be raised to eternal life on the last day (Jn 6:54; cf. Jn 5:24-29). Jesus underscores the significance of these words by reiterating them with a variation: "Those who eat my flesh and drink my blood remain in me, and I in them" (Jn 6:56).

Jesus' imagery is repulsive and scandalous, and he intends it so. For it is language that speaks of his bloody sacrifice, and anyone who desires eternal life must eat and drink nourishment found in him alone. Just as it is that our lives are sustained daily by taking the life of that which we eat, so it is that eternal life is ours only by eating true bread and drinking true drink that gives its life for us. The Word who became flesh gives his flesh and his blood for our eternal sustenance. This is sacrifice. It is dramatized every day as we eat and drink our meals, for we derive life from that which gives its life that we might live. This is why Jesus appoints a meal to memorialize symbolically his great sacrifice. Those who eat his flesh and drink his blood have eternal life, and he will raise them up on the last day (Jn 6:54). Offense and revulsion at the literal level must be overcome by believing in Jesus Christ, for only those who believe eat his flesh and drink his blood and thus have his life now and forever. We must not sanitize Jesus' gospel; we must not remove the scandal of either his sacrifice or his call to eat his flesh and drink his blood.

We would also be misguided to suppose that we acquire eternal life and salvation by drinking the wine and eating the bread of the Lord's Table. We must not stumble over Jesus' metaphors as the Jews did. They presumed that they were safe before God because they ate bread and drank living water in the wilderness. Faith nourishes itself on the reality, not the shadow. It is by believing that we understand Jesus' metaphors for faith; by believing we receive eternal life in him. Augustine of Hippo stated it well: "Believe, and you have eaten."[47]

Disciple imagery. Though we will not engage a lengthy discussion here, it is crucial to demonstrate that when Jesus calls for people to become his disciples, he is urging them to believe in him and to follow him. His call for disciples is another biblical image for belief, and, like other metaphors, it also contributes significant qualities toward a definition of Christian faith.

We have already noticed the connection between belief and being Jesus' disciple in John 8:31-32. To Jews who believed in him, Jesus says, "If you continue in my word, then truly you are my disciples; and you will know the truth, and the truth will liberate you" (Jn 8:31). Some believe that Jesus' words in this text distinguish between a call to be his disciple and the gospel's call to believe in Jesus Christ.[48] They contend that all Jesus' disciples are believers, but not all believers are his disciples.[49] They argue that the call for disciples adds con-

---

[47]Augustine's Latin is *"Crede, et manducasti."* (In *Evangelium Johannis tractatus [Tractates on the Gospel of John]* 26.1).

[48]See, for example, Charles C. Ryrie, *So Great Salvation: What It Means to Believe in Jesus Christ* (Wheaton, Ill.: Victor, 1989), pp. 104-6. Cf. also Hodges, *Gospel Under Siege,* pp. 42-43.

[49]Ryrie says, "If the examples of disciples in the Gospels may be carried over into today, then we would have to conclude that there will be some disciples who learn a little, some a lot; some who are totally committed, some who are not; some who are secret, some who are visible; some who persevere, some who defect. But all are believers" (*So Great Salvation,* p. 105).

ditions that go beyond simple faith, so that it would become a "salvation by faith plus works."[50] Unfortunately, they draw a distinction that the Bible does not, and they fail to recognize that Jesus uses the disciple's submission to the teacher as a vivid image of the kind of belief he requires. Thus, when Jesus says, "If you continue in my word, then truly you are my disciples," two things become apparent. First, as we observed earlier, when John says that "many believed in him" (Jn 8:30), the remainder of the narrative clarifies that he does not mean that their belief was genuine. Second, this is evident in Jesus' choice of words. He carefully distinguishes "true disciples" from "false disciples" by using the adverb *truly*. Jesus distinguishes "true disciples" from "spurious disciples." True disciples "remain in Jesus' word." Spurious ones defect from Christ because they do not truly believe in him (Jn 6:64-66). Likewise, there is also true faith and false faith.

The Synoptic Gospels agree with John. Jesus calls us to become his disciples when he says:

> I tell you the truth, . . . no one who has left home or brothers or sisters or mother or father or children or fields for me and the gospel will fail to receive a hundred times as much in this present age (homes, brothers, sisters, mothers, children and fields—and with them, persecutions) and in the age to come, eternal life. (Mk 10:29-30 NIV)

Because Jesus links his call with receiving eternal life, it is readily apparent that any attempt to distinguish between *believer* and *disciple* is misguided. Mark's Gospel makes it clear that Jesus' call to discipleship is nothing other than a call to obedient faith that lays hold of eternal life. His call for disciples provides rich images of the kind of belief he requires.

> If any want to become my followers, let them deny themselves and take up their cross and follow me. For those who want to save their life will lose it, and those who lose their life for my sake, and for the sake of the gospel, will save it. For what will it profit them to gain the whole world and forfeit their life? Indeed, what can they give in return for their life? Those who are ashamed of me and of my words in this adulterous and sinful generation, of them the Son of Man will also be ashamed when he comes in the glory of his Father with the holy angels. (Mk 8:34-38)

---

[50]Zane Hodges, *The Gospel Under Siege* (Dallas: Rendención Viva, 1981), p. 37 (all subsequent references are to the second edition of this book; see chap. 3, n. 35 above).

Belief in Jesus Christ entails denying oneself both gratification of sinful appetites and any pleasure, though not evil in itself, that steals affection for Christ. One who believes in Jesus Christ picks up one's own cross, an instrument of death to sin, and follows after him. Apart from denying ourselves and putting sinful desires to death, we will lose our souls.

Endowment imagery. Though there are other metaphors for faith that we could consider, the endowment or gift metaphor is the final one we will ponder. We have already encountered this familiar imagery in the words "as many as received him" (Jn 1:12). John's Gospel uses *receive* several times in place of *believe* (Jn 1:16; 3:11, 32-33; 5:43-44; 13:20; 17:8). The act of believing in Jesus Christ is stretching forth the hands to receive the heavenly gift. When John replaces *believe* with the word *receive,* his metaphor draws an implicit comparison between the act of believing and the outstretched arms that receive a gift: God's gift of his Son Jesus Christ (Jn 1:12) and the Spirit (Jn 7:39). John the Baptist expresses this fundamental principle: "No one can receive anything except what has been given from heaven" (Jn 3:27 NRSV). So to believe is to open the hand to receive God's heavenly gift, his Son.

However, a thoughtful reading of John's Gospel recognizes that belief in the Son is itself a heavenly endowment. Not only is God's Son the heavenly gift, but belief in him also is a divine endowment, though John does not explicitly call faith a gift. Instead, the Fourth Gospel uses various imagery to make it clear that belief in Jesus Christ is a gift from God. We have already seen hints of this in John's Gospel. Earlier we promised to return to Jesus' dialogue with Nicodemus. Jesus says, "Very truly, I tell you, no one can see the kingdom of God without being born from above" (Jn 3:3 NRSV). In response to Nicodemus's bewilderment at this statement, Jesus explains, "Very truly, I tell you, no one can enter the kingdom of God without being born of water and Spirit. What is born of the flesh is flesh, and what is born of the Spirit is spirit" (Jn 3:5-6 NRSV). It is evident that belief in God's Son, metaphorically portrayed as seeing and entering God's kingdom, does not cause our being born again. Rather, our entrance into the kingdom by belief in Jesus Christ is brought about by being born of the Spirit. This is crucial, for it could hardly be more clearly asserted that our very entrance into God's kingdom is a gift; belief in

Jesus Christ is a heavenly endowment. Faith is the breath of life that God has breathed into us, just as when he breathed life into the nostrils of Adam. This is the point of Jesus' choice of words: "born from above." To be born from above is to become "children of God," who were born in the likeness of Adam but now are born "not of blood or of the will of the flesh or of the will of man, but of God" (Jn 1:13 NRSV).

In a variety of ways John's Gospel reasserts that belief in Jesus Christ is God's gift of heavenly breath. Consider several reaffirmations in the Fourth Gospel that faith is as much God's endowment as is eternal life. We have already mentioned each of the following passages for other purposes.

In John 5:25-29, the imagery recalls the first creation when God breathed life into Adam's lifeless body (Gen 2:7). Jesus says, "Very truly, I tell you, the hour is coming, and is now here, when the dead will hear the voice of the Son of God, and those who hear will live" (Jn 5:25 NRSV). Our hearing, which is a metaphor for believing, is caused by Jesus' creative power to infuse eternal life into us. Jesus has authority to say this because, "just as the Father has life in himself, so he has granted the Son also to have life in himself" (Jn 5:26 NRSV). When he says this, Jesus lays claim to deity, because the power to give life is a quality that belongs to God alone.

Jesus expressly attributes our believing unto eternal life to God's creative power when he says, "No one can come to me unless the Father who sent me draws him, and I will raise him up at the last day" (Jn 6:44 NIV). Many people stumble over these words from the bread of life discourse, just as many of Jesus' first disciples stumbled over them and departed from him. Jesus means to claim nothing less than this: belief unto eternal life is a gift from God above. The only reason any of us believes in Jesus Christ is that God's Spirit implants life in us. As Jesus says, "The Spirit gives life; the flesh counts for nothing. The words I have spoken to you are spirit and they are life. Yet there are some of you who do not believe" (Jn 6:63-64 NIV). How can unbelief be explained where Jesus has spoken words that are, in themselves, spirit and life, which means they have the power to create life? Jesus explains unbelief and continued deadness among those who have heard his words of life: "For this reason I told you that no one is able to come to me unless it has been given to him from the

Father" (Jn 6:65). Who comes to Jesus Christ? That is, who believes in Jesus Christ? Jesus' answer is, those who come to him are only those to whom the Father gives faith.

Again, in Jesus' discourse with those who professed belief in him (Jn 8:30), he says, "If I tell the truth, why do you not believe me? Whoever is from God hears the words of God. The reason you do not hear them is that you are not from God" (Jn 8:46-47 NRSV). Jesus does not say, "The reason you are not from God is that you do not hear." Rather, when Jesus explains unbelief by using the figure of speech "do not hear," he asserts that the reason people fail to hear his words is that they are not born from God. This is exactly what Jesus says again when he uses the imagery of the shepherd and the sheep. Unbelieving Jews say to Jesus, "If you are the Christ, tell us plainly." He answers, "I have told you, and you do not believe. The works that I do in my Father's name testify to me; but you do not believe, because you do not belong to my sheep" (Jn 10:25-26 NRSV). Many invert Jesus' words here without realizing it. One explains, "These Jews are not His sheep because they do not believe."[51] But that is not what Jesus says. Hearing (i.e., believing) is not the cause of becoming a sheep; being one of Jesus' sheep is the cause of our hearing his words. As it is the nature of sheep to hear and follow their shepherd, so now it is our nature to hear the voice of God's Son and follow him obediently because God has made us to be his sheep.

Not only does Jesus affirm by his teaching that believing in him is God's gift, he also does so by dramatizing this reality with signs. Consider his last two signs in the Fourth Gospel. When Jesus encounters the man who had been born blind, he announces, "While I am in the world, I am the light of the world" (Jn 9:5 NIV). Why did he reassert this earlier claim (cf. Jn 8:12)? It is because he was about to perform a creative act that God alone can do, namely, make seeing eyes for the man who had none. Jesus dramatizes his creative authority. As he who is the light of the world creates eyes that see for him who had never seen, so he gives eyes of belief to ones who have never believed in the God who gives life eternal. So it is as John's prologue affirms: "Through him all things were made; without him nothing

---

[51] Hodges, *Gospel Under Siege*, p. 49.

was made that has been made. In him was life, and that life was the light of men" (Jn 1:3-4 NIV).

Jesus had expressly announced in John 5:25, "The hour is coming, and is now here, when the dead will hear the voice of the Son of God, and those who hear will live" (NRSV). He acts this out when he raises Lazarus from the dead. The dead receive no sensory impulses with their ears, yet Lazarus emerged from the tomb, for when Jesus said, "Lazarus, come out!" his word was effective to restore life to the lifeless body. So it is when the Son of God speaks life to spiritually dead people, they also emerge from their tombs. It is the creative power of the Son's voice that breathes eternal life into whomever he desires to raise from spiritual death. We hear echoes from Genesis 2:7. Because Jesus breathes life into us, we believe. His voice has the power to enliven us to hear him command us to arise from the sleep of death. God gives to us the very belief by which we have eternal life. The breath of life we breathe is belief.

One final portion in the Fourth Gospel contributes significantly to the endowment metaphor concerning belief. Earlier we quickly passed over John 12:37-40, but now we must pause to ponder its importance. As John closes his narrative of Jesus' signs, he explains widespread unbelief among the Jews as a fulfillment of Isaiah's prophecy (Is 53:1; 6:9-10). John declares, "For this reason they were not able to believe, because again Isaiah said, 'He has blinded their eyes and hardened their hearts, lest they see with their eyes and understand with their hearts and turn, and I heal them' " (Jn 12:39-40). God alone enables people to believe in the Son of God. The ability to believe in him is not a quality that is inherent to humans; it is a God-endowed capacity. Unless God enables, no one will believe in Jesus Christ and be saved.

Paul also regards faith in Jesus Christ to be a divine gift. Of Paul's texts, Ephesians 2:8 quickly comes to mind: "For it is by grace you have been saved, through faith—and this not from yourselves, it is the gift of God" (NIV). However, anyone who has learned Koine Greek knows that the pronoun in the phrase "this not from yourselves" does not correspond to the gender of its antecedent, namely, "faith." Because this is so, some suppose that faith, for Paul, is not a divine gift. It is true that Paul's antecedent likely refers to the whole clause, "for it is by grace you have been saved, through faith," but even then faith is included as an aspect of the gift. Notwithstanding Ephesians 2:8, Paul does make it clear elsewhere that faith, in his theological understanding, is God's gift.[52] He says to the Philippians, "For it has been granted to you on behalf of Christ not only to believe on him, but also to suffer for him" (Phil 1:29 NIV). Likewise, Paul says to the Romans, "For by the grace given me I say to every one of you: Do not think of yourself more highly than you ought, but rather think of yourself with sober judgment, in accordance with the measure of faith God has given you" (Rom 12:3 NIV). Words could hardly be more clear: whatever measure of faith in God we have, it has been allotted to us by God as a gift of grace.

Faith, therefore, is not only the hand that we stretch out to receive God's gift of eternal life; the outstretched hand itself is a gift from God. Spiritually our senses toward God were as dead as Lazarus's ears were to the wailing of the mourners at his tomb. Yet, just as Jesus spoke life into Lazarus in order that he might obey the command, "Lazarus, come out!" so God has "made us alive together with Christ" (Eph 2:5). We are his new creation to whom he has given the gifts of faith and of salvation, in order that we might do the good deeds he has ordained for us to do (Eph 2:8-10).

Conclusion

Christians are as inclined as anyone else to reduce complex ideas to simplistic formulas and slogans. Popular evangelical instruction and preaching tend to reduce the intricate elegance and multifaceted glory of the gospel of God's salvation to a naive notion that stunts biblical knowledge, impairs spiritual growth, dulls Christian worship and, worst of all, misleads some to presume safety rather than trust in Jesus Christ. Like the hardening of the arteries of the human body, the categories by which we understand and explain the gospel too easily become calcified. Once "hardening of the categories" sets in, one is prone to reduce all complex concepts to simplistic notions.

In chapter two we showed how the biblical writers conceive of salvation with a variety of metaphors or images, each of which has two reference points: now and not yet. If one fails to account for both

---

[52]See counterarguments by Gary L. Nebeker, "Is Faith a Gift of God? Ephesians 2:8 Reconsidered," *Grace in Focus*, July 1989.

aspects of salvation by divorcing them, by collapsing the not yet into what is already possessed or by relegating salvation only to the last day, one also tends to commit the same error concerning the complex biblical concept of faith. Just as eternal life is at once both a gift we already possess and a prize we have not yet won, similarly faith is a gift we receive and an action we exert. We all have been prone to reduce the biblical concept of faith to a simplistic notion, an idea around which we can wrap our minds. As we endeavored in chapter two to correct misconceptions about salvation, so our task in this chapter has been to do the same concerning the faith that the gospel requires of us in order that we might be saved.

The faith that the gospel requires penetrates beyond what is seen to understand that the things that are seen are temporary images of the things that are unseen and permanent. By faith we acknowledge that created things are signs that point to the God who made them all. By faith we grasp what cannot be held with our hands or scrutinized with our eyes. By faith we set our hope on God, who is invisible yet eternally more substantial than anything our senses apprehend. People who look through things created and see the Creator are people who believe that God is and that he rewards all who seek him. They are the people with whom God is pleased and for whom he has prepared an eternal city in which they shall dwell.

Because faith is like a multifaceted jewel, its radiance and splendor can be captured only by viewing it from all its angles in the light of God's revelation. This we have only begun to do in this chapter as we have examined several of faith's facets through a variety of metaphors that define faith. Because each of these biblical metaphors contributes qualities that define the kind of faith God requires, it is imperative that we be careful lest we err in one of two directions. We must guard against negating the metaphors by imposing a predefined notion of faith on them and ignoring their implicit clarifying contributions. We must be equally careful not to exaggerate the metaphors, either by forgetting that metaphors are implicit comparisons or by literalizing them as actuality.

A full array of metaphors provides definition to the abstract concept of faith. To believe in the God who rewards whoever seeks him is to taste, in advance, the glorious salvation of the age that is yet to come. To believe is to engage in strict self-discipline, to compete in the good competition of faith, to run, to land blows on oneself, to look to the Son of God for life, to eat of his flesh and to drink of his blood, to hear and follow his voice. All these and more provide contour and texture to our understanding of what faith is. At once these metaphors call us to act in obedient faith to the heavenward call of God in Christ Jesus and provide a standard by which we may know that our faith is authentic, though not perfect.

Lest we think of ourselves more highly than we ought, Scripture reminds us that whatever measure of faith is ours is as much a gift from God as eternal life is (Rom 12:3). God's grace gives what his gospel requires of us in order that we might be saved. This is the glory of the gospel. God's grace provides what God's grace demands. God's grace gives birth to faith. Whoever the Son of God calls to emerge from the tomb of sin and death into eternal life does so because his powerful voice gives spiritual ears to hear his call. When he calls for the dead to rise, his voice is the effective and creative word of new creation. If we believe in the Son of God and look to him for eternal life with persevering faith, it is because he has given us eyes to see what is unseen and ears to hear what others fail to hear. All this we receive by grace; therefore, we must speak of our faith as a divine gift.

4

RUNNING TO WIN THE PRIZE

Heeding God's Admonitions & Warnings

Do you not know that in a race the runners all compete,
but only one receives the prize?
Run in such a way that you may win it. (1 Cor 9:24 NRSV)

Of the eight chapters in this book this one is the most crucial, for it is here that we distinguish our interpretation of biblical warnings and admonitions from the four views we surveyed in chapter one. How do God's warnings and admonitions relate to his promises of assured salvation for his people? This is the primary question that determines the shape one's doctrine of perseverance and assurance will take. We began this book by describing four popular explanations of this relationship and showed why none of the four views adequately explains the biblical evidence of both promise and warning. In chapter one we briefly teased readers with three crucial perspectives on biblical warnings that distinguish our interpretation from the other four. Now we will unpack those perspectives fully.

First, how the warnings relate to God's promises will not be properly understood unless we ask the primary question concerning their function. Biblical warnings and promises must be allowed to have their respective functions within their contexts. Tempting as it is to superimpose God's warnings on the promises or the promises on the warnings, as the other four views do, however unwittingly, we resist the temptation. Instead, we engage careful and detailed interpretive work in the grammar and context of major passages where admonition and warning are present as we seek to show that these passages must be granted their full force without qualifying them with God's promises. We believe that God's promises of assured salvation have their proper function to ground our faith in God and to assure us that God faithfully keeps his promises to his children. We also believe that God's admonitions and warnings have their distinctive function to evoke faith that perseveres in holy devotion to God's heavenly call on us in Christ Jesus. Thus, God's warnings do not conflict with God's promises. His warnings serve his promises, for his warnings elicit belief and confidence in God's promises.

Second, crucial to a proper understanding of biblical warnings and admonitions is the need to recognize the conditional or suppositional nature of them. The conditional warnings and admonitions complement the conditional promises of the gospel's sustained call for persevering belief. God's warnings function to reinforce God's promise of the gospel that is conditioned on persistent belief. The conditional promise of the gospel—"Let anyone who wishes take the water of life as a gift" (Rev 22:17 NRSV)—expresses the gospel's initial command to believe. The conditional warning—"If anyone takes away from the words of the book of this prophecy, God will take away that person's share in the tree of life and in the holy city" (Rev 22:19 NRSV)—expresses a corollary to the promise as it elaborates and sustains the call of the gospel for faithfulness and loyalty to Christ that endures to the end.

Third, another essential ingredient for properly holding a biblical relationship between God's promises and warnings without qualifying either, as the other four views do, is to embrace the biblical tension between the already and not-yet aspects of God's gracious gift of salvation. This is necessary, for biblical warnings are prospective and evoke faith that perseveres to the end in order to lay hold of the eternal prize of life at the end of the race that is set before us. If we will accept the biblically designed functions of both God's promises and warnings, it is imperative that we correctly embrace the biblically conceived relationship between the already and not-yet aspects of God's gift of salvation. Salvation is already ours as heirs, issuing in confidence and assurance, for we already have God's gift of the Spirit, who is his "pledge of our inheritance toward redemption as God's own people" (Eph 1:14 NRSV). God has pledged our redemption, but we yet await it. This already-but-not-yet orientation is indispensable for a right understanding of how God's warnings correlate with his promises, for both his promises and his warnings are fundamentally oriented to the eschatological or last day, the day of salvation and judgment. This is why our discussion of that theme in chapter two is foundational to everything we will do in this chapter.

Another crucial aspect for properly embracing God's promises and warnings is a biblical understanding of faith. Thus, in chapter three we demonstrated from Scripture that all who confess the name of Jesus Christ are in the arena of faith running to win the prize, which is eternal life. We showed that the kind of belief the gospel requires is multifaceted in nature. This is why the Bible uses many images or metaphors to describe faith. Faith does not exist without altering behavior. Where faith is active, there is repentance, confession of sin, obedience, love, kindness, striving after holiness and a pursuit of eternal life as God's crowning gift.

As we have reflected on the Christian life as a race, we have considered both the prize of eternal life and how we must run to win that prize. Throughout chapter three we took notice of God's promises that assure the reward of eternal life to all who believe, for God is pleased with everyone who "believes that he exists and that he rewards those who seek him" (Heb 11:6). God promises to give salvation to all who believe and to them alone. Yet, at the same time, another observation emerges from the biblical text concerning Christian faith. Christian belief must be obedient in order for us to receive eternal life. If this conclusion is true, then it follows that we should expect the gospel to exhort and warn us in order that we might persevere in obedient faith. That is what we find throughout Scripture.

Now we turn our attention to examine the primary source of motivation to run to win the imperishable wreath. We devote this chapter to examine how biblical admonitions and warnings motivate Christians to persevere in belief. As we set out to do this, it is proper to acknowledge that we are taking up one of the most difficult tasks in reading the Scriptures. There seems to be a tension between biblical texts that warn and admonish us and texts that promise us great confidence and assurance of salvation. On the one hand we read the severe, perhaps frightening, warning of Hebrews 6:4-6: "For it is impossible for whoever were once enlightened, who have tasted the heavenly gift and have been granted to be partakers of the Holy Spirit and have tasted the good word of God and the powers of the coming age and who have fallen away, to be renewed unto repentance, because they crucify the Son of God again for themselves and they hold him in contempt." On the other hand, in the same chapter, we read words of strong encouragement to confident assurance: "We intently desire each of you to show the same diligence for full assurance of hope until the end, lest you become slothful, but be imitators of ones who inherit the promises through faithfulness and longsuffering" (Heb 6:11-12). And this "assurance of hope" that belongs to "the heirs of the promise" is based on nothing less than "the promise" and "the oath" of God, who cannot lie (Heb 6:17-20).

How should we understand the relationship between promise and assurance over against threat and warning? Do they contradict each other? One can readily recognize the apparent tension between promise and warning, but one may not as readily grasp the resolution. How should we understand this alleged tension? The Bible assures us that we who are heirs of the promise will surely receive what God has promised. Yet the Bible sternly admonishes us lest we fall short of the grace of God (Heb 12:15). What is the function of biblical admonitions and warnings? Should believers take seriously biblical cautions against apostasy and eternal destruction? If we should, how do we do this and, at the same time, retain assurance of salvation? Is assurance of faith possible for a believer? Do the Bible's warnings call on believers to doubt whether their faith is genuine? When Scripture sounds an alarm that persistence in sinful behavior will end in eternal death, is this alarm for us who believe, or is it for unbelievers? It is evident that how we understand the relationship between promise and warning has profound importance for Christians as well as immense pastoral implications.

Readers may want to refresh their minds concerning our overview of four popular explanations of the relationship between biblical warnings and promises in chapter one. What we do in this chapter interacts extensively with those four views. Against the backdrop of our survey of those four views, we will do two things in this chapter. First, as we seek to uncover the function of biblical warnings and admonitions, we will interact with several selected passages from the

New Testament. We have chosen these passages because they are crucial texts to which the four views appeal for support. Throughout our inductive consideration of these biblical warnings, we will also interact with each of the interpretive views, commenting on their strengths and weaknesses to explain the biblical texts. In order to present our understanding of the relationship between promise and warning, it is necessary to go fairly deeply into the biblical text with some detailed exegesis that may tax the reader's patience. We trust that patience will be rewarded. Second, after our inductive overview of biblical warnings, we will summarize our explanation of the apparent tension between admonition and assurance as we offer some counsel on how to make use of both promises and warnings without presuming upon God's promises or despairing because of the warnings.[1]

With that as a background, we turn our attention to examine the function of biblical warnings by considering several examples of admonitions. Our focus will be on the writers of the New Testament because they continue to use the same kind of grammatical structure as the Old Testament does when the prophets formulate God's covenant stipulations with conditional language. Therefore, our New Testament focus affirms continuity with the covenants of the Old Testament, for though the stipulations of the new covenant are different from God's former covenants, the way God expresses his stipulations remains the same with the ever-present conditional admonitions and warnings. This greater emphasis on the New Testament is for the obvious reason that it clearly announces the gospel by which we Christians come to faith in Jesus Christ and by which we persevere in that faith. As we take this inductive excursion through biblical passages that administer warnings, we will also engage each of the interpretive views we have already surveyed. We will evaluate their power to explain the biblical texts we examine. Also, it will become apparent that we cannot avoid foreshadowing other aspects of our beliefs concerning the relationship between promise and warning or admonition and assurance. We only trust that our readers find us fair and evenhanded as we endeavor to explain the Scriptures

---

[1] See also Thomas R. Schreiner, "Perseverance and Assurance: A Survey and a Proposal," *Southern Baptist Journal of Theology* 2 (1998): 32-62.

accurately. Furthermore, we will not pretend to be exhaustive, but we will address major biblical warnings over which Christians have long disagreed. Therefore, the biblical texts we have selected for consideration are passages in which the language of the warnings creates considerable tension with God's promises of assurance.

Admonition and Warning in Matthew 10 and Mark 13

In order to do justice to the Synoptic Gospels with regard to warnings and promises, much more space is needed than we can allot in this chapter. Thus we have chosen to concentrate our work on two crucial texts, Matthew 10 and Mark 13, as representative of the Synoptic Gospels.

"The one who perseveres to the end will be saved." Though these words appear in the familiar Olivet discourse of Matthew 24:13 or Mark 13:13, the text we will discuss is Matthew 10:22: "The one who perseveres to the end will be saved." Jesus spoke these words to his disciples when he sent them out to preach the advent of God's kingship. He extends this consolation and promise to them because he has just announced that they will face persecution and hatred on account of him and the gospel. Jesus formulates his promise as a proverb, which explains why these words adapt well to other settings, such as the Olivet discourse. The function of this verse is like the conditional promise of Revelation 21:6-7 that we considered in chapter one, for Jesus promises salvation, but he conditions the promised salvation on perseverance "to the end."

It is crucial for us to recognize that Jesus specifies three matters that make many evangelicals nervous. First, Jesus denotes a condition for salvation but does not use the word *faith*. He says that salvation will belong only to "the one who perseveres." This kind of talk worries many evangelicals because it sounds like salvation by works to them. Second, Jesus also formulates this conditional promise with a focus on "the end." This is instructive because many Christians have formulated salvation almost exclusively in terms of the beginning, namely, conversion in one's personal history, not in terms of consummation as in the text we are considering. Third, Jesus uses the future-tense verb—"will be saved"—in his conditional promise. For many evangelicals, salvation is punctiform. That is to say, they conceive of salvation as a point, not a continuum that includes beginning, process and consummation. Because many think of salvation as happening in a moment, we frequently hear Christians say, "Sanctification comes after salvation." This way of speaking of salvation betrays one's failure to grasp the already-but-not-yet accent of the New Testament. The evangelical lexicon employs the verb *save* almost exclusively in the past tense, such as, "Tell me how you got saved."[2] In Christian conversation, evangelicals have learned to reserve the future tense, "will be saved," to use with reference to the unsaved, such as, "Believe and you will be saved."

In chapter two we made the case that Christians tend to adjust the Bible's portrayal of salvation. Christians are inclined to overstate possession of salvation already and minimize, if not eliminate, the not-yet aspects. However, not all make the same adjustments. Consider how the various interpretations that we surveyed in chapter one understand Jesus' conditional promise to conform to their way of reading the Bible.

Those who hold the loss-of-rewards view of biblical warnings are fond of pointing out that it is naive to believe that every use of the verb *save (sōzō)* refers to salvation from sin and wrath. Thus, when they address these proverbial words of Jesus, they prefer to comment on Matthew 24:13 because there it is somewhat easier to make their case. Wilkin comments, "The context makes it clear that 'the end' of which Jesus was speaking was the end of the Tribulation, not the end of their lives. Verse 22 shows that the 'salvation' of verse 12 [sic] refers to surviving the Tribulation alive, not to deliverance from hell."[3] The reason Jesus' words have nothing to do with salvation is that this would make salvation based on works.

Admittedly, the New Testament does use the verb *save (sōzō)* with reference to earthly things, such as being saved from perishing at sea (Mt 8:25; 14:30; cf. Acts 27:44). Matthew uses *sōzō* three times for healing in the episode about the woman who hoped, "If only I touch his cloak, I will be healed" (Mt 9:21-22). Matthew's Gospel also uses *sōzō* four times in the crucifixion narrative, in the taunts of the jeering onlookers: " 'He saved others,' they said, 'but he can't save himself!'"

---

[2]We showed in chapter two that when the New Testament uses the verb *save (sōzō)* and the noun *salvation (sōtēria sōtērion)* with reference to deliverance from sin and wrath, it is predominantly future oriented.

[3]Robert N. Wilkin, *Confident in Christ: Living by Faith Really Works* (Irving, Tex.: Grace Evangelical Society, 1999), p. 266 n. 5.

(Mt 27:42).[4] However, one must ask why Matthew uses *sōzō* to denote healing, particularly when he could and does use other words that expressly denote healing, such as *therapeuō* (Mt 8:7; 10:1, 8; 12:10) or *iaomai* (Mt 8:8, 13; 15:28). Until one comes to recognize that, for biblical writers, earthly things are copies and shadows of heavenly realities, as we discussed in chapter three, one will fail to understand the relationship between the woman's being healed and being saved. Just as her prolonged physical malady is a portrait of the ravages of sin that lead to eternal death, so her miraculous healing is an earthly representation of deliverance from the clutches of sin and of death. So, when Matthew uses *sōzō* in the place of verbs for healing, he does so to help his readers recognize that Jesus' act to save a woman from physical illness points, as a sign, to his power to save his people from their sins (Mt 1:21). In any case, the context of Matthew 10 ensures that salvation from sin is intended; the threat of eternal destruction in Matthew 10:28 demonstrates that Jesus refers to eschatological salvation. The same is true of the use of "will be saved" in Matthew 24:13, despite objections to the contrary. For, as Marshall observes, "a physical sense would give a tautology: he who endures to the end shall not die before the end."[5]

Not only does Marshall properly acknowledge that Jesus' proverbial words concern eschatological salvation, but he also correctly observes the conditional nature of the promise. He states, "The condition for salvation is that 'steadfast endurance' which does not give way under temptation but remains loyal to God and His will. This is accented by the phrase 'to the end.' "[6] Again, Marshall is correct to note, "There will be no salvation for the person who gives up."[7] However, Marshall takes both a giant leap and a false step when he says, "Although this possibility is a slight one on the whole, nevertheless it is a real possibility, and we have no right to deny its existence in the interests of a preconceived

---

[4]Note the irony. In their derision, Jesus' antagonists ironically identify him correctly as "King of the Jews!" Likewise, his enemies sarcastically express a profound truth, "He saved others, but he can't save himself!" (Mt 27:42). Little did they realize that if he had saved himself he could not save others.

[5]I. Howard Marshall, *Kept by the Power of God: A Study of Perseverance and Falling Away* (1969; reprint, Minneapolis: Bethany Fellowship, 1974), p. 74. He actually comments on Mk 13:13.

[6]Ibid. Marshall explains the "to the end" saying, "It probably indicates not so much endurance to the very end of the period of tribulation but rather endurance to the very limit, even to the point of death" (p. 74).

[7]Ibid., p. 75.

theory."[8] Without any explanation, Marshall converts Jesus' conditional promise of salvation into a declarative announcement of possible apostasy. Marshall has inverted the function of the words Jesus designs to console his followers who face persecution and death on his behalf. His inversion turns them into words that express uncertainty and doubt about the outcome. We believe that this is an unwarranted conclusion from the text, for suppositions in themselves do not function to indicate anything about possibility.[9] We also believe that such a reading of conditional promises is subversive to Christian faith and confidence, not affirmative or consoling, as Jesus intended his words.

Many who hold a Reformed understanding of salvation are nervous about works-righteousness concerning texts on perseverance. They are also anxious about conceiving of salvation with a reference point

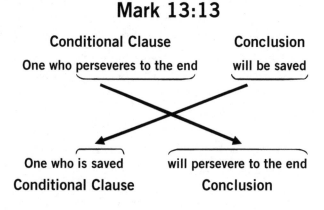

Mark 13:13

Conditional Clause	Conclusion
One who perseveres to the end	will be saved

One who is saved	will persevere to the end
Conditional Clause	Conclusion

Figure 4.1. Reformed conversion of perseverance

[8]Ibid.

[9]The supposition of Mt 10:22 uses the substantival participle *ho hypomeinas* in a conditional relationship to the verb. For the category see the discussion by Daniel B. Wallace, *Greek Grammar Beyond the Basics* (Grand Rapids, Mich.: Zondervan, 1996), p. 688.

other than the beginning of faith. Furthermore, they believe that certainty of salvation is bound up with conceiving of salvation almost exclusively in retrospective terms that focus on justification. They focus on the already aspects of salvation to the neglect of the not-yet aspects. Conceptually they transpose Jesus' conditional promise by inverting the two clauses, as illustrated in figure 4.1.

The result is that they convert the consequence of perseverance (salvation not yet attained) into the cause of perseverance (salvation already possessed). With this conceptual reorientation, one comments: "Jesus, speaking to His disciples, said, 'It is the one who has endured to the end who will be saved' (Matt. 10:22; cf. 24:13). Now at first glance that appears to contradict the truth that God is going to keep us saved, but it doesn't. We are energized to endure by the indwelling Spirit. The mark of justification is perseverance in righteousness to the very end."[10] This is a remarkable comment, characteristic of many Calvinists, for without realization or intention, anyone who explains the text this way inverts the two elements of the conditional promise. This explanation essentially reads the text as saying, "The one who is saved will persevere unto the end." This is both biblically and theologically accurate, but the text we are examining does not say that. It is a case of good theology but from the wrong verse. Rather, the text says, "The one who perseveres to the end will be saved."

Jesus' words indicate that perseverance to the end is the necessary condition. Perseverance is a means that God has appointed by which one will be saved.[11] To invert the clauses is to turn perseverance into proof or evidence that one is saved, which other biblical texts do indicate.[12] However, this interpretation turns inside out the

---

[10] John F. MacArthur Jr., *Saved Without a Doubt* (Wheaton, Ill.: Victor, 1992), p. 149. Cf. Millard J. Erickson, *Christian Theology*, 2nd ed. (Grand Rapids, Mich.: Baker, 1998), p. 996. Erickson states, "In speaking of eschatological matters, Jesus indicated that endurance is the distinguishing mark of the true believer" and quotes Matthew 24:12-13 (with Mt 10:22 and Mk 13:13) to establish his case.

[11] At times we will use the words *condition* and *means* interchangeably. When we use the word *means*, we use it in the sense that perseverance is a necessary means that God has appointed for attaining final salvation. See *Merriam-Webster's Collegiate Dictionary*, 10th ed. (Springfield, Mass.: Merriam-Webster, 1993), p. 720.

[12] We agree with Calvinists that perseverance in faith is evidence that one possesses salvation and new birth. However, the text under consideration, Matthew 10:22, does not affirm this truth. Other biblical passages, such as 1 John 2:29, make it clear that perseverance is proof that one is born of God: "If you know that he is righteous, you also know that everyone who practices righteousness has been born of him."

orientation of Jesus' words in Matthew 10:22.

So what is Jesus saying? He is saying that perseverance to the end is God's means by which anyone will be saved.[13] At the same time his words assure all who persevere and remind us that there is no other way to face persecution, even unto death, if we want to be saved in the final day. It is really this simple! But you ask, "What if I fail to persevere to the end?" The answer from the context is simply that you will not be saved, if you fail to persevere to the end. Again you may ask, "So, are you telling me that Jesus' words mean that it is possible for me to lose my salvation?" No, that is an unwarranted conclusion to draw either from the text or from our explanation of the text. Jesus' words say nothing about the possibility of losing one's salvation; that is not the function of his conditional promise. Rather, his words function to assure you that you will be saved, if you persevere. You must persevere if you want to be saved. You ask once more, "So are you saying that if I do not persevere to the end, that will prove that I was never truly saved in the beginning?" Though the theological answer is "Yes," it inverts Jesus' words. Here, Jesus does not give us a test of perseverance by which we may know whether or not we are saved. Notice his orientation. He is prospective, not retrospective. He uses the future tense, for he says "will be saved." It is true that the Bible does teach that all who are justified will persevere and be glorified (Rom 8:30), but this is not what Jesus is saying in Matthew 10:22. Also, it is true that the Bible teaches that people who failed to persevere by remaining in the church proved by their departure that they never were truly Christians (1 Jn 2:19). However, that also is not what Jesus is saying in this text. Jesus' words fit a different category of passages; his words express a promise that includes a condition. The promise of salvation is for everyone who perseveres.

When Jesus calls on us to "persevere to the end," he is calling us to

---

[13]William Cunningham summarizes well the explanation we develop concerning biblical warnings: "their proper primary effect evidently being just to bring out, in the most impressive way, the great principle of the invariableness of the connection which God has established between perseverance, as opposed to apostasy, as a means, and salvation as an end; and thus to operate as a means of effecting the end which God has determined to accomplish,—of enabling believers to persevere, or preserving them from apostasy; and to effect this in entire accordance with the principles of their moral constitution, by producing constant humility, watchfulness, and diligence" (*Historical Theology*, [1862; reprint, London: Banner of Truth Trust, 1969], 2:500-501).

persistent belief, for his words in Matthew 10:22 function as a corollary to the initial call of the gospel, just as we saw concerning Revelation 21:6-7 in chapter one. His conditional promise does not confound the gospel by adding another condition for salvation, as if belief were insufficient. Rather, his conditional promise explains and amplifies the gospel's call for belief by making the point that no one who will be saved in the end can ignore the requirement of persistent faith and devotion to Jesus Christ. To make this point, Jesus does two things in Matthew 10:22. First, he uses a metaphor to depict the kind of faith he requires of us. It is belief that does not quit when it encounters the pain of persecution or stares death in the face on account of Christ. Second, Jesus focuses his conditional promise on the end of faith's race, not the beginning. Jesus underscores this later in the text when he complements the conditional promise with a warning.

"Whoever disowns me before men, I will disown him." Jesus follows his conditional promise with an admonition to fear God, not humans, for the most their persecution can do is kill the body, but God can "destroy both soul and body in hell" (Mt 10:28 NIV). Therefore, Jesus admonishes us to fear God, whose providential care for his own exceeds his attentive purpose for the insignificant sparrow that falls in the woods or a strand of hair on one's head (Mt 10:29-30). His admonition to fear God establishes the basis for his following warning. So from consolation and assurance in the conditional promise and admonition to fear God, Jesus shifts his tone to urgency and cautionary threat. Continuing to warn the Twelve about the hostility they will face in the mission of the king, Jesus admonishes them, "Whoever acknowledges me before men, I will also acknowledge him before my Father in heaven. But whoever disowns me before men, I will disown him before my Father in heaven" (Mt 10:32-33 NIV). His warning complements his earlier conditional promise and admonition (Mt 10:22), for he reinforces the urgency and necessity of perseverance in order to receive eschatological salvation. His warning also explains his conditional promise by unpacking what he means both by "persevere to the end" and by "will be saved."[14] According to Jesus' warning, to persevere is to acknowledge Christ and not disown him.

---

[14]In the warning, two relative pronoun clauses ("whoever . . .") function as conditional clauses, whereas in the conditional promise a substantival participle functions conditionally.

The phrase "will be saved" means that "before [the] Father in heaven" Jesus will "acknowledge" all who persevere to the end. This speaks of eschatological salvation in the day of judgment, when the end has come. Jesus expands on his conditional promise as he urgently calls for perseverance under persecution by using two suppositional clauses: (1) "whoever acknowledges me before men" and (2) "whoever disowns me before men." The warning, therefore, serves Jesus' conditional promise by reinforcing the necessity of perseverance, but it does this by reasserting the conditional promise with synonyms and then stating the inverse of it.

As with the conditional promise, the temptation for Christians is to interpret the warning from a framework of an overrealized view of salvation that severs the biblical connection between the already and the not yet—the linkage between persevering and being saved in the end. The result is that warnings lose their prospective orientation and function, taking on both a retrospective focus and introspective function as tests that expose impostors, people who are not true believers. Thus, to explain what Jesus means by his reference to those who disown him, one writer says, "Here our Lord is talking specifically about false disciples, people who claim to be Christians but are not."[15] Without realizing it, this author transposes Jesus' warning from a prospective incentive for perseverance to the end into a retrospective test that exposes pseudodisciples by their past behavior. How does this transposition occur? It begins with conceptual discomfort because conditional warnings and admonitions suspend God's judgment in the last day on perseverance in this age. Then one logically slides the conditionally expressed verdict of the final day (to be disowned by Christ) forward, into the present. This conceptually nullifies Jesus' suppositional warning, for now one thinks of the verdict as if it were already disclosed. Thus, the not-yet verdict in Jesus' warning has become a verdict already determined in one's mind.

Partly owing, perhaps, to a penchant for conceptual ease, partly to linguistic unguardedness and largely to habits of the way we tend to think, Christians adjust biblical warnings and conditional promises to conform to their theological commitments. When Christians do this,

---

[15]John F. MacArthur Jr., *The Gospel According to Jesus* (Grand Rapids, Mich.: Zondervan, 1988), p. 200.

it is doubtful that they intend to do any damage to the gospel of Jesus Christ, for they may not be aware that they modify the function of these passages. Were they to realize this, surely they would make the necessary adjustments. It is our objective to help others recognize the need to make some crucial adjustments.

"Whoever loses his life for my sake will find it." One more segment of Matthew 10 begs for attention, for Jesus is not yet finished with his instructions to the twelve disciples in preparing them for their mission. Jesus tells them plainly, "Do not think that I have come to bring peace to the earth; I have not come to bring peace, but a sword. For I have come to set a man against his father, and a daughter against her mother, and a daughter-in-law against her mother-in-law; and one's foes will be members of one's own household" (Mt 10:34-36 NRSV).[16] Here Jesus reiterates his earlier prophecy that his gospel will provoke family strife (cf. Mt 10:21). Just as prediction of betrayal of one's family members introduces his conditional promise of perseverance in order to be saved, so he prefaces his call to bear a cross by speaking of family hostility. Jesus emphasizes that because "one's foes will be members of one's own household," this calls for persevering loyalty to him. So Jesus appeals to us to endure faithfully by saying, "Whoever loves father or mother more than me is not worthy of me; and whoever loves son or daughter more than me is not worthy of me; and whoever does not take up the cross and follow me is not worthy of me. Those who find their life will lose it, and those who lose their life for my sake will find it" (Mt 10:37-39 NRSV). As he does in 10:32-33, Matthew records Jesus' call for disciples by using relative-pronoun clauses.

Christians are prone to commit one of three interpretive errors concerning this passage. The first error is to think that Jesus speaks of merit. Zane Hodges, representative of the loss-of-rewards view of warnings, insists that it is imperative to distinguish Jesus' requirements for discipleship and the gospel's offer of eternal life.[17] Unfortu-

---

[16] Jesus' quotation from Micah 7:6 stands in stark contrast to Luke's use of Malachi 4:5-6 in connection with John the Baptist (Lk 1:16-17).

[17] Hodges, *Absolutely Free! A Biblical Reply to Lordship Salvation* (Grand Rapids, Mich.: Zondervan, 1989), pp. 67-88. Elsewhere he states his concern: "It is an interpretive mistake of the first magnitude to confuse the terms of discipleship with the offer of eternal life as a free gift" (*The Gospel Under Siege: A Study on Faith and Works,* 2nd ed. [Dallas: Rendención Viva, 1991], p. 41).

nately Hodges imputes the notion of merit or "earning power" to Jesus' call to be his disciple, a call that includes conditions or demands.[18]

The second mistake is to turn Jesus' call for disciples into a big stick that drives people away from Christ. John MacArthur asks, "Why is this language so severe? Why does Christ use such offensive terms? Because He is eager to chase the uncommitted away and to draw true disciples to Himself. He does not want half-hearted people deceived into thinking they are in the kingdom."[19] While Hodges adopts an extreme reading of the text, MacArthur overstates Jesus' call for disciples. Precisely because Jesus formulates his words as a condition that projects one toward the future, they function as an incentive for loyalty, not an indictment that banishes.

The third mistake that some commit is to find in Jesus' words a suggestion that it is possible for a genuine disciple to turn away from Christ and to love one's family members more and consequently to lose one's life and perish eternally. They think that they find this in Matthew 10:39: "Whoever finds his life will lose it, and whoever loses his life for my sake will find it" (NIV). However, this interpretation shifts the function of the conditional admonition from incentive for faithfulness and confidence to inducement of doubtfulness and uncertainty. Furthermore, it transforms Jesus' invitation to trust in the God who promises into words that incite preoccupation with self and with one's own passions and weaknesses.

What, then, is Jesus saying in Matthew 10:37-39? Three features deserve brief comment. First, when Jesus says, "Whoever loves father . . . more than me is not worthy of me" (Mt 10:37 NRSV), he restates his words of Matthew 10:32-33. To love family more than Christ is "to disown me before men." To be "not worthy of me" is to be disowned before the heavenly Father.

Second, Jesus explains his call for loyalty by drawing on the image of a death march on the way to the place of crucifixion, under the weight of one's own cross beam. He frames his call as a warning:

---

[18]Ironically, while Hodges and his associates with the Grace Evangelical Society argue that their view is the only one that avoids a system of works-righteousness, they introduce "merit theology" into the Christian life. Cf. Michael Horton, "Don't Judge a Book by Its Cover," in *Christ the Lord: The Reformation and Lordship Salvation*, ed. Michael Horton (Grand Rapids, Mich.: Baker, 1992), p. 33.

[19]MacArthur, *Gospel According to Jesus*, p. 201.

"Whoever does not take up the cross and follow me is not worthy of me" (Mt 10:38 NRSV). Jesus' followers must voluntarily pick up the instrument of death as they follow their Lord, who also marches on to his death. Clearly, mention of the cross foreshadows how Jesus will die, and no disciple is above one's master (Mt 10:24).

Third, by way of a riddle Jesus restates his call to bear one's cross: "Whoever finds one's life will lose it, and whoever loses one's life for my sake will find it" (Mt 10:39). To decipher this riddle we need to determine what is meant by "one's life." Matthew's phrase seems to substitute for the pronoun *oneself,* for Matthew records Jesus' riddle again (Mt 16:25), and Luke's parallel account uses *oneself* in place of Matthew's less clear expression, "one's life" (cf. Lk 9:24). The sense of Matthew's phrase, however, seems to denote respectively the earthly and then the heavenly as two contrasting domains of existence. Whoever preserves the earthly life by refusing to bear one's cross for Christ forfeits the heavenly life. Alternatively, whoever picks up one's cross and gives up the earthly life for Christ will gain the heavenly life.

"False messiahs and false prophets will arise. . . . Be alert!" Now we turn our attention to Mark 13 for two reasons. First, there is a heavy concentration of warnings in this chapter. Second, Mark 13:22-23 holds together two distinct expressions from Jesus, a strong word of consolation followed by a sharp admonition.

Mark 13 records the longest uninterrupted discourse from Jesus in this Gospel. The discourse sometimes bears the designation the "Little Apocalypse" or the "Olivet discourse" because Jesus delivers it on the Mount of Olives. It occupies a significant place in Mark's Gospel because it bridges Jesus' public ministry, which has come to an end (Mk 1:14—12:44), and the Passion narrative, where conflict with the religious authorities is the occasion of Jesus' condemnation and death, reversed by his resurrection (Mk 14:1—16:8).

In Mark's Gospel this discourse functions as Jesus' farewell address. Here he provides instruction and comfort for his disciples prior to his arrest and crucifixion. The purpose of this discourse is not to offer details about the future but to provide assurance of Christ's eschatological conquest and to give incentive for faithfulness to the end. This is apparent from Jesus' numerous admonitions to "Watch!"

(Mk 13:5, 9, 23, 33, 35, 37). In other words, Jesus' Olivet discourse does not encourage calculation but vigilance.

As they pass by the temple, the disciples comment on the massive stones and buildings that make up the temple complex. This prompts Jesus to say, "Do you see these great buildings? Not one stone will be left here upon another; all will be thrown down" (Mk 13:2 NRSV). When they reach the Mount of Olives, four of the disciples ask Jesus, "Tell us, when will this be, and what will be the sign that all these things are about to be accomplished?" (Mk 13:4 NRSV). Jesus' response comes in two large segments (Mk 13:5-23, 24-37). Jesus brackets his first segment with warnings against being deceived by false messiahs (Mk 13:5-6, 21-23). We will focus on the latter of these two warnings.

Jesus tells his disciples of intense afflictions that will occur in the future, afflictions so terrible that nothing previous will compare (Mk 13:19). Thus, he repeatedly warns his disciples to watchfulness lest they yield to the temptation to forsake him for another one who will call himself "the Christ." Their salvation is at stake, for Jesus says, "But the one who endures to the end will be saved" (Mk 13:13 NRSV).[20] For the sake of the ones he has chosen to receive salvation, Jesus says, those days of affliction will be shortened, otherwise no one would be saved (Mark 13:20).[21] Then Jesus mingles assuring promise and warning admonition in Mark 13:21-23. He says to his disciples, "If anyone says to you at that time, 'Look! Here is the Messiah!' or 'Look! There he is!'—do not believe it. False messiahs and false prophets will appear and produce signs and omens, to lead astray, if possible, the elect. But be alert; I have already told you everything" (NRSV).

Jesus plainly says that false christs and false prophets will use signs and wonders in their attempt to seduce God's chosen ones to follow after them. To be seduced, of course, is hardly inconsequential, for to yield to their claims would be to forsake Jesus Christ and to perish eternally. No one who believes in Jesus Christ can divide loyalty to him with another christ. But Mark offers consolation and assurance to believers by noting carefully that Jesus says that these seducers

---

[20]See our earlier discussion of Matthew 10:22.
[21]For our discussion of divine election, see chapter eight.

will attempt "to lead astray, if possible, the elect" (Mk 13:23). At this point the temptation is to modify either Jesus' warning with his words of assuring promise or his consoling promise with his stern warning against being deceived. Mark, however, expects his readers to receive both the warning and the promise without modifying either. Jesus reminds us of the nature of our pilgrimage in this present age. Jesus holds before us both his assuring promise to preserve the elect and his warning admonition that calls for vigilant perseverance in order to be saved. Is there an unbearable tension between them? What is the relationship between the two? Does election swallow up warning? Or does warning devour election?

It is precisely at this point that many slip to one side or the other. I. Howard Marshall opts for the latter as he claims, "for the Church as the heir of Israel's election, her election is conditional upon her desire to retain it."[22] For Marshall, God's election of us is only as sure as our vigilance. Others want to adjust the warning by smothering it with election so that they transmute the warning into either a test of genuine faith or simply a warning for hypocrites. Neither view does justice to the biblical text, because Mark intends both warning and promise to retain their full functions for believers. What is the relationship, therefore? Election is not conditioned upon perseverance, nor does election nullify the necessity of perseverance. Rather, Jesus fully intends for us to understand that God, who elected his own for salvation, secures them from apostasy and preserves them through afflictions by use of warnings that caution watchfulness, wariness and vigilant steadfastness.

Jesus uses two suppositional clauses when he speaks of the elect. First, he indicates that not even the elect would be saved through the afflictions of those days if the Lord did not abbreviate the time for endurance (Mk 13:20). A fair reading of this verse acknowledges that Jesus affirms that his chosen ones will be saved from yielding to false christs, but not without emphasizing that apart from God's favor, apostasy would eventuate. Second, Jesus says that the false Christs and false prophets will exploit signs and wonders in their effort "to lead astray, if possible, the elect" (Mk 13:22 NRSV). One could retrans-

---

[22]Marshall, *Kept by the Power of God,* p. 71. He cites H. H. Rowley for support. Cf. Morna Hooker, *The Gospel According to St. Mark,* Black's New Testament Commentaries (Peabody, Mass.: Hendrickson, 1991), p. 317.

late the words, "to lead astray even the elect, supposing it to be possible." The point Jesus makes is that the pseudo-Christs and pseudo-prophets will make a valiant and powerful attempt to seduce the elect, because they suppose it to be possible. Therefore, so far from suggesting possible apostasy of God's elect, Mark 13:22 actually affirms the opposite, but only by emphasizing that the elect will undergo severe efforts to lead them astray.

Both Jesus and Mark assume complete compatibility between assurance and urgent warning against apostasy. There is no unbearable tension between the two. For anyone who believes these two are incompatible, Mark 13:23 increases the tension for two reasons. First, upon administering his words of consolation and assurance, Jesus immediately returns to a warning, "You, be alert!" Second, Jesus grounds his warning to the disciples on the fact that he has told them everything before it comes to pass. The fact that Jesus gives his disciples prior knowledge of both the promise and warning by telling them everything in advance only multiplies the sense of tension between promise and warning. So before the time of affliction arrives, Jesus both assures and warns his disciples. Does Jesus warn despite his promise to the elect? Does Jesus give his promise of assured salvation so that his elect will not be annoyed by his repeated and strong warnings? No, Jesus warns his own disciples precisely because he assures them that God will save his chosen ones through the coming intense affliction. Why? It is because his warnings function as the means God uses to secure the salvation that he promises them with the assurance that God will surely save his chosen ones.

Admonition and Warning in Paul's Letters

Although we have already shown in chapter two how New Testament writers have a dual orientation in their concept of salvation, including both already and not yet, it may be helpful to summarize briefly Paul's perspective. We do so primarily because, since the Reformation, many Protestant Christians have tended to overstate Paul's doctrine of justification, so that it swallows up all other metaphors for salvation. The consequence has been to exaggerate salvation's already aspects with the effect that Paul's orientation on salvation as not yet fully realized has virtually collapsed into an overrealized view that the whole of salvation is already fully ours.

Always orienting his view of salvation eschatologically, that is, toward the last day, Paul announces in his gospel that God has revealed his righteous judgment in the present time (Rom 3:21-26). God has already begun his good work in us (Phil 1:6) by calling us to believe "in him who raised Jesus our Lord from the dead" (Rom 4:24). God has brought the verdict of the day of judgment forward, into the midst of redemptive history, for God has graciously revealed his righteousness through the gospel (Rom 1:17), which announces that God's obedient son, Jesus Christ (Rom 5:19), has already appeared in the flesh (Rom 1:3-4) and has already borne God's wrath for us by becoming a sin offering on our behalf (Rom 8:3). Because God condemned his own Son in our place, he has already rendered his judgment, vindicating his own righteousness, so that he now justifies all who embrace Jesus Christ (Rom 3:26). Thus, God already gives the eschatological gift of righteousness in advance of the day of judgment (Rom 5:17). Therefore, as far as the believer is concerned, the verdict of God's judgment is already in, though the day of judgment has not yet arrived. The verdict is acquittal (Rom 5:1; 8:1). This verdict is irrevocable for all whom God has called to believe (Rom 8:30), for because Christ Jesus died and was raised and now intercedes for us, God's verdict is final; God will not hear any further charges against his chosen ones, for his verdict stands (Rom 8:34).

True as it is that Paul's gospel announces that God's judgment is already rendered in Christ at the cross, the apostle never relinquishes the Old Testament eschatological orientation toward the coming day of judgment, for God's Son has come and will appear again to call everyone to judgment (Acts 17:31). For Paul, justification remains fundamentally the eschatological verdict of acquittal. For although God has already revealed his righteousness by subjecting his own Son to his wrath (Rom 3:25), God discloses his final justice at the present time only in the gospel that explains what God did in Jesus Christ on that dark and dreadful day of his death to save sinners. Further, although God presently reveals his wrath against human unrighteousness "from heaven" (Rom 1:18), that is, from a distance and not as he will in the last day, he restrains his wrath in the present time as he patiently abides those who spurn his kindness. Those who snub God's kindness accumulate wrath against themselves in preparation for the day of God's wrath, when he will reveal his righteous judgment (Rom

2:5; cf. 12:14-21) and will execute judgment in keeping with the secrets now concealed in human hearts (Rom 2:16).

We who believe in Jesus Christ receive God's righteous verdict of forgiveness before the day of judgment arrives, but not publicly, as we will on the day of judgment, when God's justice and wrath will come upon all who disobey the gospel and will also give us relief from our present afflictions (2 Thess 1:5-10). Though it is true that God has summoned us all to give account of ourselves (Rom 14:12), the day of judgment, when the eternal Judge will announce his verdict in keeping with our deeds, has not yet arrived. Until that day, we now stand justified in God's courtroom by faith only. By his Spirit, whom he gives to all who believe, already God secretly speaks acquittal, life, peace, reconciliation and adoption (Rom 5:1-11; 8:1-17). Therefore, Paul admonishes us who believe to fasten our gaze on the day of judgment in hope that we shall receive the promised salvation (Rom 2:6-10; 8:23-25; 13:11-14). For the day of judgment is the day of salvation for all who believe. It is the day of redemption (Rom 8:23; Eph 1:14; 4:30). It is when our adoption as God's children will be complete (Rom 8:23). It is the point of entrance into eternal life (Rom 2:7; 6:22; Gal 6:8). It is the day of salvation that has drawn closer than when we initially believed (Rom 13:11), the day when salvation will be ours (Phil 2:12; 1 Thess 5:8-9) and when God will reveal our justification, which we now have secretly by faith, as he crowns us with justification, openly and publicly (2 Tim 4:8). For although we have already received God's justifying verdict by faith, by faith we yet await through the Spirit the hope of receiving this same verdict in that day (Gal 5:5).[23]

As we proceed with our discussion of Paul's doctrine of salvation and propose our own explanation of his theology of perseverance, we will interact with three viewpoints that differ with our understanding of the apostle's teaching. In particular, each of these three perspectives raises objections that we must address. Furthermore, we will show that each of these viewpoints tends to interpret all of Paul's warnings through a biased reading of their selected texts.

I. Howard Marshall, an advocate of the loss-of-salvation view, suc-

---

[23]For a succinct and corroborating summary of the already-but-not-yet tension in Paul's metaphors for salvation, see James D. G. Dunn, *The Theology of Paul the Apostle* (Grand Rapids, Mich.: Eerdmans, 1998), pp. 466-72.

cinctly frames a question all must answer: "Does the verdict that we have been justified by grace through faith mean that we are certain to be justified on the day of judgment or must there remain an element of doubt until the final sentence of acquittal or of guilt is passed?"[24] In response to his own question, Marshall concludes that "the need for exhortation shows that there is a possibility of failure to work out salvation."[25] He fails to recognize the proper origin of exhortation. Consequently, he believes admonition has a negative function: to imply possible failure of faith. However, exhortation is not grounded in our extensive weakness and fragility as sinful creatures. Exhortation derives from God's power, which he displays in the gospel that calls for sinful humans to believe the good news (Rom 1:16). God designed the exhortations of his gospel to secure the obedience of faith, not to imply possible failure of faith. Exhortation is inherent to God's good news. Admonition is necessary, for the gospel is the message by which God calls us to himself, giving us faith and sustaining us until we draw our last breath. The gospel exhorts us all along the way on the basis of its announcement of God's redemption in Christ.

Nevertheless, the question Marshall raises continues to dominate most theological discussions concerning the place of warnings and admonitions in a biblical doctrine concerning perseverance. Its dominance is largely due to two assumptions on the part of many evangelicals. Generally evangelical theologians have assumed that the question Arminians pose is primary and also that conditionally expressed admonitions and warnings may imply uncertainty. Attempts to answer the Arminians' question yield both the loss-of-rewards and the tests-of-genuineness views. Each view locates its own text in Paul's letters that serves as the key by which it explains the place of warning in his theology. The loss-of-rewards view uses its own reading of 1 Corinthians 3:5-17 as the interpretive lens to explain Paul's admonitions and warnings. As a result, warnings and admonitions are truly prospective, but they only warn against loss of rewards, not the loss of salvation.[26] The tests-of-genuineness

---

[24]Marshall, *Kept by the Power of God*, p. 100. This is similar to one of the questions the disciples of Jacobus Arminius raised in their Remonstrance of 1610 against the Reformed ministers in Holland.

[25]Ibid., p. 125.

[26]See, e.g., the notes in *The New Scofield Reference Bible* (New York: Oxford University Press, 1967), p. 1, 235.

approach lays Paul's exhortation from 2 Corinthians 13:5—"examine yourselves to see if you are in the faith"—as an interpretive grid over his warnings and exhortations, so that all of them function as tests calling for self-examination. Warnings, therefore, turn us around to examine both our past walk and our heart's motives.[27]

Though we believe that Marshall's question is legitimate and demands a response, it is not the first question that we need to answer with regard to Paul's admonitions and warnings, as we stated in chapter one. We will not answer this question fully within our discussion of Paul's teachings. We will, however, answer the question as much as it concerns the many admonitions and warnings that Paul administers to the churches, but only after we address the first question that should dominate our focus. The first question concerns the function of Paul's warnings and admonitions.[28]

Romans 2. In chapter three we noticed that Paul closely associates faith and obedience when he brackets the letter to the Romans with his expression "obedience of faith" to denote his goal in preaching the gospel (Rom 1:5; 16:26). In our earlier discussion it became apparent that Paul's phrase is best understood to speak of "obeying the gospel, which is stated more plainly, faith." This is so because the apostle interchanges the verb *obey* for *believe* (Rom 6:17; cf. 10:16), for faith expresses itself in obedience. It is understandable, therefore, to find Paul unpacking his gospel in the letter to the Romans with much to say about perseverance in obedience.

Paul's gospel proclaims both the necessity and the assurance of perseverance for all who believe. He announces the necessity of perseverance by using conditional promises (Rom 2:5-10) as well as conditional warnings and admonitions (e.g., Rom 8:12-17; 11:19-24). On the other hand, Paul's extended affirmation of assured perseverance, grounded on God's unconditional love, perhaps is the strongest expression of Christian assurance in the New Testament (Rom 8:29-39). Therefore, like the other biblical writers we have considered thus far, Paul also juxtaposes warning and promise or admonition and assurance.

---

[27]See, e.g., John F. MacArthur Jr., *Faith Works: The Gospel According to the Apostles* (Dallas: Word, 1993), pp. 141, 162, 166.

[28]Space constrains us, so we restrict our discussion to four of Paul's letters: Romans, 1 Corinthians, Philippians and Colossians. We are convinced that the passages we do address are the ones we must address. Our desire is to assist readers to draw inductive conclusions from the exegetical evidence we present.

With this background in mind, we begin with Paul's conditional promises in Romans 2:7-10 and 13. Paul solemnly avows that when God judges, he will reward everyone according to his or her deeds.

> To those who by persevering in a good work seek glory and honor and incorruptibility, he will give eternal life. But upon those who act out of selfish ambition and who disobey the truth and instead submit to unrighteousness, he will inflict wrath and anger. There will be tribulation and distress for every person who does what is evil, both the Jew first and also the Greek, but there will be glory and honor and peace to everyone who accomplishes what is good, both to the Jew first and also to the Greek. For there is no partiality with God. (Rom 2:7-11)

Using two sets of designations—"eternal life" and "glory and honor and peace"—Paul affirms twice in this passage that God will reward perseverance in good deeds with "salvation." This causes no small dilemma for interpreters who want to avoid the notion that the apostle contradicts his own clear statement that "no flesh will be justified by the works of the law" (Rom 3:20).[29] However, the dilemma is in the eye of the reader, for Paul plainly affirms that the principle of God's impartial judgment is integral to his gospel, for he speaks of "the day when, according to my gospel, God shall judge the secrets of humans through Christ Jesus" (Rom 2:16). So judgment according to one's deeds is not alien to Paul's gospel but an essential element of it. Paul echoes the principle of Ezekiel 18, for both the apostle and the prophet insist that God is an impartial judge who will render his judgment in keeping with one's deeds. Paul confronts the same problem Ezekiel faced: Israelites who possess the law but fail to obey it. This is what Paul denounces in Romans 2. But in the midst of his prosecution of disobedient possessors of the law, he reaffirms God's thoroughly impartial principle of justice that holds out hope for all who do the things the law requires, because "not the hearers of the law are righteous before God, but the doers of the law shall be declared righteous" (Rom 2:13).

This is not a fictional offer that no one attains, nor is this salvation

---

[29]See Thomas R. Schreiner, "Did Paul Believe in Justification by Works? Another Look at Romans 2," *Bulletin for Biblical Research* 3 (1993): 131-39, for a survey of interpretive views that have arisen in efforts to deliver Paul from alleged self-contradiction. For an opposing view to ours that has long been held by both Reformed and Lutheran commentators see Douglas Moo, *Romans 1–8*, Wycliffe Exegetical Commentary (Chicago: Moody Press, 1991), p. 142.

based on one's own works. Though it is true that he speaks of judgment and justification, here Paul is not speaking of the legal basis or ground of justification, for that basis is the obedience of Christ alone (Rom 5:12-19). Rather, he speaks of the kind of person whom God will justify in the day of judgment. It is the obedient, not the disobedient, person. It is the doer of the law, not the possessor of the law. Who are these "doers of the law"? At the close of chapter 2 Paul explains their identity. They are people who, though they may not even have the law, do the things the law requires. They are ones who, though perhaps not circumcised in the flesh, have hearts circumcised by the Spirit of God. Therefore, Paul succinctly summarizes his argument of Romans 2 by reiterating the principle of his gospel that the true Jew is not one who possesses the law and who is circumcised in the flesh; the true Jew is one who keeps the requirements of the law from a heart circumcised by the Spirit. This person will receive praise from God, which is another way of saying "will be justified" (Rom 2:13) or "will be reckoned as circumcision" (Rom 2:26).[30]

Therefore, since Paul indicts unfaithful Israelites for failing to keep the law, which they possess by privilege from God, and since Paul orients his discussion to the eschatological day of judgment, his primary concern is to answer one question: Who will be justified? Like the prophet in Ezekiel 18:21-23, the apostle Paul answers that the one who will be justified in the heavenly courtroom of God is the person who does what God requires. The promise of eternal life is conditional, but the condition must not be confused with the basis of one's right standing before God. This is because Paul does not confuse the two. He makes it clear that God's righteous judgment laid his wrath on Christ Jesus in order that God might be just when he justifies all who belong to Jesus Christ (Rom 3:21-26). Therefore, Paul does not answer the question "On what basis will one be justified?" until Romans 3:21-31. In Romans 2 Paul

---

[30]Cf. Thomas R. Schreiner, *Romans,* Baker Exegetical Commentary on the New Testament (Grand Rapids, Mich.: Baker, 1998), p. 144. *Epainos* "denotes an eschatological reward from God (cf. 1 Cor. 4:5; 1 Pet. 1:7 . . .). The reward should not be construed as something given above and beyond eternal life. Romans 2:26 suggests that eternal life itself is the reward since there the uncircumcised person who observes the law 'will be reckoned' as circumcised, as a member of God's covenant people. Most likely, the reference to *[epainos]* communicates the same thought. Those who are truly God's people may be hidden now, but in the last days those who are truly Jews in secret and circumcised in heart will be revealed and rewarded by God with eternal life (cf. 2:7)." See also Schreiner, "Did Paul Believe in Justification by Works?" pp. 139-55.

makes one thing clear: God's promise of salvation is conditional. On the day of judgment God will award eternal life to those who persevere in good works (Rom 2:7, 10), because God does not justify hearers of the law but doers of the law (Rom 2:13). Praise from God belongs to all who keep the requirements of the law, to all who obey from hearts circumcised by the Spirit (Rom 2:26, 29).

Because our concern is not to establish the legal basis on which God justifies sinners without losing his reputation as being just and righteous, we pass over much of Paul's argument, especially Romans 3:21-31. Yet it is important to recognize that this portion of Paul's case for his gospel is vital to his argument in Romans 5:1-11, the passage we consider next, for Paul grounds his statements in Romans 5:1-11 on what he has said in 3:21–4:25.

Romans 5–6. In Romans 5:1-11 Paul offers believers assuring confidence that there is unbroken continuity between the already and not-yet aspects of salvation, even though this continuity runs through the afflictions of this present age. Paul contends that as believers, because we already stand justified in God's grace, we rightly boast with two orientations. First, our exultant rejoicing casts a confident eye to our eschatological "hope of the g lory of God" and the praise that God will give to all who are circumcised by the Spirit (Rom 2.29). This glory, of which all fall short (Rom 3:23), seems to be the same "glory and honor and immortality" that believers seek (Rom 2:7, 10) and sinners spurned (Rom 1:23).

Second, our exultant joy looks with confidence upon our present afflictions, for Paul says, "We know that affliction brings to completion perseverance; likewise, perseverance brings to completion tested character, and tested character yields hope. And this hope does not put us to shame, because God's love has been poured out into our hearts through the Holy Spirit, who was given to us" (Rom 5:3-5). It is significant to note that Paul does not insert a condition into this unbroken chain. It certainly is true that one will only advance from affliction to hope if one perseveres in faith through present afflictions. However, why does Paul not include such a condition? Paul leaves a conditional clause out because his purpose is not to place before us a conditional promise, as in Romans 2:6-10, but an unconditional assurance that everyone of us who already stands justified in God's grace will also participate in the glory that is not yet ours but for which we seek and hope.[31] For a reader to insert a condition here would invalidate the apostle's intention. (This passage both grammatically and conceptually foreshadows the unbroken chain of Romans 8:28-30.) Paul reinforces the certainty of this hope by reiterating that it is entirely grounded on Christ's death for us who were ungodly and sinners (Rom 5:6-8). Then he draws his conclusion that moves from that which is certain to that which is even more certain (an a fortiori argument) when he argues, "Much more, then, since we have been declared righteous by his blood we shall be saved from wrath through him. For while we were enemies, we were reconciled to God through the death of his Son; much more, since we have been reconciled, we shall be saved by his life" (Rom 5:9-10). Paul follows this with his profound comparison and contrast between Adam and Christ as he makes the case that all who receive grace and the gift of justification will surely reign over sin and death through Christ Jesus (Rom 5:17). So Paul insists that there is unbroken continuity between the justification we already have in Christ by faith and the public vindication from God's wrath in the final day, which we do not yet have (Rom 5:19). This unbroken continuity between the already and the not yet lays the foundation for Paul's moral exhortations throughout the next three chapters, for this continuity runs through present afflictions that call for perseverance in faith, thus accounting for Paul's admonitions that we will examine next.

Throughout Romans 6—8 Paul pastorally applies this unbroken continuity to Christians when he builds his argument on what is already true of us in Jesus Christ. He appeals to us to become what we now are in Christ in order that we might receive the inheritance that is not yet ours. So both aspects—already and not yet—punctuate Paul's exhortations throughout Romans 6—8. Thus, Paul's argument oscillates between using the indicative mood to argue what Christ has already accomplished for us and the non-indicative mood to exhort us to become what we are in Christ.[32] Thus, Paul exploits the indicative

---

[31]See Schreiner, *Romans,* p. 256.

[32]Biblical scholars use grammatical nomenclature—indicative and imperative—as a shorthand expression to speak of how ethical instruction uses the indicative mood to argue the theological basis and principles upon which biblical writers exhort Christians to action by use of the imperative mood for exhortations. See, e.g., the discussion of Rom 6:2-14 in Schreiner, *Romans,* p. 300. Schreiner makes the point that the indicative mood dominates Rom 6:2-10, while the imperative mood dominates Rom 6:11-14.

mood to argue that in Christ, sin has already lost its tyranny over believers who died with him and will also be resurrected with him (Rom 6:2-10). Then the apostle uses the imperative mood to admonish believers to take dominion and mastery over sin precisely "because sin will not master you, for you are not under law but under grace" (Rom 6:14). Note how the indicative mood of verse 14 functions as the basis for all the exhortations of verses 11-13.

It is significant that Paul begins his sequence of exhortations by appealing to believers to "count yourselves dead to sin but alive to God in Christ Jesus" (Rom 6:11). This entire admonition calls for a response that corresponds to God's justifying verdict concerning all for whom Jesus Christ died. Paul's admonition uses the verb *count* or *reckon (logizomai)*, the same verb that he repeatedly uses to express God's declarative verdict of justification for all who believe (e.g., Rom 2:26; 4:3-6, 8, 10-11, 22-23). Here, however, the verb *reckon* denotes the human act of faith. So, Paul argues, our slavery to sin has been broken because God has justified us from sin by reason of our death with Jesus Christ (Rom 6:6-7), who can never be mastered by death again but is alive to God forever more (Rom 6:8-10), so we ought to reckon ourselves "dead to sin but alive to God in Christ Jesus" (Rom 6:11).[33]

Therefore, it is evident in Romans 6:2-11 that Paul weaves the renewal metaphors of resurrection and life together with the legal metaphors of justification and manumission in order to augment his admonition that summons us to "be righteous" on the basis that we are already "reckoned righteous." Likewise, Paul also makes a transition from the kingdom imagery of ruler-subject, so prominent in chapter 5 (Rom 5:14, 17, 21), to the master-slave imagery that he introduces in Romans 6:6 and 9. So, Paul admonishes, "Therefore do not let sin reign in your mortal body so that you obey its evil desires.

---

[33]Note that in Rom 6:7 Paul uses the verb *justify (dikaioō)* in an unusual manner, for he speaks of being "justified from sin." Most translations and commentators regard Paul's expression *dedikaiōtai apo tēs hamartias* as equivalent to "freed from sin." Admittedly the expression is difficult (cf. Acts 13:38-39), but it seems unwise to regard this one use of the expression to be out of character with Paul's doctrine of justification (e.g., Moo, *Romans 1–8*, pp. 376-77). Had Paul simply intended to say "freed from sin," he could have used the same expression he later uses in Rom 6:18, *eleutherōthentes apo tēs hamartias* ("having been set free from sin"). See John R. Stott, *Romans: God's Good News for the World* (Downers Grove, Ill.: InterVarsity Press, 1994), p. 177.

Do not offer the parts of your body to sin, as instruments of wickedness, but rather offer yourselves to God, as those who have been
brought from death to life; and offer the parts of your body to him as
instruments of righteousness. For sin shall not be your master,
because you are not under law, but under grace" (Rom 6:12-14 NIV).

Lest anyone suppose, on the basis of his words, that sinning is
inconsequential, Paul emphatically denies such an inference (Rom
6:15). Paul appeals to us to recognize that, whether the metaphor is
one of judge-defendant as in Romans 2:6-10 or master-slave as in
Romans 6:15-23, the principle of God's justice is irrevocable. Using
the interrogative mood, Paul explains why licentiousness has no
place in his gospel: "Don't you know that the one to whom you
present yourselves as slaves for obedience, you are slaves of the one
whom you obey, whether of sin leading to death or of obedience leading to righteousness?" (Rom 6:16). Precisely because God has established this inviolable connection, the apostle's reminder is both a
warning and an admonition that functions as one of God's means to
bring about our salvation. Paul's reminder functions as a warning
without suggesting that it is possible for Christians to return to slavery to sin and perish in eternal death. For the apostle's words project
a mental conception that affirms God's sacred principle of justice,
that anyone who submits as a slave to sin will perish in death. That is
God's inviolable principle of justice. Paul rejoices that his readers are
no longer slaves to sin, for God has already freed them from slavery
to sin and "handed them over" to be "slaves of righteousness." This is
God's work, and he uses the gospel, the gospel Paul preaches, as the
means to accomplish this enslavement to righteousness, for they
"obeyed from the heart" the "pattern of teaching" to which God
"handed them over."[34]

The indicative that expresses God's redemption of slaves from sin's
mastery and placement of them under the mastery of righteousness
(Rom 6:17-18) forms the basis for Paul's exhortation of verse 19. In
short, "The indicative of God's work does not rule out human activity
or suggest that human decisions are unnecessary."[35] Again Paul calls

---

[34]On the expression "handed them over," it is significant to contrast its use in Rom 6:17
with its use in Rom 1:24, 26, 28, where bondage to sin also is the metaphor Paul
employs. On the expression "pattern of teaching," see Schreiner, *Romans*, p. 336.
[35]Ibid., p. 337.

attention to the fact that God uses means to secure obedience from his slaves, for they are not automatons or robots. Just as we formerly presented our "members as slaves to impurity and to greater and greater iniquity," now it is necessary to present the particulars of ourselves "as slaves to righteousness for sanctification."[36] In Romans 6:20-23, Paul offers further support for this exhortation, for the wage that master sin pays is death, but the outcome of being enslaved to God is eternal life, God's free gift in Christ Jesus our Lord.

Romans 8:1-17. Paul continues his pastoral use of the indicative and non-indicative moods in Romans 8 to unpack the powerful transformation his gospel brings to us. As he portrays salvation under the image of a change of masters in Romans 6:14-23, so Paul uses the imagery of two mutually exclusive realms or domains—flesh and Spirit—in Romans 8. Flesh and Spirit, as Paul contrasts the two in this chapter, sustain the contrasting categories he has expanded throughout Romans 5—7. They correspond to his two categories of earthly and heavenly powers and domains that stand in opposition to one another, in that the salvation of the age to come has already broken into the present time. Throughout Romans, but especially in chapters 5—8, the apostle conceives of a cosmic clash between two worlds that have both temporal and spatial qualities. The head of the old era and domain is Adam, with Christ as the head of the new. Adam's allies are sin, death, the law and the flesh. Allied with Christ are righteousness, grace, life and the Spirit. This cosmic conflict between the old humanity and the new humanity is a clash that includes not only two domains of existence but also two ages that overlap the interval between the two advents of Christ. So for Paul, flesh represents the realm of corruption, depravity, death with decay and hostility toward God that characterizes the old age and dominion under sin, all of which came by way of Adam's act of transgression and disobedience (Rom 5:19). On the other hand, Spirit represents the realm of renewal, righteousness, life and reconciliation to God that marks the new age and dominion under grace, which comes by way of Jesus

---

[36]Romans 6:19 "opens an interesting window on the Pauline conception of slavery to sin. Unbelievers are totally subservient to sin as a power that exerts authority over their lives, but the slavery envisioned is not coercion. People do not submit to sin against their will. Rather, they 'freely' and spontaneously choose to sin. In other words, unbelievers are slaves to sin in that they always desire to carry out the dictates of their master" (ibid.).

Christ's one act of righteousness and obedience (Rom 5:19).[37] By becoming believers we find ourselves in the midst of this great conflict between these two realms and ages.

With this introduction, albeit brief, we are prepared to consider Paul's argument in Romans 8, where he also weaves both warning and assurance of triumphant perseverance with his common threads of already and not yet that encompass both the temporal and spatial dimensions we spoke of above. While Paul embeds his already-but-not-yet motif into the whole fabric of Romans 8, one aspect or the other tends to dominate each segment. So in Romans 8:1-17 Paul accents the fact that we are already God's children, because we have the Spirit. In Romans 8:18-39 Paul emphasizes that we are not yet fully revealed as God's children, for we yet endure suffering in anticipation of glory.

The opening paragraphs of the chapter reiterate Paul's triumphant conclusion in Romans 5 that for all who are in Christ Jesus righteousness and life have replaced condemnation and death. For us who believe, Jesus Christ has already commuted the sentence of condemnation and death that otherwise would have been announced openly on the day of judgment. By his obedience Jesus Christ revoked our condemnation in Adam (Rom 8:3). The verdict of the day of judgment is already a reality for us ahead of time, and it is good news, for we are justified because we have been set free from the law that stirs up sin and executes one to death. Just as Paul argues in Romans 6 that we who are in Christ no longer serve sin as a taskmaster but are slaves of righteousness, so in Romans 8 Paul insists that Christ has broken the dominion of the flesh over us and has made us subject to the Spirit. All who are subject to the Spirit also have a new mindset. Paul contrasts the two mindsets: the mind set on the flesh results in death, but the mind set on the Spirit results in life. When Paul speaks of death and life, he gives them their fullest sense. He means death and life both now and not yet, as throughout Romans 5—8. Death

---

[37]James Edwards nicely summarizes the corrective to the popular interpretation of Paul's flesh and Spirit antithesis. He says, "Spirit and flesh are rather two exclusive realms, two authorities or governing powers. One is either in the Spirit or in the flesh, but not in both at the same time" (*Romans,* New International Biblical Commentary [Peabody, Mass.: Hendrickson, 1992], p. 204). For another helpful and readable discussion of these concepts, see C. Marvin Pate, *The End of the Age Has Come: The Theology of Paul* (Grand Rapids, Mich.: Zondervan, 1995), esp. pp. 43-70.

entails living under God's condemning wrath both now and forever. Likewise, life is both the present reality and future hope of all who stand justified in Christ. Therefore, being of the flesh or being of the Spirit has eternal consequences, for there is an irrevocable connection between what we are in this present age and what we shall be in the age to come (cf. 1 Jn 3:2-3).

Thus, in Romans 8:5-8 Paul describes the profound difference between one who is in Christ and one who is not. In verse 9 he begins to move from description toward the exhortation in verses 12-13, but first Paul draws his readers into the course of his argument by interacting with his sequence of four suppositions. Contrary to popular belief, fanned by theological commitments and propagated even by scholars, Paul's conditional language expresses neither doubt nor confidence concerning his readers.[38] Rather, the four suppositions of Romans 8:9-11 function to compel us to answer some questions for ourselves: "What about me? Do I have the Spirit? Do I belong to Christ? Will I be raised to eternal life in the day of resurrection?" The apostle assumes for the sake of his argument that his readers will answer the implied questions affirmatively.[39] Having drawn us into his reasoning by moving from theological description (Rom 8:5-8) to responsive suppositions (Rom 8:9-11), Paul is ready now to exhort us: "So then, brothers and sisters, we are debtors, not to the flesh, to live according to the flesh—for if you live according to the flesh, you will die; but if by the Spirit you put to death the deeds of the body, you will live" (Rom 8:12-13 NRSV).

In Romans 8:12 Paul uses the indicative to affirm the fact that

---

[38]James D. G. Dunn commits two grammatical fallacies, first when he says that *eiper pneuma theou oikei en hymin* in Rom 8:9 implies some uncertainty whether Paul's readers are in the Spirit, and then when he claims that *ei de Christos en hymin* in Rom 8:10 could be translated "since" (Dunn, *Romans 1–8*, Word Biblical Commentary 38a [Dallas: Word, 1988], pp. 428-30). *If*, in itself, even in conjunction with other Greek particles such as *per*, never implies uncertainty. On the other hand, *if*, in itself, never implies certainty. Cf. Moo, *Romans 1–8*, p. 490. See the excellent discussion in Wallace, *Greek Grammar Beyond the Basics*, pp. 690-94.

[39]The first-class condition in the Greek New Testament functions to express an assumption for the sake of the argument being made. It says nothing about its likelihood of failure or success. See A. B. Caneday, "Deity, Conditional Language, and Human Response: An Apostolic Grammar Lesson" (paper presented at the 49th annual meeting of the Evangelical Theological Society, Santa Clara, Calif., November 20-22, 1997), pp. 3-13. This paper is available from Theological Research Exchange Network at < www.tren.com >.

according to his gospel, no one who has the Spirit has any obligation to the flesh. Then Paul changes to the non-indicative or supposition when he attaches verse 13 to explain why we have no obligation to the flesh. By using two more conditional clauses he succinctly explains why obligation to the flesh is finished. Paul's conditional warning finds varied explanations. We will briefly interact with three.

Because the passage affirms that death and life are conditioned on human action, many contend that Paul at least implies that it is possible for a believer, who has the Spirit, to return to live in the flesh and to perish eternally.[40] Others, such as Zane Hodges, argue that the conditional statements indicate that Paul places "two possibilities" before Christians—perseverance and apostasy—and that the "level of probability is the same for both."[41] Hodges uses Romans 8:13 to prove his argument that "the countless warnings of the New Testament against failures of every kind ought to be sufficient to show that such a guarantee [assured perseverance] is not Biblical."[42] Yet Hodges insists that a Christian can live according to the flesh and that the death Paul speaks of is not eternal death.[43] Against these two interpretations, others insist that Paul's admonition does not suggest doubt but certainty. MacArthur explains the suppositions by saying, "Those are axiomatic statements—self-evident truths that need no proof. The unbeliever is headed for eternal death, the believer to life eternal."[44] He further explains what Paul means by the second conditional clause: "If you're a person who is killing the deeds of the body in the power of the Spirit, that's evidence of your salvation."[45] All three explanations of the text stumble over Paul's conditional statements. The first two views mistakenly presume that conditions indicate an uncertain outcome. The third interpretation distorts the text in two ways. First, MacArthur converts Paul's conditional warning into a sterile axiom. To do this, he abbreviates the supposition "if you live

---

[40]Cf. Marshall, *Kept by the Power of God,* p. 242 n. 44, where he cites Michel, *Der Brief an die Römer* (Göttingen: Vandenhoeck & Ruprecht, 1957), p. 135 n. 4, to make his case for him. Cf. also Grant R. Osborne, "Exegetical Notes on Calvinist Texts," in *Grace Unlimited,* ed. Clark Pinnock (Minneapolis: Bethany House, 1975), pp. 177, 187-88 n. 41.

[41]Hodges, *Gospel Under Siege,* p. 11.

[42]Ibid.

[43]Ibid., pp. 27, 71, 113, 175-76 n. 21.

[44]MacArthur, *Saved Without A Doubt,* p. 137.

[45]Ibid.

according to the flesh" to "the unbeliever," and he shortens the second supposition, "if by the Spirit you put to death the deeds of the body," to "the believer." Then MacArthur makes the second conditional clause retrospective rather than prospective. So while Paul's focus is on putting to death sinful deeds through the Spirit, with an orientation toward gaining eternal life in the eschatological day of judgment, MacArthur turns the supposition around so that it is retrospective with an eye that looks for evidence that one is already saved. By so doing, he has collapsed Paul's not-yet orientation toward the implied day of judgment into a present verdict. In addition, he has altered Paul's concern with God's means for experiencing the not-yet aspect of eternal life into evidence of present possession of salvation.[46]

By now our view of Paul's warning should be rather apparent. Therefore, we will only summarize our interpretation. Paul clearly addresses his warning to believers, for he assumes for the sake of his argument that his readers concur that his suppositions of Romans 8:9-11 are true of them. Therefore, he appeals to his readers as "brothers and sisters" (v. 12). His conditional warning of verse 13 suggests nothing about possibility or probability of fulfilling either supposition. Paul includes his warning for one fundamental purpose, namely, to urge us to resist the temptation to live according to the way of the flesh now and die in the last day, and instead, through the Spirit, to die to one's desires now in order that in the day to come we might attain life.

Four features of the text beg for brief comment. First, note Paul's chiasm (a crisscross literary pattern) in the text.

If you
A   live according to the flesh,
    B   you will die;
        C   but if by the Spirit
    B′   you put to death the deeds of the body,
A′   you will live.

This chiasm draws attention to the contrast between action in the present and consequence in the eschatological day. Inherent in this is the second feature we should note. Paul expresses his warning

---

[46]See ibid.

paradoxically: to live now will result in death then; to die now will result in life then. This certainly echoes the admonition Jesus gives in the form of a riddle: "For those who want to save their life will lose it, and those who lose their life for my sake will find it" (Mt 16:25 NRSV). Third, Paul's warning also echoes the call of Jesus: "If any want to become my followers, let them deny themselves and take up their cross and follow me" (Mt 16:24 NRSV). Both Jesus and Paul call on us to put to death the desires of our mortal bodies in order that we might be raised to eternal life in the age to come (cf. Rom 8:11, 23). Fourth, Paul's warning expresses a profound assumption of compatibility between exhorting humans to do what God alone enables them to do. It will not do to suggest that Paul admonishes his readers that since God has done his part now they must contribute their part and "put to death the deeds of the body."[47] Paul has no place for synergism in his theology, for it is only "through the Spirit" that the believer is able to "put to death the deeds of the body."[48] It also will not do to turn Paul's warning into a mere axiom, as if God has already done everything, as if passivity were in order for Christians. There is no unbearable correlation between the activity of the Spirit on our behalf and God's requirement for us to act in order that we might have life, since our "putting to death the deeds of the body" is possible only on account of the Spirit who works in us to do it. Also, there is no unbearable tension between the assurance of triumph through the Spirit (Rom 8:11) and the warning to "put to death the deeds of the body through the Spirit" (Rom 8:13). Assurance and warning stand compatibly together, for the warning is a significant means that God uses, through his Spirit, to secure his promised salvation in us.

In Romans 8:14-17 Paul reinforces the significance of his warning.

---

[47]Cornelius Van Til comments, "Synergism takes for granted that there can be no truly personal relation between God and man unless the absoluteness of God be denied in proportion that the freedom of man is maintained. Synergism assumes that an act of man cannot be truly personal unless such an act be impersonal. By that we mean that according to synergism, a personal act of man cannot at the same time but in a different sense, be a personal act of God. Synergism assumes that either man or God acts personally at a certain time, and at a certain place, but they cannot act personally simultaneously at the same point of contact" (*A Survey of Christian Epistemology*, vol. 2 of *In Defense of Biblical Christianity* [Phillipsburg: N.J.: Presbyterian & Reformed, n.d.], p. 68).

[48]The dative *pneumati* is best taken as a dative of agent: "through the Spirit" (Moo, *Romans 1–8*, p. 495).

He assures all who "put to death the deeds of the body" because they "are led by the Spirit of God" that they are "God's children" (Rom 8:14).[49] In verses 15-16, Paul offers support for this conclusion as he expands briefly on the relationship between having the Spirit and being God's adopted child. The Spirit we have received has nothing to do with slavery that leads to terror of judgment but has to do with "adoption as children," for it is by the Spirit that we acknowledge that God is our "Abba," our Father. Still, Paul's emphasis falls on the Spirit who breaks the power of sin in all who are God's children, who works in their hearts obedience and who then assures those characterized by obedience that they bear the traits of their heavenly Father (Rom 8:16).

From this assurance that we are God's children, Paul draws the conclusion that we are heirs. In Romans 8:17 he uses conditional clauses in two ways. First, he says "if children, then heirs" to reason from evidence to inference that all to whom the Spirit gives assurance of being God's children are God's heirs and Christ's joint heirs, which is to say that the inheritance is ours only through our union with Jesus Christ. Then, in preparation for the remainder of chapter 8, Paul attaches another conditional clause to this inference by saying, "if, in fact, we suffer with him in order that we may also be glorified with him" (Rom 8:17). He insists that the inheritance will be ours as God's children, but only if we suffer with Christ. This condition expresses a cause-effect relationship. However, we must not mistake this cause to be the ground of our inheritance. This is because Paul's condition—"if, in fact, we suffer with him in order that we may also be glorified with him"—connects with a more ultimate expression, namely, our being "joint heirs with Christ." Christ alone has established the basis of our inheritance. So the cause-effect relationship does not concern the ground of our inheritance but the means by which God gives the inheritance. God will give the inheritance of the age to come only to those who suffer with Christ in this world. Jesus has established the order: suffering first and then glory (cf. Lk 24:26). So Paul expresses with the family metaphor of inheritance what Jesus conveys with the imagery of the cross when he calls on all who would

---

[49]When Paul speaks of "being led by the Spirit of God," he does not refer "to guidance for everyday decisions in determining the will of God" (Schreiner, *Romans*, p. 422).

be his disciples to pick up the instrument of death to worldly passions, to lose one's life now, to wear Christ's shame in this world, in order that we might share his glory when he comes again (Mk 8:34-38).

1 Corinthians. More than any of Paul's other letters to churches, his first letter to the Corinthians reflects the things taking place in the church that prompted his correspondence to them. Numerous problems existed in the church and beckoned the apostle's intervention by personal visits, by sending envoys and by sending letters (cf. 1 Cor 5:9-10; 16:10-12; 2 Cor 2:4-14; 7:5-16; 13:1). Church members sent a letter to Paul to ask him several questions (cf. 1 Cor 7:1; 8:1; 12:1; 16:1). Nevertheless, the issues the apostle addresses first are his own concerns: factious disputes and unbridled gratification of sensual appetites. Though several portions in 1 Corinthians call for attention, we will focus on one significant admonition in 9:23-27.

One cannot properly understand what Paul is saying in 1 Corinthians 9:23-27 without recognizing the continuity of his argument from 8:1—11:1 (see paragraphs in the NIV). In 1 Corinthians 8:1-13 Paul addresses whether or not the Corinthians should eat food offered to idols in pagan temples. It is an issue of Christian liberty, a liberty some have by knowledge but others do not yet have. Therefore, love, not knowledge, must govern the use of this liberty. Throughout 1 Corinthians 9 Paul appeals to his own refusal to use liberties that are his and presents himself as a model for the Corinthians to follow. Paul explains three rights he has as an apostle: (1) to food and drink (1 Cor 9:4); (2) to have a wife (1 Cor 9:5); and (3) to expect the churches to provide financial support (1 Cor 9:6). It is his apostolic right to be relieved of supporting himself that becomes his focus in 1 Corinthians 9:6-18. Paul explains how he relinquishes such rights in order that he may gain converts to the gospel of Jesus Christ (1 Cor 9:19-22). Within this context of voluntarily not exercising his rights in the ministry of the gospel, Paul frames an urgent appeal on the athletic metaphor of training and then of the boxer and runner (1 Cor 9:23-27).

> I do all things on account of the gospel, in order that I might be a fellow partaker of it. Don't you know that those who run in a race all run, but one receives the prize. Run in such a manner that you might win. And everyone who competes in the arena engages in rigorous self-discipline

in all things. Therefore, they do it to receive a perishable wreath, but we do it for an imperishable one. Therefore, I run in such a manner as not to be aimless; I box in such a manner as not to punch the air; but I punish my body and enslave it, lest after I have preached to others, I myself should be a reprobate. (1 Cor 9:23-27)[50]

We leave to commentaries the finer points of the text.[51] Interpretation of Paul's purpose for raising this athletic metaphor, with a focus on his own surrender of rights for the sake of the gospel, hinges on how we should understand his use of the word *adokimos* ("disqualified, reprobate") in verse 27. Fear to become *adokimos* motivates Paul to be diligent and deliberate in perseverance, even to withdraw himself from legitimate desires and rights, lest they hinder his pursuit of the goal. What does Paul mean by *adokimos*? Too easily many interpreters assume that this question has only two alternative responses: either Paul fears that he might lose his salvation, or he is afraid that he might lose a reward that has no bearing on salvation.[52]

One can readily find advocates for either view. Unfortunately, some scholars seem to get mired in two things: Paul's imagery and a desire to avoid the idea of loss of salvation.[53] For example, Judith Gundry Volf contends that Paul makes such cautious and rigorous efforts, not out of any concern for his own salvation, but to avoid becoming disqualified in his apostolic ministry.[54] So, she claims, "Paul does not want to lose this divine approval in his ministry."[55] Because she excludes application of Paul's athletic imagery to the Corinthians, Gundry Volf's interpretation remains unconvincing. She exaggerates

---

[50]We recognize that current editions of the Greek New Testament and modern versions place 1 Cor 9:23 with the paragraph before. We have placed verse 23 with verses 24-27 only to show the coherence of Paul's concern with spiritually benefiting from the gospel he preaches.

[51]For a commentary that fairly explains the text, see Gordon Fee, *The First Epistle to the Corinthians*, New International Commentary on the New Testament (Grand Rapids, Mich.: Eerdmans, 1987), pp. 431-41.

[52]See, e.g., Craig Blomberg, *1 Corinthians*, NIV Application Commentary (Grand Rapids, Mich.: Zondervan, 1994), p. 185.

[53]Two examples of this are Judith M. Gundry Volf, *Paul and Perseverance: Staying In and Falling Away* (Louisville, Ky.: Westminster John Knox, 1990), pp. 233-47; and Blomberg, *1 Corinthians*, p. 185.

[54]Gundry Volf, *Paul and Perseverance*, p. 247. She also says, "According to the proposed interpretation . . . Paul's rigorous efforts in apostolic ministry do not serve to secure his own salvation but to make him the gospel's partner in fulfillment of his calling" (p. 253).

[55]Ibid., p. 247.

Paul's singular use of the word *defense (apologia)* in 1 Corinthians 9:3, so that all of chapter 9 becomes an apologetic for his ministry, according to her view. But this remarkably misses the continuity with both chapters 8 and 10. Paul's concern is not to offer a defense of his apostolic ministry. Rather, he speaks of a "defense" *(apologia)* in 9:3 only in terms of his freedoms and rights as an apostle. He presents his conduct in apostolic ministry as a model, calling on the Corinthians to imitate his behavior as they ponder how to behave toward one another concerning the issue of food offered to idols.

Aside from the strain Gundry Volf's interpretation puts on the individual pieces of the texts, this view leaves one wondering why Paul wrote chapter 9, if he is not calling on the Corinthians to imitate his own perseverance in the gospel. If one adopts her view that it is an apology for his apostolic ministry, chapter 9 is a misplaced intrusion into an otherwise coherent argument. To sustain her interpretation, she finds it necessary to regard chapter 10 as loosely following Paul's words in 1 Corinthians 9:27 rather than to explain why the apostle includes his own model of self-limitation on rights and freedom in chapter 9.[56]

So what is Paul saying in 1 Corinthians 9:23-27? There is a strong connection between Paul's words in verses 23 and 27, for Paul's concern is the same in both verses.[57] In verse 23, Paul announces that his goal is to participate with others in the blessings of the gospel he preaches.[58] Paul does not express this goal to show that he is self-serving. Rather, he chooses his words carefully to encourage the Corinthian Christians to identify themselves with him in his pursuit of salvation. The apostle's objective is for those to whom he has preached God's saving power in the gospel to adopt his posture con-

---

[56]Ibid., p. 239. Gundry Volf appeals to I. Howard Marshall (*Kept by the Power of God,* p. 121) to lend support to her case. But her case begs the question, for contrary to her assessment Paul's use of *gar* ("for") in 1 Cor 10:1 does link the two chapters, so that the apostle's concern in chapter 10 explains his inclusion of chapter 9. This is further supported by the fact that Paul purposely uses the verb *eudokēsen* ("was [not] well pleased") in 1 Cor 10:5, a cognate of *adokimos* ("disqualified, reprobate") in 9:27, to draw a link to what precedes.

[57]See Gundry Volf, *Paul and Perseverance,* pp. 247-54. In these pages Gundry Volf focuses on 1 Cor 9:23 because she acknowledges that this verse poses a serious problem for her interpretation of 1 Cor 9:27. She notes that most interpreters understand Paul's words in verse 23 to speak of attaining final salvation.

[58]Fee, *First Epistle to the Corinthians,* p. 432. Cf. C. K. Barrett, *Commentary on the First Epistle to the Corinthians,* Harper's New Testament Commentaries (New York: Harper & Row, 1968), p. 216.

cerning rights in order that they, too, may share in the gospel's blessings. Thus, Paul presents himself as a model to be followed by all, for
if Paul the apostle, who preaches the gospel, is concerned to relin-
quish his rights and freedoms in order that he might partake of the
salvation he proclaims, how much more should the Corinthians be
cautious how they behave?

Both verses 23 and 27 express Paul's singular concern. Note the
two verses in parallel.

> I do all things on account of the gospel, in order that I might be a fellow
> partaker of it. (1 Cor 9:23)

> But I punish my body and enslave it, lest after I have preached to oth-
> ers, I myself should be a reprobate. (1 Cor 9:27)

The whole context makes it clear that to be *adokimos* ("reprobate")
is the opposite of being a "fellow partaker" *(synkoinōnos)* of the gospel.
In the context of the athletic arena, a runner was judged *adokimos* for
breaking the rules of the games, including training (cf. 2 Tim 2:5). For
the apostle, then, *adokimos* metaphorically represents reprobation,
eternal loss. Paul uses the athletic imagery, therefore, to make it clear
to the Corinthians that for him also there is no salvation without perseverance. There is continuity between the starting blocks and the
finish line, but only by running the race with diligent and deliberate
perseverance in the arena of faith.[59]

As we have noted before, the questions we ask concerning the biblical text either guide us to understand the text's meaning or obscure
it. Unfortunately, exegetes tend to exclude the necessary and right
question concerning 1 Corinthians 9:23-27. If Paul's text yields support for only one of two alternative questions that exegetes tend to
ask, it is not surprising that dispute swirls about the passage. However, we are not bound to answer only two questions: (1) Does Paul
fear that he might lose his salvation? (2) Or is he afraid that he might
lose a reward that has no bearing on salvation? Not only does this set
up a false disjunction, it also frames the question by begging the question.[60] The first question we should ask concerning Paul's passage is,

---

[59]Paul always uses *adokimos* to refer to reprobation (Rom 1:28; 1 Cor 9:27; 2 Cor 13:5, 6,
7; 2 Tim 3:8; Tit 1:16).

[60]For discussion of these kinds of fallacies in the work of interpretation, see D. A. Carson, *Exegetical Fallacies,* 2nd ed. (Grand Rapids, Mich.: Baker, 1996), pp. 90-92, 105-6.

What function does Paul intend for his athletic metaphor in 1 Corinthians 9:23-27? It functions as a warning. Paul wants the Corinthians to adopt his own posture with regard to things that are not sinful in themselves. He has already made it clear that he wants the Corinthians to act out of love for the welfare of others, particularly toward those who are weak in conscience, lest they cause the weak to stumble to their eternal destruction (1 Cor 8:1-13). Paul has also reinforced this concern from his own self-restrictions of exercising his apostolic prerogatives (1 Cor 9:1-22). Then the apostle beckons the Corinthians to adopt his posture with regard to his own salvation. Under the athletic imagery, he has made it clear that he voluntarily forgoes rights and freedoms available to him, in order that he might attain salvation and not be a reprobate on the day of judgment. Thus, the passage functions to admonish and warn the Corinthians lest they perish by insisting on using their rights, even against their own spiritual welfare.

Now we are ready to ask whether the apostle Paul fears that he might lose his salvation. Before we answer, it is important to note that this passage is distinctive because Paul has plainly placed himself in the midst of his warning metaphor. The significance of this should not escape us, for this passage should function as a paradigm for understanding all similar warnings in Paul's letters. Here is the question: Does the apostle Paul fear that it is possible that God will reject him as a reprobate on the day of judgment? If we answer yes, we must be prepared to demonstrate that Paul also doubts God's faithfulness to his promise to preserve his people to the end, so that now he can believe that it is necessary to persevere with diligence to the end in order to be saved. He must doubt God's faithfulness so that he can believe God's warning.[61] Of course, this is incorrect, for Paul is the one who calls on the Corinthians to believe in God's steadfastness to confirm his own children to the end (1 Cor 1:8-9). Yet this is precisely

---

[61]It is worth noting that Robert Shank imposed such reasoning upon his reading of G. C. Berkouwer's *Faith and Perseverance*. Shank argues that Berkouwer "implies that the 'consolation' passages and the 'alarming admonitions' cannot be viewed with complete sincerity at one and the same time, for a person cannot be motivated by the 'alarming admonitions' until he abandons his confidence in the 'consolation' passages—the (supposed) promises of God that perseverance is inevitable and apostasy is impossible" (*Life in the Son: A Study of the Doctrine of Perseverance,* 2nd ed. [Springfield, Mo.: Westcott, 1976], p. 167).

what we must affirm if we hold that Paul fears that God might reject him as a reprobate on the day of judgment.[62]

Properly read, Paul's words serve to warn both himself and all Christians, without calling on us to doubt whether God will preserve all his children safely to the end. Rather, his warning is entirely compatible with his affirmations of confidence in God's preserving his own people to the end. Precisely because the apostle believes in God's power to secure his own, Paul also believes that it is necessary to warn both himself and us that God requires us not only to leave the starting blocks but also to run faithfully to the end. There is an inseparable continuity between the start and the finish line, and it runs through the exigencies and pressures of life in this present world as it demands faithful endurance from us.

Philippians. As we examine Paul's letter to the Philippians, we do so not because there are no other admonitions and warnings in 1 or 2 Corinthians or in Galatians. Indeed, there are several important passages that we would like to address (e.g., Gal 5:1-5; 6:7-10), but two passages in Philippians stand out and demand careful attention: Philippians 2:12-13 and 3:8-16.

Following his exalted presentation of Christ's unique and willing humiliation to serve as God's atoning sacrifice (Phil 2:6-11), Paul admonishes the Philippians, "Therefore, my beloved, just as you have always obeyed me, not only in my presence, but much more now in my absence, work out your own salvation with fear and trembling; for it is God who is at work in you, enabling you both to will and to work for his good pleasure" (Phil 2:12-13 NRSV). Many evangelicals get nervous with the apostle Paul, the champion of grace, when he speaks as he does in verse 12. He combines three expressions that seem oxymoronic to many: "you obeyed," "work out" and "your own salvation." We have already seen in our discussion of Romans 6:17 that for Paul, belief in Jesus Christ is properly expressed as obedience to Christ, not in the sense of adhering to regulations but of coming fully under

---

[62]This seems to be the reason Marshall qualifies his statements of uncertainty when he says, "The possibility is, therefore, seriously to be entertained that in 1 Corinthians 9:27 Paul raises the question of his own failure to pass the test and rejection on the Day of Judgment. . . . But although this theoretical possibility is raised, there is little doubt that Paul felt no severe temptation from this quarter (1 Corinthians 7:7), and his overwhelming feeling is one of confidence regarding his own salvation" (*Kept by the Power of God,* p. 121).

Christ as Lord, of wholehearted devotion to him. This is the obedience Paul calls for here.

Evangelical nervousness, however, has generated two rather popular, though novel, explanations of Philippians 2:12, one with a focus on "work out," the other on "your own salvation." We may dispense with both rather quickly. Both arise from a desire to avoid the idea of salvation by works. Some have devised the rather clever catch-phrase, "work outwardly what God has worked inwardly."[63] However, Paul's verb *katergazesthe* ("work out") does not bear the sense of exteriority but rather of thoroughness. Paul's imperative "work out your own salvation" means "bring to accomplishment your own salvation."[64] Others assuage their theological anxiety by arguing that salvation here refers to a sociological well-being of the whole church, not of the individual. Gerald Hawthorne even translates, "Obediently work at achieving spiritual health."[65] It is true that salvation can denote health (e.g., Acts 27:34), just as the verb *save* may (e.g., Mt 9:21-22). But Paul always uses the noun *sōtēria* to refer to spiritual or eschatological salvation, and this includes his use in Philippians 1:19 and 1:28.[66]

Thus, Paul's admonition is clear. He urges the Philippians and us to "bring your own salvation to completion." To this he adds a qualifying phrase: we are to bring our salvation to completion "with fear and trembling" *(meta phobou kai tromou)*. The Greek Old Testament (LXX) uses this phrase in a variety of texts (esp. Ex 15:16; Ps 54:5 [English 55:5]; Is 19:16). Paul also uses it elsewhere, and wherever he does, it

---

[63]See, e.g., Charles H. Welch, *The Prize of the High Calling* (Surrey, U.K.: Canning, n.d.), pp. 113-16; and Lewis S. Chafer, *Systematic Theology* (Dallas: Dallas Theological Seminary, 1948), 3:312.

[64]For fuller discussion of this text, see Moisés Silva, *Philippians*, Wycliffe Exegetical Commentary (Chicago: Moody Press, 1988), pp. 134-42.

[65]Gerald F. Hawthorne, *Philippians*, Word Biblical Commentary (Waco, Tex.: Word, 1983), p. 96. Hawthorne takes Paul's imperative, *katergazesthe*, to mean "work at" instead of "work out to its conclusion" (see also pp. 98-99). Zane Hodges reasons, "It is clear that if the 'salvation' Paul speaks of here refers to escape from hell, then obedient works are a condition for that. . . . It follows that Paul must be talking about something quite different from the salvation he speaks of in Ephesians 2:8, 9 and Titus 3:4-7. As a matter of fact he is" (*Gospel Under Siege*, p. 96).

[66]Cf. Marshall, *Kept by the Power of God*, p. 124; Silva, *Philippians*, pp. 78, 96, 138; Peter T. O'Brien, *The Epistle to the Philippians: A Commentary on the Greek Text*, New International Greek Testament Commentary (Grand Rapids, Mich.: Eerdmans, 1991), pp. 277-79.

signifies a posture of obedience to God in view of our frailties and weaknesses (1 Cor 2:3; 2 Cor 7:15; Eph 6:5).[67] By urging "fear and trembling" Paul does not call on Christians to adopt an attitude of anxiety and dread, because Philippians 2:13 supports not shaken confidence but steadfast assurance. Such a frame of mind does not arise from doubt toward God or mistrust of his faithfulness, for it is humble and conscious of weakness. Therefore, it is also opposed to self-reliance. This fear does not paralyze one with dread or terror toward God; it is fear that gives rise to caution that looks away from self to God, who is the source of faith (cf. Phil 1:29).

Philippians 2:13 provides the basis for Paul's whole exhortation in verse 12, as indicated by his conjunction "for" *(gar)*. In other words, "because God is the one who mightily works in us both our desiring and our working unto his good pleasure," Christians therefore must "bring to accomplishment their own salvation with fear and trembling." Paul's choice of words and phrases accents the priority of God's work without minimizing the necessity of the believer's obedient act. Paul makes it clear, then, that God is the one who performs or causes *(ho energōn)* two things in the believer, both "the desire" *(to thelein)* and "the working" *(to energein)*. Therefore, Paul does not tell us to do our part in salvation because God has done his part. Nor does the apostle say that God has done everything so that all we should do is passively wait for God, as in the familiar slogan: "Let go and let God." Paul calls on the Christians at Philippi to bring to accomplishment their own salvation precisely because God is the one who mightily works in them at two levels, both their willing and their working.

God's working in us is not contingent on our desiring or doing, for God's working brings about our willing and working, though not mechanically. There is no mechanistic connection between conversion and final salvation. God works in us through exhortation and warning. God is at work in us causing us to desire and to work for his good pleasure, and God is at work through the gospel by urging us onward with the command to bring to completion our own salvation. From the inception of our desires toward God to their fulfillment in

---

[67]S. Pedersen, "'Mit Furcht und Zittern' (Phil. 2,12-13)," *Studia Theologica* 32 (1978): 17-21.

obedience, the work is of God so that it might be ours. This is surely a mystery that we must carefully guard against misstating. But it is evident from this text not only that exhortation is not contrary to God's mighty working in us to cause us to persevere, but also that God's working in us is the very basis on which the gospel exhorts and warns us. No text, perhaps in the whole Bible, makes it more plain that exhortation does not call into question the assurance of God's continual work in us to bring about our perseverance in obedience to Christ.[68] Assurance of God's work in us is not only completely compatible with God's urgent appeals to us to persevere in salvation; assurance of his work in us is the basis for admonishing and warning us to obey.[69]

A second passage in Paul's letter to the Philippians that demands our attention is Philippians 3:8-16. Paul is fond of the metaphor of the arena, and particularly of the footrace, for he uses it several times. As he used it in 1 Corinthians 9:24-27 to depict his own contest for salvation, so he uses it in this passage. In the former context Paul appealed to his own perseverance as a model for setting aside rights and freedoms in deference to others that he might participate in the life the gospel promises. In this passage he exploits his experience in terms of the athletic metaphor in order to warn against being enticed by anyone who is fascinated with circumcision for salvation, as preached by Judaizers.

With biting irony he warns, "Beware of the dogs! Beware of the evil workers! Beware of the mutilation!" (Phil 3:2).[70] Because Paul was con-

---

[68]G. C. Berkouwer writes, "Only because of the unbreakable connection between our faith and God's grace, between our love and God's love, is it understandable that there is such a serious admonition here. Anyone who busies himself with these connections in a logicistic fashion plunges himself into the abyss of pride or of frivolity. But faith and love turn their ear to the Scriptural admonition. It does not suggest a falling away from true faith, nor (which is the same) a falling away from the love of God; but it accents the relatedness in faith of the entire life to the grace of God" (*Faith and Perseverance*, trans. Robert D. Knudsen [Grand Rapids, Mich.: Eerdmans, 1958], pp. 121-22).

[69]John Eadie states it well when he says that "the divine purpose does not reduce a man to a machine, but works itself out by means in perfect harmony with the freedom and responsibility of his moral nature, so that every action has a motive and character" (*A Commentary on the Greek Text of the Epistle of Paul to the Philippians* [Edinburgh: T & T Clark, 1894], pp. 135-36).

[70]Paul turns on the Jews their own words for Gentiles. He won't even bring himself to dignify them as "the circumcision" *(hē peritomē)*, for he reserves that designation for believers (Phil 3:3). He refers to those who are fascinated with circumcision as "the mutilation" *(hē katatomē)*.

verted from heading down the eternal cul-de-sac of looking to the law as the basis for righteousness before God, he holds up before the Philippians his own Jewish pedigree, his former zeal for the law and his advancements in Judaism, then dashes all of it before them as utter loss and rubbish on account of Christ Jesus. Paul says something that sounds remarkable: "I regard them as rubbish, in order that I may gain Christ and be found in him" (Phil 3:8-9 NRSV). He expresses his desire with one continuous clause with two parallel segments: "in order that I may gain Christ and that I may be found in him." Paul's use of the verb "be found" echoes several Old Testament uses, such as "Noah found favor in the sight of the Lord" (Gen 6:8; cf. Ex 33:12-17; 34:9). Paul's two phrases—"in Christ" and "be found in him"—indicate that he is using the judicial metaphor of justification before the judgment seat of God, for he explains what he means in the remainder of verse 9: he wants to be found "not guilty." To "be found in him" means "not having a righteousness of my own that comes from the law, but one that comes through faith in Christ, the righteousness from God based on faith" (Phil 3:9 NRSV).

Wasn't Paul already "in Christ"? Wasn't he already justified? Certainly, but the apostle is expressing the interplay between the already and not-yet aspects of justification in Christ Jesus. This is similar to Paul's language in Galatians 5:5: "For through the Spirit, by faith, we eagerly wait for the hope of righteousness" (NRSV). Paul does not conceive of justification before God to be strictly past or future, for his concept of righteousness before God's judgment bar is vast enough to include both. Consequently, we need to be careful not to reduce his already-but-not-yet concept to one or the other. Paul is modeling for the Philippians the posture they must ever take if they desire to have God's justifying favor rest on them, whether now or in the day of Christ Jesus. There is never a time in our Christian lives that we can regard any of our achievements to be a basis for commendation before God. Christ alone is our hope of being found righteous before God. Clearly, the words of Philippians 3:10 clarify that to pursue Christ is to be wholly identified with Christ in both his sufferings and his resurrection unto life: "I want to know Christ and the power of his resurrection and the sharing of his sufferings by becoming like him in his death" (NRSV).

At first blush it seems remarkable that Paul continues to unpack his quest to "be found in Christ" in the day of judgment. For in his subsequent verses, using the race metaphor from the athletic arena, he speaks of his untiring pursuit of Christ, the prize to be won, while finding no satisfaction in present or past attainments. Evangelicals are certainly correct to protect against misunderstanding Paul's words as if he were suggesting that (1) by his quest he merits God's approval; or (2) because of his conditional language, he is uncertain whether he will attain final salvation. However, anxiety over these two concerns not only leads some to novel and excessive interpretations of this passage but also distracts many from understanding the apostle's meaning.

Any presumption that Paul implies ideas of meriting something from God should melt away in our discussion of the text. However, notions of uncertainty or certainty, derived from Paul's suppositions themselves, need some attention. For example, Paul says, "if somehow I may attain unto the resurrection from the dead" (Phil 3:11). Scholars debate whether Paul's "if somehow" expresses doubt or confidence. Therefore, exegetes attempt to cover for the alleged intrusion of doubt into Paul's expression of hope. Many scholars presume that Paul's expression "if somehow" *(ei pōs)* indicates doubt or uncertainty. But what is uncertain? Some argue that Paul does not indicate uncertainty about the outcome; he only expresses tentativeness to reflect humility and lack of self-trust to counteract the teachings of his perfectionist opponents.[71] Others claim that Paul is not calling into question the certainty of his resurrection but only that the means of his resurrection is uncertain, whether by martyrdom or by transformation at the coming of Christ.[72] In verse 12 Paul uses another conditional clause: "Not that I have already arrived or have already been perfected, but I pursue it, if I also may lay hold of that for which I was laid hold of by Christ Jesus." Again, some scholars contend that Paul is expressing the same self-distrust as in verse 11.[73] Yet others insist that his supposition indicates expectancy.[74]

---

[71]For example, Gundry Volf, *Paul and Perseverance,* pp. 254-58. See also Hawthorne, *Philippians,* p. 146; and Silva, *Philippians,* pp. 192-93.

[72]O'Brien, *Epistle to the Philippians,* pp. 412-13. S. Lewis Johnson assumes that Paul expresses doubt as he attempts to make a case that the apostle is speaking of his uncertainty whether or not he will participate in a rapture before the tribulation ("The Out-Resurrection from the Dead," *Bibliotheca Sacra* 110 [1953]: 140-41).

[73]Silva, *Philippians,* p. 201.

[74]Gundry Volf, *Paul and Perseverance,* pp. 258-59; Gordon D. Fee, *Paul's Letter to the Philippians,* New International Commentary on the New Testament (Grand Rapids, Mich.: Eerdmans, 1995), p. 345.

However, with all due respect to scholars, this debate whether Paul's conditional clauses—"if somehow I may attain" and "if I also may lay hold of"—imply doubt or confidence is misdirected. For, as we have demonstrated before, the Greek first-class condition itself says nothing about doubt or confidence nor about uncertainty or certainty. Even I. Howard Marshall admits, "There is, therefore, no uncertainty in this passage about Paul's own perseverance in the faith, and this passage must accordingly be removed from any list of passages which express doubt about final perseverance."[75] Doubt or confidence must derive from other contextual indicators, and in the context of Philippians 3:8-16, Paul expresses confidence. But before we proceed, we cannot pass over the significance of Marshall's candid admission, for it would seem that he admits that conditional statements, in themselves, do not imply doubt. Nevertheless, elsewhere he does derive doubt on the basis of conditional statements themselves (e.g., Mk 13:22). This demonstrates how easy it is to impose one's theological bias on the text. In a text such as Mark 13:22, Marshall takes the condition itself to imply doubtfulness of perseverance, but in Philippians 3:11-12, he sees no such inference. Why not? The suppositional structure is the same; both are Greek first-class conditional expressions. In the case of Philippians 3:11-12, Marshall lets other contextual indicators override his ordinary presumption based on conditional statements themselves.

What does Paul mean by using the conditional clauses in Philippians 3:11-12? In both verses, he assumes the suppositions to be true for the sake of the argument he is making. So he assumes for the sake of his argument that he will attain unto the resurrection from the dead, and he assumes for his argument that he will lay hold of that for which Christ laid hold of him. Of course, Paul's two assumptions do not declare his assumptions to be true, even though they may be true. The very function of his two conditional clauses is to assume his statements to be true for the advancement of his argument. Therefore, we are misguided to get mired in a discussion of whether or not Paul expresses doubt or confidence. If we do, we will miss the very point he is making.

What is that point? As he did with the Corinthians (1 Cor 9:23-27),

---

[75]Marshall, *Kept by the Power of God*, p. 120.

Paul poses as a model of perseverance for the Philippians. In view of this, his athletic metaphor functions to advance his initial expressions concerning his quest to be found in Christ. To the Philippians, he presents his own quest of being found in Christ, and as he advances his argument he portrays his own view of the reality of attaining that quest in terms of suppositions. To underscore the point that he, an apostle of Jesus Christ, has not yet fully attained his quest, he accents this by using conditional clauses. Between him and his goal—"being found in Christ"—lies the course through which he must persevere in both his initial disdain for past and present attainments and in keeping the eyes of faith fastened on Christ alone, who is the prize. When he entered this race in quest of Christ, he discounted the value of any previous achievements. Now, while he runs as a believer, he purposes to forget about things that lie behind him while he strains forward to attain the goal that lies ahead, "the prize of the upward call of God in Christ Jesus" (Phil 3:14). Paul's use of the athletic imagery is masterful, for no one running a race can let one's mind muse with fondness the distance attained and the speed maintained. Anyone satisfied with present achievement while the goal still lies ahead will surely lose the race for being irresolute. Thus, Paul continues to discount his Christian attainments, for they also have no power to commend him to God in the day of Christ Jesus.[76]

Paul's whole pursuit is Christ, and the metaphor from the athletic arena assists him in presenting his own quest as a model for the Philippians. As one enters this race in pursuit of Christ by faith, one sets the feet in the starting block. As one leaps from the block, singular faithfulness to the "upward call of God in Christ Jesus" will attain the goal. The whole devotedness of the runner with the eye set on the goal and giving no thought to the starting block or the lengthening distance that lies behind is an apt portrayal of Paul's own quest for Christ. Similarly, he applies this to the Philippians by saying, "As many as are perfect, let us think like this. And if someone thinks differently, God will reveal this understanding to you also. Only let us

---

[76]Though we disagree with Gundry Volf on the conditional clauses, we do agree with her when she says, "In the present context, commendation of moral endeavor would play right into the hands of those who have confidence in the flesh (cf. 3:3, 4). Rather, instead of glorying in his achievements in Judaism as the opponents do, Paul denigrates what he once considered to be 'gain' and embraces the single aim of knowing Christ, the one all-surpassing value (3:5-10)" (*Paul and Perseverance,* pp. 259-60).

live up to what we have already attained" (Phil 3:15-16).

Paul intends a play on the word *perfect,* for while he calls on "as many as are perfect" *(teleioi)* to join him in his quest, he also disclaims perfection: "Not that I have already arrived or have already been perfected" *(teleleiōmai;* Phil 3:12). By exhorting "as many as are perfect" to adopt his posture after his disclaimer ("not yet perfected"), he implicitly rebukes any who are flirting with the perfectionist teaching that threatens believers at Philippi. He calls them to renounce illusory contentment with past and present attainments, much as he renounced his own pedigree and achievements in Judaism (Phil 3:7-8). Also, with tongue in cheek, he recovers the category perfect from the false teachers as he preserves the designation circumcision for Christians and gives Judaizers the epithet mutilation. Therefore, Paul's wordplay accents the already-but-not-yet orientation that he wants his readers to adopt with him. Paul's already-but-not-yet orientation on salvation not only corrects the temporal error (perfected already) but also the spatial error of earthly mindedness, for Paul continues by contrasting the "enemies of the cross of Christ" who have "their minds set on earthly things" with believers whose "citizenship is in heaven" (Phil 3:19-20). Therefore, perfection is not a present possession but the prize that believers pursue by faith. As with a runner in the arena, the prize at the goal determines present conduct. In sum, the verse with which Paul began to pose as a model of perseverance—"For it is we who are the circumcision, who worship in the Spirit of God and boast in Christ Jesus and have no confidence in the flesh" (Phil 3:3 NRSV)—governs the whole admonition. Unlike the backward and earthly oriented Judaizers, who put confidence in the flesh, believers already live in the heavenly Spirit and, therefore, are both prospective and upward in orientation as they pursue Christ.

Colossians 1:21-23. Colossians 1:21-23 is one of several biblical texts to which many arguments about perseverance have turned. Paul writes:

> Once you were alienated from God and were enemies in your minds because of your evil behavior. But now he has reconciled you by Christ's physical body through death to present you holy in his sight, without blemish and free from accusation—if you continue in your faith, established and firm, not moved from the hope held out in the gospel. (Col 1:21-23 NIV)

As we consider how interpreters read this passage, we note two points of contention: whether the apostle expresses doubt or confidence, and whether the orientation should be prospective or retrospective.

Like Philippians 3:11-12, this passage uses the Greek first-class condition. Also, both passages use intensified forms of the supposition (*ei pōs,* Phil 3:11; *ei ge,* Col 1:23). The tendency among scholars is to overinterpret such texts, either to exclude doubt or to accent doubt, depending largely on one's theological commitments. S. Lewis Johnson, for example, comments, "The *ei* (AV, 'if'), it may be noted, introduces a first-class condition, determined as fulfilled. The apostle assumes the Colossians will abide in their faith."[77] Other scholars pass the error on in their commentaries. Thus James D. G. Dunn suggests that Paul's conditional suggests "confidence more than doubt."[78] It is conceivable that scholars can be wrong, and they are in error frequently concerning the first-class condition. Paul's use of the intensified condition "if indeed" *(ei ge)* has its ordinary intensive function; it lays great stress on the condition as absolutely essential for the attainment of being presented holy in God's sight (Col 1:22).[79] Neither doubt nor certainty resides in the condition itself. Paul's condition means Christ "will present you holy before him . . . assuming for the sake of the argument (and that is precisely what I am doing) that you persevere in your faith."[80]

We do not need to say much about Paul's orientation. Though Dunn wrongly introduces confidence into Paul's conditional admonition, he is correct when he identifies Paul's orientation: "But final

---

[77]S. Lewis Johnson, "Studies in the Epistle to the Colossians: IV. From Enmity to Amity," *Bibliotheca Sacra* 119 (1962): 147.

[78]J. D. G. Dunn contributes to the longstanding confusion about first-class conditions when he says that *ei ge* "may denote confidence more than doubt. . . . But final acceptance is nevertheless dependent on remaining in the faith" (*The Epistles to the Colossians and to Philemon,* New International Greek Testament Commentary [Grand Rapids, Mich.: Eerdmans, 1996], p. 110). Gundry Volf extends this confusion further by saying, "Paul does not convey doubt with the words 'provided that you continue in the faith . . .' (1:23), but expects that the Colossians will do so, as the indicative mood following *[ei ge]* suggests" (*Paul and Perseverance,* p. 197 n. 231).

[79]Cf. J. D. Denniston, *The Greek Particles,* 2nd ed. (Oxford: Clarendon Press, 1946), p. 146. See also William Sanday and Arthur C. Headlam, *A Critical and Exegetical Commentary on the Epistle to the Romans,* 4th ed., International Critical Commentary (Edinburgh: T & T Clark, 1900), p. 96.

[80]D. A. Carson agrees: "In a first-class condition the *protasis* [if] is assumed true for the sake of the argument, but the thing actually assumed may or may not be true. To put it another way, there is stress on the reality of the assumption, but not on the reality of the content that is assumed" (*Exegetical Fallacies,* p. 77). Cf. E. D. Burton, *Syntax of the Moods and Tenses in New Testament Greek,* 3rd ed. (1898; reprint, Grand Rapids, Mich.: Kregel, 1976), pp. 100-103.

acceptance is nevertheless dependent on remaining in the faith."[81] But Johnson thinks Paul's orientation is retrospective, for he mistakenly concludes that Colossians 1:21-23 functions as a test of faith, for "if faith fails, that is the evidence that the faith was not valid saving faith (cf. 1 Jn. 2:19)."[82] Although this is certainly the truth that 1 John 2:19 expresses, it is an inadequate explanation of Paul's meaning, for the apostle's admonition is clearly forward looking, not retrospective. His orientation is on the day of judgment as Colossians 1:22 indicates: "to present you holy in his sight, without blemish and free from accusation" (NIV). Thus, once again Paul admonishes us to remain steadfast in faith in order that we may attain unto salvation in the last day.

Admonition and Warning in Hebrews

No discussion of biblical warnings and admonitions would be complete apart from considering the urgent warnings in Hebrews. Here one finds five warning passages: Hebrews 2:1-4; 3:1—4:13; 5:11—6:12; 10:19-39; 12:12-29.[83] As one studies these five passages, it becomes apparent that there is a crescendo effect, for the preacher, the author of Hebrews, intensifies each warning. The preacher begins with a caution lest we "ignore so great salvation," an act compared to the imperceptible drifting of a ship whose anchor fails to grasp the sea floor (Heb 2:1-4). With each warning the preacher makes the call more urgent and severe to avert increasingly more defiant responses to God's final revelation by his Son in these last days (cf. Heb 1:1-4). Figure 4.2 illustrates how the five warnings intensify.

The warnings escalate in their tone of urgency, for the first begins by warning against careless failure to hear Christ speak (Heb 2:1-4), but the last warns against defiant refusal to hear Christ who speaks from heaven (Heb 12:12-29).

As we consider the warnings of Hebrews, we will discuss them together, for they all reflect the same four components. Each passage (1) warns (2) the hearers lest they (3) sin by forsaking Christ

---

[81] Dunn, *Epistles to the Colossians and to Philemon*, p. 110.

[82] Johnson, "Studies in the Epistle to the Colossians," p. 147.

[83] Scholars vary on how they identify the warnings. For example, Scot McKnight identifies the five warnings: 2:1-4; 3:7—4:13; 5:11—6:12; 10:19-39; 12:1-29 ("The Warning Passages of Hebrews: A Formal Analysis and Theological Conclusions," *Trinity Journal* n.s. 13 (1992): 22.

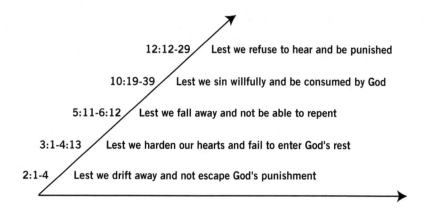

Figure 4.2. Ascending strength and urgency of warnings in Hebrews

Jesus and (4) fall subject to the dreadful consequences of apostasy.[84] Because each subsequent warning intensifies the preacher's urgent admonition, each one contributes distinctive features to the preacher's "word of exhortation" (Heb 13:22). Nonetheless, because the sin against which the author warns is the same—it is apostasy ranging from carelessness to defiance—it is right that we should consider all five passages together rather than separately.

Framing the right question. The questions we ask concerning the biblical text guide the course and outcome of our interpretive work. We need to listen to the text so that we might recognize the primary question we should address. Both Wayne Grudem and Scot McKnight raise the same primary questions but come to opposing conclusions. Grudem asks, "Were these people really saved in the first place? And if they were, does this passage prove that true Christians can lose their salvation?"[85] Likewise, McKnight asks, "Who are the subjects? Are they genuine believers? Or, are they false or pretentious believ-

---

[84]Cf. ibid., p. 25. McKnight also identifies four essential elements in the warnings, but he presents them differently.

[85]Wayne Grudem, "Perseverance of the Saints: A Case Study of Hebrews 6:4-6 and the Other Warning Passages in Hebrews," in *Still Sovereign: Contemporary Perspectives on Election, Foreknowledge, and Grace,* ed. Thomas R. Schreiner and Bruce A. Ware (Grand Rapids, Mich.: Baker, 2000), p. 133.

ers?"[86] Though both handle the biblical text with skill and ably present their respective interpretations, each seems to bias his case from the outset by posing the question that fails to address the purpose of the warning passages. It is not surprising, then, that Grudem concludes that Hebrews 6:4-6 refers to people who "had never truly been saved in the first place" or that he extends this conclusion to all five warnings in Hebrews.[87] On the other hand, one should not be surprised that McKnight concludes, "we can 'lose' the present dimensions of salvation that have already been inaugurated and experienced. . . . But, we certainly need to be careful of what we are saying if we say that the author of Hebrews states that we can 'lose salvation' because, for him, salvation is largely a future state of affairs."[88]

As we have demonstrated earlier, the questions Grudem and Mc-Knight ask are not primary, and they tend to beg the question, for the very questions they raise imply their respective conclusions. Therefore, the first question we should ask concerning the five passages in Hebrews concerns the function of each passage. What purpose or objective does it serve? What was the author's intention? To what end were these passages penned? In the titles of their essays, both Grudem and McKnight refer to these five segments of Hebrews as "warning passages," yet neither poses the fundamental question in terms of the function of warning. Both frame their primary questions not in terms that seek to uncover the warning function of the passages, but in terms that protect their own theological commitments. How do the questions they ask bias the outcome of their interpretations?

How wrong questions bias interpretation. Consider the approach that Grudem takes concerning Hebrews 6:4-6. Grudem's interpretation of this passage stands in a long tradition that extends at least back to John Calvin.[89] However, more influential is the commentary on Hebrews by Puritan scholar and preacher John Owen, who has convinced many Calvinists to adopt the tests-of-genuineness approach to

---

[86]McKnight, "Warning Passages," p. 27.

[87]Grudem, "Perseverance of the Saints," p. 173; cf. p. 179.

[88]McKnight, "Warning Passages," p. 58.

[89]John Calvin, *Commentary on the Epistle of Paul the Apostle to the Hebrews,* trans. John Owen (reprint, Grand Rapids, Mich.: Baker, 1979), pp. 135-40.

biblical warnings.[90] Owen's introductory comments outline the direction his exposition of the verses will take. He sets out to correct the idea "that they are real and true believers who are" spoken of in these verses.[91] Owen, therefore, argues that a person may be "enlightened," yet this light does not "renew, change, or transform" the person "as a gracious saving light" does.[92] Likewise, one may "taste of the heavenly gift," which is the Holy Spirit, and still not experience the saving work of the Spirit. Those who do so only taste the gift for an "experiment" or "trial" but do not eat or drink.[93] So also, some may receive a "share of the Holy Spirit," which refers to spiritual gifts, and fail to receive salvation, just as Simon Magus did (Acts 8:21).[94] Owen claims the same is true of the words "tasted the goodness of God's word, and the powers of the age to come."[95] He concludes that the text makes it apparent that Hebrews 6:4-6 addresses people who "are not true and sincere believers," and he believes that the absence of any reference to faith or believing in their description confirms his conclusion.[96]

Owen's influence on current advocates of the same view is clear. For example, Roger Nicole claims that the experiences the text describes "may have been chosen by design to describe those who have received the greatest possible external exposure to the truth, including a temporary profession of allegiance to it."[97] Wayne Grudem also echoes Owen's interpretation of the warning.[98] Like Owen, Grudem argues that if the biblical author had described the people under question with distinctively Christian characteristics such as faith, hope or love, and if the author had described them as people who had entered God's rest, whose sins had been forgiven and whose consciences had been cleansed, then "we could rightly say, 'No more

---

[90]John Owen, *An Exposition of the Epistle to the Hebrews,* ed. W. H. Goold (1855; reprint, Grand Rapids, Mich.: Baker, 1980), 5:69-91. Owen follows John Calvin's reading of the text as addressing people who fall short of being authentic believers.

[91]Ibid., p. 70.

[92]Ibid., p. 76.

[93]Ibid., pp. 79-80.

[94]Ibid., pp. 80-81.

[95]Ibid., pp. 82-83.

[96]Ibid., p. 84.

[97]Roger Nicole, "Some Comments on Hebrews 6:4-6 and the Doctrine of the Perseverance of God with the Saints," in *Current Issues in Biblical and Patristic Interpretation: Studies in Honor of Merrill C. Tenney Presented by His Former Students,* ed. Gerald F. Hawthorne (Grand Rapids, Mich.: Eerdmans, 1975), p. 362.

[98]Grudem, "Perseverance of the Saints," pp. 133-82.

clear description of genuine Christians could be given.' "[99] But finding no such descriptions, Grudem concludes "that persons other than genuine Christians are being described here."[100]

One may think that the other four warnings in Hebrews address believers because the descriptive language in them is the kind that Grudem looks for in Hebrews 6:4-6 but does not find there. For example, in Hebrews 2:1-4, the author even includes himself within the warning by saying, "Therefore, we must give attention more closely to the things we heard, lest we drift away" (Heb 2:1). Likewise, in Hebrews 3:6 the author says, "and we are his house if we hold firm the confidence and the pride that belong to hope" (NRSV). Grudem explains, however, "Rather, the purpose is always to warn those who are thinking of falling away or have fallen away that if they do this it is a strong indication that they were never saved in the first place."[101] One would also think that the people addressed in Hebrews 10:26-31 must be Christians, because the text says they have "received knowledge of the truth" and were "sanctified." But once again, Grudem explains that receiving knowledge of the truth is a synonym for "enlightened" (Heb 6:4), and neither expression denotes "saving faith."[102] Neither should anyone regard the word *sanctify* to indicate that the people addressed are believers, because the word can be used to describe outward or ceremonial cleansing (e.g., Heb 9:13; Mt 23:17, 19; 1 Tim 4:5). Thus, the warning addresses people who have been outwardly sanctified, or cleansed, but not inwardly cleansed by faith. Therefore, Grudem concludes that the warning "refers to someone who heard and understood the gospel, and joined in worship before God with the assembly of Christians, but who rejected this great privilege and therefore became liable to 'a fearful prospect of judgment' (10:27)."[103]

Nicole, on whose interpretation Grudem draws to support his own, takes all of the descriptive traits in Hebrews 6:4-6 to refer to people who are not real Christians. Most glaring is his handling of the final description, repentance. He recognizes that those warned in Hebrews

---

[99]Ibid., p. 170.
[100]Ibid.
[101]Ibid., p. 176.
[102]Ibid., pp. 176-77.
[103]Ibid., p. 179.

6:4-6 had once repented ("restore again to repentance," v. 4) and that this "confront[s] us with greater difficulties than any of the other seven descriptions."[104] Nicole proposes two possible interpretations: (1) John Owen's distinction between authentic or internal repentance and external repentance, and (2) William Gouge's distinction between profession of repentance and a state of repentance. Then Nicole plays his theological trump card: "Neither of these explanations appears entirely free of difficulty, although one may prefer to have recourse to them rather than be forced to the conclusion that regenerate individuals may be lost."[105] McKnight properly points out, "What Nicole is saying is that he prefers an explanation that is extremely difficult . . . over giving up his theological position!"[106]

The question that controls Nicole's and Grudem's interpretative work (as with Calvin, Owen and Gouge) draws them away from understanding the passages as warnings that project consequences that will invariably follow persistent departure from Christ, whether by imperceptibly drifting away from him through ignoring the salvation announced by the Lord (Heb 2:1-4) or by blatantly refusing to hear him who speaks and warns from heaven (Heb 12:25). Instead, because Grudem asks, "Were these people really saved in the first place?" he redirects the orientation of the passages from prospective warnings to retrospective characterizations of certain people whom the author of Hebrews singles out and addresses. Therefore, for Owen, Nicole and Grudem, the warnings of Hebrews have two retrospective functions. First, the warnings call on readers to examine whether their conversion is genuine. Second, the warnings tell the readers that apostasy will reveal that they were never genuine Christians. We believe that both of these themes are found in the New Testament. However, we do not believe that this properly explains the warnings in Hebrews, which are prospective: if you apostatize, then you will not inherit the promised salvation. It is a case of correct theology from the wrong text.

The root problem with Grudem's interpretation of the warnings in Hebrews is that he fails to acknowledge that salvation, according to Hebrews, is fundamentally future oriented, as McKnight correctly

---

[104]Nicole, "Some Comments on Hebrews 6:4-6," p. 361.
[105]Ibid.
[106]McKnight, "Warning Passages," p. 52.

demonstrates (cf. Heb 1:14; 2:3, 10; 5:9; 9:28).[107] Because Grudem conceives of salvation in terms of the past rather than the future, he reads the consequences (the apodosis) of the warnings retrospectively. He imposes a grammatical and theological misunderstanding of the consequence (apodosis) on the conditional clause (protasis), so that the whole warning, expressed as a supposition, becomes little more than an indicative description of the apostate. It turns out, therefore, that the warning simply declares that these people "were never saved in the first place."[108]

McKnight correctly recognizes not only that the author of Hebrews primarily portrays salvation as a future reward, but also that the author's warnings urge the readers to persevere to attain final salvation, which is not yet fully realized: "Thus, for the author, salvation, though experienced now in its inaugurated form, is something reserved for God's persevering people until the return of Jesus Christ (9:28)."[109] Nevertheless, because McKnight, like Grudem and Nicole, begins with the wrong question, he also overextends his interpretive work, but in the opposite direction. Because McKnight begins with the same primary question that Grudem asks, he also answers the question from his theological commitments more than from the warnings themselves. Consequently, he also takes an exegetical leap. We agree with McKnight that Hebrews warns believers against "the drastic consequences of eternal damnation if a person does not persevere in the faith."[110] However, we contend that if Grudem converts conditional warnings about prospective salvation and destruction into retrospective indications of false profession of faith, McKnight converts conditional warnings into declarative announcements of possible apostasy on the part of authentic believers.[111] As we have shown before, this is an unwarranted conclusion from the text, because conditional warnings in themselves do not function to indicate anything about possible failure or fulfillment. Instead, the conditional warnings appeal to our minds to conceive or imagine the invariable consequences that come to all who pursue a course of apostasy from Christ.

---

[107]Ibid., pp. 55-58.
[108]Grudem, "Perseverance of the Saints," p. 176.
[109]McKnight, "Warning Passages," p. 58.
[110]Ibid., p. 54.
[111]Ibid., p. 55.

We also believe that McKnight's use of conditional warnings in Hebrews is subversive to Christian belief and confidence, not encouraging or consoling, as the preacher intends them to be (Heb 13:22). Why is it subversive to the faith and confidence that Hebrews exhorts? It is because if McKnight's interpretation of the warnings is correct, we would have to doubt whether or not we will inherit God's promised salvation in order that we might feel the full impact of the warnings both to believe them and to avoid God's judgment and inherit salvation. We would have to cast aside confidence in God's faithfulness to keep his promise to us (Heb 10:22-23), in order to obey God's warning lest we "willfully persist in sin" and "fall into the hands of the living God" and be consumed along with his enemies (Heb 10:26-31).

Warnings as God's means of salvation. All the warnings in Hebrews are clearly future oriented, with the possible exception in chapter 3. Both Hebrews 3:6 and 14 pose some difficulty. Respectively, the two verses read "Christ, however, was faithful over God's house as a son, and we are his house if we hold firm the confidence and the pride that belong to hope" and "For we have become partners of Christ, if only we hold our first confidence firm to the end" (NRSV). In both verses something is contingent on perseverance: "we are his house," and "partners of Christ." Although verse 6 uses the present tense ("we are his house") in the consequent or apodosis of the supposition, this is no obstacle, for the present tense can bear a future sense (cf. 1 Cor 15:2).[112] Verse 14 is more difficult because the consequent of the supposition uses the perfect tense. Because of the perfect-tense verb, Carson says, "we have become . . . partakers of Christ if we now, in the present, hold firmly to the confidence we had at first."[113] Carson concludes, then, that perseverance is "the evidence of what has taken place in the past."[114] Carson is saying that perseverance is the consequence of "sharing in Christ."[115] Therefore, one may be tempted to read this supposition not as an admonition to persevere in order to be a partaker of Christ, but as an exhorta-

---

[112]Wallace, *Greek Grammar Beyond the Basics*, pp. 535-37.

[113]Carson, *Exegetical Fallacies*, pp. 84-85.

[114]Ibid., p. 85.

[115]Ibid. Carson says, "If persevering shows we have (already) come to share in Christ, it can only be because sharing in Christ has perseverance for its inevitable fruit." We agree with the theology, but we do not believe that Heb 3:14 proves it.

tion to persevere in order to demonstrate that you are a partaker of Christ already.

However, there are three problems with this interpretation. First, the verb "we have become" in Hebrews 3:14 does not bear the sense "prove to be" sharers in Christ. Rather, as Hebrews 3:14 reiterates the admonition of Hebrews 3:6, the perfect-tense verb "we are become" replaces the present-tense verb of 3:6, "we are." Second, the grammar of Hebrews 3:14 is against taking perseverance as the consequence of sharing in Christ. Rather, sharing in Christ is the consequence of perseverance. The fact that the consequent of the supposition uses the perfect tense ("we have become") does not permit us to shift the future-oriented condition ("if we hold firmly . . . unto the end") to function as if it were the consequent of sharing in Christ. Stanley Porter agrees, for he contends that "the author draws a timeless conclusion" from his mention of the rest God gives his people.[116] The supposition is "If we hold firm the beginning of our confidence unto the end, then we are become partakers of Christ." Because Hebrews 3:14 says that sharing in Christ is contingent on holding firm to the end the confidence we had at the beginning, the orientation of the consequent is to the future, to the end. While the supposition is clearly future oriented, the conclusion itself is timeless. The point of the exhortation, then, is that if we retain the beginning of our confidence firm to the end, whether the end be now or not yet, we "are become partakers of Christ." The third problem with Carson's explanation of the text is the intensified conditional (*eanper* in both Heb 3:6, 14). This intensified conditional may be represented by translating it "if only we hold firm." This stresses the necessity of fulfilling the supposition in order that the consequent may be realized. In Hebrews 3:14, the emphasized supposition entails retaining the beginning of our confidence to the very end, a clear future orientation.

We conclude, therefore, that the admonition of Hebrews 3:14 has the same orientation and objective as the warning of Hebrews 3:12-13: "Watch out, brothers and sisters, lest there be in any of you an evil, unfaithful heart by turning away from the living God, but exhort

---

[116]Stanley E. Porter, *Verbal Aspect in the Greek of the New Testament, with Reference to Tense and Mood,* Studies in Biblical Greek 1 (New York: Peter Lang, 1989), p. 269.

one another daily, as long as it is called 'today,' lest any of you be hardened by the deceitfulness of sin. We are become partakers of Christ, if only we hold firmly the beginning of our confidence to the end" (Heb 3:12-14). Both the warning and the admonition function to encourage us to persevere in order that we may receive salvation. Salvation or "sharing in Christ" is ours as a consequence of resolute perseverance in holding firm our first confidence unto the end. Rather clearly, the admonition of Hebrews 3:14 functions in the same way as the exhortation in Hebrews 6:11-12: "We want each one of you to show the same diligence so as to realize the full assurance of hope to the very end, so that you may not become sluggish, but imitators of those who through faith and patience inherit the promises" (NRSV). Both call for us to endure faithfully to the end, for salvation belongs only to those who persevere to the end.

Each of the five warning passages in Hebrews contributes its own particular features to the sustained and escalating urgency of the call for perseverance. Yet all the passages carry a singular message: promised salvation is the inheritance that comes only to those who, after entering into salvation, persevere in faithfulness to the end (Heb 1:14—2:4; 3:11-14; 6:12; 9:15; 10:36; 11:39), for God reserves his promise until the second advent of Jesus Christ (Heb 9:28).

As intense as the warnings are in Hebrews, they do not nullify or contradict equally strong admonitions to bold confidence. In fact, Hebrews intermingles admonitions to bold confidence with warnings against eternal perishing. This is particularly noteworthy in both Hebrews 6 and 10. In Hebrews 6, after warning the audience against falling away, the preacher concedes that there are grounds to believe that they have not taken the fatal step of departing from Christ because God is not unjust to abandon his people (Heb 6:9-10). Then we read, "We want each one of you to show the same diligence so as to realize the full assurance of hope to the very end, so that you may not become sluggish, but imitators of those who through faith and patience inherit the promises" (Heb 6:11-12 NRSV). The preacher follows this by assuring the readers that when God made his promise to Abraham he swore an oath in order to show "the heirs of the promise the unchangeable character of his purpose" (Heb 6:17). We who are Abraham's heirs have God's promise and oath to assure us that the promised salvation is a sure hope, "a sure and steadfast anchor of the soul" (Heb 6:19). Clearly, the preacher expects us to take to heart both the warning against perishing (Heb 6:4-8) and the admonition to confidence (Heb 6:9-20) without any sense of contradiction. Spurgeon poses a question about the function of *if* in 6:4-6:

> If God has put it in, he has put it in for wise reasons and for excellent purposes. Let me show you why. First, O Christian, it is put in to keep thee from falling away. God preserves his children from falling away; but he keeps them by the use of means. . . . There is a deep precipice: what is the best way to keep any one from going down there? Why, to tell him that if he did he would inevitably be dashed to pieces. In some old castle there is a deep cellar, where there is a vast amount of fixed air and gas, which would kill anybody who went down. What does the guide say? "If you go down you will never come up alive." Who thinks of going down? The very fact of the guide telling us what the consequences would be, keeps us from it. Our friend puts away from us a cup of arsenic; he does not want us to drink it, but he says, "If you drink it, it will kill you." Does he suppose for a moment that we should drink it. No; he tells us the consequences, and he is sure we will not do it. So God says, "My child, if you fall over this precipice you will be dashed to pieces." What does the child do? He says, "Father, keep me; hold thou me up, and I shall be safe." It leads the believer to greater dependence on God, to a holy fear and caution, because he knows that if he were to fall away he could not be renewed, and he stands far away from that great gulf, because he knows that if he were to fall into it there would be no salvation for him.[117]

Hebrews does not call on us to doubt our inheritance of God's sworn promise in order to heed God's urgent warning against falling away and perishing without hope of renewed repentance. God uses warning and consolation or threat and promise together to secure us in the way of salvation.[118]

Likewise, in Hebrews 10 the preacher urges us on to great confidence and then warns us sternly lest "we willfully persist in sin after having received the knowledge of the truth" (Heb 10:26 NRSV). Ponder the confidence and assurance to which the preacher calls us:

> Therefore, my friends, since we have confidence to enter the sanctuary by the blood of Jesus, by the new and living way that he opened for us

---

[117]Cf. Charles Spurgeon's sermon on Heb 6:4-6 ("Final Perseverance," in *The New Park Street Pulpit*, posted on The Spurgeon Archives [2000] < www.spurgeon.org/sermons/0075.htm >).

[118]Cf. Berkouwer, *Faith and Perseverance*, pp. 118-19.

through the curtain (that is, through his flesh), and since we have a great priest over the house of God, let us approach with a true heart in full assurance of faith, with our hearts sprinkled clean from an evil conscience and our bodies washed with pure water. Let us hold fast to the confession of our hope without wavering, for he who has promised is faithful. And let us consider how to provoke one another to love and good deeds, not neglecting to meet together, as is the habit of some, but encouraging one another, and all the more as you see the Day approaching. (Heb 10:19-25 NRSV)

Strong as these admonitions are, the warning that follows hardly suggests that one has to doubt either one's "confession of hope" or that "he who has promised is faithful" to secure us for the approaching day of salvation and judgment (Heb 10:23, 25). Without any hint of contradiction the preacher thoroughly integrates the call for bold confidence with the intense warning that follows. The preacher's admonition to steadfast confidence before God and warning lest we perish by willful persistence in sin work together as God's means to preserve us loyal to Christ unto the end. Therefore, the preacher commingles calls for confidence and perseverance again by saying, "Do not, therefore, abandon that confidence of yours; it brings a great reward. For you need endurance, so that when you have done the will of God, you may receive what was promised" (Heb 10:35-36 NRSV).

Conclusion: The Function of Warnings and Admonitions

How does the Bible correlate God's promises and threats? How does the Bible hold together God's assurance of salvation and his warnings lest we fail to persevere and thus perish? This chapter has interacted with the four popular explanations of biblical warnings and admonitions we first introduced in chapter one. We have argued that none of the four views adequately explains the biblical evidence concerning the correlation between divine promise and warning. The first three viewpoints assume that suppositional warnings and admonitions raise doubts concerning the faith of those they address. All three deduce too much from biblical warnings and admonitions, but each view has its distinctive explanation. First, both the loss-of-salvation view and the loss-of-rewards view presume that the warnings are disingenuous if they do not indicate that it is entirely possible for genuine Christians to fail to persevere or apostatize. Their primary disagreement, we noted, concerns what is lost: salvation or rewards.

Those who hold that believers may lose salvation argue that the Bible warns us in spite of the fact that the Bible also assures believers of God's saving protection. Those who claim that only rewards may be lost believe that biblical warnings and admonitions only concern rewards and have no correlation to the Bible's assurances of salvation to those who believe. Others, who explain the warnings and admonitions as tests of genuine faith, also believe that warnings (e.g., Heb 6:4-6) raise doubts and that admonitions (e.g., Col 1:23) assure certainty about people they address. Advocates of this view associate biblical warnings and promises as flip sides of one another: promises assure believers, but warnings expose disingenuous believers. The fourth interpretation gets its designation—"hypothetical view"—from its explanation of the suppositional language used by biblical warnings, especially those in Hebrews. Champions of this view explain warnings as follows: if a believer could apostatize, it would be impossible for that one to be saved again.

We are not convinced that any of these four views has the power to explain biblical warnings and admonitions satisfactorily. Biblical evidence indicates that warnings function harmoniously with promises, not against or in spite of promises. This is true whether the promise is conditional or unconditional. So far from implying that warning and promise are incompatible, the biblical writers presuppose that the two stand compatibly together.[119] We will conceive of warning and promise as opposites or as contrary to one another "only if we misunderstand the nature of perseverance and treat it in isolation from its correlation with faith."[120] Conditional promises and warnings do not contradict the assurance of unconditional promises. Furthermore, we believe that an evenhanded reading of the biblical text does not support the idea that gospel warnings expose unbelief or indicate what would happen if a believer could fall away. For a proper grasp of the

---

[119]Concerning this relationship Berkouwer astutely observes, "We will never be able to understand these words if we see the divine preservation and our preservation of ourselves as mutually exclusive or as in a synthetic cooperation. Preserving ourselves is not an independent thing that is added paradoxically to the divine preservation. God's preservation and our self-preservation do not stand in mere coordination, but in a marvelous way they are in correlation. One can formulate it best in this way: our preservation of ourselves is entirely oriented to God's preservation of us" (ibid., p. 104).

[120]Ibid., p. 111.

correlation between God's warnings and his assurance of preservation, it is precisely the warning that is significant. By way of conditional appeals, God arrests our attention to understand that he preserves us by using warnings, admonitions and conditional promises.[121] Indeed, if we persevere we will be saved; if we fail to persevere we will perish. The suppositional language of warnings and admonitions sustains the initial call: if you believe in the Lord Jesus Christ, you will be saved; if you fail to believe, you will perish. Just as we began the Christian pilgrimage by receiving Christ by faith, so we must walk in him, an image of persistent belief (Col 2:6-7). Therefore, warnings and admonitions function to extend the initial call of the gospel on throughout our lives, relentlessly calling us to be faithful to Jesus Christ and as road signs always pointing out the narrow pathway to salvation but also clearly marking the wide road to destruction.

Furthermore, our persevering in faithfulness to Jesus Christ "does not imply that we contribute our part and that God contributes His."[122] Anyone who supposes that our perseverance is an action independent of God's grace and love will invariably represent this in terms of earning a reward from God, as the loss-of-rewards view does. However, biblical admonitions and warnings imply nothing about earning or meriting something from God. Rather, the unconditional promise grounds both the conditional promise and the conditional warning in God's grace, for the biblical testimony is that God's grace and love precedes and creates all human faith and obedience (Eph 2:10) and that perseverance is possible only through belief that is born from grace. The gospel explains and sustains its initial call for

---

[121]Louis Berkhof states, "There are warnings against apostasy which would seem to be quite uncalled for, if the believer could not fall away. . . . But these warnings regard the whole matter from the side of man and are seriously meant. They prompt self-examination, and are instrumental in keeping believers in the way of perseverance. They do not prove that any of the addressed will apostatize, but simply that the use of means is necessary to prevent them from committing this sin" (*Systematic Theology*, 4th ed., rev. and enlarged [Grand Rapids, Mich.: Eerdmans, 1974], p. 548). William Lane Craig, a renowned contemporary Christian philosopher, wrote an essay that contends that the classical Reformed explanation of biblical admonitions and warnings actually agrees with Luis Molina's "middle knowledge view." For those interested in the essay, see William Lane Craig, " 'Lest Anyone Should Fall': A Middle Knowledge Perspective on Perseverance and Apostolic Warnings," *International Journal for Philosophy of Religion* 29 (1991): 65-74. We assess Craig's argument in an appendix to this book.

[122]Berkouwer, *Faith and Perseverance*, p. 105.

faith by its multifaceted warnings, admonitions and conditional promises in order that we may persevere in belief to the very end and be saved. The gospel warnings and admonitions continually point out the pathway of salvation.[123] The pathway is faithfulness to Jesus Christ.

Warnings and admonitions do not say anything about what is possible in the sense of "capable or likely to happen." The words *possibility* or *possible* are not suitable to capture the intention and function of conditional warnings and admonitions because they are too ambiguous. The words *possible* and *possibility* may denote something as capable of being anticipated, considered or imagined. However, as we have demonstrated, many theologians mean more than this. We have shown that advocates of both the loss-of-salvation view and the loss-of-rewards view insist that the warnings speak of possibility in the sense of something that is capable or likely to occur. Warnings and admonitions, however, express what is capable of being conceived with the mind. They speak of things conceivable or imaginable, not of things likely to happen. In fact, this is the objective of warnings and admonitions. They appeal to the mind to conceive how actions have consequences. Warnings and exhortations project a supposition that calls us to imagine that a particular course of action has an unequivocal and inviolable consequence. Because they are suppositional, warnings and admonitions appeal to our imaginations. They fundamentally form a conception, because warnings and admonitions are conceptual. They project concepts that have not yet come to pass. They appeal to our minds to conceive of cause-and-effect relationships or of the relationship between God's appointed means and end. They warn us on the basis of God's inviolable promise and threat proclaimed in the gospel: salvation is only for those who believe to the end. Thus, all the warnings caution us concerning conceivable conse-

---

[123]Berkouwer captures well the biblical perspective on warnings. He states, "The doctrine of the perseverance of the saints can never become an *a priori* guarantee in the life of believers which would enable them to get along without admonitions and warnings. Because of the nature of the relation between faith and perseverance, the whole gospel must abound with admonitions. It has to speak thus, because perseverance is not something that is merely handed down to us, but it is something that comes to realization only in the path of faith. Therefore the most earnest and alarming admonitions cannot in themselves be taken as evidence against the doctrine of perseverance" (ibid., pp. 110-11).

quences. They do not confront us with an uncertain future. They do not say that we may perish. Rather, they caution us lest we perish. They warn that we will surely perish if we fail to heed God's call in the gospel.

Road signs caution against conceivable consequences, not probable consequences. Every day people choose certain courses of action based on conceivable ideas of action and consequence, not on the basis that the action and consequence are likely to happen. As we drive along highways, we make decisions that affect our safety. Signs along the highway warn of curves ahead or of slippery bridges or of falling rocks. Their purpose is not to cause me to doubt my capability of driving. Their function is not to call into question my ability to drive by frightening me that I might crash. Rather, warning signs project cautions concerning various road hazards, and these projected cautions appeal to my capability to imagine the consequences of failing to heed the warning. The idea of possible occurrence enters only because highway departments generally post warning signs where road dangers or hazards usually do occur, such as curves or where a highway cuts its course near the base of a rocky cliff. Were they to post warning signs indiscriminately, who would heed them? But any suggestion of possibility, in this case, does not bear on my capability to drive but concerns the likely existence of road hazards, not that it is likely that I will fail to drive safely and crash.

Rock climbers ponder conceivable consequences, not probable consequences. Consider another example. A prudent mountain climber does not dwell on the possibility of falling to one's death as one prepares for a climb. One will study the annual *Accidents in North American Mountaineering* to examine why and how other climbers have made tragic mistakes in order to avoid them. Climbers do this not to frighten themselves but to sharpen their perception of dangers and to avoid taking risk. A mountaineer who ponders the likelihood of falling rather than the danger of falling will soon yield to fear and paralysis, for to focus on the possibility of falling generates introspection, anxiety, lack of confidence and nervousness. To approach a mountain in that state of mind, if one even dares to climb, eventually overwhelms one with severe doubt that leaves one paralyzed on the face of the mountain. A wise climber approaches a mountain with other climbers who have nurtured the virtues of caution: climbers who (1) cross-check each other's harnesses, ropes, knots, anchors; (2) do not hesitate to warn one another against bad judgment or risky moves or of falling rocks; and (3) have the courage and skills to rescue fellow climbers from danger.[124] Think of two climbers of equal skill who approach a mountain. One has taken every precaution, and one has not. One approaches the rock face pondering, "It is possible that I will fall." The other approaches the climb conceiving, "If I fall, the consequences are deadly." The latter comes to the climb with confidence, guided by fear against falling to her death. The other climber approaches the same mountain with doubt and lack of confidence, controlled by fear that he will likely fall and perish. Only one understands the proper function of caution.

The truthfulness of a warning or admonition does not depend on whether or not the thing supposed may come to pass. That is not how suppositional exhortations and warnings function. Rather, they function by supposing a particular course of action that has an invariable and inviolable consequence. The supposition either warns us to avoid a course and its consequence or admonishes us to take a course of action in order that the consequence might be attained.

The Bible warns of conceivable consequences, not of probable consequences. Consider a biblical example that includes both assurance of certain arrival to one's destination and warning lest one fail to attain one's assured destination. The passage is Acts 27.

During Paul's journey to Rome as a prisoner, the ship in which the apostle sailed got caught in a violent northeaster storm (Acts 27:14). Luke tells us that after several days of being violently tossed about by the winds and the sea, "all hope of our being saved was at last abandoned" (Acts 27:20 NRSV). Precisely at this desperate hour, Paul came forward with encouragement:

> I urge you now to keep up your courage, for there will be no loss of life among you, but only of the ship. For last night there stood by me an angel of the God to whom I belong and whom I worship, and he said, 'Do not be afraid, Paul; you must stand before the emperor; and indeed, God has granted safety to all those who are sailing with you.' So keep up your courage, men, for I have faith in God that it will be exactly as I

---

[124]We are grateful to our editor, Dan Reid, who is a mountain climber, for suggestions to strengthen our mountaineering illustration. Our illustration implicitly reflects his knowledgeable influence.

have been told. But we will have to run aground on some island. (Acts
27:22-26 NRSV)

Two essential features stand out in Paul's encouraging words: (1)
"there will be no loss of life among you, but only of the ship," and (2)
"we will have to run aground on some island." He specifies both the
end (saving of all lives on board) and the means to the prophesied
end (running aground on an island).

Though Paul had consoled and assured the ship's crew, passengers
and military unit that every life on board would be saved by means of
running aground on an island, fear overwhelmed the sailors. After
enduring fourteen nights of being driven aimlessly about, the sailors
determined that they were approaching land. For fear that they
would perish on rocks, the sailors made an attempt to escape from
the ship in the dinghy. Paul, however, discovered their scheme and
urgently warned that the shipboard skills of the sailors would be
needed if the passengers and others on board should survive: "Paul
said to the centurion and the soldiers, 'If these men do not remain in
the ship, you will not be saved" (Acts 27:31). In response, "the soldiers
cut the ropes that held the lifeboat and let it fall away" (Acts 27:32
NIV).

Was the apostle speaking with tongue in cheek? Or was Paul's warning genuinely serious? Was he being truthful? If he was truthful, did his
warning deny the assured safety he prophesied earlier? If his prophecy
was sure to be fulfilled, did this make his warning superfluous and hol-
low? Does Paul's warning trade on the possible failure of God's promise? Does his warning appeal to the possibility that God's promise may
fail? Or does his warning appeal to the mind to conceive the dire consequences of failing to abide by God's promise announced earlier? Is the
apostle's warning against loss of life contrary to God's promise to preserve every life? Expressed another way, does Paul's warning call on
the centurion and the soldiers to doubt God's promise of preservation,
in order that they might believe and act on his urgent warning against
loss of life? The relationship between assured promise and urgent
warning in this story is precisely the correlation we find in biblical
promises that assure us of final salvation and biblical warnings and
admonitions that require us to persevere in faithfulness to Jesus Christ
in order that we might be saved in the day of judgment.

Paul's warning was genuine. His urgent appeal was entirely truthful, for Paul had previously announced the means by which all lives on board would be saved. Salvation would be realized by running aground on an island, and in such a situation, the skills of sailors would be essential. Paul's warning does not nor could it deny the promised salvation, for God himself assured the promise to Paul. Who is God that he should go back on his word or change his mind?

But someone may object that the threat is senseless. One may ask, "Why would God warn the centurion and the soldiers to take action to stop the sailors' scheme when God had already assured them that they would all be saved?" Someone may even ask, "Why should God warn people not to do something that he has assured them will not happen?" Ah! But the questioner fails to recognize that God accomplishes his promised purposes by use of means. Paul understood this. He recognized that God's promise included both the end (all lives will be saved) and the means (run aground on an island). Therefore, Paul urgently warned that deliverance could not be achieved apart from the use of God's appointed means. He framed his warning in keeping with the promise. Thus, the warning reminded the centurion and soldiers of the promise, which included running aground on an island, in which case the skills of the sailors would surely be needed (cf. Acts 27:33-41). Recalling Paul's promise that was assured from God, the centurion and soldiers could imagine the consequences of failing to keep the sailors in the ship. They recognized that the consequences would be deadly. Immediately, they understood and acted to prevent their departure, lest they themselves should perish in the sea.

In other words, while God assured the end (deliverance), the end would not be realized apart from the means (remaining in the ship). If the means should fail, the end would fail. Does Paul speak of possible failure of the thing promised? No. He does not indicate likely failure. Rather, he calls for his hearers to conceive of the consequences of failing to act on the means. It is a statement that appeals to one's imagination, for God has given humans the capability to project cause and effect, means and end, or course and outcome. Therefore, Paul appealed to the centurion's and soldiers' fear of dying to get them to act quickly to prevent the sailors from leaving the ship. By his warning, Paul did not incite doubt concerning God's promise. Rather, his whole purpose was to strike fear in them not to neglect the necessary means of deliverance announced in the promise; his objective was to provoke them to believe the promise and to act on it.

To feel the full force of the warning, those aboard the ship did not have to doubt the promise of God. In order for the warning to do its work, the promise was not set aside. Rather, Paul's warning works to accomplish the promise God announced through Paul. God's promise and God's warning are harmonious. They are not at enmity. God secures the things he promises by use of means, and urgent warning is one of those means that God uses to accomplish his promises.

Thus, Acts 27 illustrates well the fact that exhortations and warnings are a significant means by which God moves humans to act so that his promises to them will be fulfilled. Yes, both the end and the events leading to the end are ordained and sure, but when God's purposes involve humans, he accomplishes his assured end by means entirely suitable to humans. That is, he appeals to our motives and fears to prompt us to act in keeping with his designed purpose. God does not coerce humans against their wills. The centurion and soldiers did not act contrary to their own desires when they stopped the sailors from abandoning the ship. There was no unseen hand that compelled them against their desires and personal interest. Indeed, if they had permitted the sailors to abandon ship, lives would have been lost, and they knew it. Therefore, they acted quickly to prevent loss of life.

Conclusion: God warns of conceivable consequences, not probable consequences. So it is with believers. The Scriptures assure us who believe that God secures all who are in Jesus Christ (Rom 8:29-39). But at the same time the Scriptures also admonish and warn us that we must persevere in obeying Jesus Christ or else die eternally (Rom 8:12-13). Are we caught in a hopeless contradiction? Is it necessary to doubt God's promise in order that we might believe and obey God's warning? No! Our God who promises salvation to all who believe in Jesus Christ also uses means to secure his promise to save everyone who believes. God secures us in Christ by using admonitions and warnings framed in the same contingent or conditional form as the initial call of the gospel. Warnings and admonitions are not the only means God uses, as we will show later in the book, yet warnings are crucial. God, who made us capable of imagining and conceiving of consequences to our choices, appeals to our minds to believe him and obey him when he admonishes and warns us. He does so without ever contradicting his promises. He also does so without ever calling on us to doubt his promises so that we might obey his warnings. This is because God warns us by calling on us to use our imaginations to conceive or envision the dreadful and inviolable consequence of failing to persevere in faithfulness to Christ. He does not frighten us by threatening that we may fall away or that it is likely that we will fail to persevere. Therefore, God strengthens our faith both by assuring us that he will preserve us safely to the end and by warning us lest we perish by failing to persevere in steadfast loyalty to Jesus Christ.

5

REFLECTING ON FALLEN RUNNERS

Who Are Those Who Have Fallen Out of the Race?

And in the case of an athlete, no one is crowned
without competing according to the rules. (2 Tim 2:5 NRSV)

O ur burden in chapter four was to demonstrate that we must take seriously biblical warnings and admonitions because they are a vital means God uses to save us, for by them he calls us and keeps us faithful to Christ. Admonitions and warnings function in the same way as the initial call of the gospel: "Believe in the Lord Jesus, and you will be saved" (Acts 16:31 NIV). They urgently call for obedient faith as they point out the only pathway to salvation. Yet the biblical material that we need to include within our doctrinal belief concerning Christian perseverance is complex. Many devout Christians disagree with the way we have explained biblical warnings and admonitions. On the one hand, some may object that the Bible speaks of real believers who fail to persevere and perish eternally. On the other hand, some may remain unconvinced by our discussion and continue to use 1 John 2:19 to explain that the Bible warns and admonishes people who are thinking about forsaking Christ that if they do, they were never truly saved.[1]

---

[1]On warnings and admonitions Wayne Grudem explains, "The purpose is always to warn those who are thinking of falling away or have fallen away that if they do this it is a strong indication that they were never saved in the first place" ("Perseverance of the Saints: A Case Study of Hebrews 6:4-6 and the Other Warning Passages in Hebrews," in *Still Sovereign: Contemporary Perspectives on Election, Foreknowledge, and Grace*, ed. Thomas R. Schreiner and Bruce A. Ware [Grand Rapids, Mich.: Baker, 2000], p. 176).

Therefore, in this chapter we seek to explain how we should understand the biblical perspective on failure to persevere. There are four kinds of passages that we need to consider. First, there are two prominent instructional passages of Scripture that speak of some who fail to persevere. Those two passages are 1 John 2:18-19 and the parable of the soils (Lk 8:11-15). Second, as a warning to Christians, several passages in the New Testament remind us of the Israelites who died in the wilderness (1 Cor 10:1-13; Heb 3:7—4:13; Jude 5). Third, there are a few biblical passages that identify, by name, individuals who have failed to persevere: Alexander, Hymenaeus, Philetus and Demas (1 Tim 1:18-20; 2 Tim 2:14-19; 4:10). Fourth, our discussion will conclude as we consider the contrast between Judas and Peter, both of whom sinned against Jesus.

New Testament Teaching on Failure to Persevere

What about those who fail to persevere? In chapter four we indicated that many Christians appeal to 1 John 2:19 to account for biblical warnings and admonitions that call for perseverance. Christians who adopt the tests-of-genuineness view are quick to use this passage to explain that the warnings of the gospel address people who never were true believers, which is why they fall away. We understand why believers are so inclined to use 1 John 2:19 this way, because formerly we also held to the same explanation of biblical warnings. However, we came to realize that the retrospective vantage point of this verse cannot explain the gospel's warnings, admonitions and conditional promises, which are clearly prospective. They direct our whole attention to the future prize to be received by all who persevere to the end, but 1 John 2:19 turns our attention backward to consider why people have failed to persevere to the end. Of course, 1 John 2:19 and passages like it should have an important function in our understanding of the Christian's race. Therefore, we will show how John's glance backward contributes an important perspective on the biblical teaching concerning perseverance. This passage provides a retrospective explanation concerning the many who once were running the race of faith alongside us but have since dropped out of the race and have failed to persevere.

In the debate whether or not all believers faithfully persevere to the end, it is right to raise 1 John 2:19 in order to explain the failure of many to persevere.[2] It was the apostle John himself who reasoned that anyone who fails to remain with the people of Christ never truly belonged to God's people. He warns and explains:

> Children, it is the last hour! As you have heard that antichrist is coming, so now many antichrists have come. From this we know that it is the last hour. They went out from us, but they did not belong to us; for if they had belonged to us, they would have remained with us. But by going out they made it plain that none of them belongs to us. (1 Jn 2:18-19 NRSV)

John does not exclude these antichrists "from us" by reason of a test of narrow group loyalty. Rather, when he says, "if they had belonged to us, they would have remained with us," the words "with us" point to our common fellowship by virtue of Christ (cf. 1 Jn 1:6-7). According to John, there is a connection between being in Christ and persevering in him and with his people, a connection that cannot be severed. On what basis does John believe this? Certainly it is no mere syllogism that leads him to this conclusion. Instead, for John the unbreakable bond between being in Christ and remaining in Christ derives from the correlation of belief and love in response to God's love. It is not our belief that forges this unbreakable continuity. Rather, it is God's love that forms this bond. As we showed in chapter three, Christian faith cannot be recognized apart from its actions.[3] Faith and love are inseparable, for whoever believes also loves, so that our love for fellow believers assures us that we have passed from death to life (1 Jn 3:14).[4] Yet it is important to note that the apostle conceives of our faith and love as having value only because we stand in God's love by virtue of his work of raising us from death to life. We stand in his love only because God first loved us and turned his wrath away from us as he poured it out on his own Son (1 Jn 3:16; 4:10, 19).

---

[2]We recognize that there are some who object to this use of 1 John 2:19, e.g., Zane Hodges (*The Gospel Under Siege: A Study on Faith and Works*, 2nd ed. [Dallas: Rendención Viva, 1991], pp. 58-59) and Robert Wilkin (*Confident in Christ: Living by Faith Really Works* [Irving, Texas: Grace Evangelical Society, 1999], p. 262 n. 5).

[3]Berkouwer correctly notes that "it is the significant thing about faith that it does not exist in itself and cannot be seen apart from its content" (*Faith and Perseverance*, trans. Robert D. Knudsen [Grand Rapids, Mich.: Eerdmans, 1958], p. 114).

[4]We are not suggesting that love alone is sufficient to assure us that we are truly born of God. Love for fellow Christians is necessary for assurance that we are God's children, but it is not sufficient in itself. Chapter seven provides a fuller discussion of the biblical grounds for Christian assurance.

Faith and love do not spring from ourselves but from God's love for us in Christ, for faith and love are born of God (1 Jn 4:7). Thus, John properly concludes that people who are against Christ forsake the assembly of Christ's people because they never truly belonged among us, for they never really belonged to Christ.

John's words, however, do not bear only a negative function designed to explain why some fail to persevere. His words also have the ring of hope and assurance to all who persevere with Christ's people, for the apostle says, "If they had belonged to us, they would have remained with us" (1 Jn 2:19 NRSV). This gives warrant for us who are born of God to have confidence that we will persevere in our faith, not by the power of our own strength, however, but because our faith and love both derive from God, who gave birth to us. Those who have true faith will not boast in their faith itself, for faith is a gift that comes to us by being born of God (1 Jn 5:1; cf. Phil 1:29).[5]

Those who believe for a while. Many who follow Jacobus Arminius and John Wesley point to Jesus' teaching in the parable of the soils to prove that believers can apostatize and perish eternally. In particular, they appeal to Luke's account. Jesus interprets his own parable by saying:

> This is the meaning of the parable: The seed is the word of God. Those along the path are the ones who hear, and then the devil comes and takes away the word from their hearts, so that they may not believe and be saved. Those on the rock are the ones who receive the word with joy when they hear it, but they have no root. They believe for a while, but in the time of testing they fall away. The seed that fell among thorns stands for those who hear, but as they go on their way they are choked by life's worries, riches and pleasures, and they do not mature. But the seed on good soil stands for those with a noble and good heart, who hear the word, retain it, and by persevering produce a crop. (Lk 8:11-14 NIV)

Jesus depicts four kinds of people who hear the gospel of his kingdom. Despite the fact that Luke faithfully records Jesus' own explanation of his parable, there is considerable disagreement on how to

---

[5]A literal translation of 1 John 5:1 reads, "Everyone who believes that Jesus is the Christ has been born of God, and everyone who loves him who gives birth also loves the one who is born of him." The participial phrase "everyone who believes" denotes action that is antecedent to the action indicated by the finite verb "has been born" *(gegennētai)*. This is so because John believes that our belief derives from our divine birth.

interpret his interpretation. No one disputes the identity of the one who hears the gospel represented by the seed on the pathway. This one's heart is callous so that the gospel falls on deaf ears without any reception. Thus, no one suggests that the first represents a believer. However, advocates of both the loss-of-salvation view and the loss-of-rewards view insist that the second and third soils represent believers. For example, Robert Shank insists that, though they only believe for a while, their faith is authentic. They have salvation for a short time and lose it because they fail to persevere.[6]

Those who hold the loss-of-rewards view agree that the rocky soil and the thorny soil represent genuine believers. Though they fall away, they do not perish. Rather, they are still saved; they will only lose rewards, not salvation.[7] Robert Wilkin identifies four arguments to support his interpretation. First, he agrees with Shank's explanation: "Jesus clearly said that the people represented by the rocky soil believed. . . . What these people believed is nothing other than the saving message, the gospel."[8] Second, he regards Jesus' description that they "received the word" as a technical phrase that means, "Those who receive the word are born again."[9] Third, Wilkin says the description "sprang up" represents new birth.[10] Fourth, to argue against the loss-of-salvation interpretation, he appeals to Jesus' words in Luke 8:12, "so that they may not believe and be saved," to indicate that "he was talking about eternal salvation." Though all these arguments agree with Shank's explanation of the parable, Wilkin will not accept his conclusion that faith may fail so that one will perish eternally. Wilkin argues that Jesus "wasn't talking about some type of

---

[6]Robert Shank, *Life in the Son: A Study of the Doctrine of Perseverance,* 2nd ed. (Springfield, Mo.: Westcott, 1976), pp. 32-33.

[7]"What is at stake are our eternal rewards . . . which only persevering saints shall receive" (Wilkin, *Confident in Christ,* p. 29).

[8]Wilkin reasons, "When Jesus said that the devil takes away the word 'lest they should believe and be saved' (verse 12), He was talking about saving faith. He said that whoever believes in Him is saved the very moment he believes. There is no minimum time requirement on saving faith. Thus, when Jesus said that these rocky soil people believed, we have no choice but to conclude that they were saved, since according to verse 12 all who believe are saved" (ibid., p. 27).

[9]Ibid., p. 28.

[10]"Only a seed that has germinated can spring up. Germination and growth are proof that life has begun. . . . The people represented by the rocky soil exercised saving faith. Whether they believed for a second or for a century, they were born again at the very moment they believed in Christ for eternal life" (ibid., p. 28).

temporary salvation that could be lost."[11] Wilkin represents well the loss-of-rewards view concerning faith, salvation and perseverance. Despite their protests, those who hold this view reduce saving faith to little more than a momentary act of detached agreement with or mental assent to the gospel.[12] Thus, Wilkin concludes, "Even if a person believes only for a while, he still has eternal life."[13]

Briefly, Wilkin's interpretation falters primarily because he fails to explain the pieces of the parable in keeping with the whole. First, Jesus does not say that the people represented by the rocky soil believe. He includes a significant qualifier: "believe for a while." Not only does he qualify their faith temporally, he also qualifies it in terms of depth: "they have no root." The imagery is an apt sketch of belief that fails to grasp the gospel and therefore does not save. Second, the phrase "receive the word" is hardly a technical expression for conversion. Luke's use of the phrase in the Acts 8:14 does not indicate that all who received the word among the Samaritans or the Gentiles were born again. The presence of Simon Magus in Samaria demonstrates this fallacy.[14] Third, Wilkin squeezes more from the verb "sprang up" (Lk 8:6) than the parable allows. Jesus' explanation of the parable provides no warrant for Wilkin to conclude, "Germination and growth are proof that life has begun."[15] In fact, Jesus designs his explanation of the rocky-soil hearers to make it clear that they do not represent those who believe and are saved. He distinguishes their response to the word from that of pathway hearers, but their end is no different. Fourth, Wilkin is correct that Jesus does not speak of "tem-

---

[11] Ibid., p. 28.

[12] It is worth noting that Wilkin's discussion of Lk 8:13 begins by objecting to a commentary on the description, "believed for a while." He writes, "The fact that they believe for a while but . . . fall away means that they only accept the facts of the Word mentally and then reject it when 'the going gets tough' " (ibid., p. 27, quoting John Martin, "Luke," in *The Bible Knowledge Commentary*, ed. John F. Walvoord and Roy B. Zuck [Wheaton: Victor, 1983, 1985], 2:225).

[13] Wilkin, *Confident in Christ*, p. 29.

[14] Acts 8:13-14 is a good example to show how the New Testament writers describe responses to the gospel. Even though Luke knew that Simon Magus had not received the new birth of the Spirit, he records, "Simon himself believed and was baptized" (Acts 8:13). Why does Luke tell the story this way? It is because he wants to make it clear that there are varied receptions of the gospel. Simon is an example of one who externally looked like a believer, for he even submitted to baptism. However, his subsequent behavior uncovered his belief to be counterfeit.

[15] Wilkin, *Confident in Christ*, p. 28.

porary salvation," but Jesus does portray a kind of belief that is temporary, that fails to endure and thus is not saving faith, and exposes its true nature by failure to persevere.

Luke's account of Jesus' explanation of the parable of the soils is distinctive, for he more than either Matthew or Mark explicitly develops a brief but consequential clarification of the kind of belief that the gospel requires for salvation. To this end Luke's Gospel explains why the devil seizes the word of the gospel from those represented by the pathway. It is "in order that they may not believe and be saved" (Lk 8:12). Neither Mark nor Matthew includes such an explicit explanation. Again, concerning the hearer represented by the rocky soil, Luke explains that the phrase "endure for a while" (cf. Mt 13:21; Mk 4:17) means "believe for a while" (Lk 8:13). Concerning the hearer represented by the thorny soil, Luke stresses their persistent failure to produce the fruit of the gospel—"they do not produce fruit to maturity"—a failure due to their being choked by anxiety, wealth and pleasure (Lk 8:14). Finally, Luke's elaboration concerning the hearer symbolized by the good soil indicates that only this kind of hearer receives the word of the gospel unto salvation. Note Luke's threefold description: (1) "they hear the word with an honest and good heart," (2) "they hold the word fast," and (3) "they bring forth fruit with perseverance."[16] Here is a portrait of a genuine believer. The heart is made good. The word finds lodging. This one who hears the word perseveres through times of testing, in contrast to the one on the rocky soil. Unlike the one among the thorns, this one does not yield to anxiety, wealth or pleasure. This one perseveres and produces mature fruit.

Though I. Howard Marshall believes that genuine believers may apostatize, he is not convinced that the parable of the soils indicates this. Because Jesus portrays them as having "no root," Marshall admits, "Their faith may not have been securely based and may not have been a total act of commitment. But there is no indication that it was unsound other than the evidence of how the men failed in a crisis."[17] He continues by saying, "We can conclude only that the character of faith is shown up by testing, and that in this case a lack of

---

[16]Cf. Luke's wording with both Matthew 13:23 and Mark 4:20.

[17]I. Howard Marshall, *Kept by the Power of God: A Study of Perseverance and Falling Away* (1969; reprint, Minneapolis: Bethany Fellowship, 1974), p. 63.

steadfastness is evident."[18] Clearly, Jesus designs this parable to distinguish authentic faith from disingenuous belief. Humans who observe others receiving the word cannot tell in advance which reception takes root and will weather opposition and persecution. Initial reception of the gospel is no sure indicator that faith will endure and prove to be genuine. It is not the reception of the word but the duration of faith that signals genuineness. Failure to persevere uncovers belief to be temporary, inadequate and insincere. Perseverance that yields fruit confirms faith's authenticity.

Luke plainly states that the issue at stake in the parable of the soils is belief unto salvation, for the devil strives to prevent belief that perseveres unto salvation (Lk 8:12). Though Satan fails to prevent all from receiving the gospel, he has allies that aid his endeavor. If the devil cannot confiscate the gospel from some, the flesh and the world will obstruct reception of the word so that faith does not endure or ripen to fruitfulness. This is the point Luke makes with the rocky-soil and thorny-soil hearers. According to Luke, some will receive the gospel with a joyous show of rapid growth only to wilt and wither when tested, because persecution exposes how shallow their reception of the word truly is. Their faith is fleeting, for it wilts as quickly as it sprang up. Jesus characterizes their reception of the gospel and apostasy as emotional and shallow. The flesh's passion for ease in this life cuts faith short. They receive the gospel jubilantly, but they quickly forsake the gospel on account of the grief it brings. Concerning those symbolized by the thorn-infested soil, Jesus does not describe their reception of the gospel as "believe for a while." Instead, he says the world's anxieties, riches and pleasures entangle and strangle their reception of the gospel, so that they produce no fruit. Jesus designs his parable to instruct us that salvation belongs only to those who hear the word, who hold it fast and who yield fruit worthy of faith and do so with perseverance. While Jesus used the parable of the soils to teach the crowd concerning the gospel of the kingdom, the varied responses portrayed in the parable were being fulfilled among those who heard him. This is true each time we read or hear this parable, for the parable is like a mirror. It reflects how we hear the gospel. It does its work as we hear it, for it rebukes the disingenuous and

---

[18]Ibid.

assures those who bear fruit with perseverance. Is it because the parable of the soils rebukes temporary believers and those entangled with the world's goods that some attempt to find consolation by convincing themselves that the second and third soils represent Christians also?

The Example of Israel's Apostasy

Three passages warn Christians lest we imitate the unfaithful Israelites who perished in the wilderness (1 Cor 10:1-13; Heb 3:7—4:13; Jude 5). Though each passage warrants its own discussion, for our purposes we will consider them together.

Our first concern is to take note of the kind of language these passages use. Jude 5 says, "Now I want to remind you, though you all know, that the Lord once saved a people from the land of Egypt and afterward destroyed those who did not believe." The author of Hebrews appeals to the example of rebellious Israelites, saying:

> Who were they who heard and rebelled? Were they not all those Moses led out of Egypt? And with whom was he angry for forty years? Was it not with those who sinned, whose bodies fell in the desert? And to whom did God swear that they would never enter his rest if not to those who disobeyed? So we see that they were not able to enter, because of their unbelief. (Heb 3:16-19 NIV)

Finally, the apostle Paul's use of Israel's apostasy is more sustained. It spans 1 Corinthians 10:1-13, but we cite only the first five verses.

> I do not want you to be unaware, brothers and sisters, that our ancestors were all under the cloud, and all passed through the sea, and all were baptized into Moses in the cloud and in the sea, and all ate the same spiritual food, and all drank the same spiritual drink. For they drank from the spiritual rock that followed them, and the rock was Christ. Nevertheless, God was not pleased with most of them, and they were struck down in the wilderness. (1 Cor 10:1-5 NRSV)

Despite all Israel's privileges—miraculous deliverance from Egypt, passage through the sea on dry ground, the presence of the Lord leading them with the pillar of fire and the cloud, bread from heaven, water from the rock—the exodus generation rebelled against the Lord and perished in the desert. Bodies that had been satisfied with miraculous food and drink now lay strewn across the wasteland of the wilderness. As Hebrews and Jude use Israel's rebellion, so Paul appeals to the Corinthians not to reenact Israel's acts of rebellion. He identifies four: idolatry (Ex 32, golden calf); sexual immorality (Num 25, with Moabite women); testing the Lord (Num 21, bronze snake); and grumbling against the Lord (Num 16, Korah and the plague).

For Paul, Israel is more than simply a historical illustration of rebellion's consequences. Paul holds the Israelites before the Corinthians, because he understands that God designed Israel's rebellion and their consequences as foreshadows or types to warn Christians and to deliver us to the promised land of salvation in the last day. The apostle provides two sets of indicators that Israel functions typologically. First, in the opening verses of 1 Corinthians 10 cited above, Paul interprets Israel's exodus from Egypt and wilderness blessings as types. Note the phrases he uses to indicate the spiritual symbolism of Israel's earthly experiences: (1) "baptized into Moses"; (2) "ate the same spiritual food"; (3) "drank the same spiritual drink"; (4) "drank from the spiritual rock"; (5) "the rock was Christ." Paul indicates that the water of the sea, the cloud, the manna, the water from the rock and the rock itself all bore symbolic significance for Israel as they pointed away from themselves to things spiritual and heavenly. But the Israelites did not believe and therefore perished in the wilderness.

Paul's second set of indicators of Israel's typological role is the brackets he places around the four acts of Israel's rebellion. Twice he expressly affirms this prefiguring function of Israel's rebellion. Paul says, "Now these things occurred as types for us, lest we be cravers of evil as they craved evil" (1 Cor 10:6). Later he reiterates, "Now these things happened to them typologically, and they were written for our admonition, for us to whom the ends of the ages have come" (1 Cor 10:11). As Paul reads the Old Testament, he understands that Scripture has a last-days orientation toward Christ and his people. The Old Testament was written for us who belong to Jesus Christ (cf. Rom 4:23-24; 15:4; cf. 1 Pet 1:10-12). Therefore, Israel's rebellion and destruction in the wilderness after God's deliverance of them from Egypt and from destruction in the wilderness foreshadows the culmination of God's salvation as he redeems the church in Christ. Paul's point is that the salvation of Christians has been the goal toward which God has been directing his redemptive and revelatory acts in history.[19] In 1 Corinthians 10:12 Paul restricts the function of this foreshadowing. He does not mean that the church will reenact Israel's past rebellion. Rather, the church comes to the same critical moments that Israel faced.

The gospel offers no ground for us to presume that we are safe. As it was for the Israelites, so also for us. Participation in external rituals such as baptism or sacred food holds no power either to give us salvation or to assure us that we possess salvation. That is why Paul emphasizes that all the Israelites who came out of Egypt "were baptized into Moses in the cloud and in the sea, and all ate the same spiritual food, and all drank the same spiritual drink." All participated in the external rites and symbols, but most perished because they did not lay hold of the spiritual reality that the rites symbolized. Their baptism, their eating and their drinking was only outward, not inward, for they rebelled against God. Paul means that their perishing in the wilderness signifies their eternal loss.

The apostle recognizes that the Corinthians are at a critical juncture, lest some in the church at Corinth presume that they can participate in both the Lord's Table and in festivals at pagan temples without incurring God's wrath (1 Cor 10:14-22). Paul realizes that some Corinthians are flirting with the false notion that salvation is theirs already apart from the need to persevere. They were in danger of presuming upon God and falling into the sins Israel committed in the wilderness, especially the sin of idolatry. The Corinthians are at a critical place, for as Israel presumed they had an inherited privilege, so Paul uses the typology of Israel's wilderness experiences to warn the Corinthians: "So let the one who takes for granted that he stands take heed lest he fall" (1 Cor 10:12). But he does not leave his admonition general; he narrows it. "Therefore," Paul says, "my dear friends, flee from idolatry" (1 Cor 10:14).

What does this discussion contribute to our understanding of how the New Testament uses Israel's rebellion to warn Christians lest we follow their habit of unbelief? An Old Testament type anticipates things to come. That is to say, a type looks for fulfillment just as any

---

[19]Space prohibits adequate explanation of 1 Cor 10:13, so we encourage readers to consult the discussion of this passage by C. Marvin Pate, *The End of the Age Has Come: The Theology of Paul* (Grand Rapids, Mich.: Zondervan, 1995), pp. 105-8.

prophetic announcement looks for fulfillment. How does Paul understand types? He gives us several clues in 1 Corinthians 10:1-5, as we have already indicated above. Consider another example of typology in Paul's theology. The apostle recognizes that God appointed Adam to have a symbolic function for all his race, for he was our representative. When he disobeyed, he brought sin and death to us all (Rom 5:12-14). But Adam was more than a symbol for all humanity; he was a symbol foreshadowing Christ, who is the one to come (Rom 5:14). Most of the analogical correspondence between Adam the type and Christ the reality entails contrast: disobedience versus obedience. However, this does not nullify the fact that from the beginning God designed Adam to foreshadow Christ by looking forward to the true representative for us who would fulfill what the first man could never accomplish on his own, namely, eternal life. Why could Adam not secure eternal life for his descendants? It is because, as a creature, his own eternal life hung on the tree of life that stood as a symbol in paradise. Was it an actual tree? Indeed it was. As long as Adam ate from that tree and not from the tree of the knowledge of good and evil, he would have life and never die (Gen 2:15-17). Likewise, the analogical relationship between Israel as the type and the church as the reality foreshadowed falls along contrasting lines. As the sanctuary was an earthly copy and shadow of the true and heavenly sanctuary, so Israel is but an earthly shadow and copy of God's true and heavenly people who are in Christ, the true seed of Abraham (cf. Jn 15:1; Gal 3:16). We need to recognize the typological relationship between Israel and the church, because the New Testament distinguishes the two as shadow is to reality. According to Paul's theology, Israel was unfaithful and rebellious, but the church is obedient and submissive to Christ (Rom 3:3; 1 Cor 10:1-13; Eph 5:22-33). Israel descended ethnically from Abraham, but all who are in Christ are Abraham's spiritual descendants (Rom 2:25—3:9; Gal 3:29).

All of this means, therefore, that we must carefully consider the language the New Testament uses to describe Israel's deliverance from slavery in Egypt and apostasy in the wilderness. For example, consider Jude 5: "Now I want to remind you, though you all know, that the Lord once saved a people from the land of Egypt and afterward destroyed those who did not believe." We would be wrong to conclude that God spiritually saved the Israelites that he brought out of Egypt. Jude is not saying that God spiritually redeemed Israel and that later in the wilderness Israelites lost the gift of salvation and perished. Rather, Jude's argument hangs on Israel's typological relationship to God's people in Christ. Israel received a type of salvation, for God redeemed them from slavery in Egypt. God filled the exodus with symbols and types that pointed away from the earthly release from slavery to spiritual and heavenly release from slavery to sin. God designed the whole Passover institution for this purpose, but Israel failed to grasp the heavenly reality by faith and preferred to live by sight, fastened on the symbols and types rather than the heavenly realities to which they point. Therefore, Jude's appeal is one that seeks to transform sight into belief, which Israel did not have.

Hebrews makes the same argument concerning the generation of Israelites whom Moses led out of Egypt and who sinned in the wilderness and died there: "So we see that they were not able to enter, because of their unbelief" (Heb 3:19 NIV). As the Corinthians came to a critical juncture, so also the readers of Hebrews did. Thus, the preacher's sermon urgently calls the Hebrew believers with the words of the ancient psalmist: "Today, if you hear his voice, do not harden your hearts as you did in the rebellion" (Heb 3:7, 15; 4:7 NIV, quoting Ps 95:7-8).

Jude, Hebrews and Paul do not contend that the Israelites had believed unto salvation only to lose God's gift of salvation by unbelief. When they use Israel's rebellion and destruction to motivate us to belief that perseveres, they ground it in the typological relationship between Abraham's earthly and heavenly descendants. Israel's rebellion is not an example of children to whom God has given spiritual birth and who nonetheless perish eternally. The New Testament writers do not use Israel to show that it is possible for God's spiritually birthed children to apostatize and perish. They appeal to Israel's rebellion to admonish us to be the true people of God that Israel was not. They use Israel to exhort us not to presume upon God's rich provisions and take it for granted that we have inherited privilege. Our inheritance will be received by faith, not by presuming it is ours. Israel's unbelief and eternal destruction testify to God's irrevocable order and sequence. Failure to believe God's promises terminates unalterably and finally in eternal death. Therefore, do not presume to test God. Without faith, it is impossible to please God.

Biblical Examples of Individuals Who Apostatized

The apostle Paul, who exhorts us with strong warnings against apostasy and unbelief, also prophesies that some will fall away from the faith as they succumb to teachings by hypocritical liars (1 Tim 4:1-2). Even as he writes the two letters to Timothy, Paul's prophecy finds fulfillment, for he identifies four men who failed to persevere in the gospel and embraced teachings contrary to the gospel. The four are Alexander, Hymenaeus, Philetus and Demas (1 Tim 1:18-20; 2 Tim 2:14-19; 4:10). Do these examples prove that it is possible for believers who receive the saving grace of God and have eternal life to apostatize and perish in eternal death? Is the passage from death to life reversible? How should we understand God's promise, as Jesus expresses it: "This is the will of him who sent me, that I shall lose none of all that he has given me, but raise them up at the last day. For my Father's will is that everyone who looks to the Son and believes in him shall have eternal life, and I will raise him up at the last day" (Jn 6:39-40 NIV)? Can the continuity between genuine initial belief in Jesus Christ and resurrection unto eternal life in the last day be broken? Were Alexander, Hymenaeus, Philetus and Demas men whom God's grace raised from death to new life in Christ?

Alexander, Hymenaeus and Philetus. In 1 Timothy 1:18-20 Paul writes:

> I entrust this charge to you, Timothy, my son, in accord with the prophecies previously announced to you, that by them you might fight the good fight, while holding to faith and to a good conscience, which some, upon repudiating, have made shipwreck concerning faith, among whom are Hymenaeus and Alexander, whom I have handed over to Satan in order that they may be taught not to blaspheme.

Paul begins his charge to Timothy in 1:3, interrupts it in 1:12-17 and resumes it in 1:18. Paul initially speaks of "some people" who have wandered off course (1 Tim 1:6), then identifies two men who have abandoned the faith: Hymenaeus and Alexander (1 Tim 1:20).[20]

---

[20] It is uncertain whether the Alexander whom Paul mentions in 1 Tim 1:20 is the same man designated "Alexander the metalworker" in 2 Tim 4:14. It may be that Paul intends to distinguish the two men by adding the appellation "the metalworker." Another Alexander, a Jew, has a role in attempting to quiet the mob action against Paul (Acts 19:33-34). It may be that this Alexander is "Alexander the metalworker" (2 Tim 4:14), especially since it was metalworkers whose livelihood was being subverted by so many conversions to Christ in Ephesus (Acts 19:23-27).

Admittedly, Paul uses strong and vivid expressions to depict their defection from the Christian gospel. They have repudiated a good conscience and they have made shipwreck of faith. Were these men, at one time, made alive in Christ? Did they subsequently cross back over from life to death?[21] Or did their repudiation of a good conscience and shipwreck of faith "merit serious divine chastening," but not eternal punishment?[22]

Our answers to these questions would be premature without also taking into consideration what Paul says of Hymenaeus in 2 Timothy 2:16-19. It is in the midst of extended exhortations to Timothy to be faithful to his charge as a minister of the gospel (2 Tim 2:1-26) that Paul associates Hymenaeus with Philetus, "whose teaching will spread like gangrene" (2 Tim 2:17). In verse 17 the apostle says these two men "have wandered from the truth" because they teach that the resurrection has already occurred. Their heresy is similar to one that Paul counters in 1 Corinthians 15, a form of overrealized eschatology. Belief that the resurrection has already happened creates a mutated version of Christianity, a version Paul does not regard to be Christianity at all. It seems that these two men believed and taught that when Christ arose resurrection was complete. They collapsed the not-yet resurrection of believers into the already resurrection of Christ, so that they believed there is no future resurrection on the last day. This heretical belief influenced and shaped how they behaved with regard to the appetites of the body. Whereas this heresy in Corinth evidently prompted some to indulge the bodily appetites (1 Cor 6:13), in Ephesus it evidently prompted ascetic prohibition of marriage and use of certain foods (1 Tim 4:1-5).[23] Their heresy strikes at the very core of Christian faith, for "if it is preached that Christ has been raised from the dead, how can some of you say that there is no resurrection of the dead? If there is no resurrection of the dead, then not even Christ has

---

[21]Marshall contends that both men were once authentic believers but that they fell away to eternal death (*Kept by the Power of God,* p. 128).

[22]Zane Hodges argues this view (*Absolutely Free! A Biblical Reply to Lordship Salvation* [Grand Rapids, Mich.: Zondervan, 1989], p. 110).

[23]Apparently there were ascetic elements in Corinth as well, in view of Paul's counsel through 1 Corinthians 7. See William L. Lane, "I Tim. iv.1-3. An Early Instance of Over-realized Eschatology?" *New Testament Studies* 11 (1965): 164-67. See also Anthony C. Thiselton, "Realized Eschatology at Corinth," *New Testament Studies* 24 (1978): 510-26.

been raised. And if Christ has not been raised, our preaching is useless and so is your faith" (1 Cor 15:12-14 NIV). Clearly, Paul extends no tolerance to the heresy embraced and taught by Hymenaeus and Philetus.

With this added information, what is the explanation of the apostasy of Hymenaeus, Alexander and Philetus? Biblical interpreters have offered three diverse responses. Some, including Shank and Marshall, conclude that the three men were believers who abandoned belief in the gospel and apostatized completely and finally.[24] They perished eternally. Others, such as Hodges and Wilkin, agree that these men were Christians who lost their faith in the gospel's promise of resurrection and may have ceased to confess faith in Christ Jesus. Nevertheless, Hodges and Wilkin insist that they remained Christians. Though they apostatized, they will not enter eternal punishment.[25] We believe a third explanation of the apostasy of these three men more fully satisfies Paul's description and theological perspective.

The church has always been an assembly of people gathered together around a common confession of faith in Jesus Christ. This common confession, however, is external. Therefore, from the beginning, many have joined the fellowship of believers though they never truly embraced Jesus Christ. We have already observed that Jesus taught us in his parable of the soils to expect a mixed assembly that includes people who only outwardly receive the gospel. Jesus also taught us that in the present age the kingdom of God is not yet purified, for wheat and weeds will grow together in the same field (Mt 13:24-29). To distinguish believers from unbelievers and to warn the unrepentant concerning their certain destiny of eternal destruction, Jesus instituted a procedure of church discipline (Mt 18:15-20). We also noted that the apostle John understood that the church is a mixed assembly, for he recognized that the presence of antichrists in the church is an indication that the last days have dawned (1 Jn 2:18-19). He accepts their exit from the assembly as an indicator of their true character, for their departure uncovers their hypocrisy. Likewise, Paul is not surprised at the presence of heretics and unbelievers in

---

[24]Shank, *Life in the Son*, pp. 176-77; Marshall, *Kept by the Power of God*, pp. 128-31.
[25]Hodges, *Absolutely Free*, pp. 108-11; Wilkin, *Confident in Christ*, p. 252 n. 8.

the congregation of the church. He cautioned the elders from Ephesus, saying, "I know that after I leave, savage wolves will come in among you and will not spare the flock. Even from your own number men will arise and distort the truth in order to draw away disciples after them. So be on your guard!" (Acts 20:29-31).

Therefore, when Paul writes to Timothy, who is situated at Ephesus, it should come as no surprise that he charges him: "I urge you, as I did when I was on my way to Macedonia, to remain in Ephesus so that you may instruct certain people not to teach any different doctrine, and not to occupy themselves with myths and endless genealogies that promote speculations rather than the divine training that is known by faith" (1 Tim 1:3-4 NRSV).[26] So Paul announces to Timothy that he had already exercised his apostolic authority when he handed Alexander and Hymenaeus "over to Satan in order that they may be taught not to blaspheme" (1 Tim 1:20). Paul's action recalls his appeal to the Corinthian church that had failed to follow the church disciplinary procedure with regard to the immoral man (1 Cor 5:1-13). He called on the Corinthians "to hand this man over to Satan for the destruction of the flesh, so that his spirit may be saved in the day of the Lord" (1 Cor 5:5 NRSV). In that case, the apostle did not give the man the benefit of the doubt, for he describes him as one "who calls himself a brother but is sexually immoral" (1 Cor 5:11), and he exhorts the Corinthians: "Expel the wicked man from among you" (1 Cor 5:13 NIV; cf. Deut 17:7). Similarly, Paul excluded Alexander and Hymenaeus from the fellowship of the church by casting them outside into Satan's domain. For Paul, excommunication has a remedial and redemptive objective: "that they may be taught not to blaspheme." It would be unwise to suppose, either with the man in Corinth or with Alexander and Hymenaeus, that Paul pronounced his final verdict over them. Clearly, he hoped that apostolic discipline would restore them.

A second reason we reject the first two explanations and adopt a third is that the apostle Paul describes the apostasy of the three

---

[26]Even Marshall agrees: "These passages [in the Pastoral Letters] bear witness to the mixed nature of the Church; it contained men who professed the faith but had never come to belief, and it also contained others who were being tempted by them to apostasy. Thus the Church included men who had no claim to the name of Christian despite their outward profession of faith and were interlopers with no right to be there" (*Kept by the Power of God,* p. 128).

men—Alexander, Hymenaeus and Philetus—by using language suitable for the situation. Paul and other New Testament writers describe apostasy from the vantage point of the mixed assembly of people who confess belief in Christ and his gospel. To all appearances, all three men made a profession of faith in Christ Jesus. Outwardly they joined the church. On the face of it they were believers. It seems evident that they even attained leadership roles in the church at Ephesus, probably as elders (cf. Acts 20:29-30). Therefore, it is fitting that Paul describes Alexander and Hymenaeus as repudiating a good conscience and making shipwreck of their faith (1 Tim 1:19). Surely Paul would not expect that the two men he describes would agree with his assessment of them. It is likely that they would have regarded themselves as true believers and Paul as the defector. It is also proper for Paul to portray Hymenaeus and Philetus as men who wandered from the truth (2 Tim 2:18), though they would hardly accept the charge. They were dangerous men precisely because they rejected what they once professed; their apostasy disclosed that they always were wolves masquerading as sheep. Paul tailors his description of the apostates in keeping with outward appearance, and he does so to caution others who profess faith in Christ, lest they follow their heretical teachings and abandonment of the gospel.

It is also instructive to consider the larger context in which Paul indicates that Hymenaeus and Philetus have abandoned the gospel as they teach that the resurrection has already happened. It is significant that the apostle begins this paragraph with a reminder: "Remember Jesus Christ, raised from the dead, descended from David. This is my gospel, for which I am suffering even to the point of being chained like a criminal. But God's word is not chained. Therefore I endure everything for the sake of the elect, that they too may obtain the salvation that is in Christ Jesus, with eternal glory" (2 Tim 2:8-10 NIV). By beginning this way, Paul makes three things clear. First, by teaching that the resurrection has already taken place, Hymenaeus and Philetus must logically deny that Jesus Christ was raised from the dead (cf. 1 Cor 15:12-14). They have abandoned Paul's gospel, for they have rejected the inner logic and coherence of his good news. Second, Paul inseparably binds together an orthodox belief in his gospel and the necessity to hold it fast by persevering through afflictions that come with embracing the gospel. Third, the apostle explains that

God's chosen ones—the elect—will be saved through the use of means, including Paul's preaching and imprisonment on account of the gospel. Then, using an early hymn, the apostle applies the necessity of perseverance through affliction to all who profess faith: "Here is a trustworthy saying:

> If we died with him, we will also live with him.
> If we persevere, we will also reign with him.
> If we deny him, he will also deny us.
> If we are unfaithful, he remains faithful,
> for he cannot deny himself. (2 Tim 2:11-13)

The hymn begins with a supposition that reasons from evidence to inference: union with Christ in his death implies that "we will also live with him." The two middle lines of the hymn express suppositions that denote a cause-effect relationship. Perseverance results in reigning with Christ. Denying Christ results in his denying us, a condition that echoes Jesus' warning in Matthew 10:33, which we discussed in chapter four. Like the first line of the hymn, the last seems to reason from evidence to inference, except here the conclusion does not logically follow from the supposition, which accounts for the attached explanation, "for he cannot deny himself."[27]

Though the last line is clear in what it says, its meaning is ambiguous. The reason for this is that its connection with the remainder of the hymn is not immediately evident. Here is the question: Does it contrast with the third line, or does the final line reiterate a thought parallel to line three? Is Christ faithful to deny and punish all who are unfaithful to him because he will not deny the justice and holiness of his character, or is Christ faithful to sustain Christians, even though they are unfaithful, because he will not deny his word of promise? Many understand the last line of the hymn as a word of reassurance: even if we are unfaithful to Christ, he will not be unfaithful to us, because he cannot deny himself.[28] Most who adopt this understanding qualify the supposition—"if we are unfaithful"—so that it is not

---

[27]On the semantic function of Greek conditional sentences, see Daniel B. Wallace, *Greek Grammar Beyond the Basics* (Grand Rapids, Mich.: Zondervan, 1996), pp. 682-84.
[28]See, for example, Hodges, *Absolutely Free,* pp. 112, 221 n. 4. See also George W. Knight III, *Commentary on the Pastoral Epistles,* New International Greek Testament Commentary (Grand Rapids, Mich.: Eerdmans, 1992), pp. 407-8; and Marshall, *Kept by the Power of God,* p. 133.

parallel to "if we deny him."[29] Others believe this conflicts with both the tenor of the hymn and the parallelism between the third and fourth lines.[30] They contend that to offer words of assurance to people who are unfaithful is out of character with the hymn and with Paul's gospel. For example, Hendriksen claims it is more likely that the last line assures us that Christ will follow through on his threats as well as his promises.[31] However, Stein persuades us that we should read verse 13 as "reassurance for sensitive Christians who are burdened with their failures and shortcomings."[32]

Therefore, the hymn assures eternal life to all who died with Christ. It admonishes perseverance in order that we may gain dominion with Christ. It also warns against denying Christ, lest he deny us. Finally, it assures believers who may be plagued with doubts on account of momentary lapses in faithfulness that God's oath of faithfulness is irrevocable. He will keep his promise to preserve us, for he cannot deny himself.

Paul's subsequent use of the hymn in 2 Timothy 2:14-19 confirms our interpretation. Paul urges Timothy, "Remind them of these things as you solemnly warn them in the presence of God not to quarrel about words, which is of no use, instead leading to the ruin of those who hear" (2 Tim 2:14). He continues by admonishing Timothy to remain faithful to the gospel and to resist those who indulge in empty speech (2 Tim 2:15-16). In this context Paul names Hymenaeus and Philetus as prime examples of men who have abandoned the gospel and destroy the faith of some. Over against their destructive influence Paul confidently affirms, "But God's firm foundation stands, bearing this inscription: 'The Lord knows those who are his,' and, 'Let

---

[29]For example, Knight translates the fourth line "although we are unfaithful" and claims that this is only "temporary unfaithfulness" (*Commentary on the Pastoral Epistles*, p. 407). Hodges, however, does not qualify the expression. He explains the clause "if we are unfaithful" in terms of a loss of faith: "Undoubtedly the Christian who has lost his or her faith may cease to name the name of Christ, and may even cease to confess Christianity" (*Absolutely Free*, p. 111). Again he states, "Indeed, their very faith in Christ may be overturned like those who . . . gave ear to Hymenaeus and Philetus" (p. 120).

[30]John Stott argues, "Yet the logic of the Christian hymn, with its two pairs of balancing epigrams, really demands a different interpretation" (*Guard the Gospel: The Message of 2 Timothy* [Downers Grove, Ill.: InterVarsity Press, 1973], p. 64).

[31]Cf. William Hendriksen, *Exposition of the Pastoral Epistles* (Grand Rapids, Mich.: Baker, 1957), p. 260; and Stott, *Guard the Gospel*, p. 64.

[32]Robert Stein, *Difficult Passages in the Epistles* (Grand Rapids, Mich.: Baker, 1988), p. 65.

everyone who calls on the name of the Lord turn away from wickedness' " (2 Tim 2:19 NRSV). Paul evidently uses Isaiah's imagery of an immovable foundation stone to represent God's purpose in Christ Jesus (Is 28:16). The foundation stone bears two inscriptions drawn generally from the Old Testament story of Korah's rebellion. The first inscription speaks of God's concealed knowledge. "The Lord knows those who are his" derives from Numbers 16:5 in the Greek Old Testament (LXX), a text that speaks of God's knowledge that discriminates between his servants and Korah with his band of rebels. Paul apparently wants Timothy to see a similarity between Korah and Hymenaeus and Philetus, so he uses the text to affirm that God acknowledges all who belong to him and will keep them safe. The inscription—"The Lord knows those who are his"—corresponds to Paul's mention of the elect, or God's chosen ones, in 2 Timothy 2:10. Paul is not using the verb *knows* in a cognitive sense, for in that sense God knows both the righteous and the wicked. Rather, as Paul uses the verb here, it signifies God's elective love for his own, a committed relationship to save his people (cf. Gal 4:8-9).[33]

The second inscription—"Let everyone who calls on the name of the Lord turn away from wickedness"—probably derives from the story of Korah as well, for just before God's judgment fell on Korah, Moses commanded the rest of the people to turn away from the wicked lest they perish (Num 16:26). Paul's admonition makes it clear that the doctrinal error of Hymenaeus and Philetus concerning resurrection is wicked. There is a connection between erroneous beliefs concerning the gospel and unrighteousness. Thus, the two inscriptions on God's immovable foundation bind together two inseparable elements of the gospel: God's secret knowledge that discriminates between the true and the spurious, and God's commandment that requires obedience, which distinguishes the righteous from the wicked.

Did Paul believe that Hymenaeus, Alexander and Philetus truly had been acknowledged by God as his own children, born of the Spirit and recipients of eternal life and salvation in Jesus Christ? No, the apostle regards them as imposters who made a confession of faith

---

[33]See S. M. Baugh, "The Meaning of Foreknowledge," in *Still Sovereign: Contemporary Perspectives on Election, Foreknowledge, and Grace,* ed. Thomas R. Schreiner and Bruce A. Ware (Grand Rapids, Mich.: Baker, 2000), pp. 183-200, esp. pp. 193-94.

that shipwrecked and thus brought out in plain view the true nature of their hearts. Does Paul regard these men as hopelessly lost forever? No, for he admonishes Timothy, "The Lord's servant must not quarrel; instead, he must be kind to everyone, able to teach, not resentful. Those who oppose him he must gently instruct, in the hope that God will grant them repentance leading them to a knowledge of the truth, and that they will come to their senses and escape from the trap of the devil, who has taken them captive to do his will" (2 Tim 2:24-26 NIV).

Demas. Demas also defected from the gospel. In a personal note, Paul appeals to Timothy to come from Ephesus to visit him in prison, especially since Timothy has access to his few treasured possessions:

> Do your best to come to me soon, for Demas, in love with this present world, has deserted me and gone to Thessalonica; Crescens has gone to Galatia, Titus to Dalmatia. Only Luke is with me. Get Mark and bring him with you, for he is useful in my ministry. I have sent Tychicus to Ephesus. When you come, bring the cloak that I left with Carpus at Troas, also the books, and above all the parchments. (2 Tim 4:9-13 NRSV)

Paul grieved over Demas, who had deserted him. Demas had been one of Paul's trusted fellows in the work of the gospel. In two letters the apostle indicates that Demas accompanied him in his earlier imprisonment (Col 4:14; Philem 24). However, near the end of his life, as Paul spends his final days in prison again, he loses his friend to the present age. Was Demas truly transformed by God's saving grace? Did he lose salvation when he deserted Paul? When Demas deserted Paul, did he forsake the gospel?

Paul says Demas "deserted me because he loved the present age." Is Paul exaggerating when he speaks like this? Did Demas simply leave Paul but not Christ? Was the aged apostle being too harsh with Demas?

Paul's gospel requires wholehearted devotion to Christ. Some may think Paul is overbearing in his expectations of Demas. For example, he tells believers in Philippi that he intends to send Timothy to them and then explains, "I have no one else like him, who takes a genuine interest in your welfare. For everyone looks out for his own interests, not those of Jesus Christ (Phil 2:20-21 NIV). However, when Paul speaks like this, he is not being overly harsh. He does not mean that

his other fellow ministers love the present world as Demas fell in love
with the world. Paul distinguishes between legitimate concerns that
marriage brings and love for the world. He makes this clear when he
encourages singleness: "I would like you to be free from concern. An
unmarried man is concerned about the Lord's affairs—how he can
please the Lord. But a married man is concerned about the affairs of
this world—how he can please his wife—and his interests are divided"
(1 Cor 7:32-34 NIV).

Demas's love, however, is not for a woman in marriage; he loves
the present age. Paul uses the phrase "this present age" three times in
the Pastoral Letters (1 Tim 6:17; 2 Tim 4:10; Tit 2:12). As he uses this
phrase, the accent falls on a temporal contrast with "the coming age"
(cf. Gal 1:4; Eph 1:21; 1 Tim 4:8). However, the contrast is not merely
temporal but also between things seen and unseen, a point Paul
emphasizes when he says, "For our light and momentary troubles are
achieving for us an eternal glory that far outweighs them all. So we fix
our eyes not on what is seen, but on what is unseen. For what is seen
is temporary, but what is unseen is eternal" (2 Cor 4:17-18 NIV).
Things seen are but earthly shadows of things to come, which is why
we must walk by faith and not by sight (2 Cor 5:7).

The treachery of Demas's departure from the gospel comes to light
when we ponder Paul's steadfast loyalty as he withstood great opposition. Demas, who "loved the present age," contrasts sharply with Paul,
Timothy and others who "love Christ's appearing" (2 Tim 4:8). So
Demas did not simply forsake the man Paul. He forsook the gospel
Paul preached, for he set his affection on the things of this age and
turned away from Christ Jesus. Evidently, he found the demands of
Paul's gospel too rigorous, for his gospel calls for all "to renounce
impiety and worldly passions, and in the present age to live lives that
are self-controlled, upright, and godly, while we wait for the blessed
hope and the manifestation of the glory of our great God and Savior,
Jesus Christ" (Tit 2:12-13 NRSV). Afflictions and troubles that come
with the gospel in this present age test one's character, and Demas's
true character finally emerged as he tended the aging apostle confined in chains on account of the gospel.

Demas failed to persevere in heeding the call of Paul's gospel, a call
he often heard and probably preached himself. Paul wrote to Timothy:

Command those who are rich in this present world not to be arrogant nor to put their hope in wealth, which is so uncertain, but to put their hope in God, who richly provides us with everything for our enjoyment. Command them to do good, to be rich in good deeds, and to be generous and willing to share. In this way they will lay up treasure for themselves as a firm foundation for the coming age, so that they may take hold of the life that is truly life. (1 Tim 6:17-19 NIV)

Paul's gospel does not endorse asceticism, for he does not despise the things of this world in themselves. Nevertheless, he recognizes that the goods of this age may be obstacles to faith that every believer must overcome. Therefore, he admonishes Timothy to instruct all who are "rich in this present age" to be "rich in good deeds" and generous with their wealth.[34] According to Paul, this is what hope in God and faith look like. Belief that takes hold of eternal life cannot, at the same time, love this present age and set one's hope on its goods.

Does Paul tell Timothy and us about Demas's departure from the gospel in order to terrify us who believe? Is the apostle telling us that perseverance and apostasy are equally likely for believers today and tomorrow? No, the apostle does not present Demas or Alexander, Hymenaeus and Philetus to show that sometimes God cannot preserve his chosen ones. Rather, the apostle points out some who have dropped out of the race to remind us that salvation belongs only to those who run the entire race. Paul's gospel requires us to persevere in the gospel in order that we might be saved in the coming age.

God does not hand us salvation and guarantee our possession of it despite unbelief, so that we have security apart from persevering faith. God's gift of salvation does not hang on a fragile thread of faith that is of human origin. This is so because "true faith is not a human contribution to salvation, but is the state of being oriented to God's grace; because it is not a grasping but rather a being grasped; because it is not a conquest, but rather a being conquered."[35] The way of faith is dynamic, not static, because perseverance "comes to realization

---

[34]Paul engages in some playful phrasing in 1 Tim 6:17-19. For example, the adjectival clause "those who are rich in this present age" *(tois plousiois en tō nun aiōni)* contrasts with the verbal clause "command them to be rich in good deeds" *(ploutein en ergois kalois)*. A third phrase plays off the same cognate, "God . . . provides all things richly for our enjoyment" *(plousiōs eis apolausin)*.

[35]Berkouwer, *Faith and Perseverance,* p. 112.

only in the path of faith."[36] Therefore, the apostasy of Demas and others reminds us that the whole message of Paul's gospel "is inseparably bound up with the living correlation between faith and God's grace."[37] Paul never reasons about God's preserving grace and our steadfastness abstracted from belief in Jesus Christ. Therefore, he calls attention to those who fail to persevere in order that we may look only to Christ for all things.

Two Kinds of Falling: Judas and Peter

Jesus foretold his disciples that they all would fall away from him (Mk 14:27). However, Jesus singled out Judas and Peter with specific prophecies. While eating the Passover with his disciples, Jesus announced, "I tell you the truth, one of you is going to betray me" (Jn 13:21 NIV). Though eleven of the disciples did not know who would be the betrayer, Jesus sent Judas out to carry out his dreadful mission (Jn 13:26-30). Likewise, Jesus foretold Peter's triple denial of his companionship with his Master: "I tell you, Peter, before the rooster crows today, you will deny three times that you know me" (Lk 22:34 NIV; cf. Mt 26:34; Mk 14:30). Mark indicates, "But Peter insisted emphatically, 'Even if I have to die with you, I will never disown you.' And all the others said the same" (Mk 14:31 NIV). Peter's protest hints that he was self-reliant and not trusting God. Though he protested, Peter did sin against his Lord, and Judas betrayed Jesus with a kiss, a symbol of friendship (Mk 14:44-45; Lk 22:48).

Both Peter and Judas fell, just as Jesus prophesied. However, Peter's fall ended in repentance and restoration, but Judas's fall plunged him into eternal night (Jn 13:30). What accounts for the difference between these two men? The answer to this question is not to be found in the personal strengths and weaknesses of each, for both had tragic falls. Judas fell completely and finally. Peter fell away but was restored, yet restoration was not within his power. Therefore, the answer to the question entangles us in the web of correlation between God's sovereignty and creature accountability. We say "creature accountability" because Satan plays a role also.

Judas, the betrayer. According to the Gospels, the Old Testament

---

[36]Ibid., p. 111.
[37]Ibid., p. 107.

prophesied that the Messiah's friend would betray him (Jn 13:18 quotes Ps 41:9). It should come as no surprise, then, that Jesus knew before he selected him as one of the Twelve that Judas would betray him, for Jesus said, "Have I not chosen you, the Twelve? Yet one of you is a devil!" (John 6:70 NIV; cf. v. 64). He also foretold his betrayal and specifically identified Judas as the betrayer (Mt 26:20-25). It is noteworthy that Jesus links his ability to foretell his betrayal with his deity, for Jesus says, "From now on I am telling you before it comes to pass, in order that when it happens you may believe that I Am" (Jn 13:19).[38] Jesus is saying that the basis for believing that he is deity is that he tells the Twelve what will befall him before it happens. So, in the presence of the Twelve, Jesus announces, "Very truly, I tell you, one of you will betray me" (Jn 13:21 NRSV).[39]

We also discover that Judas is "the son of perdition" (Jn 17:12), an expression that within the context means Judas was destined by God for eternal loss.[40] We find this in Jesus' prayer, when he expressly prays for the ones the Father had given him out of the world, excluding Judas (Jn 17:2, 6, 9, 12, 14-16). The Fourth Gospel also indicates another player in the drama: the devil not only prompted Judas to betray Jesus but also entered into him (Jn 13:2, 27). During his last meal with the Twelve, Jesus gave a sign to indicate who would betray him: " 'It is the one to whom I will give this piece of bread when I have dipped it in the dish.' Then, dipping the piece of bread, he gave it to Judas Iscariot, son of Simon. As soon as Judas took the bread, Satan entered into him" (Jn 13:26-27 NIV).

What should we conclude from this evidence? First, when Judas betrayed Jesus, he fulfilled God's prophesied plan (Ps 41:9). Second, he carried out precisely Jesus' prediction, for over protests to the contrary, John's Gospel rather unambiguously indicates not only that Jesus knew from the beginning that Judas would betray him but also

---

[38]John 13:19 is one of five passages that use the construction "I Am" *(egō eimi)* as a rather clear claim of deity, reflecting the Old Testament name of the Lord and laying claim to a quality that belongs to God alone (cf. Is 43:10). See also John 6:20; 8:24, 58; 18:5-6.

[39]Remarkably, John Sanders argues that Jesus did not know that Judas would betray him (*The God Who Risks: A Theology of Providence* [Downers Grove, Ill.: InterVarsity Press, 1998], pp. 98-99).

[40]Cf. D. A. Carson, *Divine Sovereignty and Human Responsibility: Biblical Perspectives in Tension* (Atlanta: John Knox Press, 1981), p. 132.

that Judas was one of his disciples who did not believe in him (Jn 6:64).[41] Third, John 6:64 means that Judas never possessed salvation, so when he fell away, his fall was not from eternal life to eternal death. Judas was a pretender from the beginning.[42] Fourth, Judas's fall was not because Jesus lacked power to preserve him from perishing. Jesus did not intercede for Judas, in order that Scripture might be fulfilled (Jn 17:12). Judas is accountable for his treachery, for he willfully conspired with the chief priests to betray Jesus (Mt 26:14-16). Fifth, Judas could not blame the devil, though the devil put it into his heart to betray Jesus. Judas willingly took the morsel of bread from Jesus, signifying that he fully knew his role in condemning innocent blood (Jn 13:27). Sixth, Judas knew his own accountability for his wicked act, for when he "saw that Jesus was condemned, he was seized with remorse and returned the thirty silver coins to the chief priests and the elders. 'I have sinned,' he said, 'for I have betrayed innocent blood.' 'What is that to us?' they replied. 'That's your responsibility.' So Judas threw the money into the temple and left. Then he went away and hanged himself" (Matt 27:3-5 NIV).

The case of Judas contradicts the idea that he possessed eternal life but lost it by betraying Jesus. Furthermore, the biblical account of Judas's defection discloses that human accountability for apostasy stands correlated with God's sovereign purpose. Judas did not act independently of God's ordained intention. His grievous sin fulfilled prophecy. The biblical writers believe that God stands behind even evil actions of his creatures without mitigating their accountability or blemishing his own character. Even the fact that Satan used Judas does not alleviate his personal responsibility. Over both Judas and the devil stands God's sovereignty, for both evildoers accomplished precisely what God had purposed, namely, the death of Jesus Christ to vanquish the devil's work (1 Jn 3:8).

Peter, the denier. Compared to Judas, Peter came to a much different

---

[41]Robert Shank argues, "John does not say here that Jesus knew that Judas would betray him when he chose him as one of the twelve, least of all that he chose him for that purpose. What he does say is that Jesus was not taken by surprise and soon saw signs of treason in Judas" (*Life in the Son,* p. 179, quoting A. T. Robertson, *Word Pictures in the New Testament* [New York: Harper, 1930], 5:379).

[42]Shank contends, "We believe the case of Judas is an instance of true apostasy, rather than of original and prolonged imposture. . . . The case of Judas, then, was one of apostasy, rather than original hypocrisy" (*Life in the Son,* p. 179).

end after disowning Jesus Christ. Why? As with Judas, Jesus foretold Peter's denial but with even greater precision: "Truly I tell you, this day, this very night, before the cock crows twice, you will deny me three times" (Mk 14:30 NRSV). Jesus predicts that Peter will be prompted to deny him three times, all before the rooster crows the second time at daybreak.[43] But even before he foretells Peter's triple denial, Jesus says, "Simon, Simon, listen! Satan has demanded to sift all of you like wheat, but I have prayed for you that your own faith may not fail; and you, when once you have turned back, strengthen your brothers" (Lk 22:31-32 NRSV). Peter was not the only disciple whose faith Satan wanted to strip away, for Jesus says, "Satan has demanded to sift all of you like wheat."[44] Nevertheless, Satan wanted to shake Peter because he recognized that he was the most prominent of the Twelve, a role he often presumed to fill, as his boast shows: "Lord, I am ready to go with you to prison and to death!" (Lk 22:33 NRSV). So Jesus predicts that Peter will sin by yielding to Satan's wishes, how often he will sin, when he will sin and that he will repent. As some people reason, if Jesus' predictions are sure to come to pass, Peter's personal accountability, his need to pray lest he fall into temptation and Jesus' intercession for him would be set aside as irrelevant.[45] But the biblical text indicates that Jesus made his precise prediction of Peter's denial in the same conversation in which he announced that he had prayed that Peter's faith not fail and that his prayer would be effective, for Peter would be restored. As in the case of Judas, without any hint of conflict, the biblical writers embrace the fact that God rules over even sinful deeds his creatures carry out and that he does this without destroying their accountability or without being tarnished in his own character.

Peter's fall was loathsome, especially since he protested with self-confidence, "Lord, I am ready to go with you to prison and to death!"

---

[43]Though Mark 14:69 appears to suggest that the same female servant prompted Peter's first two denials, according to Matthew 26:71, the second who provoked him is "another female servant." On this, see William Hendriksen, *The Gospel According to Mark* (Grand Rapids, Mich.: Baker, 1975), pp. 619-20.

[44]On the plural *you* here and the singular in the clause "But I have prayed for you, Simon," see Darrell L. Bock, *Luke,* Baker Exegetical Commentary on the New Testament (Grand Rapids, Mich.: Baker, 1996), 2:1,742.

[45]Advocates of open theism argue this. For example, see Sanders, *God Who Risks,* pp. 135-36.

(Lk 22:33 NRSV). He aggravated his sin by sleeping instead of praying lest he be tempted, as Jesus exhorted him in the garden (Lk 22:39-46). Evil as his behavior was, after the rooster rebuked Peter, Jesus arrested Peter's faith from failing completely (Lk 22:60-62). It was not the strength of Peter's faith in and love for Christ that preserved him from destruction, for his confidence rested on his own strength to endure. When it appeared that only chaff remained after Satan's sifting of Peter, when he had focused solely on the preservation of his earthly life and when the confidence of his readiness to die for Christ crumbled as he swore an oath of denial, it was only Jesus Christ's intercession that saved him.[46] Thus, Christ's love and grace brought repentance and restored faith so that Peter "went outside and wept bitterly," for he recognized the impotence and sinfulness of his presumptuous vow of loyalty. This is what distinguished Peter from Judas, for Judas also felt remorse, but he found no way to quell his conscience other than to return the blood money and to hang himself (Mt 27:3-5). Peter's faith persisted because Jesus interceded for him, but Judas plunged into eternal darkness as he fulfilled prophecy (Acts 1:16-20).

It was the intercession of Jesus—both his prayer for Peter and his gaze at him when the rooster crowed—that saved the overconfident apostle. Jesus did not intercede for Judas, for otherwise he, too, would have been saved. Such is the power of Jesus' intercession. Likewise, all of us who belong to Christ find that, while we are not of the world but still in the world, our only hope of persevering in faithfulness to Christ is his intercession on our behalf. It is not for the world but for all whom the Father has given him that he prays, "I ask you to protect them from the evil one. . . . Sanctify them in the truth; your word is truth" (Jn 17:15, 17 NRSV). As Jesus prayed for Peter, so he prays for us to persevere to the end, for he asks, "Father, I want those you have given me to be with me where I am, and to see my glory, the glory you have given me because you loved me before the creation of the world" (Jn 17:24 NIV; cf. v. 20). His prayer does not extend merely through today or on through tomorrow; it reaches to the last day, for he asks the Father to preserve us to dwell with him forever. Paul also assures us that Christ Jesus continues to intercede

---

[46]Cf. Berkouwer, *Faith and Perseverance,* p. 145.

on our behalf, for he says, "Who is he that condemns? Christ Jesus, who died—more than that, who was raised to life—is at the right hand of God and is also interceding for us" (Rom 8:34 NIV). Our perseverance in faithfulness to Jesus Christ inherently flows from a humble confession of reliance on him alone. None for whom Jesus intercedes will fall further than Peter did; none will perish. Nothing "will be able to separate us from the love of God that is in Christ Jesus our Lord" (Rom 8:39 NIV).

Conclusion

Who are the fallen runners strewn along the racecourse? Who are those who have failed to persevere? They are people who had varied responses to the gospel, but all proved, by their failure to persevere, to be impostors. Some receive the gospel with a show of joy, believe for a while and then fall away abruptly when persecution on account of the gospel comes to them. Others receive the gospel but entangle themselves in the world's anxieties by pursuing wealth and pleasure. Consequently, they never bring forth fruit worthy of the gospel. Such were Alexander, Hymenaeus, Philetus and Demas. They all, along with Judas, fell away from the gospel and showed by their defection from Christ that they never truly belonged to him. All these who have fallen, including Israel, stand as warning signs along the pathway of faith. They do not prompt us who believe to doubt whether or not God will preserve us to the end of the race. Rather, they remind us that we do not run in our own strength, that we are powerless to persevere in faith unless the one who has called us to faith sustains us by his grace and love.

Readers who suppose that possession of wealth itself is what constitutes entanglement in the world's anxieties need to remember that owning riches itself is not the enemy of godliness. Abraham, Job and Barnabas were all men of considerable wealth. They were also devout men. With the parable of the soils, Jesus does not assault possession of wealth but rather wealth's possession of us. The parable's concern is our response to the word of the gospel. As Jesus says elsewhere, "You cannot serve God and wealth" (Mt 6:24 NRSV).

Peter's fall and restoration remind us of two things. First, we must be aware how frail we truly are in ourselves and therefore drink deeply of the water of life in the Spirit. Second, it is God's grace alone that distinguishes us from those who have fallen and perished along the way. It is as Paul says, "For who makes you different from anyone else? What do you have that you did not receive? And if you did receive it, why do you boast as though you did not?" (1 Cor 4:7 NIV). Here is what distinguishes true perseverance from disingenuous perseverance. We must look to Christ to strengthen our weak knees and to cut a straight course to the goal (cf. Heb 12:12-13), for to vow presumptuously as Peter did is to put confidence in our strength and not in Christ, who intercedes effectually for us.

God has said,
  "Never will I leave you;
  never will I forsake you."

So we say with confidence,
  "The Lord is my helper; I will not be afraid.
  What can man do to me?" (Heb 13:5 NIV)

6

DRAWING ON GOD'S GRACE

Going the Distance by God's Power

Even youths will faint and be weary,
  and the young will fall exhausted;
but those who wait for the LORD shall renew their strength,
  they shall mount up with wings like eagles,
they shall run and not be weary,
  they shall walk and not faint. (Is 40:30-31 NRSV)

I n the previous chapter we examined those who did not finish
the race, those who began to run but quit when the race proved
to be arduous and long. Those who drop out of the race, John
tells us, were never truly a part of the people of God (1 Jn 2:19). Persevering in Christ is the mark of authenticity. By leaving the church
they testify that their so-called faith was not genuine saving faith. We
have also seen in previous chapters that people must run the race
until the end to receive the prize of eternal life. Persevering in faith is
not optional but essential. Believers must meet the conditions stated
in the Scriptures to obtain what God has promised. But how do believers satisfy the conditions that are necessary to attain eternal life? The
Scriptures inform us that we do not do so in our own strength. We
cannot and will not make it to the end of the race in our own power.
We need the power of God to finish the marathon that we run, and we
have the promise of God that he will supply the necessary power.
Thus, we can be certain that every believer will most certainly finish
the race and obtain the prize. In this chapter we shall focus on God's

promise to sustain us to the end. We shall call four witnesses to the witness stand to defend the thesis that God promises to sustain until the end those who are genuinely part of the people of God.

Peter

We saw in the last chapter that although Peter denied Jesus, the Lord did not abandon him. Therefore, it is fitting that our first witness is Peter. We will appeal to only one verse from his letters, but we will also consult a text from Luke in which Jesus makes a promise to Peter. The verse from 1 Peter is a very important one and thus must be investigated carefully. Peter says that believers "are being protected by the power of God through faith for a salvation ready to be revealed in the last time" (1 Pet 1:5 NRSV). The salvation envisioned here is eschatological, since it will "be revealed in the last time." *Salvation* is another term for the end-time "inheritance" that is reserved for believers and that nothing can blemish (1 Pet 1:4). The terms *reserved* (1 Pet 1:4) and *protected* (1 Pet 1:5) are alternate ways of communicating the idea that God preserves the inheritance for believers.[1] The word *protected (phroureō)* is often used in military contexts (cf. Judith 3:6; 1 Esdras 4:56; Wisdom 17:16; 2 Cor 11:32) to denote the guarding or fortifying of something. We are guarded by God's power so that we will obtain the eschatological inheritance, and thus we receive the inheritance because of his might and not because of our strength. Of course, 1 Peter 1:5 says that we are protected by God's power "through faith." Is it warranted to conclude, therefore, that one must exercise faith to receive end-time salvation? Apparently so, for the final inheritance is not obtained whether or not faith exists but through faith. Since faith is linked to our final inheritance, it is also clear that faith is "understood as continuing trust or faithfulness."[2] Peter does not restrict himself to the initial act of faith but conceives of a faith that lasts to the end. Now, if ongoing faith is a condition for obtaining the final inheritance, then the verse could be construed to say that God will protect us until the end as long as we continue to exercise faith. Some might conclude that if persistence in faith is necessary to be saved, then we cannot be certain of our end-time salva-

---

[1] J. Ramsey Michaels, *1 Peter*, Word Biblical Commentary (Waco, Tex.: Word, 1988), p. 22. The translation is taken from the NASB here.
[2] Ibid., p. 23.

tion. God will do everything he can to protect us from unbelief, but he cannot compel us to believe, and thus keeping us is God's part and faith is our part.

The interpretation just presented has a serious flaw and should be rejected. We agree that there is no final salvation apart from continued faith, and thus faith is a condition for obtaining the eschatological inheritance. The flaw is to conclude that God's protection can be kept in a separate compartment from our believing. We can get at the issue by asking, "How are we protected through God's power?" All of 1 Peter clarifies that we are not exempted from suffering or even death because of the power of God, since the church experienced persecution. God's power does not shield believers from trials and sufferings, but it does protect us from that which would cause us to fall away. What would prevent us from maintaining our allegiance to Christ until the end? Surely the answer is sin, and we know that sin stems from unbelief, in failing to hope in God during our earthly sojourn.[3]

God's power, to be effective at all, must guard us from sin and unbelief. If his power plays no role in our faith, then it seems that his power accomplishes nothing in our making it to the end—since it is precisely unbelief and failure to hope in God that causes us to fall away from God. If God's power does not protect us from unbelief, it is hard to see what it does. How is God protecting us until the end if his guarding plays no role in our continuing faith? We are suggesting that 1 Peter 1:5 contains a glorious promise. God's power protects us because his power is the means by which our faith is sustained. Ernest Best rightly discerns that the ultimate reason for our preservation must be God's gift rather than our faith, since otherwise "the reference to God's power" is "unnecessary and provides no assurance to the believer since what he doubts is his own power to cling to God in trial."[4] We should not use this verse to deny that believers must maintain their faith until the end. Its function is to encourage believers with the truth that God will preserve their faith through sufferings and the vicissitudes of life. Faith and hope are ultimately gifts of God, and he fortifies believers so that they persist in faith and hope until the day that they obtain the eschatological inheritance.

---

[3]Supporting the centrality of hope in 1 Peter is John Piper, "Hope As the Motivation of Love: 1 Peter 3:9-12," *New Testament Studies* 26 (1980): 212-31.

[4]Ernest Best, *1 Peter*, New Century Bible (Grand Rapids, Mich.: Eerdmans, 1971), p. 77.

Jesus' words to Peter in the Gospel of Luke also remind us that persistence in faith is a gift of God. Jesus' death is imminent, and he forecasts that all the disciples will deny him in an hour of peril. Nevertheless, Jesus assures Peter with these words, "But I have prayed for you, Simon, that your faith may not fail. And when you have turned back, strengthen your brothers." Satan has asked for Peter, to sift him as wheat and destroy his faith (Lk 22:32 NIV). The hour of testing has arrived in which prayer is needed so that the disciples will triumph during the ordeal (Lk 22:46). Judas surrenders to the enemy during this time, and Peter faces a severe test. Jesus assures Peter, however, that he will persist despite the severity of the testing and despite his denials of Christ. Even though Peter denies Christ, his faith does not fail forever. He is given the grace to repent and continue on the journey of faith. The faith of Peter is not optional. Jesus is not saying that Peter will be saved no matter what he does, even if he never repents. Peter must continue to exercise faith in order to survive the time of testing. Satan sifts Peter like grain so that he can destroy Peter's faith, and Peter's faith must emerge intact for him to be considered part of the people of God.

Faith, of course, is a human choice. Thus, we can legitimately say that Peter must choose to exercise faith to obtain the final inheritance. Luke does not conceive of Peter defeating the power of Satan apart from the decision of faith. Yet such faith is ultimately the gift of God. Faith is Peter's portion because Jesus prayed for him. Jesus' effective prayer is the foundation of Peter's faith. Jesus prays for Peter so that his faith will survive and Peter will receive end-time salvation. Because Jesus prays for Peter, Luke is suggesting, Peter's faith will emerge from the hour of testing and continue to the end. Luke, then, does not conceive of perseverance without the continuance of faith, but such endurance is conceived to be the result of Jesus' prayer. We think here of the intercessory work of Christ for all believers. In Romans 8:33-34 the intercession of Christ is linked to the surety of final vindication on the day of judgment. Similarly, in Hebrews 7:25 the completeness and finality of our salvation is secured through the priestly and intercessory work of Christ. It seems probable, therefore, that in Luke 22:32 and the other texts that speak of Christ's intercessory work an effective intercession is intended. Those for whom Christ intercedes will continue in faith and persevere until the day of redemption.

John

The second witness supporting the preservation of believers by the Father is John. Before examining the promises that speak of God's preserving work, we must recall that John continually exhorts his readers to continue in obedience. The promises of preservation must not be used to cancel out these exhortations. The threat that those who do not abide in the vine will be cast away is a real one (Jn 15:2, 6). John warns of the danger of a sin that brings death (1 Jn 5:16-17). We cannot discuss in detail the various interpretive theories here, but it is probable that the sin warned against is apostasy.[5] Believers must guard against that which will separate them from the living God (1 Jn 5:21). We know that we belong to God if we keep his commandments (1 Jn 2:3-6; 3:4-10), love our brothers and sisters (1 Jn 2:7-11; 3:11-20; 4:7-21) and believe that Jesus is the Messiah come in the flesh (1 Jn 2:18-23).

The warnings and threats addressed to believers are genuine, yet John also has some of the most significant promises of divine preservation in the New Testament. One of the notable texts is in John 6:37-40:

> All that the Father gives me will come to me, and whoever comes to me I will never drive away. For I have come down from heaven not to do my will but to do the will of him who sent me. And this is the will of him who sent me, that I shall lose none of all that he has given me, but raise them up at the last day. For my Father's will is that everyone who looks to the Son and believes in him shall have eternal life, and I will raise him up at the last day. (NIV)

The text begins by asserting that all whom the Father has given to the Son "will come" to the Son. This coming to the Son is equivalent to believing in the Son. We know this from John 6:35, where Jesus says, "I am the bread of life. He who comes to me will never go hungry, and he who believes in me will never be thirsty" (NIV). It is obvious in this sentence that *comes* and *believes* are synonyms, since the one who "comes to" or "believes in" Jesus satisfies his or her hunger and thirst. Therefore, when Jesus says in John 6:37 that those given by the Father "will come" to the Son, he means that they "will believe" in the Son. We know, however, that not all believe in

---

[5]See I. Howard Marshall, *Kept by the Power of God: A Study of Perseverance and Falling Away* (1969; reprint, Minneapolis: Bethany Fellowship, 1974), p. 186.

or come to the Son, so the Father only gives some human beings to the Son. Those who are given, however, will certainly come, and those who have believed in Jesus will never be driven away by the Son. What Jesus means by this is expressed more clearly in John 6:39: "I shall lose none of all that he has given me, but raise them up at the last day" (NIV). No one whom the Father gives to the Son will perish; that is, not one believer will ever be lost. Jesus pledges that each one without exception will be preserved, and he also specifies to what they will be preserved when he says that he will "raise them up at the last day." When Jesus says they will be raised on the last day, he means that they will attain the resurrection. They will enter fully into the life of the age to come.

John 6:40 clarifies this as well. Those who look to the Son and believe in him "have eternal life." That is, they already enjoy the life of the age to come. Thus it inexorably follows, says Jesus, that "I will raise" such people up "at the last day." No one who now has eternal life will fail to experience the end-time resurrection. Jesus promises that they will experience the resurrection because of his preserving work. Those whom have been specially given to him shall never be lost. This same theme is reiterated in John 6:44: "No one can come to me unless the Father who sent me draws him, and I will raise him up at the last day" (NIV). Here Jesus complements what he said in John 6:37. There he said that those given by the Father will come to the Son. Here he emphasizes that those who are not given cannot come to the Son. The idea, of course, is not that they sincerely desire to come to Jesus but the Father prevents them from doing so. Rather, they cannot come because they do not have any desire to believe in Jesus. They are naturally repelled by him. On the other hand, those drawn by the Father are given the desire and will to believe, and once they believe they are guaranteed that Jesus will raise them up at the last day. The emphasis here is on the power of God's grace. He grants people the desire to come to Jesus, and once they come he ensures that they will never depart from him. These promises provide tremendous comfort and strength to believers. We know that we are prone to wander, but we have the promise that Jesus will never lose us, that the work he began he will also complete on the day of our resurrection.

One might question whether what has been said above is true. Is it genuinely the case that there are no exceptions, that every single person given to the Son by the Father will be preserved until the end? Some have said that Judas is an exception, and if there is one exception there may be others.[6] Judas is adduced as an exception from John 6:70-71: "Then Jesus replied, 'Have I not chosen you, the Twelve? Yet one of you is a devil!' (He meant Judas, the son of Simon Iscariot, who, though one of the Twelve, was later to betray him)" (NIV).[7] On first glance the case of Judas seems to contradict the claim that no one is lost whom the Father gave to Jesus. Jesus chose him, yet he turned out to be a devil. A more thorough investigation, however, indicates that Judas is not an exception at all. He was never one of those given by the Father to the Son. In the same discourse where Jesus asserts that all those given by the Father will come to the Son, he attests that Judas was never part of the saving community: " 'Yet there are some of you who do not believe.' For Jesus had known from the beginning which of them did not believe and who would betray him. He went on to say, 'This is why I told you that no one can come to me unless the Father has enabled him' " (Jn 6:64-65 NIV). The progression of thought in these verses should be carefully noted. Jesus begins by noting that some do not believe in him as the bread of life. Then John observes that Jesus knew from the outset who would not believe and who would betray him. In other words, even when Jesus chose Judas, he knew that Judas would abandon him.

At this juncture in the argument those who believe that some of the chosen may apostatize might observe that Jesus foreknows which of the chosen will forsake him. But John 6:65 rules out this interpretation, for Jesus explains why some do not believe and why Judas would betray him. He does not say, "The reason some do not believe, even though they have been initially chosen, is that they choose to forsake me later. They do not have the persistence and courage to follow me to the end." Instead he says, "This is why I told you that no one can come to me unless the Father has enabled him" (Jn 6:65 NIV). When Jesus accounts for Judas's betrayal, he explains that Judas (and others!) do not come to him because the Father has not given them the ability to do so. Indeed, the words "come to me" demonstrate that

---

[6]Grant Osborne, "Soteriology in the Gospel of John," in *The Grace of God, the Will of Man: A Case for Arminianism*, ed. Clark H. Pinnock (Grand Rapids, Mich.: Zondervan, 1989), pp. 249, 254.

[7]See the previous chapter for a complementary discussion on Judas.

Judas had never come to Jesus for salvation. The text does not say that Judas came to Jesus initially but now was forsaking him. On the contrary, Jesus remarks that Judas had never placed his belief in him as the bread of life, and the reason he had not done so was because the Father had not enabled Judas to do so. We see, therefore, that Jesus' foreknowledge of what was about to happen in verse 64 is based on what the Father had decided would occur according to verse 65. It is also clear that even though Jesus chose Judas, such choosing never involved salvation for Judas, for he was never given the grace that would enable him to come to Jesus.

Further evidence supporting the idea that Judas was never genuinely part of the people of God is found in John 13. The washing of the disciples' feet symbolizes the cleansing that believers receive when saved. This symbolic dimension comes to the forefront when Peter objects vehemently to Jesus washing his feet (Jn 13:6, 8). Jesus, however, insists that Peter must humble himself and allow his feet to be washed by Jesus because "unless I wash you, you have no part with me" (Jn 13:8 NIV). In other words, if Peter does not let Jesus wash his feet, he has no inheritance or place in the kingdom of God. The washing symbolizes being cleansed by Jesus and receiving forgiveness of sins. Peter then responds by asking Jesus to wash his whole body (Jn 13:9). But Peter continues to misunderstand the symbolism at work, so Jesus explains, " 'A person who has had a bath needs only to wash his feet; his whole body is clean. And you are clean, though not every one of you.' For he knew who was going to betray him, and that was why he said not every one was clean" (Jn 13:10-11 NIV).[8] When Jesus says "you are clean," he is obviously not speaking of the physical condition of their feet! His point is that all of them have received a saving washing and are part of the people of God. He proceeds to qualify the assertion that all are clean. The betrayer, Judas, stands out as an exception. He is not clean. In other words, Judas has never received the saving washing that the other eleven enjoyed. Judas was never part of the people of God. It follows, then, that Judas cannot function as an exception to the promise to preserve all believers. He is not an exception because he was never

---

[8]There is a textual problem in this verse that makes it quite difficult to interpret, but the point we derive from the text stands regardless of how one resolves the textual problem or interprets the difficulty attending to it.

cleansed by the Son in the first place. He never came to the Son in belief and faith. Judas can scarcely function as an example of genuine apostasy if he never had saving faith.

The situation of Judas should be explored from another angle. John emphasizes that his betrayal was a fulfillment of Scripture and what God had predicted would occur (Jn 6:64; 13:1-3, 18-19; 17:12; 18:1-4, 9-11). In other words, Judas had a preordained role to fulfill regarding the person of Jesus. Of course, John does not conclude from this that Judas is exempt from responsibility for his actions. The biblical writers never draw the philosophical conclusion that if human choices are preordained, then we are not responsible for what happens (see Acts 2:23; 4:27-28). In John 17 Jesus returns to the theme of divine protection and preservation of those given to him by the Father. The Son gives "eternal life to all those you have given him" (Jn 17:2 NIV). The language hearkens back to John 6:37 and 6:44. Those drawn by the Father and given to the Son receive the gift of eternal life. Jesus then prays for those who have believed, and he particularly prays that the Father will protect or keep them (Jn 17:11-12, 15) so that they will be spared from the power of the evil one and so that ultimately they will "be with me where I am, and . . . see my glory" (Jn 17:24 NIV). What Jesus prays for here is nothing less than the perseverance of faith until the end. He asks God that those believers given to him will be sustained in their faith until the day they can be with him and see his glory. What John wants to communicate to the church in recording this prayer is the certainty of an answer. Those who belong to the Son because of the Father's decision will certainly persist in faith until the end, and the reason they will maintain their allegiance is because Jesus prayed for them. When Jesus in the midst of the prayer says, "While I was with them, I protected them and kept them safe by that name you gave me. None has been lost except the one doomed to destruction so that Scripture would be fulfilled" (Jn 17:12 NIV), this should not be understood to say that some who belong to the Son will ultimately be lost. Jesus' very point in bringing up Judas is that he was an exception from the beginning. He was never, as we have seen, among those given by the Father to the Son. He was never washed and cleansed in the saving bath. It was prophesied from the outset that he would fulfill the role of betrayer. Thus, Jesus did not lose a single one of those given to him by God, and we are strengthened immeasurably when we realize that this prayer of Jesus will certainly be answered. God will keep us to the end and will unquestionably answer the prayers of his Son.

One more text needs to be explored in terms of Jesus losing none of those given to him. When Jesus is arrested, he intervenes so that his disciples are not taken into custody with him (Jn 18:8). John adds an editorial comment to Jesus' intervention: "This happened so that the words he had spoken would be fulfilled: 'I have not lost one of those you gave me' " (Jn 18:9 NIV). This aside seems astonishingly irrelevant at first glance. Should we interpret all of Jesus' promises about not losing any of those given in terms of being rescued from arrest and possible execution by the Romans? Certainly not, for this would do violence to the contexts in which the other sayings occur. It is imperative to recognize that John often clothes spiritual truths in physical events (the washing of the disciples feet!).[9] D. A. Carson rightly explains the significance of this verse:

> In one sense, the disciples' safety is secured by Jesus' arrest and death. But this is not simply the substitution of physical safety for eternal salvation. Rather, it is the symbol of it, an illustration of it—more, it is the first step in securing the eschatological reality.[10]

The physical preservation of the disciples symbolizes their eschatological preservation. The events in John 18 are the beginning of the fulfillment of Jesus' prayer in John 17.

None of those given by the Father to the Son will ever be lost. They will certainly attain the resurrection of the dead. They will persevere to the end because the Son prays for them. The Son's prayer for believers that they will be spared from contamination from the evil one (Jn 17:15) has another connotation. Jesus prays for them because they must maintain their allegiance to him until the end in order to see his glory (Jn 17:24). Persistence in faith is not a matter of indifference. Nonetheless, believers know that they will not make shipwreck of their faith because the Son prays for their endurance until the end.

Assurance of future bliss is also promised in John 10:27-29: "My sheep listen to my voice; I know them, and they follow me. I give

---

[9]For the significance of symbolism in John's gospel, see Craig R. Koester, *Symbolism in the Fourth Gospel: Mystery, Meaning, Community* (Minneapolis: Fortress, 1995).

[10]D. A. Carson, *The Gospel According to John* (Grand Rapids, Mich.: Eerdmans, 1991), p. 579.

them eternal life, and they shall never perish; no one can snatch them out of my hand. My Father, who has given them to me, is greater than all; no one can snatch them out of my Father's hand" (NIV). Jesus the Good Shepherd has a flock, and this flock listens to his voice and obeys his summons. Because they are part of his flock, they believe in him (Jn 10:26). Jesus, during this present evil age, grants them the life of the age to come, namely, eternal life. Eternal life by definition is inviolable, for those who have it will "never perish." However, the emphasis is not on the inherent efficacy of eternal life but on the powerful grasp of the Good Shepherd. No one can dislodge the sheep from his hand. Nor does the Son work alone. He works in concert with the Father so that the sheep are under the protection of both the Father and the Son. The flock can never be removed from their saving grasp. Osborne maintains that the warnings against apostasy in John's Gospel show that eternal life is not a "future certainty."[11] Human choices, he insists, must be factored into the equation since assurance works "with faith-response."[12] Osborne is correct that the promises can never be used to nullify the warnings. Believers must pay heed to the warnings in order to attain to the resurrection of the last day. But he incorrectly deduces that warnings cancel out future certainty and that human decisions and divine sovereignty are coequal.

The correlation between human belief and divine preservation becomes clear when we examine the teaching of John 10. John maintains that the sheep listen only to the shepherd's voice and therefore follow only the shepherd (Jn 10:3-4). They flee from strangers because they do not recognize them (Jn 10:5). John does not envision a situation in which some have eternal life even though they give allegiance to thieves and robbers (Jn 10:8). The sheep must listen to and follow the shepherd to obtain eternal life. Human choices and decisions are crucial in the process of salvation. The issue before us,

---

[11]Grant Osborne, "Exegetical Notes on Calvinist Texts," in *Grace Unlimited*, ed. Clark H. Pinnock (Minneapolis: Bethany Fellowship, 1975), p. 172.

[12]Osborne, "Soteriology," p. 251. Marshall (*Kept by the Power of God*, pp. 174-83) is a bit more restrained than Osborne and does not make a definite decision. He says that "logic breaks down" and believers "know" that they are "safe in the care of Jesus" but also know that they have an obligation "to abide continually in Jesus" (p. 183). Cf. also Robert Shank, *Life in the Son: A Study of the Doctrine of Perseverance*, 2nd ed. (Springfield, Mo.: Westcott, 1976), p. 59.

however, is this: What finally accounts for the belief and the obedience of the sheep? Are human decisions and divine summoning
coequal? John 10:26 specifically rules out this possibility: "You do not
believe because you are not my sheep" (NIV). The text does not say
that "you are not my sheep because you do not believe." In one sense,
of course, that statement is true. But John has a different intention
here. He locates the unbelief of his opponents ultimately in the fact
that they are not part of the flock. In other words, those who believe
do so because they have been chosen to be part of Jesus' flock.
Human beings must believe in order to be saved, but such belief is a
gift of God, and those who come to faith do so because they are part
of Jesus' flock (cf. Eph 2:8; Phil 1:29). Similarly, the protecting work
of the Father and Son by which they prevent anyone or anything
from snatching the sheep from their hands is ultimate. Believers must
follow after the shepherd, but Jesus promises that they will most certainly do so because of the protecting work of the Father and the Son.
The sheep listen to the shepherd's voice precisely because they are
safe in his hands, and he never relaxes his grip so that anyone
escapes from his firm hold. We must not wrench perseverance and
assurance apart so that one has the latter without the former. Nonetheless, we must also see that the reason we make it to the end is
because Jesus' power guarantees we will do so. Those who are swept
up into his powerful embrace invariably hearken to his voice.

Jude

The third witness supporting the preserving power of God is Jude.
Jude writes to counter false teachers afflicting the community. What
especially marks these people is their licentious behavior (Jude 8-16),
and Jude assures his readers that these interlopers will experience
eschatological judgment (Jude 4-7). The entrance of these people into
the church is no surprise; the apostles predicted this very state of
affairs (Jude 17-18). There is also no doubt about the status of these
people: "These are the men who divide you, who follow mere natural
instincts and do not have the Spirit" (Jude 19 NIV). Since these people
do not have the Spirit, they are not part of the people of God. Jude
does not consider their aberrant behavior as a temporary lapse or
backsliding. He expresses confidence that those troubling the church
are not believers at all. We see once again that when New Testament

writers look retrospectively at those who were part of the church and then have abandoned the faith, they identify such as unbelievers.

Of course, this does not mean that the status of every single person in the church is clear. There are some suffering from doubt who are in need of mercy (Jude 22), and there are others in mortal danger who can still be snatched from the fire (Jude 23). The spiritual state of the false teachers is apparently clearer than the status of those who are under the interlopers' influence. Even the inspired writer is unclear about whether some of those in the church are truly believers, so we should not be surprised that such certainty is not granted to us today. Often God does not intend for us to know about the spiritual state of others, so that we can make a pronouncement about their spiritual state. Warning passages are given so that we can admonish people to continue in faith, not so that we can discern who is truly part of the people of God. Most of us would like to know the future destiny of others, but God does not reveal such information to us when some are straying from the Lord. We are to help them in the most practical way possible, not by speculating on whether they will go to heaven, but by helping them to get back on the pathway to heaven.

In verses 20-21 Jude turns to the readers and gives them an exhortation: "But you, beloved, building yourselves up on your most holy faith; praying in the Holy Spirit; keep yourselves in the love of God, waiting anxiously for the mercy of our Lord Jesus Christ to eternal life" (Jude 20-21 NASB). The structure of these verses is instructive. The central admonition stands out with the only imperative verb in the two verses: "keep yourselves in the love of God." The three participles explain how we can keep ourselves in God's love: (1) by building ourselves up in our holy faith; (2) by praying in the Holy Spirit; and (3) by waiting for the coming of the Lord Jesus Christ. The summons to keep ourselves in God's love is another way of saying, "Do not commit apostasy." We are to maintain our allegiance to God until the end and not stray from his love. When we examine the three participles we see that we can preserve our faith until the end in tangible ways. First, we keep ourselves in God's love by building ourselves up in the faith. The word *faith* stands here for the content of the Christian faith. Those who wish to avoid apostasy must grow in their knowledge of the truth. Second, we are to pray in the power of the

Holy Spirit. Fervent and consistent prayer prevents our hearts from growing cold towards God. Third, we are to await eagerly the coming of our Lord Jesus Christ. Why is this important? Because Jude indicates that when Jesus comes we will receive "eternal life." Here the not-yet dimension of eternal life comes to the forefront. In this life we are deeply conscious of our need for God's mercy, since we will obtain perfection only at the coming of Christ. Those who long for eternal life reveal that the center of their existence is not this world but the next one.

This strong admonition from Jude where he exhorts his readers to keep themselves in God's love prepares us for the concluding doxology: "To him who is able to keep you from falling and to present you before his glorious presence without fault and with great joy—to the only God our Savior be glory, majesty, power and authority, through Jesus Christ our Lord, before all ages, now and forevermore! Amen" (Jude 24-25 NIV). On the one hand, Jude exhorts the readers to keep themselves in God's love. They must certainly exert effort and diligence to do so. Yet finally and ultimately those who escape from apostasy do so because of the grace of God. He is the one "who is able to keep you from falling."

Some understand falling to refer to a failure to live a productive Christian life instead of apostasy. They offer in defense of this the fact that Jude speaks of being presented before God "without fault." Such an interpretation veers away from the context of the letter of Jude. The concern of Jude throughout the letter is apostasy. He ominously reminds the readers that even though Israel was liberated from Egypt those who sinned failed to reach the land of promise (Jude 5). Angels who sinned have no second chance (Jude 6), and Sodom and Gomorrah serve "as an example of those who suffer the punishment of eternal fire" (Jude 7 NIV). Jude does not introduce Sodom and Gomorrah to titillate his readers. He is concerned that they do not presume upon grace and think that they will be spared from the judgment that leveled those cities. The infiltrators remind Jude of Cain, Balaam and Korah (Jude 11), who are all men destined for eternal judgment. Similarly, these men are those "for whom blackest darkness has been reserved forever" (Jude 13 NIV). They will experience the fierce judgment that Enoch threatens (Jude 14-15). Thus, when Jude says that God can keep believers from falling and present them without fault, he means that God can keep believers from apostasy. "Without fault" here does not mean sinless; the point is that these believers have stayed true to God until the end. This is the reason for their limitless joy. Jude preserves the tension between divine sovereignty and human responsibility well. Believers must keep themselves in God's love by diligently growing in their faith, praying in the Holy Spirit and awaiting the coming of Jesus the Messiah. Yet behind all this work is the keeping and sustaining grace of God. He is the one who prevents us from falling into apostasy. Jude concludes with this doxology because he does not want the believers to be paralyzed with uncertainty or to feel that all depends on them. The God who called them and set his love upon them (Jude 1) will keep them and preserve them, and thus the glory belongs to him alone (Jude 25).

Paul

Our fourth witness is the apostle Paul. In a number of texts Paul affirms emphatically that those whom God has redeemed will certainly obtain the final inheritance. One of the most famous passages in this regard is Romans 8:29-39. We begin by examining Romans 8:29-30:

> For those God foreknew he also predestined to be conformed to the likeness of his Son, that he might be the firstborn among many brothers. And those he predestined, he also called; those he called, he also justified; those he justified, he also glorified. (NIV)

The word *foreknew* designates those on whom God has set his covenantal affection, those whom God has chosen to belong to the people of God.[13] Those who are foreknown are also predestined to be like Jesus. In other words, they are predestined to obtain the eschatological inheritance, for likeness to the Son will be ours at the end time. We can be sure that not all people are foreknown or predestined, since the text is chained together in such a way that all those who are foreknown are also glorified. Evidence that the list is limited to believers is also found in verse 30: "those he called, he also justified."

---

[13]For a convincing defense of this view of foreknowledge, see S. M. Baugh, "The Meaning of Foreknowledge," in *Still Sovereign: Contemporary Perspectives on Election, Foreknowledge, and Grace*, ed. Thomas R. Schreiner and Bruce A. Ware (Grand Rapids, Mich.: Baker, 2000), pp. 183-200.

We know that not all people are justified, for only those who exercise faith are righteous (Rom 5:1), and not all people believe. Nonetheless, all those who are called are justified. If all the called without exception are justified, then it also logically follows that not all are called. It is also clear that the word *calling* cannot mean "invited to believe," for it is obvious that many of those invited to believe fail to do so. We conclude, therefore, that calling is an effectual calling that creates a justifying faith.

Paul concludes this "golden chain" with the assertion that those who are justified are also glorified. Glorification is a future reality for believers, yet Paul uses an aorist verb to convey the idea that the future glorification is certain for believers.[14] All those who are foreknown, predestined, called and justified will invariably and without exception be glorified (cf. Rom 5:9-10; 2 Thess 2:13-14). Since God initiates faith, he will also bring it to completion. Some interpreters insert the idea that we will be glorified if we continue in the faith but that continuance in the faith is uncertain.[15] However, this violates the intention of the text, for Paul constructs the chain precisely because it cannot be broken. What God began in the past (foreknowing us as his people) will not be disrupted in the future (glorification). Since he began the process of salvation in foreknowing and predestining us and continued it in calling and justifying us, he will surely complete it in glorifying us.[16]

The same certainty and confidence toward the future is trumpeted in the concluding verses of Romans 8, where Paul celebrates the inviolability of the believer's relationship to Christ:

> Who shall separate us from the love of Christ? Shall trouble or hardship or persecution or famine or nakedness or danger or sword? As it is written: "For your sake we face death all day long; we are considered as sheep to be slaughtered." No, in all these things we are more than conquerors through him who loved us. For I am convinced that neither

---

[14]Perhaps the aorist is gnomic. For the options, see Judith M. Gundry Volf, *Paul and Perseverance: Staying in and Falling Away* (Louisville, Ky.: Westminster John Knox, 1990), p. 12.

[15]So Marshall, *Kept by the Power of God,* p. 93: "We simply are not told here that God's calling inevitably produces faith in men." Contrary to Marshall, this is the implication of the text, since those who are called are justified.

[16]For a more detailed interpretation of the text, see Gundry Volf, *Paul and Perseverance,* pp. 9-14.

death nor life, neither angels nor demons, neither the present nor the
future, nor any powers, neither height nor depth, nor anything else in
all creation, will be able to separate us from the love of God that is in
Christ Jesus our Lord. (Rom 8:35-39 NIV)

Paul deliberates on what could possibly sever us from Christ's love,
and those things that are most apt to remove us from his saving grasp
are introduced: the pressures of life, persecution, starvation, lack of
food and clothing, the prospect of death because of one's adherence
to the gospel, fearsome realities in the present and the future, angelic
powers and the like. The worst that life can throw at us is contemplated, for it is precisely these things that would be most likely to
detach us from Christ's love. Paul affirms with confidence, however,
that none of these things will prevail over the love of God and Christ.
He is convinced that there is nothing in the created world that can
uncouple us from Christ. Indeed, we are "more than conquerors"
through Christ. Why does Paul say that we are more than conquerors
instead of just saying that we are conquerors? Probably because God
takes the things that are most frightening, hurtful and harmful and
turns them to our good. This is confirmed by Romans 8:28. All things
are woven together for the good of those who are called by God, and
the good in the context is not necessarily a comfortable life on earth
but conformity to Jesus the Son. We are more than conquerors
because God uses the painful things in life for our holiness and glorification. Since God has already given us the supreme gift in his Son,
he will also "graciously give us all things" (Rom 8:32). That is, everything in life will turn out for our benefit, even if it is not intrinsically
pleasant. This is confirmed by 1 Corinthians 3:21-22, where Paul
declares that all things are ours and includes in the things that belong
to believers "the world or life or death or the present or the future"
(NIV). Even death, though it is the last enemy (1 Cor 15:26), is simply
a stepping stone to our triumph. We are more than conquerors
because God turns our enemies into his servants and uses them for
our benefit. A God who uses even the most terrible things for our
good will see to it than none of these things remove us from his love.
Indeed, he will use them to make us feel his love more profoundly
and deeply.

Some object to the interpretation proposed here by saying that
none of these external things can separate us from the love of Christ

but that we ourselves with the power of our free choice can detach ourselves from his love.[17] They affirm that Christ's love is always present but that we can turn against his love and deny him forever. Such an interpretation is incorrect because Paul reflects on the very things that might propel believers to deny Christ. Paul introduces persecution, famine, the possibility of martyrdom and present and future troubles because these are the elements of life that conspire to snuff out the faith of believers. These are the things that taunt believers with the horrible thought that God does not care, that Christ does not love them. A temptation to depart from the faith does not occur in a vacuum. The sufferings of everyday life and the pressures that mount up are the things that could cause believers to renounce Christ. Paul's point here, however, is that the most terrible things that one can conceive of will not have that effect in the lives of believers. They will never deny Christ or shrink back from him. They will "hang on" not because of the strength of their will and their indomitable courage in the midst of difficulties and sufferings; they will persist because the love of God will never let them go. We are all keenly conscious of our weakness, our inability to make it through even relatively minor afflictions. But we do not go it alone. We will persevere in faith because God's love has grasped us and will hold us securely in the midst of the vicissitudes of life. If this passage merely says that God loves believers no matter what happens but that we may still depart from his love, then it is cold comfort indeed, for our prime concern is not that God will cease loving us. We know he will be faithful to the end. What worries us is that we will deny him, that we will turn our backs on the faith and renounce our first confession. This text assures us that we will not do so. We will remain true to God, not because we are so noble, but because Christ is so loving, because Christ's love is relentless. Nothing, not even ourselves—especially ourselves—can ever cause us to renounce the love of God that has invaded our lives.[18]

The inviolability of God's work is also communicated through the metaphors of sealing and deposit. Two texts convey this thought. In

---

[17]Marshall, *Kept by the Power of God*, pp. 94, 114; Osborne, "Calvinist Texts," p. 179; Shank, *Life in the Son*, p. 208.

[18]In support of the interpretation suggested here, see Gundry Volf, *Paul and Perseverance*, pp. 57-58; Michael A. Eaton, *No Condemnation: A New Theology of Assurance* (Downers Grove, Ill.: InterVarsity Press, 1995), p. 194.

2 Corinthians 1:21-22 Paul says, "It is God who makes both us and you stand firm in Christ. He anointed us, set his seal of ownership on us, and put his Spirit in our hearts as a deposit, guaranteeing what is to come" (NIV). In Ephesians a similar idea emerges: "You also were included in Christ when you heard the word of truth, the gospel of your salvation. Having believed, you were marked in him with a seal, the promised Holy Spirit, who is a deposit guaranteeing our inheritance until the redemption of those who are God's possession—to the praise of his glory" (Eph 1:13-14 NIV). In both texts God is said to have sealed believers, and in Ephesians the seal is identified as the Holy Spirit of promise (cf. Eph 4:30). The metaphor of the seal indicates that God protects and guards his people. The protective symbolism of the seal is supported by Revelation 7:1-8, where the 144,000 are sealed and thus preserved from God's wrath. The background to the Revelation text is Ezekiel 9, where God's servants in Jerusalem are sealed to protect them from the avenging angels when the city is devastated. It is also clear that the sealing metaphor cannot be segregated from the deposit metaphor. Those who are protected by God and owned by him are also given the Holy Spirit as a deposit or down payment. Ephesians 1:14 clarifies that the Spirit is a down payment or guarantee for the eschatological redemption of the body. The endtime dimension of the deposit is also apparent in 2 Corinthians 1:22. Both the seal and the deposit emphasize that God will guard, protect and finish what he has started. As 2 Corinthians 1:21 says, "It is God who makes both us and you stand firm in Christ." The God who makes us stand firm is also the one who has given us the Spirit as a seal and down payment of our future redemption. The end-time gift of the Spirit is a guarantee that there is more to come, that the salvation inaugurated will be consummated. Likewise, the metaphor of the seal assures us that God will protect us until the end. We belong to him, and he will never take away from us the stamp of his ownership.[19]

We have maintained in this book that believers must endure to the

---

[19]For an excellent discussion of the seal and deposit metaphors in Paul, see Gundry Volf, *Paul and Perseverance,* pp. 27-33. Marshall (*Kept by the Power of God,* p. 98) and Osborne ("Calvinist Texts," p. 181) are certainly right in saying that these promises should not be used to deny the need for perseverance. Where they go astray, however, is in failing to see that these texts promise that believers will indeed persevere.

end in order to be saved. The issue before us, however, is how believers fulfill the admonitions and warnings to maintain their faith. Paul argues, most emphatically, that Christians continue in the faith through the powerful work of God. He says in 1 Corinthians 1:8-9, "He will keep you strong to the end, so that you will be blameless on the day of our Lord Jesus Christ. God, who has called you into fellowship with his Son Jesus Christ our Lord, is faithful" (NIV). Believers must continue in the faith until the end, but it is God who will keep them strong so that they can fulfill what is demanded. Being blameless on the day of the Lord does not suggest sinless perfection in this life. The idea is that believers will have maintained their allegiance to God until the end of their lives. They will be blameless because they have continued in the faith. What Paul highlights, though, is that such continuance is ultimately God's work. Paul does not deny that believers must continue in the faith; what he indicates here is that they do so only through the power of God and, moreover, that they will most certainly do so by God's grace. The God who called us effectually to saving fellowship with his Son Jesus Christ is a faithful God. He will complete what he has started.

Philippians 1:6 affirms the same truth. Paul is confident "that he who began a good work in you will carry it on to completion until the day of Christ Jesus" (NIV). What good work was inaugurated in the Philippians? The good work is nothing less than belief in the gospel, trust in Jesus Christ. Paul is obviously thinking of the conversion of the Philippians, and there is no conversion in Pauline thinking without faith. Paul informs us here that this good work of believing was begun by God himself. In other words, faith is a gift of God. If he began the good work and the good work is nothing other than faith, then our faith is a gift from his hand (cf. Eph 2:8-9). The focus, however, is not on the inauguration of faith but on its completion. The same God who fanned faith into a flame in our lives will keep the flame of faith burning until the end. He will carry it out to completion until the day of Christ Jesus.

Once again, some interpreters contend that even though God is faithful, we humans are not.[20] God is faithful, but we may prove to be faithless. Such an objection fails to understand the verses. The very

---

[20]Marshall, *Kept by the Power of God,* p. 98; Osborne, "Calvinist Texts," pp. 182-83.

point of the verses is that God will continue what he has started. If he did not inaugurate faith, then he will not continue it. But if God did not grant the gift of faith, then in what way did he begin the good work in the lives of believers? How can the good work be attributed to him in any meaningful way if the credit ultimately devolves on human beings who made the decision? To put it another way, if God does not sustain the faith of human beings, then he plays no role in our good works in the Christian life, for all good works flow from faith. On this view, God simply encourages from the sidelines, saying, "I hope you continue in the faith. I will continue to be here until the end. But persevering in the faith is your role." Such a picture contradicts this text. God provides the energy and strength to keep playing in the game. Even the desire to maintain allegiance to Christ comes from God, for as Paul says, "It is God who works in you to will and to act according to his good purpose" (Phil 2:13 NIV). We would never run to the end of the race without divine resources. Those resources, however, guarantee that we will finish the race we have begun.

We have already seen in several texts that Paul's assurance of God's work in us until the end does not nullify our need for perseverance. Instead, our necessary perseverance is established by and grounded in God's work in our lives. This theme is so pervasive in Paul that we need to observe it in several other texts. For example, near the end of 1 Thessalonians Paul writes, "May God himself, the God of peace, sanctify you through and through. May your whole spirit, soul and body be kept blameless at the coming of our Lord Jesus Christ. The one who calls you is faithful and he will do it" (1 Thess 5:23-24 NIV). We have already argued earlier in this book that blamelessness and sanctification on the day of the Lord Jesus are not optional for believers. We must be blameless and sanctified to secure an eternal inheritance. Notice, however, that Paul prays that God will answer this prayer. Believers must be sanctified to inherit end-time salvation, yet Paul asks God to fulfill such a condition in the lives of believers. Not only does Paul ask God to do so, but he is also convinced that God will. Since God is the one who called them initially to salvation, he will do what is necessary to fulfill that calling, namely, sanctify the Thessalonians. Once again, it will hardly do to say that since believers must persevere the promise is uncertain. The very point of the text is that God is the one who will help believers fulfill the necessary conditions; that is why he is invoked in prayer. Nor does Paul abstract God's work from our role so as to discourage human willing. Precisely the opposite. God's work encourages us to will and work.

The same dynamic is evident in 1 Corinthians 10:1-13. In verses 1-12 Paul warns the Corinthians against idolatry, reminding them that the wilderness generation did not enter the land of promise. Neither will the Corinthians inherit the kingdom if they turn aside from God. They should beware of a presumptuous arrogance in which they consider themselves immune from any need for vigilance: "So, if you think you are standing firm, be careful that you don't fall" (1 Cor 10:12 NIV). God's promises are prostituted if they are used to undermine the need for ongoing obedience and striving after the Lord. In the same context in which Paul advances a strong warning, he also includes a powerful promise: "No temptation has seized you except what is common to man. And God is faithful; he will not let you be tempted beyond what you can bear. But when you are tempted, he will also provide a way out so that you can stand up under it" (1 Cor 10:13 NIV). The promise and the warning should not be played off one another here.[21] Believers need to heed the warning and to strengthen themselves with the divine promises of sustenance. The warning is the means by which the promise reaches its fulfillment. It is also the case that the promise will surely be fulfilled. An examination of the context (1 Cor 10:1-12, 14-22) indicates that the temptation specifically in Paul's mind here is idolatry or apostasy. The Lord will not allow his people to fall prey to apostasy. The reason they can be assured of continuance is because "God is faithful." He will never allow the temptation to become so great that believers surrender their faith. He will provide strength in the midst of the difficulties so that believers will endure the time of testing.[22] We must endure to avoid eschatological judgment, yet such endurance is ultimately a gift of God.

When the Thessalonian believers were tested by the afflictions that accompanied conversion, Paul emphasized that believers must stand the test in order to be saved (cf. Acts 14:22; 1 Thess 3:2-3). Those who

---

[21]See the helpful exegesis of Gundry Volf, *Paul and Perseverance,* pp. 70-74.

[22]Some interpreters claim that believers will be delivered out of the situation instead of being given the strength to endure in the midst of it. In either case, God promises to sustain us.

perish do not love the truth (2 Thess 2:10-12), but those who have been chosen by the Lord will be glorified (2 Thess 2:13-14). On this basis Paul exhorts believers to adhere to apostolic traditions and prays that God will fortify them for every good work (2 Thess 2:15-17). Paul knows that ultimately it is God's work that sustains believers to the end, and he is confident that God will complete such a work: "The Lord is faithful, and he will strengthen and protect you from the evil one" (2 Thess 3:3 NIV). Believers will make it because God is faithful, and his faithfulness manifests itself in strengthening and protecting them from the evil one. Paul does not envision a situation in which believers attain to the resurrection and succumb to evil at the same time. Obtaining the eschatological inheritance is dependent upon being spared from the ravages of the evil one, and it is God who ultimately oversees and fortifies believers to escape from the evil one's power.

Conclusion

We must finish the race to obtain the prize. No believer who quits the race halfway through will receive the prize. We cannot deceive ourselves with the thought that disobedience and faithfulness are idle matters. When we see what is at stake we tremble (and well we should), since many have gone before us who have been heedless of divine warnings. Yet we also may feel intimidated when we consider our own resources in finishing the race. We keenly realize that our strength is slight and our willpower inadequate. At this juncture in the race we take courage from the promises of God. He pledges that all those who are called and chosen will obtain the prize. He will provide the strength needed to finish the race. He will fortify our weakened knees and faltering resolve so that we do not apostatize. We will most certainly obtain the crown that is set before us, for the same God who propelled us onto the racetrack will complete the good work he has started. He is faithful to us as his covenant people, and thus we receive strength and encouragement to continue our journey to the heavenly city.

7

RUNNING
WITH CONFIDENCE

Being Assured That We
Shall Win the Prize

Let us hold fast to the confession of our hope without wavering,

for he who has promised is faithful. . . .

Therefore, do not cast aside your confidence,

which possesses a great reward. For you have need of perseverance

in order that, after you have done God's will,

you may receive the promise. (Heb 10:23, 35-36)

We have insisted throughout this book that the New Testament directs its admonitions and warnings to believers. We have also argued that these warnings do not merely threaten believers with losing rewards but that eternal life itself is at stake. Biblical writers frequently warn believers that if they turn away from Jesus Christ they will experience eternal judgment. If believers apostatize their destiny is the lake of fire, the second death, hell. These warnings cannot be waved aside and relegated to those who are not genuine Christians. They are directed to believers and must be heeded for us to be saved on the last day. We will win the prize of eternal life only if we run the race to end. If we quit during the middle of the race, we will not receive eternal life.

If we are correct in saying that the warnings and admonitions of Scripture are for believers, and if we are right in saying that eternal life is at stake, then how can believers have any assurance of salvation in the present? Some who understand the warning passages to be directed to believers maintain that we cannot and should not have assurance that we will run the race to the end. We cannot know how we will respond to situations in the future, according to this view, and thus there is no certainty that we will persevere to the end. All we know, these people say, is that we will be saved if we keep trusting God until the end. The warnings indicate, however, that we could depart from God in the future. We have assurance for today, according to this line of thought, and uncertainty about tomorrow, since we do not know for certain how our lives will turn out. The very presence of the warnings, these people insist, demonstrates that we may apostatize and deny Jesus Christ. Denial of the faith may be unlikely, yet the admonitions and warnings show that it is indeed possible. Those who espouse this view contend that lack of assurance is the inevitable byproduct of taking the warnings seriously. If the warnings are genuine and address believers, then it follows that we cannot possess a firm confidence in our final salvation.

Contrary to the above view, we believe that the Scriptures teach that we can have a firm confidence and assurance in our final salvation. Assurance of our inheritance does not nullify the force of the admonitions and warnings in Scripture. The admonitions and warnings of the Scriptures threaten believers with eternal judgment for apostasy, but these warnings do not violate assurance and confidence regarding final salvation. Our thesis is that the warnings do not cancel out assurance for believers. The exhortations and admonitions are, in fact, compatible with assurance regarding final salvation. We would go further. The warnings, admonitions and exhortations are a means of producing a firm and assured confidence in believers. The warnings do not rob us of assurance. They are signposts along the marathon runner's pathway that help us maintain our confidence. Our confidence in our future inheritance increases when we pay heed to the exhortations delivered in the Scriptures. In this chapter we will endeavor to explain the biblical view of assurance and to defend the idea that such assurance fits with the idea that the warning passages of the Scriptures should be taken with utter seriousness.

Assurance Is Integral to Saving Faith

There is considerable debate as to whether assurance regarding final salvation is inevitably involved in and correlated with saving faith. Those who maintain that believers can apostatize would certainly dissent from such an idea. If believers can actually forsake salvation, then there can be no firm confidence that they will persist until the end. We have argued, however, in the previous chapter that the notion that believers will not persevere to the end is mistaken. The Scriptures promise that God will keep those whom he has called, that those who have eternal life will never forsake their God and that God will consummate the good work he has inaugurated.

Others concur that God will empower believers so that they will endure to the end. But they contend that assurance is separable from saving faith and subsequent to it. This view was defended by the Puritans and is evident in the Westminster Larger Catechism: "Assurance of grace and salvation not being of the essence of faith, true believers may wait long before they obtain it; and, after the enjoyment thereof, may have it weakened and intermitted, through manifold distempers, sins, temptations, and desertions; yet are they never left without such a presence and support of the Spirit of God as keeps them from sinking into utter despair."[1]

More recently, Martin Lloyd-Jones has defended this view, arguing that the witness of the Holy Spirit that confirms that we are God's children (Rom 8:16; 1 Jn 3:24; 4:13), the sealing of the Spirit (2 Cor 1:22; Eph 1:13) and the outpouring of God's love in our hearts through the Holy Spirit (Rom 5:5) occur after our conversion and assure our hearts that we truly belong to God.[2] We are gripped with God's love in an indescribably powerful way, and we know experientially that we are God's children. Lloyd-Jones compares such an experience to a child walking side by side with his father. The child knows his father

---

[1] See the Westminster Larger Catechism in *The Westminster Confession of Faith* (Rossshire, U.K.: Free Presbyterian Publications, 1976), pp. 171-72. Joel R. Beeke argues that Calvin and the Calvinists who succeeded him did not differ substantially—only in emphasis—in their understanding of assurance (Beeke, *The Quest for Full Assurance: The Legacy of Calvin and His Successors* [Carlisle, Penn.: Banner of Truth, 1999]). It is not our intention here to interact with Beeke's thesis. He adduces significant evidence to support his view. Even if he is correct, the difference in emphasis could lead to a difference in focus in the lives of believers. Our goal is not to resolve the debate on whether Calvin's successors departed from him but to explain the biblical evidence.

[2] For a defense of the view of Lloyd-Jones with extensive citations from the Puritans in support see D. M. Lloyd-Jones, *Romans: An Exposition of Chapter 8:5-17. The Sons of God* (Grand Rapids, Mich.: Zondervan, 1974), pp. 285-399.

loves him and enjoys fellowship with him. But as they are walking the father suddenly sweeps the child into his arms, hugs him and tells him how much he loves him. Now the child knows in a fresh and powerful way the breadth of his father's love for him. The witness and the sealing of the Spirit are like this, according to Lloyd-Jones. They are experiences in which believers are ushered into God's presence in unforgettable ways. They experience his presence, power, holiness and love in ways that transcend their earlier relationship with him. Lloyd-Jones documents this by providing the experience of many well-known persons in church history, especially from the Puritan tradition, in which they recount special occasions in which they encountered God. Such experiences, says Lloyd-Jones, are the witness and the sealing of the Spirit. On these occasions the love of God is poured out into our hearts through the Holy Spirit (Rom 5:5). Such experiences give us assurance that we are truly God's children. Lloyd-Jones believes that it is crucial that we do not correlate assurance with our initial faith in Christ. Such assurance, he contends, is subsequent to conversion. God in his sovereignty pours his grace upon us, and we experience his presence and power dramatically. It also follows from Lloyd-Jones's view that not all Christians have assurance, for not all believers are given the special experiences of God's love and presence that he recounts. No one, he maintains, can follow a sequence of steps to arrive at assurance. There is no formula that secures the experience of the sealing and the witness of the Spirit. Believers must seek the Lord and pray diligently, but ultimately such encounters with God are the prerogative of God in his sovereignty. Some believers enjoy these inestimable encounters and others do not. Thus, some believers have assurance, while others do not.

Contrary to Lloyd-Jones and some in the Puritan tradition, we believe that assurance of salvation is joined indissolubly with saving faith. Such assurance is coincident with faith in Jesus Christ, and thus it is the joyful experience of all believers. Supporting the close connection between saving faith and assurance is Hebrews 11:1: "Now faith is being sure of what we hope for and certain of what we do not see" (NIV). This sentence is not necessarily a definition of faith. It may simply designate how faith expresses itself. Commentators disagree as to whether the verse focuses on the expression of faith or the subjective assurance that constitutes faith.[3] Even if the objective view is correct, Hagner rightly observes that "the objective understanding of this verse, of course, presupposes the reality of subjective assurance . . . as the wellspring of acts of faith."[4]

It is a mistake, in any case, to segregate the objective and subjective elements in this verse. The subjective confidence and assurance of believers propels them to trust God in the circumstances of life. We see from the rest of Hebrews 11 that faith necessarily involves assurance regarding the trustworthiness of God's word. The heroes of faith who preceded us based their lives on God's promises, no matter how improbable they seemed to be. Thus, Noah built an ark though it had not yet rained on the earth (Heb 11:7), Abraham left his country for a better one, though he did not know where his new homeland would be (Heb 11:8-16), and offered up Isaac with the assurance that he would receive him back (Heb 11:17-19), and Moses renounced the pleasures of Egypt for the coming reward (Heb 11:24-29). The promise that the author of Hebrews features for his readers is their future salvation (Heb 10:35-39): "But we are not of those who shrink back and are destroyed, but of those who have faith and keep their souls" (Heb 10:39 RSV). The contrast here is between destruction *(apōleian)* and keeping of the soul *(peripoiēsin psychēs)*. Since destruction is opposed to the keeping of the soul, it is clear that future salvation itself is at stake here (cf. Heb 10:39 in the NIV). The reward envisioned here is salvation itself. This reward is later described as "the city with foundations" (Heb 11:10) and a heavenly country (Heb 11:16) and the future perfection of believers (Heb 11:40). The author of Hebrews argues that Abraham and Moses were in actuality looking forward to the same eschatological reward as the readers, and these two men of faith endured suffering and pain because they were convinced and assured that an eternal reward lay before them.

Thus, we are not misusing the text in Hebrews 11 when we relate it to assurance regarding end-time salvation. Our ancestors in the faith themselves put their faith in the end-time reward that awaited them. Hebrews 11:1 informs us that believers expressed their faith in God in

---

[3]See, e.g., Philip Edgcumbe Hughes, *A Commentary on the Epistle to the Hebrews* (Grand Rapids, Mich.: Eerdmans, 1977), pp. 438-41; and Donald A. Hagner, *Hebrews* (New York: Harper & Row, 1983), pp. 161-63.

[4]Hagner, *Hebrews*, p. 161.

tangible and concrete ways because they were confident about the future and assured that God's promises were true. In other words, faith must include assurance to be saving faith. Saving faith involves confidence in the trustworthiness of God's promises regarding the future. If one does not have confidence in and assurance of receiving God's promises, one does not have saving faith.

One of the most important texts in all of Scripture on the nature of saving faith is Romans 4:17-22. Paul argues in Romans 1–3 that righteousness with God comes through faith, not works. He introduces Abraham as an exemplar of righteousness by faith in Romans 4. Since Abraham is the model and pattern for saving faith, it is imperative to grasp the nature of Abraham's faith. The kind of faith that saves from God's wrath is faith like Abraham's. An extended citation from Romans 4:17-22 will open a window on the nature of Abraham's faith:

> He believed [in] God who gives life to the dead and calls things that are not as though they were. Against all hope, Abraham in hope believed and so became the father of many nations, just as it had been said to him, "So shall your offspring be." Without weakening in his faith, he faced the fact that his body was as good as dead—since he was about a hundred years old—and that Sarah's womb was also dead. Yet he did not waver through unbelief regarding the promise of God, but was strengthened in his faith and gave glory to God, being fully persuaded that God had power to do what he had promised. This is why "it was credited to him as righteousness." (NIV)

Abraham's faith was not vacuous and unformed, with no particular content. He believed in the God who could raise the dead ("who gives life to the dead," Rom 4:17), so that even if Isaac died at the hands of his own father he would be raised to life again in fulfillment of the promise that Abraham's descendants would be multiplied through Isaac (Gen 17:15-22; 21:12).

Abraham also believed in the God who could call into existence that which did not yet exist (Rom 4:17). That is, God could produce children via the bodies of Abraham and Sarah despite the fact that they were too old to beget children any longer. Abraham had a sure confidence (i.e., "hope" Rom 4:18) regarding the future, for God had promised him innumerable descendants (Gen 15:5). Abraham's confidence did not spring from his own abilities or resources. He was keenly aware of his old age and Sarah's barren womb (Rom 4:19). He did not deny the facts about his own resources; he faced them and reflected on them. The weakness of himself and Sarah, however, did not dispel his faith, for his faith was not based on his own ability but on God's promise (Rom 4:20). He became strong in his faith because his faith was in God himself. He knew that his God was the God who could create out of nothing and raise the dead. Thus, when he considered the promise, he became stronger in his faith. His faith "gave glory to God" because he was "fully persuaded that God had power to do what he had promised." Abraham's faith honored God because it reckoned him as the all-sufficient one, able to do all that he had promised.

Note that the text says that Abraham was "fully persuaded" that God could fulfill his promises. In other words, the faith of Abraham was a faith that included assurance or confidence—and it is precisely this kind of faith that is necessary to be right with God, for Romans 4:22 explains the connection between Abraham's assurance of faith and his relationship with God: "This is why 'it was credited to him as righteousness.' " In other words, Abraham was counted as righteous because he had an assured faith, a faith that had confidence in God's future promises. Paul specifically draws the connection between Abraham and believers in Jesus Christ in Romans 4:23-25. Believers must also have the same kind of faith as Abraham, trusting in the God who can fulfill his promises for our happy future. God has exercised his power in the present era by raising Jesus from the dead. Saving faith in Jesus Christ is a confident faith, a faith that is full of assurance and hope.

If assurance is part and parcel of faith, does it follow that Abraham's assurance of faith was perfect? Romans 4:19-20 says that he did not "weaken" or "waver" in unbelief, which might suggest, on first glance, that Abraham's faith was always strong. The problem with this interpretation, however, is the text of Genesis itself. Abraham's faith did waver when he lied about Sarah being his wife (Gen 12; 20) and when he resorted to having a son through Hagar (Gen 16). Does this contradict Paul's claim that Abraham's faith did not waver? No, for Paul considers Abraham's life as a whole. He maintained his assurance of faith until the end. This does not mean that there were no valleys in Abraham's journey of faith. He was not a perfect exemplar in the sense that he never deviated from God's ways. The dominant note in his life, however, was one of believing and trusting the promise. Abraham did not waver in faith in the sense that he persisted in faith until the end, and faith rather than faithlessness characterized his life. His willingness to sacrifice Isaac attests to the persistence and growth of his faith. When we say, therefore, that assurance is integral to faith, we are not arguing for perfect faith. But we are insisting that saving faith is faith like Abraham's and faith like that described in Hebrews 11. It is a faith that endures to the end, faith that is the dominant motif of a believer's life. Such faith is inevitably correlated with assurance, for faith by definition involves confidence in God and a belief that he has promised a glorious future for us.[5]

That assurance is inevitably correlated with faith is supported by John Calvin.[6] Calvin says, "Now we possess a right definition of faith if we call it a firm and certain knowledge of God's benevolence toward us, founded upon the truth of the freely given promise in Christ, both revealed to our minds and sealed upon our hearts through the Holy Spirit."[7] Faith cannot be separated from assurance, according to Calvin, for those who come to God must be certain that God loves them, and such a belief is the work of the Holy Spirit. The use of the word *sealed* also suggests that the sealing of the Spirit occurred at conversion, in Calvin's thinking. The Spirit seals to our hearts that God has good in store for us. Calvin remarks elsewhere, "He alone is a believer who, convinced by a firm conviction that God is a kindly and well-disposed Father toward him, promises himself all things on the basis of his generosity."[8] Again, genuine belief involves "firm conviction," and one must be "convinced" of God's goodness and

---

[5]For a practical and immensely helpful development of this theme, see John Piper, *The Purifying Power of Living by Faith in Future Grace* (Sisters, Ore.: Multnomah, 1995).

[6]For an exposition of Calvin's view, see Randall C. Zachman, *The Assurance of Faith: Conscience in the Theology of Martin Luther and John Calvin* (Minneapolis: Fortress, 1993), pp. 174-87. Zachman argues that the view of Luther was fundamentally the same as Calvin's (see esp. pp. 54-68). We shall touch on the view of Luther later. William Cunningham also agrees that Luther and Calvin understood assurance to be of the essence of faith, though he disputes the credibility of their view. See his *Reformers and the Theology of the Reformation* (London: Banner of Truth Trust, 1967), pp. 111-48.

[7]John Calvin *Institutes of the Christian Religion* 3.2.7. This understanding of assurance in Calvin is supported by Zachman *(Assurance of Faith)* and R. T. Kendall, *Calvin and English Calvinism to 1649* (Oxford: Oxford University Press, 1979), p. 25. However, Kendall (pp. 25-26) is not as convincing as Zachman (pp. 188-203) in explaining the role that obedience plays in assurance.

[8]Calvin *Institutes* 3.2.16.

beneficence toward us. Genuine faith means that we believe that God promises happiness to us in him. In his commentary on 1 Corinthians Calvin expresses a similar idea: "There we may know that this is the nature of faith, that conscience has, by the Holy Spirit, a sure witness of God's good will toward itself, and relying on this, it confidently calls on God as Father."[9] We should note that contrary to some Puritans the witness of the Spirit here is identified with saving faith. The Holy Spirit stamps on our heart the truth that God loves us so that we can invoke him as our kind Father. Saving faith, according to Calvin has "firm assurance" of the good that is ours both in the present and the future.[10] Faith without assurance is like having flowers without soil. It will not live long, and it is not the biblical idea of saving faith.

Growing in Assurance

Assurance is integral to saving faith, but we should not conclude from this that assurance is a static entity in the lives of believers. Believers may doubt that they belong to God and question whether they are saved even when there are no good grounds for such tormenting thoughts. To say that assurance is constitutive of faith does not and should not lead to a simplistic view of the Christian life. Believers suffer from doubts, temptations, depression and uncertainty on occasion. The Christian life is a journey with ups and downs and some fierce attacks on our faith. In addition, since assurance is not a static entity, it can wax and wane for believers. While we are traveling on our faith journey—or, perhaps better, while we are running the marathon to obtain the prize—assurance is not a fixed entity. On the whole, it should grow and increase. Our growth in assurance is like a spiral, not in a direct and straight line upwards, but overall there is more certainty about our status with God as we run the race. At times we may regress in our assurance, but the general pattern is one of progress and advancement. Our assurance in faith depends on a three-legged stool: (1) God's promises (2) the fruit of the Spirit in our lives and (3) the witness of the Holy Spirit. We ponder these successively.

---

[9]John Calvin, *1 Corinthians*, ed. David W. Torrance and Thomas F. Torrance, trans. John W. Fraser, Calvin's New Testament Commentaries (Grand Rapids, Mich.: Eerdmans, 1960), 9:59.

[10]Calvin *Institutes* 3.2.28.

The promises of God. In a three-legged stool each of the legs is equally important, and thus the analogy is not a perfect one, for the promises of God are the most important leg for the assurance of faith. The promises include, but are not limited to, those that we set forth and explained in the previous chapter, namely, God's promises to preserve and keep his people until the end so that they obtain final salvation. The promises are of paramount importance because our confidence and certainty about our status before God in the future rests ultimately not on ourselves but on God himself. The fundamental reason we have confidence that we shall finish the marathon in which we run is not our strength, our godliness or our endurance. We are confident that we shall obtain our inheritance because God has promised that we shall do so.

To rehearse the texts of the previous chapter would be superfluous. What we need to grasp at this juncture is the role these promises play in our confidence about our final redemption. Some believers are prone to introspection and contemplate their own capacities for perseverance. They may be paralyzed with fear as they realize their inadequacy and tendency to wander from the grace of God. They are keenly aware of their own shortcomings and begin to despair of ever finishing the course on which they have embarked. The error of such an approach does not lie in the despair that surfaces over one's own ability to sustain faith until the end. The misstep is in focusing on ourselves rather than God. Our attention should be fixed on the lighthouse of God's promises rather than the fog of our own capacities, because the former is the sure path for assurance. God's promises cut through the mist of uncertainty and reveal to us the truth about our own situation.

The Puritans were right in forging a connection between assurance and the fruit of the Spirit (more on this below). Yet if the fruit of the Spirit becomes the fulcrum by which we discern our relationship to God, an unhealthy and destructive introspection is almost sure to follow. Despite the many strengths of the Puritans, those who become immersed in reading them today need to be wary of becoming excessively introspective and self-focused. The reason for this is that the promises of God may no longer be the fulcrum for our assurance in faith. Biblical assurance rests fundamentally on God and his promises. When we come to faith, we surrender any notion that our works are the basis upon which we can be right in God's sight. Similarly, any good works we do subsequent to faith can never be the basis of our right standing before God. We believe that salvation is of the Lord. We will be saved on the last day because of God's sovereign work, for the one who elected and called us will also glorify us (Rom 8:29-30).

Some traditions doubt that believers can have assurance that they are right with God.[11] Biblical writers, however, are eager to see that such assurance permeates the lives of believers. John, for example, writes, "This is the testimony: God has given us eternal life, and this life is in his Son. He who has the Son has life; he who does not have the Son of God does not have life. I write these things to you who believe in the name of the Son of God so that you may know that you have eternal life" (1 Jn 5:11-13 NIV). The apostle writes 1 John to assure believers that they truly belong to God. John's church (or possibly churches) was troubled because some members of the church had seceded and probably formed a new congregation. Those who remained were perplexed and wondered whether they were genuinely part of the people of God.[12] John's purpose throughout the letter is to assure them that they truly belong to God and that their faith has not been a facade. That assurance is the primary goal of the letter is vindicated by 1 John 5:13, where John says that he writes to those "who believe in the name of the Son of God so that you may know that you have eternal life."

John does not want his readers to be uncertain or despairing of their status before God. He desires them to have full assurance that they belong to God and are his children. Thus, in 1 John 3:1 he emphasizes that we are the children of God now. He marvels at the Father's love that we are called God's children and then observes, "And that is what we are!" (NIV). Believers can and should know with certainty that they are presently God's children. The process has not yet been completed because we are not yet perfectly like Jesus; this will occur when "we shall see him as he is" (1 Jn 3:2 NIV). Meanwhile, however, we can be confident that we are God's children and are part

---

[11]See, e.g., *Catechism of the Catholic Church*, no. 1861 (New York: Doubleday, 1994), p. 508.

[12]For this understanding of 1 John, see D. A. Carson, "Reflections on Assurance," in *Still Sovereign: Contemporary Perspectives on Election, Foreknowledge, and Grace*, ed. Thomas R. Schreiner and Bruce A. Ware (Grand Rapids, Mich.: Baker, 2000), pp. 274-75.

of his family. John provides similar assurance to his church in 1 John 2:12-14. The children (believers who are young in faith), young men (believers who are growing stronger in faith) and fathers (mature believers) can be sure that their sins are forgiven, that God's Word is triumphing in their lives and that they "have known him who is from the beginning" (1 Jn 2:13, 14). John does not want believers to be paralyzed with uncertainty about their status before God. He longs for them to be full of confidence and joy, knowing that God is their beloved Father. Believers are already God's children now, and they do not comprehend fully what they shall be (1 Jn 3:2-3). Even now, however, they are God's children, confident that Jesus' appearance will consummate what has already begun.

A comparable word of assurance is declared by Jesus in John 5:24: "I tell you the truth, whoever hears my word and believes him who sent me has eternal life and will not be condemned; he has crossed over from death to life" (NIV). Those who believe now can be certain that they will not be condemned on the last day. The life of the age to come has invaded history and become theirs, and thus they have nothing to fear from death. Death has already been conquered by Jesus the Messiah. We are reminded again of the texts that we examined in the previous chapter, such as John 10:28-29, where the inviolability of eternal life is taught. All who believe in Jesus as the Christ have eternal life and will never perish.

What torments believers most with regard to assurance is the knowledge of their sins. Are they truly forgiven? Our conscience may remind us of our sins and proclaim that we are not right with God, that our sins are still remembered in the divine law court. The Scriptures assure us repeatedly that we are forgiven by virtue of Christ's sacrifice on the cross. Some of the most powerful words in this regard are found in Hebrews 10:19-22:

> Therefore, brothers, since we have confidence to enter the Most Holy Place by the blood of Jesus, by a new and living way opened for us through the curtain, that is, his body, and since we have a great priest over the house of God, let us draw near to God with a sincere heart in full assurance of faith, having our hearts sprinkled to cleanse us from a guilty conscience and having our bodies washed with pure water. (NIV)

We have confidence to enter the presence of our holy God, not because of our works or virtue, but because of the blood of Jesus that has definitively cleansed us from our sins (Heb 9:15—10:18). Thus, we can enter God's presence "in full assurance of faith," since the blood of Christ has cleansed us from a guilty conscience. Of course, the forgiveness of sins through Jesus' work on the cross is a staple of New Testament teaching (cf., e.g., Mt 26:28; Rom 3:21-26; Gal 2:16-21; 3:10-14). The foundation for our assurance is objective and not subjective. Believers do not base their assurance on their own works or their perception of their advancement in godliness. The basis of assurance is the atoning death of Christ by which he satisfied the anger of God against sin (Rom 1:18-25; 3:21-26). Of course, God himself, because of his great love, sent Christ to appease his own wrath.

Understanding that the primary leg of assurance is founded on God's promises and the objective work of Christ is of tremendous practical significance. We may often feel that we are not right with God. Our consciences may tell us that we are too unworthy to stand before him on the day of judgment. Martin Luther, in particular, grasped the importance of this truth. He says, "Our feelings must not be considered, but we must constantly insist that death, sin, and hell have been conquered, although I feel that I am still under the power of death, sin, and hell."[13] In other words, what it means to walk by faith is to believe what God says about death, sin and hell instead of believing our own subjective feelings about these things. We may feel that we are still guilty before God. But the truth is that if we have believed in Jesus we are free from God's wrath and stand clean before him. The declarations of God's Word are accepted as true, even though we experience moments of anguish during trials in which we believe that we are still guilty before God. Luther's pastoral strength was at its height here, for when believers experience tribulation (*Anfechtung*), they do not feel God's presence with them. Indeed, it seems as if God has vanished and left them alone. Everything in us cries out for God, yet he seems far from us, and we question whether we are really God's children. Luther insightfully observes that during these situations we are tempted to reintroduce the notion that we are righteous on the basis of our works or to appeal to the lives of others to salve our consciences:

Therefore when you feel your sin, when your bad conscience smites

---

[13]Martin Luther, *Sermons*, as cited in Zachman, *Assurance of Faith*, p. 56.

you, or when persecution comes, then ask yourself whether you really believe. At such times one is wont to run to saints and helpers in cloisters and in the desert for succor and relief, crying, "O dear man, intercede for me! O dear saint, help me! O let me live! I promise to become pious and do many good works!" That is how a terrified conscience speaks. But tell me, where is faith?[14]

Faith rests on the objective work of Christ, trusting that he has forgiven our sins by his work on the cross. We are forgiven because the Scriptures assure us that we are right in God's sight by virtue of Christ's death and resurrection.

Our consciences may tell us that Christ is going to serve as our judge instead of our savior. Of course, Luther believes that Christ acts as judge for those who are separated from him.[15] What he warns against, though, is the notion that our feelings are the final arbiter in this matter. We easily fall into the trap of believing that the voice of our conscience and our feelings are the voice of Christ. We must take our stand here on the promises of Scripture. Those who confess their sins are forgiven (1 Jn 1:9). We who believe are cleansed by the blood of Christ. We can draw near in full assurance of faith because of Christ's cleansing work (Heb 10:22). Our authority and our beacon is the Word of God rather than our subjective impressions. Luther helps us to fight the fight of faith by telling us how to argue against our feelings: "Flesh and Satan, you are lying; for God has spoken and has made a promise. He will not lie, even if the opposite happens or I die in the meantime."[16] Overcoming these moments of doubt is difficult because we are inwardly convinced that our subjective feelings constitute reality. We think our feelings of condemnation mirror what God really thinks and that the promises of Scripture are pious delusions.[17] Luther reminds us that what is hidden is often what is true, while what is visible and felt is often false: "For it is the wisdom of the saints to believe in the truth in opposition to the lie, the hidden truth in opposition to the manifest truth, in hope in opposition to hope."[18]

---

[14]Martin Luther, *Sermons on the Gospel of St. John: Chapters 6–8*, in *Luther's Works*, ed. Jaroslav Pelikan and Daniel Poellot (St. Louis: Concordia, 1955-1986), 23:75.

[15]See the discussion in Zachman, *Assurance of Faith*, pp. 64-65.

[16]Luther, *Works*, 5:205.

[17]Calvin also teaches that such feelings spring up in those who are believers (*Institutes* 3.2.17). Cf. Zachman, *Assurance of Faith*, pp. 183-87.

[18]Luther, *Works*, 4:357.

Calvin says something remarkably similar:

> Our circumstances are all in opposition to the promises of God. He
> promises us immortality: yet we are surrounded by mortality and cor-
> ruption. He declares that He accounts us just: yet we are covered with
> sins. He testifies that He is propitious and benevolent toward us: yet
> outward signs threaten His wrath. What then are we to do? We must
> close our eyes, disregard ourselves and all things connected to us, so
> that nothing may hinder or prevent us from believing that God is true.[19]

We must pronounce what our feelings say to us to be a lie and
acknowledge that the Scriptures are the truth. Our perceptions about
reality as we contemplate the visible world do not match the truth.
This is the case because the already of God's redemption is veiled and
hidden by the not yet that surrounds us.

We are deceived into thinking that God will not be merciful to sinners who come to him for forgiveness and that he could not and
would not have mercy on people like us. The Scriptures must be used
as a sword here to wield off the lies of Satan. Faith embraces the
promises of Scripture to be true, believing that we are right in God's
sight, forgiven, accepted and beloved because of the work of Christ.
Calvin remarks, "For nothing so moves us to repose our assurance
and certainty of mind in the Lord as distrust of ourselves."[20] Our feelings may tell us otherwise, but our feelings are badly mistaken.
Assurance first and foremost does not depend on our subjective
impressions but on the objective work of Christ whereby he secured
and will secure our salvation.

We have focused on the promises that inform us that we are presently right with God, for if one does not have assurance now, then the
promises that we surveyed in the last chapter—where God promises
to complete the good work he started—will be of little comfort. We
will scarcely benefit from God's promises to sustain our faith until the
end if we are unsure about our status before God in the present. Our
assurance in both instances rests on the work of God in Christ. We
must consistently console and fortify our souls with the truth of what
God has done instead of relying first and foremost on our subjective

---

[19]John Calvin, *The Epistles of Paul the Apostle to the Romans and the Thessalonians,* ed.
David W. Torrance and Thomas F. Torrance, trans. Ross Mackenzie, Calvin's New Testament Commentaries (Grand Rapids, Mich.: Eerdmans, 1960), 8:99, on Rom 4:20.
[20]Calvin *Institutes* 3.2.23.

feelings. Faith rests on the promises of God and pronounces feelings that contradict these promises to be lies. Doubts, trials and depression will come, but we will stand fast and endure not by gazing on ourselves but by placing our trust in the promises of God's Word. He tells us that we are forgiven of ours sins through the blood of his Son and that we will make it to the end by the power of his grace.

The fruit of the Spirit. The promises of God are fundamental for the confirmation of our assurance. We must focus our attention outside of ourselves to the work of God and his promises to discern our status before God. Yet it would be a mistake to posit an absolute discontinuity between the objective and subjective poles in assurance. We will be led astray if we attempt to base our assurance on our own goodness or capacity to stay true to the end. On the other hand, it would be equally fallacious to deny that our assurance is confirmed and strengthened by the transformation wrought in us by the Holy Spirit. Our primary focus must be on the promises of God in Christ and his objective work on our behalf. Yet this objective work does not float free from our own lives so that there is no connection between God's promises and our everyday lives. The already has entered history, and thus we have been changed by the coming of the kingdom in this present evil age. Biblical writers encourage us to confirm our assurance by reflecting on the transformation that has occurred in us by the power of the Holy Spirit. We have said that assurance is a three-legged stool and that the fundamental leg is the promises of God. Nonetheless, we must not conclude from this that the other legs of the stool are superfluous. Even though the promises of God are primary in establishing our assurance, it would be a serious mistake to expel the necessity of believing obedience to confirm assurance. We must beware of an either-or mentality that brings the promises of God to center stage and eliminates the role of human obedience. We must adhere to the balance presented in the Scriptures, where both God's promises and human obedience play a role, although the promises of God have the lead and fundamental role.

As believers who experience tribulation, we need to cling to the promises of God to sustain our faith, which is buffeted by doubts and perils. On the other hand, New Testament writers are also concerned about those who claim to believe and yet do not match their confession of faith with believing obedience. Woven throughout the New

Testament is the insistence that a transformed life is evidence of and necessary for salvation. Such a theme permeates John's first epistle. John says, "We know that we have come to know him if we obey his commands" (1 Jn 2:3 NIV). That is, we can be assured that we are Christians if we keep the commandments. John does not merely say that we know we are Christians if we profess Jesus to be the Christ, though, of course, such a confession is indispensable as well (1 Jn 2:20-23). Confessing Jesus as the incarnate Messiah is a necessary but insufficient condition for assurance. John says that there must also be the transformation of our lives. We must keep God's commands. As John says, those who obey God's word have really had God's love completed in them (1 Jn 2:5). John then adds, "This is how we know we are in him." We know we are in him if we obey his Word and keep his commandments. Those who disobey his commands are liars in claiming to know him (1 Jn 2:4). They walk in the darkness of Satan's realm, even though they claim to have fellowship with God (1 Jn 1:6).

The verses we have cited are representative of 1 John, for John hits on this theme again and again. For example, in 1 John 2:28—3:10 there is a sustained emphasis on the righteousness of those in the light. We know that "everyone who does what is right has been born of him [God]" (1 Jn 2:29 NIV) and that "no one who sins has either seen him or known him" (1 Jn 3:6 NRSV). Notice that John does not say that those who live righteously are especially good Christians. He says that those who sin are not believers at all! They have not seen God or known him. John drives the theme home in 1 John 3:7-10 (NRSV):

> Little children, let no one deceive you. Everyone who does what is right is righteous, just as he is righteous. Everyone who commits sin is a child of the devil; for the devil has been sinning from the beginning. The Son of God was revealed for this purpose, to destroy the works of the devil. Those who have been born of God do not sin, because God's seed abides in them; they cannot sin, because they have been born of God. The children of God and the children of the devil are revealed in this way: all who do not do what is right are not from God, nor are those who do not love their brothers and sisters.

John sets forth the opposition between the wicked and righteous in stark terms. Those who sin are of the devil, and those who are born of

God "do not" and "cannot sin." The children of the devil and the children of God are manifested by their works.[21] We should note once again that we cannot limit these statements to super-spiritual Christians who have reached a level that ordinary Christians have not attained, for John says that the triumph over sin described here is true of all those born of God, that is, all Christians.

It is tempting to domesticate these verses, but John at the very least insists that those who are believers demonstrate that they belong to the people of God by the quality of their lives. We must remember that John wrote this to a church that was troubled about their status before God. They were concerned that the secessionists who had formed a new church were perhaps the genuine people of God. John assured those who remained in the church (cf. 1 Jn 2:19) that they were genuinely the people of God. In other words, John expected his readers to see themselves when he spoke of the righteousness of their lives. He did not write these words to frighten believers about whether they were authentic believers but to assure them that they were born again. It is as if John were saying, "You know that you are believers; look at the change in your lives. And you know the secessionists are not of God; look at the moral dissolution of their lives." These secessionists were likely proto-Gnostics who denied that they were sinners but actually lived licentiously and without regard for moral norms (1 Jn 1:6-10). We overinterpret John, therefore, if we understand passages like 1 John 3:7-10 to require moral perfection as a prerequisite for assurance. Indeed, if one were to argue that moral perfection is the topic here, then one must conclude that such perfection is necessary to be a Christian at all! For John says that those who "cannot sin" are those who are born of God (1 Jn 3:9; cf. 5:18). John has elsewhere said that perfection is not the lot of those who are in the light (1 Jn 1:6-10). Indeed, he informs us that as we walk in the light the blood of Jesus cleanses us from all sin (1 Jn 1:7). It follows that walking in the light is not perfect obedience, for one would not need to be cleansed from sin if walking in the light

---

[21] Amazingly, Zane C. Hodges completely evacuates these verses of any force. He says that if a believer does evil, then that believer conceals the fact that he or she is really a believer (*The Gospel Under Siege: A Study on Faith and Works,* 2nd ed. [Dallas: Rendención Viva, 1991], pp. 67-68). But John is giving us a means to discern whether one is of God or of the devil. This is the natural way to interpret his words.

precluded all sinning! We must hold in balance the tension in John's teaching. Believers are not sinless, yet there is a dramatic change in our lives. Our lives are no longer characterized by sin. There is substantial, significant and observable evidence that we belong to God. Such changes in our lives confirm to us that we are truly the children of God.

Someone might ask how to distinguish good and moral people who do not confess Christ from Christians. We have already suggested that the secessionists lived licentiously. They were probably proto-Gnostics who dismissed the need for moral rigor in everyday existence. John responds that one discerns the children of God and the children of devil by the way one behaves. John is not calling for perfection, but he is insisting that the direction and orientation of one's life must bear the marks of the Spirit's work. To put it in Pauline terms, those who belong to the people of God manifest the fruit of the Spirit. Are there not many nonbelievers, however, who live morally commendable lives? Should we conclude, then, that they also belong to the people of God?

The question is an important one because John identifies those who belong to the people of God by their behavior. Where we make a mistake is in abstracting any one of John's "marks" by which we discern whether one belongs to people of God from the other marks. If we isolate one mark from another, we do violence to the epistolary situation that called forth the letter of 1 John. John argues that people know they are believers if they keep the commandments (1 Jn 2:3-6; 2:28—3:10), love brothers and sisters (1 Jn 3:11-18; 4:7-21) and confess Jesus as the Messiah (1 Jn 2:20-23; 4:1-3; 5:6-7). One cannot wrench these three themes apart and isolate them so that any one mark can function outside of the others. Thus, people who live moral lives but deny that Jesus is the Messiah are not Christians. Fulfilling each of the conditions is necessary to belong to the people of God. John wrote his letter to a specific situation in which the secessionists who left the church were immoral, loveless and denied Jesus as the Messiah who came in the flesh. He counters by saying that we can be assured we are part of the people of God if we are righteous, love brothers and sisters and confess Jesus as the Christ. He was not addressing a situation where people met some of the marks but not others. In any case, to separate one mark from another is to abstract the letter of John from the specific circumstances that it addressed. All three marks work together in concert to determine the authenticity of one's profession of faith. Indeed, even if one meets all three of these conditions today, it does not follow that one is a believer. These conditions are necessary conditions to belong to the people of God, but they are not sufficient conditions.[22] John did not intend to write a comprehensive treatise on how to discern whether one is a believer. He wrote to address the circumstances his flock experienced, and his words are part of what we need to include in assessing whether one truly belongs to Christ.

Some of the qualifications discussed above, although essential, may hinder us from seeing John's major point. Those who are born of God and know God show it by the way they live. Those who claim to know God and live in sin are liars. If it is a mistake to abstract living righteously from confessing Jesus as the Messiah, the converse is also true. That is, if one professes to believe in Jesus as Messiah but there is no corresponding change of life, then that person has no warrant to say that he or she is a believer. We must take John's words seriously and not dilute them in an attempt to salve our consciences with the idea that there is "peace, peace, when there is no peace."

We have already mentioned that John also teaches that love is the mark of the people of God. He says, "We know that we have passed from death to life, because we love our brothers. Anyone who does not love remains in death. Anyone who hates his brother is a murderer, and you know that no murderer has eternal life in him" (1 Jn 3:14-15 NIV). Once again John could scarcely be clearer. Those who love have already entered the age to come, whereas those who hate and murder are not Christians. Zane Hodges proposes a very unlikely interpretation.[23] He says that passing from death to life does not refer to conversion despite the similar wording in John 5:24. He also confines the "we" here to the apostles, when it is most naturally interpreted to refer to all believers. One can appreciate that Hodges wants to say that a murderer can still obtain eternal life. Surely John is not saying that whoever murdered anyone at anytime is headed for

---

[22]For instance, John did not explicitly say that one must confess the deity of Christ, presumably because the opponents did not deny it Yet evangelicals would agree that the deity of Christ is a nonnegotiable element for genuine Christian faith.

[23]See Hodges, *Gospel Under Siege,* pp. 69-70.

destruction. Yet Hodges's exposition here domesticates the text by introducing an unlikely disjunction between the words *have* and *abide*. Hodges ends up saying that believers can murder and hate, whereas John seems to say precisely the opposite. It certainly should cause us to pause when the interpretation presented appears to turn the actual words of the text around. When David sinned, he was worried about his future inheritance (Ps 51). That is why he prayed that God would not remove the Holy Spirit from him (Ps 51:11). If David thought like Hodges, he would not have bothered to pray such a prayer.

A similar notion is expressed in 1 John 4:7-8: "Dear friends, let us love one another, for love comes from God. Everyone who loves has been born of God and knows God. Whoever does not love does not know God, because God is love" (NIV). The stark opposition that characterizes John's writing continues here. Those who love brothers and sisters know God and have been born of God, but those who fail to love do not know God.[24] Finally, in 1 John 4:19-21 the apostle says, "We love because he first loved us. If anyone says, 'I love God,' yet hates his brother, he is a liar. For anyone who does not love his brother, whom he has seen, cannot love God, whom he has not seen. And he has given us this command: Whoever loves God must also love his brother" (NIV). How do we know that we are believers? By our love for brothers and sisters. Those who hate, John affirms, are liars and deceivers.

The link between love and assurance is forged in 1 John 3:19-24. In verse 18 John exhorts believers to love in word and deed and not just with oral protestations of love. Love must manifest itself in the nitty gritty of life, according to John. John then adds, "This then is how we know that we belong to the truth, and how we set our hearts at rest in his presence whenever our hearts condemn us. For God is greater than our hearts, and he knows everything" (1 Jn 3:19-20 NIV). The link between verses 18 and 19 is absolutely crucial here. When John

---

[24]Hodges says about 1 John 4:7 that the unloving person "does not really know God at the level of real fellowship and intimacy with Christ." Note how Hodges wriggles away from the words of the text here, for John speaks of being "born of God," which surely means having new life and being a Christian. Hodges refers to "fellowship" and "intimacy," but John refers to being "born of God" (*Gospel Under Siege*, p. 71). Hodges dances away from the text to sustain his view that one can hate and still be a Christian.

declares in verse 19 that "this" is how we know that we are of the truth and "this" is the way we can have confidence before him, he refers back to the genuine love spoken of in verse 18 (and the previous verses as well). John specifically ties our assurance of faith to the love that we show in tangible ways to others. Assurance does not rest only on God's promises; it also is confirmed by the way we live. Are we showing love and kindness to our brothers and sisters in the Lord?

The other instructive element in this text is 1 John 3:20. When we are loving others, we assure ourselves that we are genuinely part of the people of God even though "our hearts condemn us." This fits with what we said about God's promises above. Our consciences may tell us that we are guilty before God, even though our lives are marked by love and good deeds! In this case, the objective presence of such love and good deeds must take precedence over our fallible consciences. We may not feel that we are genuinely believers, but "God is greater than our hearts, and he knows everything" (1 Jn 3:20 NIV). Our feelings are not the ultimate umpire that determines the truth. What is happening in our lives is the means by which we should judge whether we are believers. If we are practicing love, says John, we need to use those good deeds to argue against feelings of condemnation that insidiously worm their way into our lives. We know that we belong to God because we demonstrate love in concrete ways to our brothers and sisters in Christ. Once again, John expects his community to see themselves in his words. He believes that those who have remained in the church are loving and that those who have left are full of hate. He hopes that those who have remained will be full of assurance because of their works, despite the doubts of their hearts, for they will perceive that they are loving.

The confirming role of good works is explicitly taught in 2 Peter 1:5-11. False teachers have infiltrated the church (2 Pet 2), and Peter defends the belief in Christ's coming and attacks the false teachers because of their licentious lifestyle. He reminds the church of the truth of the gospel and cautions them from succumbing to the corrupting influence of the infiltrators. Peter leaves no doubt in chapter 2 that the false teachers are headed toward eschatological destruction. They will experience judgment, as did the disobedient angels (2 Pet 2:4), the flood generation (2 Pet 2:5) and Sodom and Gomorrah (2 Pet 2:6). Peter warns the church against falling prey to the same fate.

Thus, Peter exhorts his readers to "make every effort to add to your faith goodness; and to goodness, knowledge; and to knowledge, self-control; and to self-control, perseverance; and to perseverance, godliness; and to godliness, brotherly kindness; and to brotherly kindness, love" (2 Pet 1:5-7 NIV). Virtuous living is not encouraged simply because it makes life on earth more fulfilling, nor is the idea that living a godly life will lead to greater rewards in heaven. These virtues are imperative to escape the fate of the false teachers. That is, righteous living is necessary to obtain entrance into the kingdom of Jesus Christ.

The interpretation proposed here is the most probable way of interpreting 2 Peter 1:8-11:

> For if you possess these qualities in increasing measure, they will keep you from being ineffective and unproductive in your knowledge of our Lord Jesus Christ. But if anyone does not have them, he is nearsighted and blind, and has forgotten that he has been cleansed from his past sins. Therefore, my brothers, be all the more eager to make your calling and election sure. For if you do these things, you will never fall, and you will receive a rich welcome into the eternal kingdom of our Lord and Savior Jesus Christ. (NIV)

Peter contends that one must practice the virtues specified in verses 5-7 in order to enter the kingdom of Christ. Devoting ourselves to godliness is not merely a good idea or a guarantee of a greater reward; it is necessary to enter the kingdom at all! It could be argued from verses 8-9, contrary to what we are suggesting, that Peter speaks of rewards given to those who live a fruitful Christian life. Such an interpretation should be rejected for a number of reasons: (1) We have already seen in 2 Peter 2 that the fate of the false teachers and those who succumb to their influence is final judgment. It is antecedently unlikely that another judgment is specified here, for Peter fears lest readers fall under the sway of the infiltrators. (2) The immediate context certifies our interpretation. The readers are exhorted "to make your calling and election sure" (2 Pet 1:10). Both election and calling do not relate to rewards beyond eternal life or fruitfulness in this life. Believers are called and elected to eternal life itself. Nowhere does Scripture relate election and calling to rewards that are beyond and in addition to eternal life. Believers are elected and called to the reward of eternal life itself. To say "make your calling and election sure" is another way of saying, "make your salvation sure." (3) When Peter says, "If you do these things you will never fall" (2 Pet 1:10), the word *fall (ptaisēte)* does not mean "if you practice these virtues, you will never sin." The verb *fall (ptaiō)* does refer to sin in other contexts (Jas 2:10; 3:2). To adopt such a meaning here, however, is quite improbable. For one thing, the sentence would be a tautology, for it is patently obvious that as long as one practices virtues one is not sinning.[25] Instead, Peter makes the same point as Jude does in verse 24 of his book. Those who practice these virtues will never fall, that is, they will obtain final salvation.[26] The word *fall* refers here, then, to apostasy. Those who practice godly virtues will not turn decisively away from the gospel of Christ. (4) Similarly, entrance into the "eternal kingdom of our Lord and Savior Jesus Christ" designates induction into the kingdom of the Lord. This expression is simply the converse of saying "you will never fall" and thus should be interpreted similarly to refer to the eternal inheritance that awaits believers.

Thus far we have argued that Peter summons the church to godly living so that they will enter the eternal kingdom. Final salvation is at stake in his call to obedience. What we want to focus on here is the relationship of this theme to assurance. Believers are to practice the virtues itemized in 2 Peter 1:5-7 "to make [their] calling and election sure" (2 Pet 1:10). Godly living, in other words, ensures that one will enter the kingdom of our Lord Christ in the future. Richard Bauckham makes this observation about the text: "This passage does not mean that moral progress provides the Christian with a subjective assurance of his election (the sense it was given by Luther and Calvin, and especially in seventeenth-century Calvinism), but that the ethical fruits of Christian faith are objectively necessary for the attainment of final salvation."[27] We agree with Bauckham that the primary purpose in this text is to say that good works must be present to enter the kingdom. Peter does not stress that one must be subjectively aware of such good works to enter the kingdom. Instead, he

---

[25] Rightly Richard J. Bauckham, *Jude, 2 Peter,* Word Biblical Commentary (Waco, Tex.: Word, 1983), p. 191.

[26] Bauckham says, "The metaphor must rather be given the same sense as in Jude 24. . . . It refers to the disaster of not reaching final salvation" (ibid.).

[27] Ibid., p. 190.

insists that these virtues must be objectively present for final salvation.

Nevertheless, the view of Calvin and Luther and their heirs is not far off the mark either, and thus we need not opt for the either-or view of Bauckham.[28] Peter certainly teaches that the virtues must be objectively present for one to inherit the future promises (2 Pet 1:3), yet his admonition to believers would be superfluous if they could not subjectively determine whether or not these virtues existed in their lives. Peter expects the readers to be able to discern whether these virtues are theirs and abounding (2 Pet 1:8), and it also follows, therefore, that they will know whether they are making their calling and election certain. Thus, Peter is at least indirectly teaching that our assurance is confirmed by godly virtues. Our growth in godliness is an indication that our calling and election are not a charade. The objective signs of growth in our lives provide subjective assurance that our faith is genuine, that we are not deceiving ourselves about our relationship with God.

When we discussed the promises of God in the previous section we emphasized that the promises are given to provide comfort and strength for us when our consciences accuse us unjustly and when we despair of ever finishing the race. New Testament writers are also concerned, however, with those who might presume upon God's grace and who would use the promises of Scripture to console their consciences, even though their lives are characterized by wickedness. Virtually every teaching in the Scriptures can be abused, and God's gracious promises could be used as a platform for a life of sin. Hence New Testament writers consistently admonish believers to good works, insisting that such good works are irrefragably linked to salvation. The famous passage in James 2:14-26 is a case in point and not at all unusual. James argues that faith without works does not save and that we are justified by works. Both Abraham and Rahab are adduced as examples of people who were justified by works. It is not our purpose to discuss this text in detail here or to resolve the many controversies that have arisen over its meaning and how it relates to

---

[28]For Calvin see *The Epistles of Paul the Apostle to the Hebrews and the First and Second Epistles of St. Peter,* ed. David W. Torrance and Thomas F. Torrance, trans. William B. Johnston, Calvin's New Testament Commentaries (Grand Rapids, Mich.: Eerdmans, 1963), 12:333-34; for Luther see *Works,* 30:158.

Pauline teaching. Perhaps it will suffice to say that the argument of our entire book attempts to show why and how Paul and James do not conflict theologically. It is highly artificial, in our opinion, to argue that salvation and justification in James do not relate to eternal life and justification before God.[29] There is no indication that James uses the terms *save* and *justify* with a meaning different from Paul's.[30] We should take the book of James at face value and in its most natural sense. Faith without works is dead, and those who lack good works will not be vindicated by God on the day of judgment. Those who claim assurance of faith but fail to produce good works contradict their profession by their lives. There is no warrant for thinking that they truly belong to the people of God.

One reason we do not linger over James is that the reader may think that James's words are unusual and distinctive. In actuality, the message of James is common in the New Testament. The exhortation of Hebrews 6:9-12 (NIV) is instructive in this regard:

> Even though we speak like this, dear friends, we are confident of better things in your case—things that accompany salvation. God is not unjust; he will not forget your work and the love you have shown him

---

[29]Hodges, *Gospel Under Siege*, pp. 20-38; R. T. Kendall, *Once Saved, Always Saved* (Chicago: Moody Press, 1983), pp. 170-72, 207-17. Kendall understands the text to refer to both enjoyment of God's blessings now and loss of rewards at the judgment seat of Christ. Kendall suggests that the "profit" mentioned in James 2:16, the "deadness" of faith without works in 2:17 and the "uselessness" of faith without works refers to the profit, vitality and utility of works for "other" people (pp. 216-17). But this view is wildly improbable, for in James 2:14 the profitability of faith without works is related to the salvation of the person who is not doing the good works. James asks, "Can such faith save him?" The word *him* demonstrates that James refers to the person who lacks the good works; the word *profit* should be interpreted similarly.

[30]This claim is controversial for the word *justify*, since some have taken it to mean "demonstrate" in the sense of proving one is right with God (Calvin *Institutes* 3.17.12; R. C. Sproul, *Faith Alone: The Evangelical Doctrine of Justification* [Grand Rapids, Mich.: Baker, 1995], p. 166). The notion that the verb *justify (dikaioō)* has such a meaning, however, is called into question by the lexical evidence, for the verb rarely has such a meaning (perhaps Lk 7:29, 35). *Justify* in this context means "to be right before God," as is customary in the New Testament. Moreover, Douglas J. Moo rightly observes that such a definition does not fit well in James's context, since "the question is not 'How can righteousness be demonstrated?' but, 'What kind of faith secures righteousness?'" (*The Letter of James: An Introduction and Commentary*, Tyndale New Testament Commentaries [Grand Rapids, Mich.: Eerdmans, 1985], p. 109). Moo goes on to say that James refers here to justification on the last day in which believers are vindicated by their works. We agree with Moo that justification in James relates to God's declaration rather than the idea of proving or demonstrating one's righteousness. Of course, such works are an evidence of genuine faith.

as you have helped his people and continue to help them. We want each of you to show this same diligence to the very end, in order to make your hope sure. We do not want you to become lazy, but to imitate those who through faith and patience inherit what has been promised.

Preceding these words of exhortation is one of the most severe warning passages in the New Testament (Heb 5:11–6:8). Nonetheless, the author is optimistic about the future destiny of the readers because their love has been fervent and their good works have been manifested in the church. In other words, the author is convinced that they belong to the people of God because of the changes that have occurred in their lives. The readers can confirm and strengthen this assurance by showing "this same diligence" in good works "to the very end, in order to make your hope sure" (Heb 6:11). The author of Hebrews does not say, "You will be saved no matter what you do in the future," but rather exhorts them to diligence in godliness to the end of their lives so that their hope is sure. In other words, their perseverance in good works will confirm their assurance. We have argued that assurance is integral to faith, but it is also true that assurance vanishes if we do not continue in the obedience that springs from faith. Continuing in the journey of faith seals to our hearts that we truly belong to the people of God.

The confirming role of good works relative to assurance is also taught by Paul. Those who live under the dominion of the Spirit manifest the fruit of the Spirit (Gal 5:22-23). In Galatians 5:19-21 the works of the flesh are described, then Paul adds this comment: "I warn you, as I did before, that those who live like this will not inherit the kingdom of God" (Gal 5:21 NIV). Paul does not guarantee that believers will inherit the kingdom regardless of how they live. He warns that those who succumb to the flesh will not enter the kingdom.[31] This fits with Galatians 6:8-9, where Paul says, "If you sow to your own flesh, you will reap corruption from the flesh; but if you sow to the Spirit, you will reap eternal life from the Spirit. So let us not grow weary in doing

---

[31]Michael A. Eaton understands the threat to relate to loss of present blessing, or it means that one is "saved through fire" (1 Cor 3:15; see *No Condemnation: A New Theology of Assurance* [Downers Grove, Ill.: InterVarsity Press, 1995], p. 112). Our examination of the overlap between the terms *kingdom, eternal life* and the like in chapter one makes Eaton's interpretation quite improbable.

what is right, for we will reap at harvest-time, if we do not give up" (NRSV). The antithesis between corruption and eternal life demonstrates that sowing to the flesh leads to judgment. That is, those who sow to the flesh will not experience eternal life on the last day, whereas those who sow to the Spirit will inherit eternal life.

Eaton understands this text to refer not to final salvation and destruction but to present enjoyment (or the forfeiting of such enjoyment) of the blessings of the kingdom.[32] Contrary to Eaton, there is no place in the Scriptures where eternal life is defined in such a way. Methodologically, one could posit the same interpretation of the verses that are understood (even by Eaton) to refer to final salvation. That is, why could we not say that the verses that say we have eternal life if we believe in Jesus Christ relate only to the present enjoyment of God's blessings? That is not our view, but we see no reason why such a gambit would be forbidden if we adopted Eaton's exegesis. Indeed, we could go further. We could then say that the verses that speak of eternal life in the future are the only ones that relate to final salvation and that those that speak of believing and having eternal life now relate only to present enjoyment of kingdom blessings. In other words, Eaton's scheme can easily be turned around to yield precisely the opposite conclusion! We cannot help but think that a presupposition has muted the New Testament texts in Eaton's scheme. Any verses that relate eternal life to works cannot (according to Eaton) really relate to eternal life. Those that connect eternal life to believing do refer to end-time salvation. It is much more satisfying to assign a consistent definition to terms like "eternal life" and to understand them within the already-but-not-yet schema of New Testament eschatology.

The same thought is expressed in 1 Corinthians 6:9-11:

> Do you not know that the wicked will not inherit the kingdom of God? Do not be deceived: Neither the sexually immoral nor idolaters nor adulterers nor male prostitutes nor homosexual offenders nor thieves nor the greedy nor drunkards nor slanderers nor swindlers will inherit the kingdom of God. And that is what some of you were. But you were washed, you were sanctified, you were justified in the name of the Lord Jesus Christ and by the Spirit of our God. (NIV)

---

[32]Ibid., p. 113.

These verses are not addressed to unbelievers. Paul admonishes the Corinthians who were indulging in frivolous lawsuits by warning them that such behavior is frightening because people who behave in such a way will not inherit the kingdom. Precisely because assurance is integral to faith, Paul insists that those who indulge in wickedness will not enter the kingdom of God; they will not experience eternal life. There is no warrant for assurance if one is doing the works of the flesh and living contrary to the will of God.

We see Paul's pastoral application of such an understanding in 1 Thessalonians. The church in Thessalonica was a recently planted church, and Paul had to leave the congregation shortly after establishing it because of pressure from the local authorities (Acts 17:1-10). Paul wondered how the church would fare during his absence, thinking that perhaps Satan would tempt them and that their faith would be smothered when pressures and tribulations arrived (1 Thess 3:1-5). He sent Timothy to investigate the spiritual state of his converts: "For this reason, when I could stand it no longer, I sent to find out about your faith. I was afraid that in some way the tempter might have tempted you and our efforts might have been useless" (1 Thess 3:5). Paul was tremendously encouraged, however, since Timothy brought news of the Thessalonians' perseverance in the gospel. He expresses his sentiments in these words: "For now we really live, since you are standing firm in the Lord" (1 Thess 3:8 NIV). Paul is filled with joy and encouragement and assurance because the Thessalonians have withstood the storm and continue to maintain their faith. In this case, of course, Paul's assurance is the subject of discussion. Nonetheless, the text indicates that assurance cannot be severed from perseverance. Assurance is strengthened and confirmed by continuing in the faith.

The strengthening of assurance through continued obedience is clearly taught in Romans 5:3-5: "Not only so, but we also rejoice in our sufferings, because we know that suffering produces perseverance; perseverance, character; and character, hope. And hope does not disappoint us, because God has poured out his love into our hearts by the Holy Spirit, whom he has given us" (NIV). The theme of Romans 5:1-11 is hope. Those who are justified should be full of hope and assurance because their destiny is future glory (Rom 5:2), and since they are now justified and reconciled, they will be spared from the wrath of God on the day of the Lord (Rom 5:9-10). Their confidence about the future causes them to exult in God through the Lord Jesus Christ (Rom 5:11). Paul does not merely say that believers can be full of confidence about the future; he also says that believers can rejoice in their present afflictions and troubles.

The reason for this extraordinary joy is charted out in Romans 5:3-5. It is not the case that believers rejoice in sufferings because suffering is now a pleasant experience! If such were the case, suffering would cease to be suffering—it would be inherently delightful. Afflictions are still painful. Believers do not rejoice in them because they have been transmuted into delightful experiences. Believers rejoice in their troubles because the pressures of life build endurance into them. They are toughened up by the trials of life. Patient endurance of afflictions in turn leads to tested character. As believers encounter the difficulties of life, they are conformed more and more to the image of Jesus (Rom 8:29). They become more and more like him in character and godliness. They become seasoned saints who have been refined and tested through the crucible of suffering. Such transformation of character in turn leads to hope.

Why does it lead to hope? Hope is begotten by transformed character because the changes in our lives testify to us that God is actually working in our lives. Occasionally, when everything in our lives is going well, we wonder if our faith is genuine. We ask ourselves if we are any different from unbelievers who live comfortable lives. But when suffering comes and we see good fruit, we know that our faith is not an illusion. We can see that we are changing and growing. Thus, we are full of hope and assurance about our future destiny. This is simply another way of saying that as we grow in godliness our assurance is confirmed and strengthened. We should not think of assurance with regard to final salvation in one-dimensional terms. Assurance is integral to saving faith, yet our assurance should grow as we progress in the journey of faith. It is solidified and deepened as we experience trials and continue to grow in godliness. We should not conceive of good works as a threat to assurance in the faith. Rather, good works are a means by which assurance is expanded and fortified.

The notion that our assurance is confirmed by good works is also taught by both Luther and Calvin.[33] For Luther the confirming role of good works applies especially to our lives before other human beings. The reason Luther forged such a distinction is that we are always aware of how far short we fall from God's perfect standards. Nonetheless, he insisted that our lives before other human beings had to be of such a character that it was clear that we are Christians.[34] Luther believed that even in God's presence our assurance was confirmed by our godly lives: "We have need of this testimony of our conscience that we have carried out our ministry well and have also lived a good life."[35] Luther did not believe that a good conscience and good works justified us, but he did believe these works strengthened our assurance:

> Although we must not rely on this, since we are justified, it puts my conscience at peace, that I do evil to no one, and thus I walk safely in God. . . . Now comes the confidence in the Lord that on the basis of this conduct we can be certain that God is well disposed toward us. . . . These are the testimonies of our conscience, if anyone has lived properly in his calling and did his duty. . . . Thus all who do good to their neighbor know that they are pleasing to God, since this is the testimony of our conscience, that we are conducting ourselves before the world in a holy manner.[36]

The wording here indicates that, according to Luther, living a godly life confirms that we are believers. Failure to manifest good works demonstrates that our faith is false and that we are not really believers.[37] On the other hand, "If this is my feeling, if I curse no one, hate no one, yes, sympathize with those who are troubled and afflicted, there we have the testimony of our conscience that we are children of God."[38] Similarly, he says, "The consciousness of a life well spent is the assurance that we are keeping the faith, for it is through works that we learn that our faith is true."[39] And, "Therefore man knows by the fruits of faith what kind of tree it is, and is proved by love and deed whether Christ is in him and he believes in Christ."[40]

---

[33]See especially here Zachman, *Assurance of Faith,* pp. 80-87, 198-203.
[34]Luther, *Works,* 51:273-74.
[35]Ibid., 27:120-21.
[36]Ibid., 17:288-89.
[37]Ibid., 24:255; 27:127.
[38]Ibid., 30:308.
[39]Ibid., 30:279.
[40]Luther *Sermons* 2:240.

Though a good conscience confirms our assurance, Luther insists that it must never be the basis of our assurance.[41] Here we rely solely on the mercy of Christ. Zachman believes that Luther's oscillation between trusting the mercy of Christ for justification and appealing to our good conscience for testimony of the authenticity of our faith is "inherently unstable."[42] Whether Luther formulated the biblical materials in the most satisfying way is certainly debatable. However, all believers must preserve the tension between not relying on their good works as a basis for salvation and the necessity of good works to be saved on the final day. Similarly, the biblical tension regarding assurance must be preserved. Assurance is integral to saving faith, yet assurance is also strengthened and confirmed by walking in godliness. Whether such a tension is "inherently unstable" is debatable, for no logical contradiction is involved here. Human beings are prone to upset the balance and emphasize one side of the tension above the other, yet the gospel calls us to live in such a way that we preserve the tension between assurance being integral to faith and the need to confirm our assurance by keeping God's commandments.

Calvin also argues that our assurance is not founded on our good works, since our works are imperfect and our only hope for mercy is the cross of Christ.[43] Nonetheless, he maintains that our assurance is confirmed by our good works: "The godly man enjoys a pure conscience before the Lord, thus confirming himself in the promise with which the Lord comforts and supports his true worshippers."[44] Note the connection between a pure conscience and the confirmation of assurance by our good works. Calvin says with reference to 2 Peter 1:10 that "calling is shown to be confirmed by a holy life."[45] Calvin rightly emphasizes that we cannot merit justification by our good works and that assurance for salvation rests only on Christ. But it would be a mistake to conclude from this that he rejects the idea that our assurance is strengthened and fortified by good works. Calvin's two-pronged distinction relative to assurance was due to his attempt to be faithful to the biblical witness. We should emulate him by also preserving the balance

---

[41]See Zachman, *Assurance of Faith,* p. 85.
[42]Ibid., p. 87.
[43]Calvin *Institutes* 3.14.18.
[44]Ibid., 3.20.10.
[45]Calvin, *Hebrews, 1 and 2 Peter,* p. 334.

between the foundation and confirmation of our assurance.

The witness of the Spirit. The foundation of our assurance consists in the promises of God that assure us that he will complete the good work he has begun. We have also seen that the fruit of the Spirit, our good works, confirm and strengthen our assurance as believers. The Scriptures also forge a connection between our assurance in faith and the witness of the Spirit. One of the central texts for this teaching is Romans 8:16. We shall examine briefly all of Romans 8:12-17 to ensure that we place the statement about the witness of the Spirit in its proper context:[46]

> So then, brothers and sisters, we are debtors, not to the flesh, to live according to the flesh—for if you live according to the flesh, you will die; but if by the Spirit you put to death the deeds of the body, you will live. For all who are led by the Spirit of God are children of God. For you did not receive a spirit of slavery to fall back into fear, but you have received a spirit of adoption. When we cry, "Abba! Father!" it is that very Spirit bearing witness with our spirit that we are children of God, and if children, then heirs, heirs of God and joint heirs with Christ—if, in fact, we suffer with him so that we may also be glorified with him. (NRSV)

Paul summons believers to a way of life free from the dominion of the flesh. He bases this injunction (note the connecting words "so then" in v. 12) on the work of Christ on the cross and the infusion of the Spirit's power (Rom 8:1-11), which liberates believers from slavery to the old Adam. Believers are no longer obliged to live under the dominion of the flesh because the powers of the coming age have invaded their lives. Yet the age to come has not yet arrived in its fullness, and thus believers live in the tension between the already and not yet. Thus, the exhortation in Romans 8:13 is still needed for Christians. Paul warns us that if we succumb to the desires of the body we will die. In order to live, that is, to obtain eternal life, we must slay the deeds of the body by the power of the Spirit. This verse informs us that the desires of the flesh are powerful enough to require concerted resistance. We must consciously and intentionally put these desires to death in order to reach our eternal destiny. Such a teaching is not

---

[46]For a more extended commentary on these verses, see Thomas R. Schreiner, *Romans,* Baker Exegetical Commentary on the New Testament (Grand Rapids, Mich.: Baker, 1998), pp. 426-27.

works-righteousness, for Paul informs us that conquering sin in this way is "by the Spirit." We must summon our wills and make decisions to triumph over the flesh, yet ultimately the subjection of the flesh comes from the power of the Holy Spirit. We ask the Spirit for strength to overcome powerful temptations. We stock our minds with the sword of the Spirit—the word of God (Eph 6:17)—to fight off the lies that come from the body. We pay heed to both the promises and threats of God's word and ask the Spirit to give us the faith to believe in them, so that we will obey because we trust that God's way is the path to a happy future.[47]

At this juncture it is crucial to see the connection between verses 13 and 14. The two verses are joined by "for," and we need to inquire about the logical relationship between the two verses. Verse 13 declares that those who slay the deeds of the body and conquer the desires of the flesh will obtain eternal life. Then, in verse 14 Paul says, "For all who are led by the Spirit of God are children of God" (NRSV). To be "led by the Spirit" in this context does not refer to guidance for everyday decisions. The connection with verse 13 demonstrates that being led by the Spirit refers to yielding to or submitting to the Spirit by putting to death the deeds of the body. To be led by the Spirit is nothing less than to obey the Spirit. Moreover, Paul tells us that those who are led by the Spirit are the children ("sons" in the Greek text) of God. In other words, those who are steered by the Holy Spirit are genuinely part of the people of God. The slavery referred to in verse 15, therefore, is the slavery of sin from which Paul says, in Romans 6, believers were freed. Believers have not received a spirit that enslaves but a Spirit that frees. As sons of God we cry out "Abba! Father," and this sonship is attested by our new obedience.

In the midst of this argument, Romans 8:16 appears, where Paul affirms that the Spirit testifies to our spirits that we are God's children. We have lingered over the previous context because the preceding verses have shown that our assurance is linked to our obedience, and in this very same context Paul's words about the witness of the Spirit occur. It is instructive that assurance is connected to both the fruit of the Spirit and the witness of the Spirit in the same context.

---

[47]For a very practical and helpful illustration of how this works out in the case of lust, see Piper, *Purifying Power,* pp. 334-36.

Paul proceeds to emphasize God's promises in Romans 8:28-39, and thus we have in one context the three legs of assurance. The intertwining of both the fruit of the Spirit and the witness of the Spirit in the same context suggests that we should not abstract one from the other so as to play the one against the other. Assurance is based both on the witness of the Spirit and the fruit of the Spirit.

But what is the witness of the Spirit? We have mentioned previously that Martin Lloyd-Jones understood it to be an experience subsequent to conversion in which one receives assurance that one is part of the people of God. The flow of thought in Romans 8:12-17 indicates that Lloyd-Jones's view is quite improbable. All believers are set free from sin and no longer obliged to the flesh (v. 12). All believers are to put to death the body's impulses by the power of the Spirit (v. 13). All those and only those who submit to the Spirit are the children of God (v. 14). Paul is certainly not suggesting that some of those who are not led by the Spirit may also be God's children. All believers have been freed from the spirit of slavery and have received the Spirit of adoption (v. 15). All believers are the children of God and therefore are also heirs of eternal glory. Thus, we can confidently say that all believers have the witness of the Spirit. We do violence to Paul's train of thought to say that we are all freed from the power of sin, led by the Spirit, adopted as God's children and heirs of eternal glory and then conclude that the witness of the Spirit is given only to some.

Nor is there any reason to think that the witness is subsequent to conversion. Paul is certainly thinking of our conversion in Romans 8:15 when he speaks of receiving the Spirit of adoption instead of the spirit of slavery. On that occasion, we acknowledge God as our dear Father, our Abba. Similarly, the witness of the Spirit is such that it testifies that we are the children of God. Now. we are not saying that the witness of the Spirit is only at conversion. We are simply insisting that it commences with conversion. Believers receive the witness of the Spirit when they are freed from the spirit of slavery, when they receive the Spirit of adoption, when they acknowledge God as their loving Father, and this witness of the Spirit remains with us as we continue in our journey of faith.

We have not really identified the nature of the witness of the Spirit. We have simply maintained that it is received at conversion and continues during our earthly sojourn. The text itself does not elaborate on what the Spirit's witness is. What we do see in the text, however, is the function of the Spirit's witness. It assures us that we are God's children. Thus, we understand the witness of the Spirit to be the work of the Spirit by which he gives us the subjective assurance that we are God's children. The promises of God and the fruit of the Spirit are extrinsic legs of the stool supporting our assurance. But the witness of the Spirit is an intrinsic leg, in the sense that it is subjectively experienced. As believers we need both the objective and the subjective dimensions of assurance. The Spirit whispers to our hearts that we are God's children. We call on God as our dear Father because we sense and feel that he is now our protector and guide. Of course, the subjective witness of the Spirit cannot be abstracted from the objective dimensions of assurance. Someone who lives like the devil and claims the witness of the Spirit is not to be granted the benefit of the doubt! Further, weaker believers can talk themselves out of the witness of the Spirit. They can be filled with so many doubts and questions that the witness of the Spirit is muffled in their lives. Here, the promises of God need to take priority so that the witness of the Spirit is not something they try to manufacture. Neither do we want to minimize the preciousness of this truth. The Spirit testifies to our hearts that we are his children; we sense and feel it is so. We know, ineffably, that we are now the children of God. We sense that he is our Father and that we are his children.[48] We rejoice that his Spirit indwells us and tells us that we are his adopted children.

It is instructive to see that John in his first letter argues along lines similar to Paul's. We have already observed that John forges a link between assurance and obedience, between assurance and loving brothers and sisters in the Lord, and between assurance and confessing Jesus as the Messiah. John would refuse to tolerate those who claim to be part of the people of God and do not match their profession by their behavior. Nonetheless, he also appeals to the gift of the Spirit as a foundation of assurance: "By this we know that we abide in him and he in us, because he has given us of his Spirit (1 Jn 4:13 NRSV). John writes to the people who have remained in the church

---

[48]The view proposed here is actually quite similar to the view of John Wesley. See William J. Abraham, "Predestination and Assurance," in *The Grace of God, the Will of Man: A Case for Arminianism,* ed. Clark H. Pinnock (Grand Rapids, Mich.: Zondervan, 1989), pp. 233-35.

and assures them that they truly "abide" in God and that God abides in them because of the gift of the Spirit. Again, the gift of the Spirit is granted at conversion. This is confirmed by the perfect tense verb *dedōken* ("he has given"), which signifies, in the context, that the Spirit was given at conversion. John's comment in 1 John 3:24 is remarkably similar: "All who obey his commandments abide in him, and he abides in them. And by this we know that he abides in us, by the Spirit that he has given us" (NRSV). We should simply observe here that the gift of the Spirit and the keeping of the commandments are conceptually distinct but practically inseparable in the lives of believers. Like Paul, John does not wrench apart the subjective and objective poles of assurance. The gift of the Spirit brings the subjective dimension to the forefront. We know that we abide in him, that is, we know we are part of the people of God because we have received the Holy Spirit. We understand the reference to the Holy Spirit to relate to the subjective dimension. John expects the readers to recognize that they are God's people because they have the Spirit within.

His argument regarding the anointing that abides in them runs along similar lines (1 Jn 2:20-27). This text is puzzling, since it seems to exclude the need for any teaching. But once we understand that John counters false teachers who claimed to have special access to the truth, it is clear that John wants to assure believers that they already know the truth and should remain in the truth because of the "anointing" they received. Thus, John does not forbid any teaching but teaching that departs from the received tradition, teaching that denies Jesus as the Christ. When John appeals to the anointing, however, it is quite probable that the Holy Spirit is at least included in the anointing.[49] What we want to observe here is that the anointing of the Spirit functions as assurance that John's converts have genuinely received the truth. John appeals to their anointing to encourage and remind them that they are genuinely part of the people of God.

The link between the internal witness of the Spirit and God's promises is well explained by Luther.[50] God's promises in his Word are sealed to our hearts by the Holy Spirit. He takes the external Word

---

[49]I. Howard Marshall argues that the Word and Spirit together constitute the anointing (*The Epistles of John*, New International Commentary on the New Testament [Grand Rapids, Mich.: Eerdmans, 1978]).

[50]See especially Zachman, *Assurance of Faith*, pp. 61-63.

and confirms that it is true in our case: "Then, when the Spirit has been received, the heart is certain and has confidence."[51] We are prone to believe, says Luther, that God is angry at us: "For because the awareness of the opposite is so strong in us, that is, because we are more aware of the wrath of God than of His favor toward us, therefore the Holy Spirit is sent into our hearts."[52] The Spirit communicates to our hearts that God truly loves us. He takes the objective promises and makes them subjectively true in our hearts.

Calvin understands the witness of the Spirit to be his supernatural work by which he persuades us of the truth of the Scriptures: "For as God alone is a fit witness of himself in his Word, so also the Word will not find acceptance in men's hearts before it is sealed by the inward testimony of the Spirit."[53] The words "inward testimony" indicate the internal and subjective work of the Spirit by which he assures us that we are God's children: "Therefore we may know that this is the nature of faith, that conscience has, by the Holy Spirit, a sure witness of God's will toward itself and relying on this, confidently calls on God as Father."[54] Calvin ratifies the understanding of the witness of the Spirit we are suggesting here; the Spirit speaks to our hearts, assuring us that God is our beloved Father.

Warnings and Assurance

Is assurance of faith compatible with the warnings and admonitions of Scripture? Many might think that our view of the warnings and admonitions destroys assurance. R. T. Kendall, for example, affirms emphatically that believers will go to heaven even if they never do any good works.[55] He worries that if the admonitions relate to salvation, then believers could not have any assurance. Thus, he claims that none of the admonitions and warnings relate to inheriting final salvation. If the warnings and admonitions are directed to believers and threaten them with eternal destruction, then it seems that believers would be cast upon the precipice of worry and fear. We would constantly be anxious about our future destiny and worry that we would

---

[51]Luther, *Works*, 30:315.
[52]Ibid., 26:381.
[53]Calvin *Institutes* 1.7.4.
[54]Calvin, *1 Corinthians*, p. 59.
[55]Kendall, *Once Saved, Always Saved*, pp. 49-59.

perish forever if we fall away from the faith.

We have discussed in some detail how to understand the admonitions and warnings in chapter four, and we will not linger here on what is treated in detail there. What we have argued, however, is that the admonitions and warnings do not function to threaten our assurance. On the contrary, admonitions and warnings fortify and build up our assurance. The New Testament authors presuppose consonance and accord between assurance and warning. The biblical evidence indicates that warnings function harmoniously with promise, not in spite of promise. Biblical admonitions and warnings do not subvert faith in God's promises. We do not doubt God's promises in order to believe and heed his warnings. This is true whether the promise is conditional or unconditional. So far from implying that warning and promise are incompatible, the biblical writers presuppose that the two stand compatibly together. We will conceive of warning and promise as opposites or as contrary to one another "only if we misunderstand the nature of perseverance and treat it in isolation from its correlation with faith."[56] Conditional promises and warnings do not contradict the assurance of unconditional promises. For a proper grasp of the correlation between God's warnings and his assurance of preservation, it is precisely the warning that is significant, for it enables believers to understand that God preserves them by using warnings, admonitions and conditional promises.

All the biblical warnings and admonitions we examined in chapter four are prospective and orient believers away from themselves to lay hold of Jesus Christ as the runner pursues the wreath of victory. Yet, even 2 Corinthians 13:5, which calls for self-examination with a retrospective orientation, does not encourage doubt or discourage assurance. Even this passage strengthens our assurance. In 2 Corinthians 13:5 Paul says, "Examine yourselves to see whether you are in the faith; test yourselves. Do you not realize that Christ Jesus is in you—unless, of course, you fail the test?" (NIV). Paul calls on believers to put themselves to the test here. They are to examine their lives to discern whether Jesus Christ genuinely indwells them. If he does not indwell them, then they fail the test and are not members of the peo-

---

[56]G. C. Berkouwer, *Faith and Perseverance*, trans. Robert D. Knudsen (Grand Rapids, Mich.: Eerdmans, 1958), p. 111.

ple of God. We maintain that the admonition to test ourselves is intended for all believers, not only for those who are weak and faltering. Appraising whether we belong to Jesus Christ is salutary for all of us. Unfortunately, however, some understand all exhortations, but especially ones like this, to be inherently depressing and defeating. They turn such admonitions into a platform for morbid introspection and self-doubt. On the contrary, the admonition to test ourselves is not intended to throw us into a tizzy of doubt. Paul expects the Corinthians to examine themselves and be assured that they are truly part of the church of Christ. Of course, the assurance that he expects to be theirs does not become a reality apart from heeding the admonition. Responding rightly to the warnings is the pathway by which we gain assurance in our "marathon of faith."

G. C. Berkouwer, in his outstanding work *Faith and Perseverance,* paves the way so that we can grasp the connection between assurance and the warnings and admonitions in the Scriptures. Berkouwer discusses the famous warning in Hebrews 6 and insists that such a text does not rob believers of their boldness and assurance.

> On the contrary, he wishes to lead the Hebrews, who are surrounded by danger on all sides, more and more to boldness (Heb. 6:1ff.). This is not a disturbing and threatening of the assurance of salvation by setting the Hebrews over the abyss of an uncertain choice between two alternatives. It is an admonition, whose purpose is to lead them to a more secure walk in the way of salvation.[57]

In other words, admonitions are intended not to threaten assurance but to strengthen it, since biblical writers construed the function of admonitions as means to secure and attain the end to which believers are called. Berkouwer, again, is very helpful in this regard:

> The congregation is not brought to a crossroads, with two equally possible directions; it is shown the one way, the one upon which they are traveling and upon which Jesus Christ has gone before them. On this road the admonition is in place to keep going along this road, a warning that comes to its sharpest expression because of the completeness and the radicality of the transition which brought them to travel along this road.[58]

We dare not abstract the warnings from their function in the con-

---

[57]Ibid., p. 119.
[58]Ibid.

text of the Scriptures. The threats and admonitions of Scripture are designed to motivate us to continue following the Lord and to turn us away from anything that would distract us from that pursuit. Indeed, the admonitions are one of the means God uses by which we continue to run the race, and thus they must be conceived as strengthening and confirming our assurance. Once again, Berkouwer is of an immense help to us: "These admonitions, too, have as their end the preservation of the Church, which precisely in this way is established in that single direction, which is and which must remain irreversible—the direction from death to life."[59]

We cannot and must not posit an assurance regarding final salvation that neglects or ignores the warnings of Scripture. Doing so abstracts one element of the biblical message from another element. We are then in danger of selecting the portion of the biblical message that suits our predispositions and preferences. The scriptural writers maintain the tension between assurance of faith and admonitions to continue in faith. Yet the tension and paradox must be located in the proper place. Paying heed to the admonitions does not, in fact, threaten assurance but is the pathway by which assurance is maintained.

What if someone were to reply that this is no assurance at all, that the only assurance that counts is ours regardless of our response to the warnings of Scripture? Such a view is guilty of the very abstraction that must be avoided. Desiring assurance without availing oneself of the means by which assurance is maintained is analogous to wanting a banana split without the ice cream. In actuality, such people do not really want a banana split, since they have a dislike for ice cream. They are like Rosie Ruiz, who in 1980 wanted to wear the victor's wreath in the Boston Marathon without running the whole course. Her glory quickly faded to disgrace when officials discovered that she cheated.[60] Similarly, those who desire assurance but reject the means by which assurance is maintained call into question whether they really want assurance, since they have separated assurance from the means by which it is preserved. The Grace Evangelical Society fails to grasp the distinctions we are introducing, and hence

---

[59]Ibid., p. 121.
[60]See the official Boston Marathon webpage at < www.baa.org/index2.htm >.

they merge the view proposed by us and Berkouwer with the popular retrospective view and the introspective Puritan view.[61]

A personal example from one of us (you can guess which one!) may help readers grasp the connection between admonitions and assurance. When I hear the threats and warnings of Scripture, I take them seriously. That is, when I read Hebrews 6 I realize that this is a word directed to me. If I apostatize, I will be cursed and experience the fierce wrath of God eternally. I tremble at such a prospect, and I say to myself, "I do not want to suffer such a punishment. I want to live with God forever." This warning reminds me that life's choices are serious. It reminds me that I must persevere in the faith to be saved. I pray, "Lord, give me the desire and strength to continue on the journey of faith." I find that the warning provokes me to follow the Lord more ardently. It snaps me out of my slumber and incites me afresh to love and good works. The net result, therefore, is that my assurance is strengthened because I see by my response to the warning that I am truly part of the church of Christ.

What About Those Who Have Lapsed?

People often ask us about the status of those who have made a profession of faith, whether in childhood or later, and who have then lapsed from the faith, or perhaps their lives ended with some dramatic sin. Those who have "fallen away" now give little indication of whether they are part of the people of God and will inherit final salvation. Often what people want to hear is that such loved ones or friends are saved despite their life to the contrary. Or people will relate the story of the sin of such people, then say, "But, of course, they are Christians." Our perspective on this situation is quite different. We do not believe it is our role to say one way or the other whether a lapsed brother or sister is saved![62] Notice first of all that the way that the issue is posed restricts salvation entirely to the past, but we have already seen that salvation is also something to be inherited at the

---

[61] See < www.faithalone.org/news/y1999/99mar1.html > .

[62] Charles C. Ryrie falls into this trap. He agrees that believers are imperfect and then extends the argument from there, asking "how much" believers can sin and still be saved. He implies that we can sin to a considerable extent and still belong to the people of God (*So Great Salvation: What It Means to Believe in Jesus Christ* [Wheaton, Ill.: Victor, 1989], p. 48). But the very attempt to provide assurance to those who are straying is misguided, nor is it our role to pronounce definitively on those who are straying.

last day. Thus, to conceive of salvation exclusively in the past is to confine the biblical evidence only to the one dimension of the scriptural witness. In any case, we are scarcely in the position to declare definitively whether someone who has by all appearances lapsed will enter the kingdom of God.

We certainly believe that some Christians for a lesser or greater period of time take backward steps. Our task in such situations is not to utter a declaration about the final destiny of such people. Who are we to play God and utter such definitive judgments? We should bring to bear the teachings of the Scriptures and simply say, "If you keep his commandments, you will be saved." Or, "If you repent and turn, you will be spared from God's wrath." James 5:19-20 confirms what we are saying here: "My brothers and sisters, if anyone among you wanders from the truth and is brought back by another, you should know that whoever brings back a sinner from wandering will save the sinner's soul from death and will cover a multitude of sins" (NRSV). Notice that James does not pronounce a negative judgment on those who have strayed from the truth. He urges fellow believers to make every effort to restore them. Therefore, we should not fall into the trap of making a static and timeless pronouncement about their status before God. We challenge them with the exhortations of the Scriptures. The Scriptures call on those who are wandering to repent and to turn again in order to be saved! Such an admonition does not necessarily lead to the conclusion that these people were not saved before! The admonition, however, is directed to where a person is now in his or her walk with the Lord. We are not privileged with a bird's-eye view of the lives of others. We merely state what the Scriptures teach, and the Scriptures themselves exhort all those who are wandering to return to the Lord and to slough off all that is holding them back from him. How tempting it is to play God in these situations and to make a pronouncement about other people's destinies. But we do not know what their destiny is as lapsed ones, because we do not know how they will respond to the admonition.

But if the above is true, then is assurance not a charade? Do we not lose assurance whenever we wander from the Lord? Once again the danger of abstracting biblical teachings out of their context is great. Assurance is integral to faith, and it is strengthened as one walks in the light. But no assurance is granted to those who turn their backs on the Lord. There is no warrant for assurance if sin is dominant in our lives. We maintain our assurance by continuing to run in the race. Those who desire assurance while they are turning away from the Lord are like runners who quit running in the middle of the race but inquire of the official if they will still receive a prize for running! The official replies, "You cannot receive the prize without continuing in the race!" Assurance is not an abstract entity that is ours regardless of what we do. That would contradict a massive amount of biblical teaching. No, our assurance in the faith is strengthened as we continue to run the race, persevering until the end to receive the prize.

8

RUNNING BY DIVINE APPOINTMENT

Who Are Those Who Run to the End & Win?

Therefore, brothers and sisters, be all the more eager to confirm
your call and election, for if you do this, you will never stumble.
For in this way, entry into the eternal kingdom of our Lord
and Savior Jesus Christ will be richly provided for you. (2 Pet 1:10-11 NRSV)

Throughout this book we have maintained that we must run to win the prize of eschatological salvation. Those who give up in the race will not inherit the kingdom of God. Some object to the thesis we advance by claiming that it smacks of works-righteousness. We reply that our conception of the race is no different from that of the author of Hebrews, who exhorts the readers not to "throw away your confidence" since "it will be richly rewarded" (Heb 10:35). The author then says, "You need to persevere in order that when you have done the will of God, you will receive what he has promised" (Heb 10:36). What is the reward and the promise that is placed before the readers here? The reward is given when Jesus comes to those who live by faith and do not shrink back from their confession (Heb 10:38-39). Hebrews 10:39 clarifies that the reward is eternal life: "But we are not of those who shrink back and are destroyed, but of those who believe and are saved" (NIV). The word used for *destroyed* (*apōleia*) is consistently used in the Scriptures to designate eschatological destruction and what happens to unbelievers at the last judgment. Thus, the author summons the readers to belief unto final salvation. If they quit the race at this juncture, they will not be saved.

What is most striking here is that continuing in the race is portrayed by the author of Hebrews as the result of faith. The famous "heroes of faith" chapter (Heb 11) follows immediately on the words of exhortation we have just examined, encouraging readers to have the same kind of faith as the men and women of faith who preceded them. Since the author of Hebrews forges a link between faith and perseverance, it is utterly fallacious to describe such perseverance as works-righteousness. The author of Hebrews conceives of running the race to the end as a pursuit of faith. After portraying in chapter 11 the dynamic and persevering faith of those who preceded us, the author uses the illustration of a race to encourage the Hebrews to continue on their journey: "Therefore, since we are surrounded by such a great cloud of witnesses, let us throw off everything that hinders and the sin that so easily entangles, and let us run with perseverance the race marked out for us. Let us fix our eyes on Jesus, the author and perfecter of our faith, who for the joy set before him endured the cross, scorning its shame, and sat down at the right hand of the throne of God" (Heb 12:1-2 NIV). We are justified in portraying the journey of faith as a marathon race, for the writer of Hebrews thinks of the Christian life as a race in which perseverance is needed. Indeed, in the succeeding verses (Heb 12:3-11) the writer teaches that the Christian life is comparable to the discipline that children receive from their fathers. Such discipline and training is not pleasant but produces the righteousness and holiness without which "no one will see the Lord" (Heb 12:14). Since the writer portrays the Christian life as a race needing gutsy endurance and a training ground in which discipline is meted out, we are correct in saying that obtaining the eschatological prize takes ardent effort. There is no call to passivity here! In order to run the race and fight the fight of faith, we must "strengthen feeble arms and weak knees" (Heb 12:12). The race will not be won without the most rigorous training, nor will we complete it without a fierce resolve to shed all that hinders us.

The pronounced emphasis on human exertion and determination could easily lead us to the conclusion that finishing the race is our work. But we have already observed that the call to perseverance sandwiches the famous chapter on faith (Heb 11). It never entered the mind of the author of Hebrews that the call for endurance to inherit salvation contradicted the idea that salvation is by faith. Indeed, in the very verses that summon us to run the race with perseverance, we are reminded that Jesus is "the author and perfecter of our faith" (Heb 12:2). With these words the biblical tension between divine sovereignty and human freedom leaps to center stage. We must run the race with dogged determination to obtain the prize of eternal life, and it takes remarkable discipline and training to make it to the end. We are keenly conscious of the faith that is needed to accomplish such things. Nonetheless, the author of Hebrews reminds us that Jesus is "the author and perfecter of our faith." The word *author (archēgos)* means that Jesus is the "originator" or "founder" of our faith.[1] In other words, our faith is the gift of God. Not only does our faith come from him, but he also sustains our faith; he is also the "perfecter" or the one who completes our faith.[2] Saying that we must run the race to the end can scarcely be called works-righteousness, since such persevering faith is ultimately the gift of God! As G. C. Berkouwer says, "Faith knows that of itself it does not produce salvation and abiding in Christ."[3]

Running the race can be exhausting, and we may grow tired and worn out, yet Isaiah also teaches us that God gives us strength to go on: "He gives strength to the weary and increases the power of the weak. Even youths grow tired and weary, and young men stumble and fall; but those who hope in the LORD will renew their strength. They will soar on wings like eagles; they will run and not grow weary, they will walk and not be faint" (Is 40:29-31 NIV). Ultimately our ability to keep running the race comes from the Lord. At the end of the day, he is the one who renews our strength and grants us the grace to soar and run and walk. To be faithful to Scripture we must preserve the biblical tension between our responsibility to exercise faith and run the race, and the truth that any faith and work we have is a gift of God. If we exclude our role as human beings, we encourage a passivity and a laxity that is contrary to the biblical calls to exertion and effort that we have been

---

[1]See Donald A. Hagner, *Hebrews* (New York: Harper & Row, 1983), p. 195.

[2]Against the view of I. Howard Marshall, *Kept by the Power of God: A Study of Perseverance and Falling Away* (1969; reprint, Minneapolis: Bethany Fellowship, 1974), p. 149; Grant R. Osborne, "Soteriology in the Epistle to the Hebrews," in *Grace Unlimited*, ed. Clark Pinnock (Minneapolis: Bethany Fellowship, 1975), p. 157.

[3]G. C. Berkouwer, *Faith and Perseverance*, trans. Robert D. Knudsen (Grand Rapids, Mich.: Eerdmans, 1958), p. 202.

investigating. On the other hand, if we rule out the idea that God is ultimately the one behind our believing and working, we introduce the
idea that salvation is ultimately and finally our work. Both ideas must
be firmly rejected. We are the ones who exercise faith and run the race,
yet when we ask ourselves, "How does this become a reality in our
lives?" the answer is that we believe and continue running the race
because God's grace has grasped us and propels us to go forward. His
work in our lives is the foundation for our work and faith.

The idea we are trying to communicate is captured nicely by Paul
in Philippians 2:12-13: "Therefore, my beloved, just as you have
always obeyed me, not only in my presence, but much more now in
my absence, bring to accomplishment your own salvation with fear
and trembling; for it is God who is at work in you, enabling you both
to will and to work for his good pleasure." Paul calls on the Philippians to work out their salvation. Note that he does not say, "You are
saved. Now work for your reward, which is in addition to salvation."
He summons the Philippians to bring to accomplishment their salvation! Effort, toil and energy are all communicated in this phrase. We
are to use all the resources at our disposal in order to be saved on the
last day. We must obey, pray, resist the flesh and yield to the Spirit to
inherit salvation. No theology is acceptable that diminishes this call to
work out our salvation. Many "evangelicals" immediately and reflex-
ively reject such a translation as promoting works-righteousness.
Such a judgment makes them "more Pauline" than Paul! Actually,
they are a lot less Pauline than Paul, for Paul consistently, as we have
seen throughout this book, considers good works as necessary to
enter the kingdom of God. Zane Hodges escapes this exegesis by arguing that salvation is not soteriological here.[4] His whole enterprise is
quite precarious because, according to Hodges, if the text connects
salvation to good works, then salvation cannot be soteriological. This
seems to be an example of a "can't lose" exegesis. It calls into question
Hodges's repeated claim that he takes the text at face value. On the
contrary, he introduces an overlay into virtually every text he handles. If the text speaks of good works being necessary for believers,
then no matter what term is used—"eternal life," "salvation," "king-

---

[4]Zane C. Hodges, *The Gospel Under Siege: A Study on Faith and Works,* 2nd ed. (Dallas:
Rendención Viva, 1991), pp. 96-101.

dom of heaven" and the like—the text cannot be soteriological.

What is truly remarkable about this pair of verses is the tension between our work and God's. We must accomplish our salvation, yet in the last and final analysis any work we do is the result of God's work in us. He is the one who enables us to do such good works. At the end of the day, any work that is pleasing to him stems from his empowering in our lives. Ultimately, our good works come from his good work in us. It is even more remarkable than this. Even the desire to do good works comes from God. We all know how difficult it is to have a desire for something we find distasteful. If we dislike broccoli, red beets or squash, we lack any desire to eat them. Similarly, if we lack the inclination or desire to love and obey God, how can such a desire be produced in us? This text tells us that God, in his grace, gives us the desire to do his will. It is a miracle of grace that we find in us a desire and an aptitude to do his will. Moreover, the desire does not fail just before the action is carried out. God also grants the ability to put the desire into action. We receive both the desire and the ability to keep his commands. Ultimately, then, the ability and desire to accomplish our salvation stems from God himself. As Philippians 1:6 says, God has begun his good work in us, and he will complete what he has started. But one can never appeal to this teaching to cancel out the call to work out one's salvation. One of us knows of a person who kept having sexual relations outside marriage; his excuse was, "God in his grace has not given me the desire to obey him. It would be legalistic of me to keep his commands without the desire." This is a prime example of going beyond the biblical tension. We are called on to work, to obey and to exert our energy. The biblical writers inform us, however, that the work and desiring that we do on God's behalf finally and ultimately come from him.

The same tension existing between our work and God's work is found in the area of faith. We know from many texts of Scripture that God calls on us to believe and trust him. Trusting God is something we do. We make a decision to place our faith and trust in God. We have emphasized human responsibility throughout this book. Here we wish to consider the other pole of God's work in us, for the Scriptures also teach that faith is God's gift. We believe, yet at the same time faith is the gift of God. That faith is the gift of God is borne out by Ephesians 2:8: "For it is by grace you have been saved, through faith—and this not from yourselves, it is the gift of God" (NIV). Paul teaches that the salvation we have experienced is not from ourselves but is God's gift. Does the gift of God include faith as well? Some would reply that faith is what we do. Of course, we exercise faith when we believe, for faith is a human decision. But the question needs to be posed more precisely. Is our faith a gift of God and not from ourselves? That is, ultimately, do we exercise faith because God has imparted to us the ability to believe? Some maintain that the only thing that is the gift of God in this verse is salvation. Faith, they contend, is what we contribute to salvation. The argument centers on the word *this (touto)* in Ephesians 2:8. The word *this* in the Greek text is a neuter pronoun, but the word *faith* is a feminine noun. Some latch on to the disparity between the genders of the two terms, claiming that Paul would have used the feminine pronoun if he were intending to teach that faith is God's gift. On first glance this argument appears impressive. When we examine the text more closely, however, its plausibility is diminished, since there is no neuter word in the text for which *this* can serve as the antecedent. The word *grace* is feminine, and the word *saved* is a masculine participle. If we insist that the word *this* must refer back to a word of the same gender, then it refers to nothing. Instead, the neuter *this* is used generally to include both salvation and faith as the gift of God. Paul uses an inclusive term so that everything mentioned in Ephesians 2:8 is conceived of as God's gift.

There are a number of passages in which Paul uses the neuter pronoun *this* to refer generally and inclusively to what has just been said (Rom 13:11; 1 Cor 6:6, 8; 7:35; 11:17; 2 Cor 1:17; Eph 5:5; Phil 1:19, 28). The closest parallel is found in Philippians 1:28, where Paul exhorts the Philippians not to be "frightened in any way by those who oppose you. This is a sign to them that they will be destroyed, but that you will be saved—and that by God" (NIV). The word *this* here is the same neuter pronoun in Greek that is translated "this" in Ephesians 2:8. The last phrase of Philippians 1:28 literally says in Greek, "and this from God." Moisés Silva rightly says about this phrase that it "probably does not refer exclusively to the word *sōteria* . . . but rather to the whole complex of ideas: conflict, destruction, perseverance, and salvation."[5] Likewise,

---

[5] Moisés Silva, *Philippians*, Baker Exegetical Commentary (Grand Rapids, Mich.: Baker, 1988), p. 93.

in Ephesians 2:8 both salvation and faith are a gift of God.

It is no small matter to maintain the tension between faith being God's gift and our responsibility to believe. If we deny the latter, then we encourage an unhealthy passivity and laxity. We may also end up teaching that it does not matter what we do, since all things come from God. On the other hand, if we ignore the truth that faith is God's gift, we may be inclined to boast that we have had the courage and wisdom to exercise faith. It is no accident that after Paul says that salvation and faith are God's gift of grace in Ephesians 2:8, he communicates God's intention in granting us these gifts. Salvation is "not by works, so that no one can boast" (Eph 2:9). If we are ultimately responsible for our faith, then we can brag about our decision to believe. Paul never doubts that we believed, but he looks further back and sees that our faith was due to God's gracious work in our lives. Similarly, in Philippians 1:29 faith is God's gift that has been bestowed on us in his grace. In other words, we run the race of faith by divine appointment; we run because God's gift of grace has invaded our lives.

We have contended in this work that we must confirm our calling and election to enter the eternal kingdom (2 Pet 1:10-11). Peter summons his readers to a tenacious diligence in pursuing godly virtues (2 Pet 1:5-7). Neither Peter nor any other biblical writer believes entrance into the eternal kingdom is obtained apart from good works. Without holiness we shall not see the Lord (Heb 12:14). Biblical writers exhort us consistently to live devoted and holy lives and teach that this is necessary for eternal life. Yet standing behind our diligent pursuit of godliness and holiness is God's predestinating work, his election of us and his call unto salvation.

Running the Race and Election

The foundational character of God's electing and predestinating work must be understood to grasp rightly the relationship between God's work and ours. One of the central texts on election is Ephesians 1:4-6: "For he chose us in him before the creation of the world to be holy and blameless in his sight. In love he predestined us to be adopted as his sons through Jesus Christ, in accordance with his pleasure and will—to the praise of his glorious grace, which he has freely given us in the One he loves" (NIV). Seven observations can be made from these verses. First, "he chose us," that is, God is the one who did the choosing. When teaching on this passage, I have often asked students what Paul means when he says "he chose us."[6] Sometimes students will essentially say that the point of these verses is that "we chose God." Now, is that not curious? The verses do not say that we chose God but that he chose us. We have a tendency to reinterpret verses so that they harmonize with our worldview in which human choice is ultimate. This text informs us that God's choice is the final determination of our salvation. He set his love on us and selected us to be his children.

Second, the choosing occurred "before the creation of the world." Some think this simply means that God saw beforehand who would choose him. But Paul's discussion of the election of Jacob rather than Esau in Romans 9:11-12 makes it plain that this is not what he means.[7] He says there, "Yet, before the twins were born or had done anything good or bad—in order that God's purpose in election might stand: not by works but by him who calls—she was told, 'The older will serve the younger.' " God chooses before people are born and before they have done any works, whether good or bad, to make it clear that his choice is not based on simply foreseeing the good they will do. He chooses before birth and before any works are done so that his "purpose in election might stand" so that it might be clear that those who are saved are saved only by virtue of God's choice, not by virtue of any good they have done or will do.

Third, Paul says that we were chosen "in him," which means that we are chosen in Christ. Paul is not suggesting here that God only chose Christ and then all those who choose Christ are saved. He does not say that God chose Christ but that he chose us "in" Christ, that is, through the work of Christ.[8] When God planned our salvation, he planned that it would only be effected through the work of Jesus Christ on the cross. In any case, 1 Corinthians 1:30 makes it clear that

---

[6]This is the experience of one of the authors; hence the first-person singular *I*.

[7]For a more technical discussion of Romans 9 and election, see Thomas R. Schreiner, "Does Romans 9 Teach Individual Election unto Salvation?" in *Still Sovereign: Contemporary Perspectives on Election, Foreknowledge, and Grace*, ed. Thomas R. Schreiner and Bruce A. Ware (Grand Rapids, Mich.: Baker, 2000), pp. 89-106.

[8]Rightly, Paul K. Jewett, *Election and Predestination* (Grand Rapids, Mich.: Eerdmans, 1985), p. 73. For a critique of Karl Barth's particular view of election in Christ see pp. 48-56.

we are "in Christ" only because of God's work in our lives, not because of our own independent choice: "It is because *of him* that you are in Christ Jesus, who has become for us wisdom from God—that is, our righteousness, holiness and redemption" (NIV, italics added). The key words here are "of him," which in Greek can be rendered literally either "of him" or "from him." We are not in Christ because of our own initiative but by virtue of God's work in our lives. In other words, we do choose to be in Christ, but we only make this choice because God has effectively worked in our lives so that we desire to make this choice.

Fourth, God chose us "to be holy and blameless in his sight" (Eph 1:4). The salvation that God has planned for us includes holiness. We have contended throughout this book that final salvation is inseparable from the experience of holiness and righteousness. What this text emphasizes is that such holiness is the result of God's choice of us, and thus the ultimate reason for our holiness is God's glorious grace (Eph 1:6). A comparable text is Ephesians 2:10, which states that we are "created in Christ Jesus to do good works, which God prepared in advance for us to do" (NIV). This text is radically misinterpreted if we read it as a call or exhortation to do good works. Of course, exhortations to do good works abound in the New Testament. Here, however, Paul concentrates on what God has done to secure our holiness. Just as he created light where there was darkness on the first day of creation (cf. 2 Cor 4:6), so too he has transformed us by his creative power, and he has ordained that certain good works will become a reality in our lives. It would be a travesty to use this verse to cancel out the many exhortations to practice godliness, yet we must also pay heed to the distinctive teaching of this text. God has prepared in advance the good works that we will inevitably do, and thus we are reminded that any good works we do are the fruit of his grace.

Fifth, the means by which God elected us is described in terms of predestination. The word *predestined* in Ephesians 1:5 is actually a participle that modifies the main verb *chose* in verse 4. This means that predestined further elaborates what is involved in choosing. The idea is quite similar to what we have already seen. God planned and ordained in advance the salvation of believers.

Sixth, that the salvation of believers is in mind is clear from the rest of Ephesians 1:5: "He predestined us to be adopted as his sons through Jesus Christ" (NIV). Adoption as sons is nothing less than induction into the family of God. If someone were to say from verse 4 that God only chose us for sanctification and not for salvation, this mistake is corrected in verse 5. God chose us to be adopted into his family as his children. We must also observe, however, that the common distinction between sanctification and salvation limits salvation to the past and ignores its future dimension. Both salvation and sanctification, as we argued in chapter two, fall under the rubric of the already but not yet, and thus sharp distinctions between the two should be avoided.

Finally, why did God choose us? So that we could have intellectual arguments about whether the doctrine of predestination is true? Surely the doctrine of election raises many questions, but the reason Paul wrote about it is so that we would "praise . . . the glory of his grace" (Eph 1:6 NASB), and so we would say, "Praise be to the God and Father of our Lord Jesus Christ" (Eph 1:3 NIV). Paul wrote this because he wanted us to feel what a glorious and merciful thing it is to be chosen by God. How we should praise and thank him for extending his mercy toward us! God gets all the glory, for salvation is wholly his work. Even our choosing of him is due to his choosing us. We, on the other hand, are filled with gladness and happiness because we experience the wonder of salvation that was given to us undeserving sinners.

Another crucial passage in Paul's theology of election is 1 Corinthians 1:26-31. We need to cite the entire passage:

> Consider your own call, brothers and sisters: not many of you were wise by human standards, not many were powerful, not many were of noble birth. But God chose what is foolish in the world to shame the wise; God chose what is weak in the world to shame the strong; God chose what is low and despised in the world, things that are not, to reduce to nothing things that are, so that no one might boast in the presence of God. He is the source of your life in Christ Jesus, who became for us wisdom from God, and righteousness and sanctification and redemption, in order that, as it is written, "Let the one who boasts, boast in the Lord." (NRSV)

One of the crucial words in this text is the word *called.* Calling (or "called") is not the same as preaching and inviting people to be saved, as 1 Corinthians 1:23-24 demonstrates. There Paul says, "We preach

Christ crucified: a stumbling block to Jews and foolishness to Gentiles, but to those whom God has called, both Jews and Greeks, Christ the power of God and the wisdom of God" (NIV). The preaching of the gospel is extended to all, Jews and Greeks, and some reject the preaching of the cross as a stumbling block or as foolishness. But those who are called accept the message and believe, finding Christ to be the power and wisdom of God. It is clear here that calling and preaching should be distinguished. Paul is not saying that he only invited and called some to believe when he preached. All heard the proclamation and were invited to believe, but only some of those who heard the gospel were called by God, that is, chosen by him.

Verses 26-28 are further evidence that calling refers to God's choice. Paul exhorts the Corinthians to consider their calling, but what is it about their calling that he wants them to consider? Namely, that God chose the foolish, weak and despised of the world. The calling is defined three times in terms of God's choice: "God chose the foolish" (v. 27), "God chose the weak" (v. 27), and "God chose the things that are not" (v. 28). Indeed, calling in Paul often refers to God's sovereign work of choosing someone, which is effected through the preaching of the gospel (cf. e.g., Rom 8:30; 9:7, 12, 24, 25; 1 Cor 1:9; Gal 1:6, 15; 1 Thess 2:12; 5:24; 2 Thess 2:14; 1 Tim 6:12; 2 Tim 1:9). Typically, God does not choose the intellectuals, the strong and the social elite. Why? Paul says in 1 Corinthians 1:29 so that "no one might boast before" God. Intellectuals and the politically powerful are liable to see themselves as people worthy of salvation. The root problem with intellectuals, those who have strength and physical ability, and the social elite is self-worship. God usually chooses those who are considered foolish and weak by the standards of the world to drive home the point that "it is because of him that you are in Christ Jesus" (1 Cor 1:30). Salvation is a gift. It is undeserved. Our wisdom, righteousness, redemption and sanctification are all gifts from God through Christ Jesus. In other words, God chose us so that we will "boast in the Lord" (1 Cor 1:31) and give him the glory and praise for what he has accomplished in our lives.

The last passage in Paul in which we will consider divine election is Romans 8:28-30 (NIV).[9]

---

[9]There are, of course, many others we could consult. See, e.g., Romans 9:1-29; 1 Thessalonians 5:9; 2 Thessalonians 2:13-14; 2 Timothy 1:9; 2:25; Titus 3:5.

We know that in all things God works for the good of those who love him, who have been called according to his purpose. For those God foreknew he also predestined to be conformed to the likeness of his Son, that he might be the firstborn among many brothers. And those he predestined, he also called; those he called, he also justified; those he justified, he also glorified.

Believers rightly prize the promise that all things work together for good, but it is imperative that we see the foundation on which this promise is based. The "for" beginning verse 29 indicates that verses 29-30 are the foundation for the great promise given in verse 28. It should be said, incidentally, that the good that is effected does not mean that God has promised believers a comfortable life without suffering. The good of verse 28 is further explained in verse 29 as being "conformed to the likeness of his Son." God uses every circumstance in our lives to make us more like his Son, Jesus Christ.

How do we know, though, that God will use every circumstance of our lives to make us become more like Jesus Christ? Romans 8:29-30 explain that God has planned the whole course of our salvation from eternity past to our future glorification. The salient parts of these verses should make this point plain. Verse 29 says that "those God foreknew he also predestined to be conformed to the likeness of his Son." Although the word *foreknew* in the New Testament on two occasions refers to knowing what will occur in the future (Acts 26:5; 2 Pet 3:17), when it refers to God's work the idea of foreordination is also included. This means that God has planned and determined beforehand what will occur. For example, Acts 2:23 says of Jesus' death that he was "delivered up by the predetermined plan and foreknowledge of God" (NASB). The word *foreknowledge* here is basically synonymous with the words *predetermined plan.* God did not merely "foresee" when Jesus would come to die for the sins of the world; he planned in advance that he would do so. Incidentally, this verse is also helpful in terms of explaining the relationship between predestination and human responsibility. If God predestined that Jesus would die on the cross, then how could the people who killed him be responsible for killing him? Many people would say that if God has determined that something will happen and it includes evil, then those who do the evil are not responsible for their actions. This seems to be a sensible objection, but it does not conform to how the biblical writers think about reality. Of course, Peter does not provide a philosophical solution to this problem. He simply affirms in the same verse that both God's sovereignty and human responsibility are true. God determined in advance that Jesus would die, and those who killed him were responsible for carrying out this wicked deed. Jesus, he says, was "nailed to a cross by the hands of godless men" (Acts 2:23 NASB). The implication follows that Peter holds them responsible for this evil deed, even though it was preplanned by God. It is, therefore, biblically false to say that if God predestined something to happen, those who carry out the deed cannot be responsible for the evil inflicted. If that is true, then those who killed Jesus would have been innocent of wrongdoing!

Returning to the subject of foreknowledge, another verse that helps us to define *foreknow* is Romans 11:2: "God did not reject his people, whom he foreknew" (NIV). The word *foreknew* here functions as the antonym to the word *reject*. What word would have the opposite meaning of the verb *reject*? A verb that means "elect" or "select." We could rephrase the verse this way: "God has not rejected his people whom he elected to be his own." This understanding of God's special saving knowledge of his people is supported by the Hebrew word for "know." For example, Amos 3:2 says of Israel, "You only have I known of all the families of the earth; therefore I will punish you for all your iniquities" (NRSV). Obviously God knew about all the other peoples on the earth. The verse is not saying that God is unaware of their existence. The point is that God has known Israel in a special way; he has chosen them to be his people. God's foreknowledge of his people means that they are the recipients of his special covenantal affection and love.[10]

Jeremiah 1:5 buttresses our conclusion in a passage in which God describes the call of Jeremiah: "Before I formed you in the womb I knew you, before you were born I set you apart; I appointed you as a prophet to the nations" (NIV). Again, the word *knew* here does not merely mean that God foresaw that Jeremiah would exist. It means that God had chosen Jeremiah to be a prophet even before he was

---

[10]Supporting this understanding of foreknowledge is S. M. Baugh, "The Meaning of Foreknowledge," in *Still Sovereign: Contemporary Perspectives on Election, Foreknowledge, and Grace*, ed. Thomas R. Schreiner and Bruce A. Ware (Grand Rapids, Mich.: Baker, 2000), pp. 183-200.

born. This understanding of *knew* is borne out by the Hebrew parallelism in this verse, for the two terms that are roughly synonymous
with *knew* are *set apart* and *appointed*. All three refer to God's choice
of Jeremiah as a prophet. He chose him, set him apart to be his own
and determined that he would be a prophet.

The last example of the word *foreknow* is from 1 Peter 1:20, where
Peter says that Christ "was foreknown before the foundation of the
world" (NASB). This cannot mean that God simply foresaw when
Christ would come. Since Christ is part of the Godhead, it had to be
planned by the Godhead when he would come into the world and
make atonement for sin. Rendering the word *foreknown* as "chose"
(NIV) is not satisfying, for then God's relationship of love with the Son
is omitted; thus, *foreknown* is more fitting than *elected* or *chose*.

To return to Romans 8:29, when Paul says "those God foreknew,"
he is speaking of God's choice to know believers in an intimate and
saving way. He has set his covenantal and saving affection on us. The
word *those* shows that he is not referring to all people but only some.
God has not set his covenantal affection on all people without exception. His saving choice is bestowed on those whom he has called.
Romans 8:30 says that "those he predestined, he also called." Previously we argued that calling in Paul refers to God's effectual and per-
suasive work in a person's heart that inevitably leads one to be saved.
What distinguishes calling from predestination is that calling occurs
in history. The preordained plan of God is carried out in history
through calling, and this calling operates through the preaching of the
gospel. The next phrase, "those he called, he also justified," confirms
that the calling is an effectual one, for all those who are called are justified. We know that not all people are justified, and we know that
people cannot be justified apart from faith (Rom 5:1). It follows, then,
that not all people are called and that calling creates faith in the
hearts of God's people. Only those who are called are justified, and all
those who are called are justified.

That our triumphing in the race is by divine appointment is supported by the last phrase in Romans 8:30: "those he justified, he also
glorified." The glorification of believers refers to our future perfection
in heaven, when we will be "conformed to the likeness of his Son"
(Rom 8:29). The past tense of the verb *glorified* is used because Paul
views the process from God's perspective. From God's perspective the

process is as good as done. Those who are righteous in God's sight will be glorified. Note that this is true of all those who are justified. There are no exceptions. God will see to it that those whom he has fore-known, predestined, called and justified will be glorified. God will give believers the strength to persevere to the end. No true believer will ever be separated from the love of Christ, as Romans 8:31-39 testi-fies. Some Christians love to teach that believers will never lose their salvation but shy away from teaching that God elects only some to salvation. These verses in Romans show that the two teachings are inseparably connected. You cannot have one without the other. The only reason believers can be assured that they will be glorified is because they have been chosen by God.

We should not miss the main point of this teaching on divine elec-tion. God chooses us as a testimony to his grace, and it is by his grace and power that we are sustained to run the race before us. Nonethe-less, the doctrine of election naturally disturbs many people because it causes them to question God's love and justice. We cannot deal with such questions in any depth here,[11] but several comments can be made in this regard. Most of us instinctively think that God is obli-gated to save people. When we remember that God could justly con-demn all to hell, then we realize that it is merciful that he saves any at all. In the United States, rights have become so prominent that it is tempting to think that we have a right to be saved. Such a conception minimizes sin and is human idolatry at its worst. Scripture clearly asserts that those who are destined for hell deserve to be sent there because of their sin and that God is utterly just in consigning them to hell. Hell is a horrible reality to contemplate, but we ought not to retract the teaching because of our own sensitivity. Hell testifies to the infinite heinousness of sinning against God's glory. Any sin against God is of infinite proportions because of his infinite majesty. Since he is infinitely glorious, the punishment is infinite in its extent.

In addition, Scripture teaches that God is absolutely sovereign and human beings are responsible. Many people today focus on human responsibility to the extent that human free will cancels out divine sovereignty. The problem with this approach is that it compromises

---

[11] For a helpful nontechnical treatment, see D. A. Carson, *How Long, O Lord? Reflections on Suffering and Evil* (Grand Rapids, Mich.: Baker, 1990).

the many verses in Scripture that teach divine sovereignty. Instead, we should acknowledge that God is completely sovereign and human beings are responsible (cf. Acts 2:23; 4:27-28). Much can be said to account for how these two relate to one another,[12] but ultimately and finally we must acknowledge that how both of these can be true is a mystery to us. We do not fully understand how absolute divine sovereignty and human responsibility can both be true. Scripture teaches that they are, and we rest in that fact. It is hardly astonishing that since God is God and we are finite human beings, some truths are beyond our comprehension. In a similar way, the doctrine of the Trinity (three persons and one God) and the two natures of Christ (fully human and fully divine) are beyond our comprehension. Asking questions is legitimate and stimulates learning, but there are some questions to which we do not know the answers.[13] God has made known to us the teaching on election so that we would praise him and thank him for choosing us and so that our hearts would be humbled, knowing that he has done all. He is worthy of all the glory for choosing us, and we tremble at the mercy of being chosen because we are so keenly conscious of being undeserving.

Therefore, biblically speaking, we are wrong to conceive of God's election as excluding anyone. One can only think that divine election excludes people if one fails to recognize that Scripture presents election as God's choice of humans to whom he intended to be gracious and to save from sin and death. Far from excluding humans from God's grace, his election is an act of inclusion, for unless God took the initiative to set his love on us, we never would have believed and we would not persevere in Christ Jesus. God chose us even before he created anything (Eph 1:4). While the apostle Paul speaks of God's choosing with the verbs *elect* and *foreknow*, John expresses the same truth by using the verb *love.* God's choosing us is his gracious and saving love, for John says, "We love because he first loved us" (1 Jn 4:19 NIV). This verse reiterates what John says earlier: "This is love: not that we loved God, but that he loved us and sent his Son as an atoning sacri-

---

[12]See, e.g., Jonathan Edwards, *The Freedom of the Will*, ed. Paul Ramsey (New Haven, Conn.: Yale University Press, 1957).

[13]But we do not want to deny that some answers can be given. For a contemporary defense of the doctrines of grace, see Thomas R. Schreiner and Bruce A. Ware, eds., *Still Sovereign: Contemporary Perspectives on Election, Foreknowledge, and Grace* (Grand Rapids, Mich.: Baker, 2000).

fice for our sins. Dear friends, since God so loved us, we also ought to love one another" (1 Jn 4:10-11 NIV). The apostle John grounds this line of reasoning on the fact that "God is love" (1 Jn 4:8, 16).

The Bible portrays God's love with distinguishable aspects.[14] Here we are particularly concerned with the biblical portrayal of God's unconditional love of election and his conditional love of saving provision for his people. It is not only vital that we maintain equilibrium between these aspects of God's love; it is also crucial that we not confound the biblical portrait of God's love. Imbalance will lead to disastrous effects pastorally. Confusion will undercut the glory of the gospel of God's grace. Evangelicals tend to invert these two aspects of God's love. Precisely where the Bible affirms that God's love is unconditional, evangelicals tend to regard his love as conditional. Also, where the Bible indicates God's love is conditional, many evangelicals conceive of his love as unconditional. This seems like a riddle. Let's sort it out briefly.

First, when Scripture says that God chose us in Christ, many insist that God chose us on the basis of some condition found in us, such as "God foreknew that we would believe." This conditions God's election of us on something in us. We already showed how this is a misreading of Romans 8:29, for it is persons whom God foreknew, that is, set his love on in advance. It is not something about us that God foreknew or attracted him to choose us. Rather, God chose us by setting his covenant affection on us without anything in us to prompt his choice (Rom 9:11-12). God elected us—he loved us—unconditionally. There was nothing lovely in us for him to love.

Second, the gospel announces God's saving love to all who receive the Son. The gospel plainly expresses conditions in order that we may receive God's saving love. John 3:16 comes to mind: "For God loved

---

[14]D. A. Carson outlines five distinguishable ways the Bible depicts God's love: (1) the unique love the persons of the Trinity have for one another, such as the Father's love for the Son and the Son's love for the Father (Jn 3:35; 5:20); (2) God's providential love and care over all his creation (he watches over even a sparrow; see Mt 10:29); (3) God's benevolent saving posture toward his fallen world (Jn 3:16); (4) God's love that marked out whom he purposed to save (Eph 5:25); (5) God's love that he expresses provisionally or conditionally toward his people—a love requiring obedience from its recipients (Jude 21) ("On Distorting the Love of God," *Bibliotheca Sacra* 156 [1999]: 3-12, esp. pp. 7-10). See also his other essays in *Bibliotheca Sacra* 156 (1999): "God Is Love," pp. 131-42; "God's Love and God's Sovereignty," pp. 259-71; "God's Love and God's Wrath," pp. 387-98.

the world in this manner so that he gave his only Son, in order that everyone who believes in him may not perish but have eternal life." God's saving love is ours if we believe in his Son. Likewise, the gospel indicates that we must persevere in God's love and kindness in order that we may be saved. Two texts readily come to mind: "Behold, therefore, God's kindness and severity—upon those who fall, severity; but upon you, God's kindness, if you continue in his kindness. Otherwise you also will be cut off" (Rom 11:22): "Keep yourselves in God's love, eagerly awaiting the mercy of our Lord Jesus Christ unto eternal life" (Jude 21). Despite these clear passages, many Christians want to affirm God's unconditional love to people who persist in sinful lifestyles without repentance.[15] Many Christians freely but wrongly hand out consolation to others living in sin, despite the fact that the Bible says that the Lord "hates the workers of iniquity" (Ps 5:5). It is in this conditional sense of God's love that we can understand a passage such as 1 Peter 5:5, which says, "God opposes the proud but gives grace to the humble" (NIV). In the sense noted above, God's love and grace are conditional.

Many find the unconditional electing love of God and of Christ repugnant, yet they properly expect this kind of love from a husband toward his wife. A husband is to love his wife unconditionally, as Christ loved the church and gave himself for her (Eph 5:25), for a husband's love is an earthly representation of Christ's elective and sacrificial love for the church. Therefore, because God has ordained marriage to be an earthly image of his electing and sacrificial love for his people, we expect a husband to love his wife with singular devotion and faithfulness. He must include only his wife in his marital affections and unwavering loyalty. Certainly, this does not mean that a husband will despise other women. Rather, he will manifest a different kind of love for other women. Such a husband is analogous to God in this respect.

Properly understood, the Bible's teaching on election and predestination is a substantial source of comfort and assurance for believers. It comforts us because the surety of our salvation, therefore, is not ultimately dependent on our faith but on God's love that he set on us

---

[15]John Piper calls this "conditional grace"; see *The Purifying Power of Living by Faith in Future Grace* (Sisters, Ore.: Multnomah, 1995), pp. 231-49. He also makes it clear that these conditions do not imply merit and that they do not contradict unconditional election.

in Christ Jesus. Election and predestination assure us that God is for us all the way. He chose us in Christ. He punished our sins in Christ. He called us to believe in Jesus Christ. He preserves us in him for the day that Christ Jesus will return for us. It is with confidence, then, that we face all the future foes to our faith, for nothing has the power to separate us from God's electing love in Christ Jesus.

Conclusion

In the final analysis, therefore, we do not pit perseverance against God's election. Rather, God's election establishes and sustains our perseverance. Without God's electing work, we would never run the race to the end. The teaching on God's election and God's prior work in our lives also demonstrates that the thesis propounded in this book cannot be dismissed as works-righteousness, for any good work we do comes from God's work in us: "We love because he first loved us" (1 Jn 4:19). Our love is a response to and the effect of his love for us. We have seen that there are many conditional texts in the Scriptures teaching that one will be saved if one perseveres in the faith, keeps God's commands or loves brothers and sisters in Christ. Many interpreters try to mute the conditional character of such texts, but we have seen that there is no warrant for doing so. On the other hand, other interpreters accept such texts as conditional but try to defend the thesis that the warnings have nothing to do with eternal life.[16] We have seen that this gambit fails as well. The passages really are conditions and really do relate to eternal life! It is precisely here that so many cry out "works-righteousness" and "legalism."

The first thing we say in response to such claims is that works-righteousness and legalism need to be defined biblically. Too many people come to the biblical text with a philosophical overlay that assumes that any conditions are contrary to the gospel. Such a view, we would contend, does not come from the Scriptures themselves, for conditions are found on virtually every page! We need to recognize that the presence of conditions for eternal life does not constitute works-righteousness or legalism. The second thing that must be pointed out, however, is that our election to salvation is unconditional. God did

---

[16]This is the mistake of Zane Hodges and his followers. For one example of Hodges making this sort of claim, see his *Gospel Under Siege,* pp. 40-41.

not elect us because he saw any good works in us, nor because he saw we would exercise faith, nor because he saw we would do good works in the future, nor because he saw that we would persevere in the faith. His election and calling produced in us faith and good works and perseverance. Thus, any idea that conditions for salvation amount to works-righteousness can be confidently waved aside. The good works we do are the work of his grace. Yet we must not nullify the biblical tension and omit the need to do good works. Similarly, one must be accurate in describing in what sense the gospel is conditional and unconditional. The exhortations to inherit salvation are conditioned upon perseverance, but our election to salvation is unconditional. In other words, we must run the marathon to the end to win the prize. We must gut it out and make it over the finish line. But those who make it over the finish line know that they have made it over the line because God has appointed them to run. He is the one who has given them the grace and energy and strength to run until the end, so he gets all the glory.

Appendix

A RESPONSE TO WILLIAM LANE CRAIG'S " 'LEST ANYONE SHOULD FALL': A MIDDLE KNOWLEDGE PERSPECTIVE ON PERSEVERANCE & APOSTOLIC WARNINGS"

I n an erudite philosophical essay[1] William Craig contends that advocates of the classical Reformed doctrine of the perseverance of the saints actually embrace a position proposed by Luis Molina.[2] Craig explains as he concludes his essay:

> To maintain that the warnings of Scripture are the means by which God guarantees the perseverance of the elect is in fact to adopt a Molinist perspective. . . . In the world He chose to actualize, believers always persevere in the faith. Perhaps the warnings in Scripture are the means by which God weakly actualizes their perseverance. That is to say, in the moment logically prior to creation, God via His middle knowledge knew who would freely receive Christ as Savior and what sorts of warnings against apostasy would be extrinsically efficacious in keeping them from falling away. Therefore, He decreed to create only those persons to be saved who He knew would freely respond to His warnings and

---

[1]William Lane Craig, " 'Lest Anyone Should Fall': A Middle Knowledge Perspective on Perseverance and Apostolic Warnings," *International Journal for Philosophy of Religion* 29 (1991): 65-74.

[2]The following sources are noted by Craig (ibid., p. 74 n. 6): Luis Molina, *On Divine Foreknowledge: Part 4 of "De Liberi Arbitrii cum Gratia Donis, Praescientia, Providentia, Praedestinatione et Reprobatione Concordia,"* trans. with introduction and notes by Alfred J. Freddoso (Ithaca, N.Y.: Cornell University Press, 1988); William Lane Craig, *The Problem of Divine Foreknowledge and Future Contingents from Aristotle to Suarez*, Brill's Studies in Intellectual History 7 (Leiden: Brill, 1988), chaps. 7-8; and E. Vansteenberghe, *Molinisme, in Dictionnaire de théologie catholique*, ed. A. Vacant, E. Mangenot and E. Amann (Paris: Librairie Letouzey et ane, 1929), vol. 10, pt. 2, cols. 2094-2187.

thus persevere, and He simultaneously decreed to provide such warnings. On this account the believer will certainly persevere and yet he
does so freely, taking seriously the warnings God has given him.[3]

How does Craig arrive at this conclusion? His essay is an excursion
in philosophical reasoning that begins with a faulty premise and,
therefore, in its argument fails to account for substantive elements in
the theological position it opposes. Thus, Craig concludes that the
classical Reformed view that God's means of preserving his children
includes biblical warnings, in essence, reduces to his own Molinist
view.

From the outset, we agree with Craig that many theological statements that advocate Christian perseverance have not articulated the
matter well.[4] Specifically, Craig quotes Louis Berkhof, with whom we
agree, as reflected in the following quote:

> There are warnings against apostasy which would seem to be quite
> uncalled for, if the believer could not fall away. . . . But these warnings
> regard the whole matter from the side of man and are seriously meant.
> They prompt self-examination, and are instrumental in keeping believ-
> ers in the way of perseverance. They do not prove that any of the
> addressed will apostatize, but simply that the use of means is necessary
> to prevent them from committing this sin.[5]

Craig uses Berkhof's statement as representative of the classic
Reformed view of perseverance and proceeds to critique this summary of the theological position concerning biblical warnings. Craig
begins by arguing:

---

[3]Craig, "Lest Anyone Should Fall," p. 73. He adds a caveat: "Of course, Molinism does
not imply the doctrine of the perseverance of the saints. The defender of middle
knowledge could hold that logically prior to creation God knew that there were no
worlds feasible for Him in which all believers persevere or that, if there were, such
worlds had overriding deficiencies in other respects. Therefore, the warnings of
Scripture do not guarantee the perseverance of believers, for believers can and do
ignore them. Nevertheless, it does seem to me that those who interpret the warnings
of Scripture as the means by which God ensures the perseverance of the saints have
abandoned the classic understanding of that doctrine and have adopted instead a
middle knowledge perspective on perseverance."
[4]Craig offers examples such as John Calvin *Institutes of the Christian Religion* 3.3.21, 24;
4.1.10; 4.24.6-11; Calvin's comments on Hebrews 6 and 10 in *Commentary on the Epistle
of Paul the Apostle to the Hebrews*, trans. John Owen (reprint, Grand Rapids, Mich.:
Baker, 1979); and Judith M. Gundry Volf, *Paul and Perseverance: Staying In and Falling
Away* (Louisville, Ky.: Westminster John Knox, 1990).
[5]Louis Berkhof, *Systematic Theology*, 4th rev. and enlarged ed. (Grand Rapids, Mich.:
Eerdmans, 1974), p. 548 (see Craig, "Lest Anyone Should Fall," p. 66).

This ingenious response raises all sorts of intriguing questions. For example, if the believer's will is so overwhelmed by God's grace that he is actually incapable of apostasizing [sic], then why give such warnings at all? Would they not be entirely superfluous? If, on the other hand, it is the warnings themselves that bring about perseverance, then is it not true that the believer is capable of falling away, even though, because of the warnings, he will not? For warnings do not seem to act as efficient causes upon the will, forcing one to act in a certain way; they can be disobeyed. Contrast, for example, my speaking English as a result of being raised by English-speaking parents: I am determined to speak English; I cannot suddenly choose to start speaking Vietnamese. I have no freedom simply to elect what language I speak. Now in the case of warnings, if they are severe enough and I am prudent, then I shall certainly heed them. But in virtue of being warned, I do not think we should want to say that my freedom has thereby been removed; it is still within my power to disregard the warnings, and if I am foolish enough, perhaps I shall do so. If then it is merely the warnings that guarantee perseverance, it seems that the believer is in fact free to disobey them and fall away, even though he will not. I shall assume, therefore, that warnings do not obviate human freedom.

What seems to be at stake in the question I am raising is a counterfactual proposition like

    1. If the warnings had not been given, the believers would have fallen away.

Does the defender of perseverance regard (1) as true or not? If he holds that (1) is true, then it seems clear that the believers are in fact capable of falling away, for in the closest possible worlds in which the antecedent of (1) is true, they do fall away.[6]

We cite Craig's opening argument in full to demonstrate that he begins his argument on a faulty premise. This faulty premise flaws his whole argument against Berkhof's position.

First, from the outset Craig assumes a false disjunction between God's grace that overwhelms the believer's will so that he or she cannot apostatize and "the warnings themselves that bring about perseverance." Craig fails to represent Berkhof's theological position correctly, for he sets God's grace over against the warnings as if there were an inherent antipathy between the two, something he has not demonstrated. This is evident in the way Craig frames the question: "For example, if the believer's will is so overwhelmed by God's grace

---

[6]Craig, "Lest Anyone Should Fall," pp. 66-67.

that he is actually incapable of apostasizing [sic], then why give such warnings at all? Would they not be entirely superfluous?" He sets up a false disjunction, for Berkhof does not separate the two. Instead, Berkhof believes that the two are compatible. According to Berkhof, God's grace uses the warnings as a means to secure whom God purposed to save and to preserve them unto the end. Craig's false disjunction seems attributable to different definitions of "God's grace."

Second, Craig assumes the validity of his disjunction between God's grace and the warnings and falls prey to reductionism by assuming, for the sake of his argument, something about the warnings with which Berkhof does not agree. Craig reasons, "If, on the other hand, it is the warnings themselves that bring about perseverance, then is it not true that the believer is capable of falling away, even though, because of the warnings, he will not? For warnings do not seem to act as efficient causes upon the will, forcing one to act in a certain way; they can be disobeyed." Here, because Craig fails to realize that he has assumed a false disjunction concerning Berkhof's position, he only sees two alternatives. So to make his argument, he then assumes that Berkhof thinks the warnings are effective in themselves to bring about perseverance. Of course, Berkhof does not hold such a position. For Berkhof, the warnings are effective only as God, in his grace, uses them effectually to preserve his chosen ones. The warnings are not effective in themselves any more than the call of the gospel to believe is effective in itself.

Third, Craig continues his assumption of a false disjunction between God's grace and the warnings as if Berkhof's position eliminates the need for believers to heed the warnings. Craig muses, "Now in the case of warnings, if they are severe enough and I am prudent, then I shall certainly heed them. But in virtue of being warned, I do not think we should want to say that my freedom has thereby been removed; it is still within my power to disregard the warnings, and if I am foolish enough, perhaps I shall do so. If then it is merely the warnings that guarantee perseverance, it seems that the believer is in fact free to disobey them and fall away, even though he will not. I shall assume, therefore, that warnings do not obviate human freedom." Berkhof agrees that the warnings do not obviate human freedom, for he says, "The use of means is necessary to prevent" apostasy.

Of course, the fundamental problem here is that Craig and Berkhof have different definitions for human freedom. Craig begs the question, for he imposes his own definition of human freedom on the discussion without addressing the significant differences between his own view and that of Berkhof.[7] If Craig's argument with Berkhof is to have merit, he must address this profound difference, but he does not.

Fourth, notice how Craig continues to beg the question as he sustains the false disjunction between God's grace and the warnings. He states, "If then it is merely the warnings that guarantee perseverance, it seems that the believer is in fact free to disobey them and fall away, even though he will not." Here Craig wrongly attributes his own view of warnings on Berkhof, with the result that he misrepresents Berkhof's position for two reasons. First, Berkhof does not lodge the assurance of perseverance in the warnings, as Craig believes he does, for the warnings are only a means God's grace uses to preserve his children. Second, the word *merely* betrays Craig's disjunctive fallacy as he settles the matter at issue by introducing a restrictive modifier into Berkhof's argument. Berkhof does not agree that "it is merely the warnings that guarantee perseverance." Berkhof's paragraph, cited by Craig, only indicates that biblical warnings are one element of "the use of means" that is necessary to keep believers from apostatizing.

Therefore, when Craig moves into the heart of his argument, he operates on the basis of a flawed premise that includes unstated assumptions concerning definitions about both human freedom and the correlation of divine sovereignty and human accountability. The remainder of his argument is also flawed because he has engaged in reductionism. He has reduced his opponent's position to a caricature, for his argument proceeds on the following premise: "If then it is merely

---

[7]Craig's essay indicates that he holds a fairly libertarian view of human freedom, as is often true of those who hold a Molinist or middle-knowledge viewpoint. Late in the essay Craig does mention the primary difference between himself and Berkhof on human freedom: "The heart of the issue lies in the efficacy of God's grace: is God's grace intrinsically efficacious or extrinsically efficacious? According to the classic doctrine of perseverance, God's grace is intrinsically efficacious in producing its result, that is to say, grace infallibly causes its effect. But according to Molina, divine grace is extrinsically efficacious, that is to say, it becomes efficacious when conjoined with the free cooperation of the creaturely will. On Molina's view, God gives sufficient grace for salvation to all men, but it becomes efficacious only in the lives of those who respond affirmatively to it" (Craig, "Lest Anyone Should Fall," p. 69).

the warnings that guarantee perseverance, it seems that the believer is in fact free to disobey them and fall away, even though he will not." His reductionism is evident as he begins, for he poses the question:

> What seems to be at stake in the question I am raising is a counterfactual proposition like
>
>   1. If the warnings had not been given, the believers would have fallen away.
>
> Does the defender of perseverance regard (1) as true or not? If he holds that (1) is true, then it seems clear that the believers are in fact capable of falling away, for in the closest possible worlds in which the antecedent of (1) is true, they do fall away.

Berkhof and the best representatives of the Reformed view—that God uses biblical warnings as a means to preserve believers—would not concede that Craig's first proposition is true as stated because he has incorrectly reasoned that "the warnings guarantee perseverance," and he proceeds from that false assumption. When Craig conceives of the classic Reformed tradition on God's means of preserving believers, he reduces those means to the warnings and assumes them to be effective; thus, his whole argument against the Reformed view takes a trajectory that will miss its mark.

Craig's invalid disjunction between God's grace and the warnings continues to show itself in various places throughout the logical propositions of his reasoning on this matter. For example, it is not surprising that Craig characterizes Berkhof's position as "theological fatalism."[8] So even though Craig believes that he has proved that Berkhof and advocates of the classic Reformed view actually adopt the Molinist perspective, he has not done so. Why? It is because the best representatives of the classical view, including Berkhof, do not accept the premise that "it is merely the warnings that guarantee perseverance," as Craig presumes.

---

[8]Ibid., p. 67. Craig argues, "Now the defender of perseverance might insist that even if (1) is true, nevertheless, given the fact that believers have, indeed, been warned, the believers cannot fall away. But this response commits an error which is prevalent in discussions of divine foreknowledge and human freedom, namely, confusing the necessity of a proposition in *sensu composito* with its necessity in *sensu diviso*. Proponents of theological fatalism often fail to distinguish these two senses in considering a proposition like

2. Whatever is foreknown by God must occur, which they take to entail a denial of human freedom.

But (2) *in sensu composito* means merely

2*. Necessarily, any event which is foreknown by God will occur."